ハヤテのごとく! 17

Hayate the combat butler

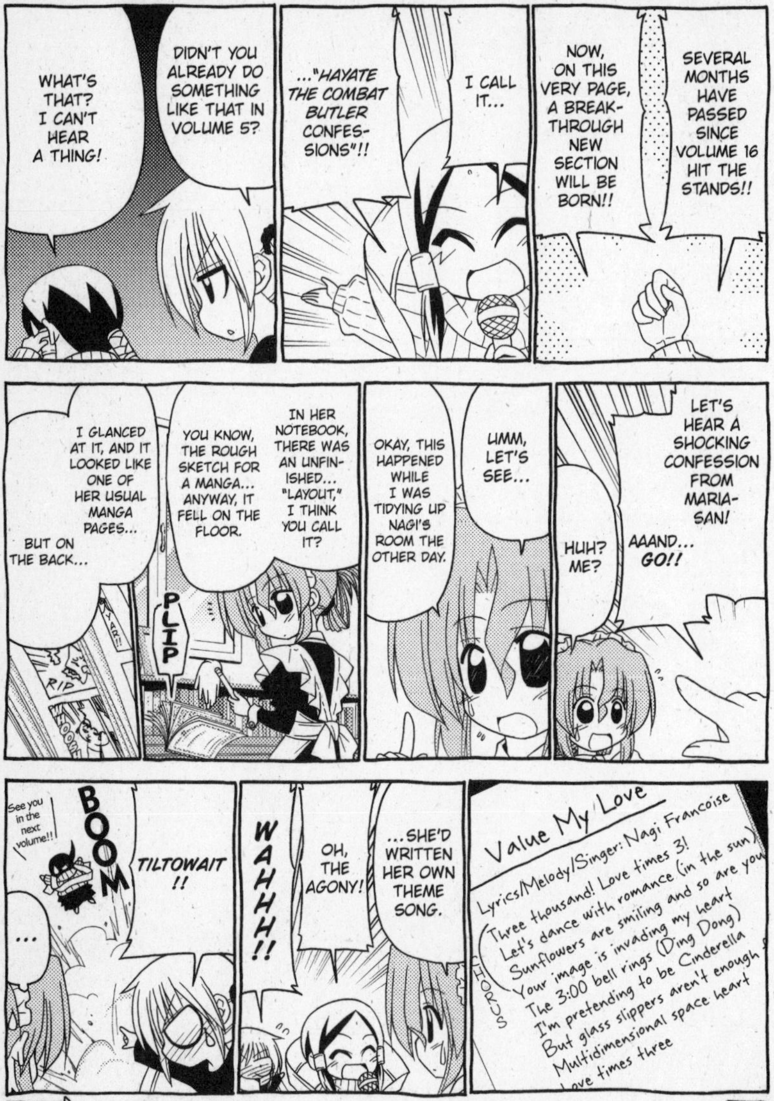

SEVERAL MONTHS HAVE PASSED SINCE VOLUME 16 HIT THE STANDS!!
NOW, ON THIS VERY PAGE, A BREAKTHROUGH NEW SECTION WILL BE BORN!!
I CALL IT...
..."HAYATE THE COMBAT BUTLER CONFESSIONS"!!
DIDN'T YOU ALREADY DO SOMETHING LIKE THAT IN VOLUME 5?
WHAT'S THAT? I CAN'T HEAR A THING!
LET'S HEAR A SHOCKING CONFESSION FROM MARIA-SAN!
AAAND... GO!!
HUH? ME?
UMM, LET'S SEE...
OKAY, THIS HAPPENED WHILE I WAS TIDYING UP NAGI'S ROOM THE OTHER DAY.
IN HER NOTEBOOK, THERE WAS AN UNFINISHED... "LAYOUT," I THINK YOU CALL IT?
YOU KNOW, THE ROUGH SKETCH FOR A MANGA... ANYWAY, IT FELL ON THE FLOOR.
PLIP
I GLANCED AT IT, AND IT LOOKED LIKE ONE OF HER USUAL MANGA PAGES...
BUT ON THE BACK...
RIP
Value My Love
Lyrics/Melody/Singer: Nagi Francoise
Three thousand! Love times 3!
Let's dance with romance (in the sun)
Sunflowers are smiling and so are you
Your image is invading my heart
The 3:00 bell rings (Ding Dong)
I'm pretending to be Cinderella
But glass slippers aren't enough
Multidimensional space heart
Love times three
CHORUS
...SHE'D WRITTEN HER OWN THEME SONG.
OH, THE AGONY!
WAHHH!!
TILTOWAIT!!
BOOM
...
See you in the next volume!!

The staff and I were dying with laughter as we came up with these lyrics.

HAYATE THE COMBAT BUTLER
VOL. 17
Shonen Sunday Edition

STORY AND ART BY
KENJIRO HATA

English Adaptation/Mark Giambruno
Translation/Yuki Yoshioka and Cindy H. Yamauchi
Touch-up Art & Lettering/HudsonYards
Design/Yukiko Whitley
Editor/Shaenon K. Garrity

The rights of the author(s) of the work(s) in this publication to be so identified have been asserted in accordance with the Copyright, Designs and Patents Act 1988. A CIP catalogue record for this book is available from the British Library.

Printed in Canada

Published by VIZ Media, LLC
P.O. Box 77010
San Francisco, CA 94107

10 9 8 7 6 5 4 3 2 1
First printing, March 2011

www.viz.com

WWW.SHONENSUNDAY.COM

PARENTAL ADVISORY
HAYATE THE COMBAT BUTLER is rated T+ for Older Teen and is recommended for ages 16 and up. This volume contains fantasy violence and crude humor.

T+ FOR OLDER TEEN

ratings.viz.com

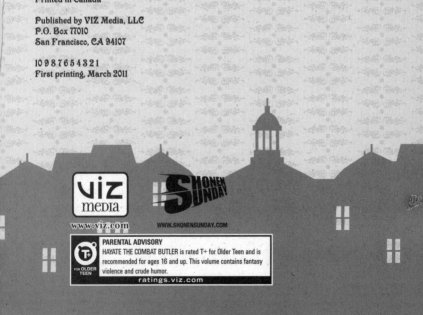

Hayate the Combat Butler

17

KENJIRO HATA

CONTENTS

Episode 1
"Even Though the Law Says 'No,' My Yearning to Watch It Won't Go Away"
5

Episode 2
"You Are Bound to Meet Most of the People You'll Need in Your Life"
21

Episode 3
"The Sweat and Tears Under the Mask Can't Be Revealed, Because I Am a Hero"
37

Episode 4
"That's the Machine That Captures Time with Light"
53

Episode 5
"THE END OF THE WORLD (1) - The 3,000 Realms You Desired"
69

Episode 6
"THE END OF THE WORLD (2) - The Castle Where God Is Said to Dwell"
89

Episode 7
"THE END OF THE WORLD (3) - The Miniature Garden of Amaterasu"
105

Episode 8
"THE END OF THE WORLD (4) - A Voice That Reaches the Entire World"
121

Episode 9
"THE END OF THE WORLD (5) - A Premonition of the End"
137

Episode 10
"THE END OF THE WORLD (6) - A Will for Power"
153

Episode 11
"THE END OF THE WORLD (7) - Proof of Love on the Left Hand"
169

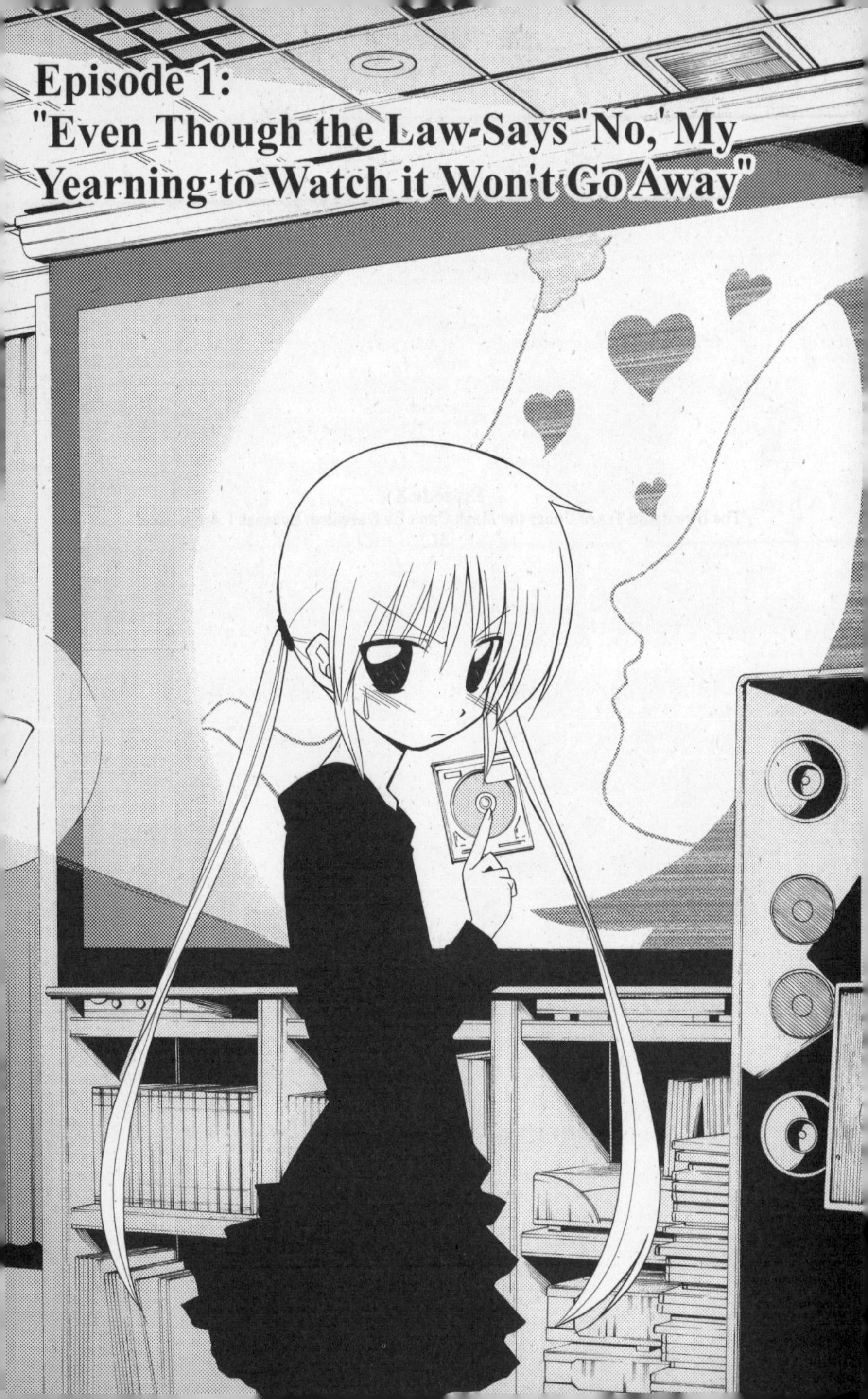
Episode 1:
"Even Though the Law Says 'No,' My Yearning to Watch it Won't Go Away"

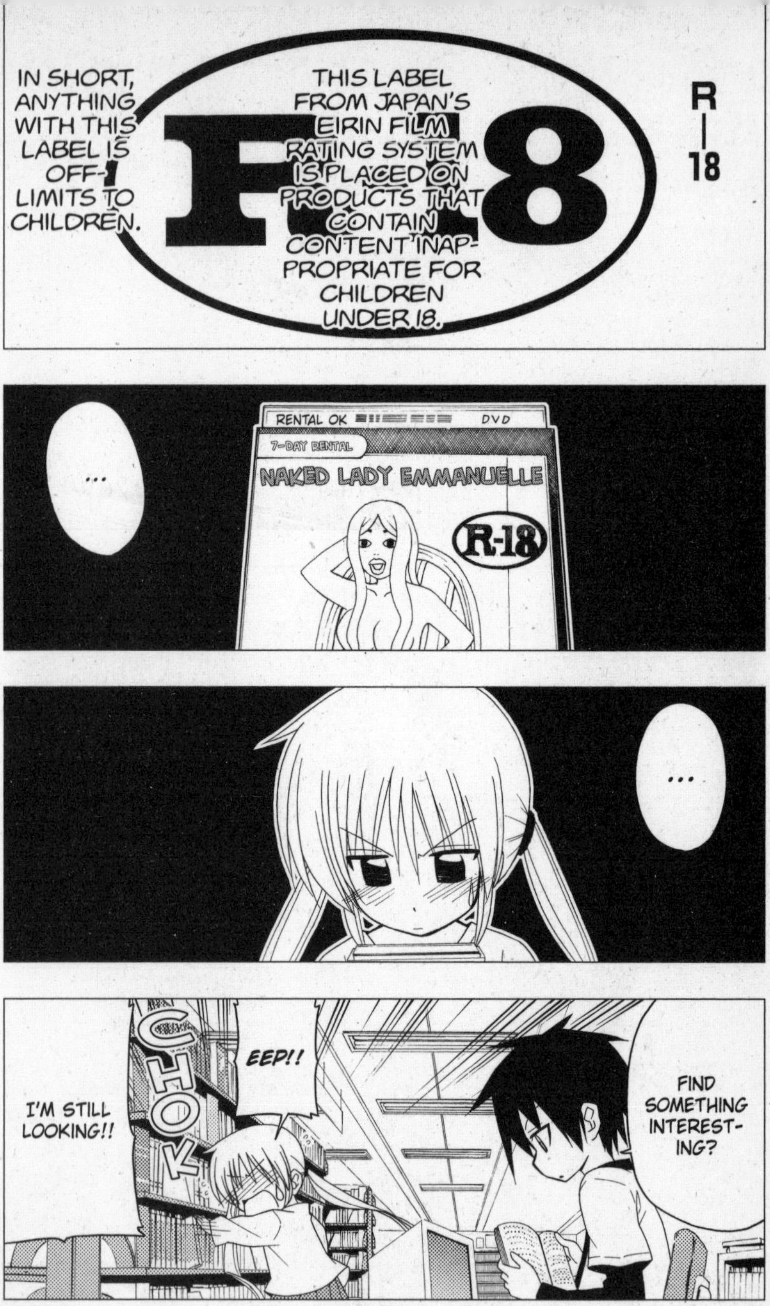
R-18
THIS LABEL FROM JAPAN'S EIRIN FILM RATING SYSTEM IS PLACED ON PRODUCTS THAT CONTAIN CONTENT INAPPROPRIATE FOR CHILDREN UNDER 18.
R-18
IN SHORT, ANYTHING WITH THIS LABEL IS OFF-LIMITS TO CHILDREN.
RENTAL OK
DVD
7-DAY RENTAL
NAKED LADY EMMANUELLE
R-18
...
...
FIND SOMETHING INTERESTING?
EEP!!
CHOK
I'M STILL LOOKING!!

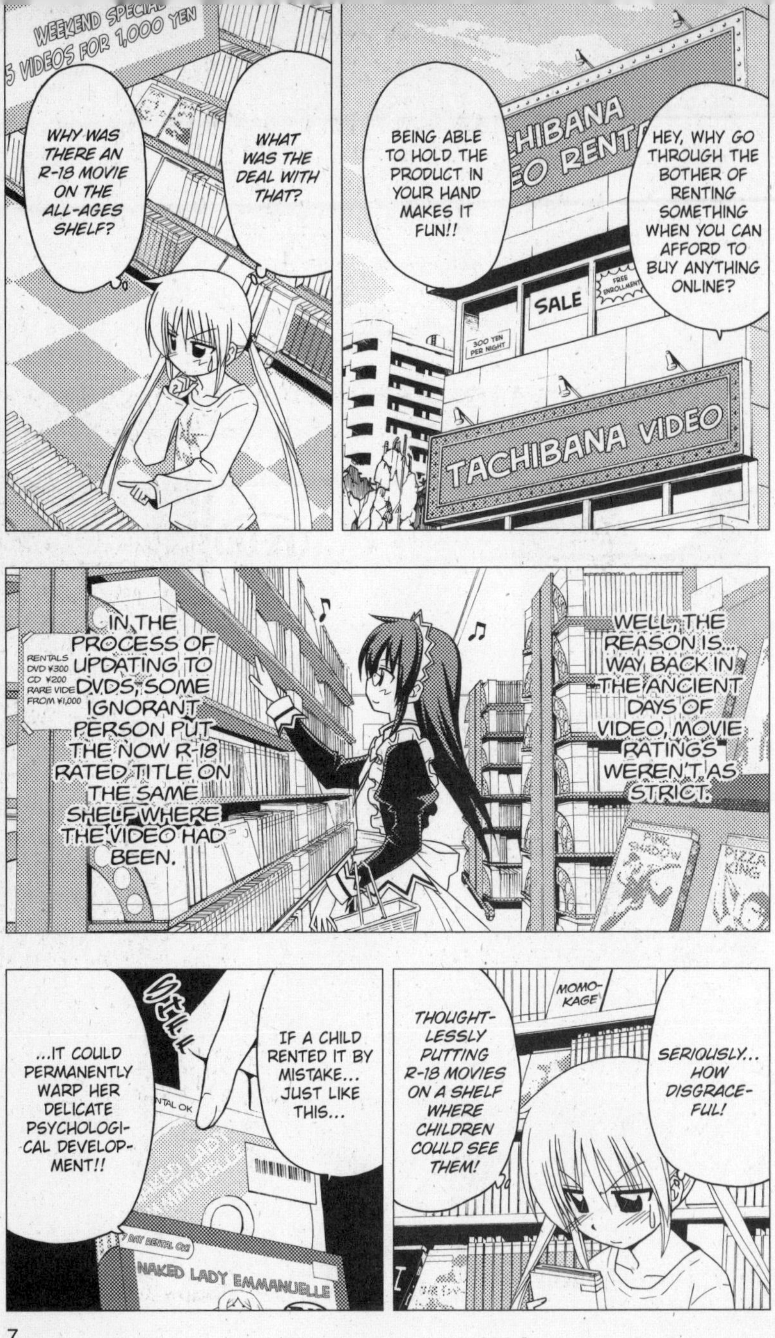
TACHIBANA VIDEO
SALE
FREE ENROLLMENT
300 YEN PER NIGHT
HEY, WHY GO THROUGH THE BOTHER OF RENTING SOMETHING WHEN YOU CAN AFFORD TO BUY ANYTHING ONLINE?
BEING ABLE TO HOLD THE PRODUCT IN YOUR HAND MAKES IT FUN!!
WEEKEND SPECIAL
5 VIDEOS FOR 1,000 YEN
WHAT WAS THE DEAL WITH THAT?
WHY WAS THERE AN R-18 MOVIE ON THE ALL-AGES SHELF?
WELL, THE REASON IS... WAY BACK IN THE ANCIENT DAYS OF VIDEO, MOVIE RATINGS WEREN'T AS STRICT.
PINK SHADOW
PIZZA KING
IN THE PROCESS OF UPDATING TO DVDS, SOME IGNORANT PERSON PUT THE NOW R-18 RATED TITLE ON THE SAME SHELF WHERE THE VIDEO HAD BEEN.
RENTALS DVD ¥300 CD ¥200 RARE VIDE FROM ¥1,000
SERIOUSLY... HOW DISGRACE-FUL!
MOMO-KAGE
THOUGHT-LESSLY PUTTING R-18 MOVIES ON A SHELF WHERE CHILDREN COULD SEE THEM!
IF A CHILD RENTED IT BY MISTAKE... JUST LIKE THIS...
...IT COULD PERMANENTLY WARP HER DELICATE PSYCHOLOGI-CAL DEVELOP-MENT!!
7 DAY RENTAL OK
NAKED LADY EMMANUELLE

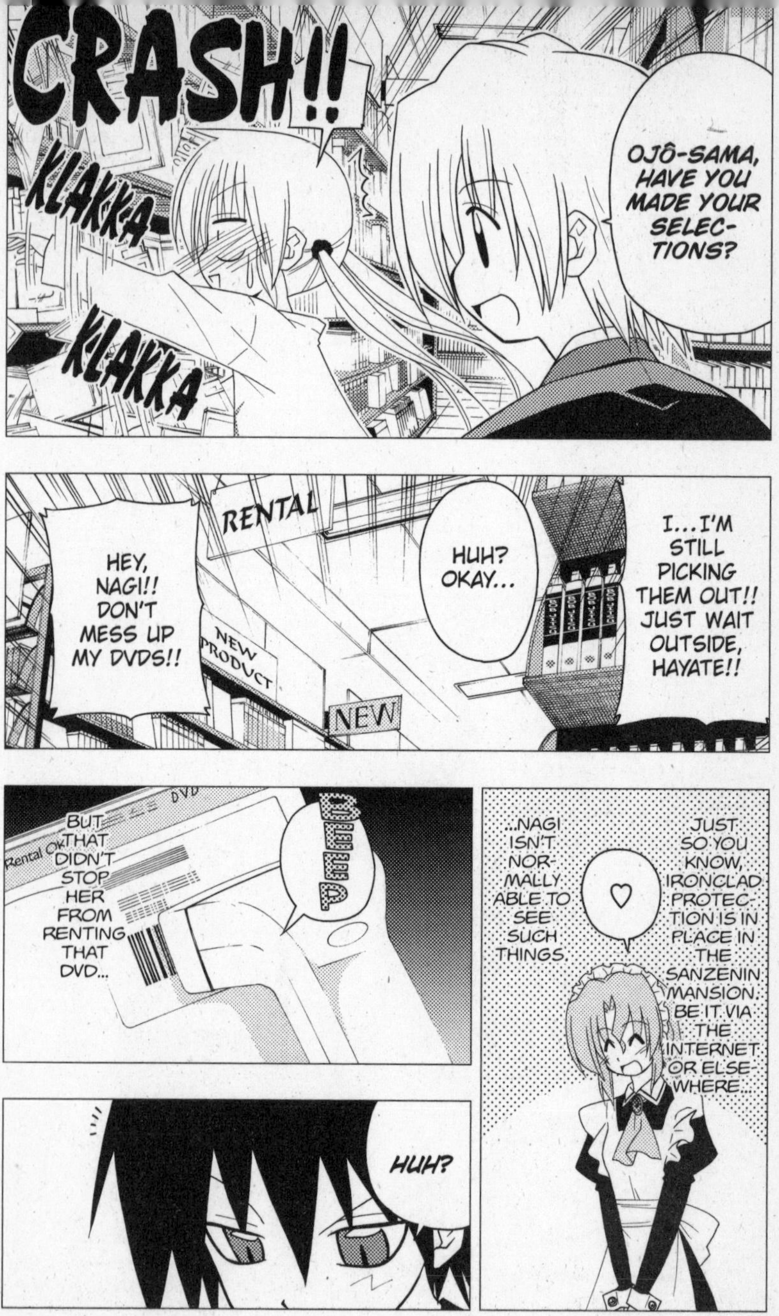
OJÔ-SAMA, HAVE YOU MADE YOUR SELECTIONS?
CRASH!!
KLAKKA-
KLAKKA
I...I'M STILL PICKING THEM OUT!! JUST WAIT OUTSIDE, HAYATE!!
HUH? OKAY...
RENTAL
HEY, NAGI!! DON'T MESS UP MY DVDS!!
NEW PRODUCT
NEW
JUST SO YOU KNOW, IRONCLAD PROTECTION IS IN PLACE IN THE SANZENIN MANSION, BE IT VIA THE INTERNET OR ELSEWHERE...
♥
...NAGI ISN'T NORMALLY ABLE TO SEE SUCH THINGS.
BEEP
BUT THAT DIDN'T STOP HER FROM RENTING THAT DVD...
HUH?

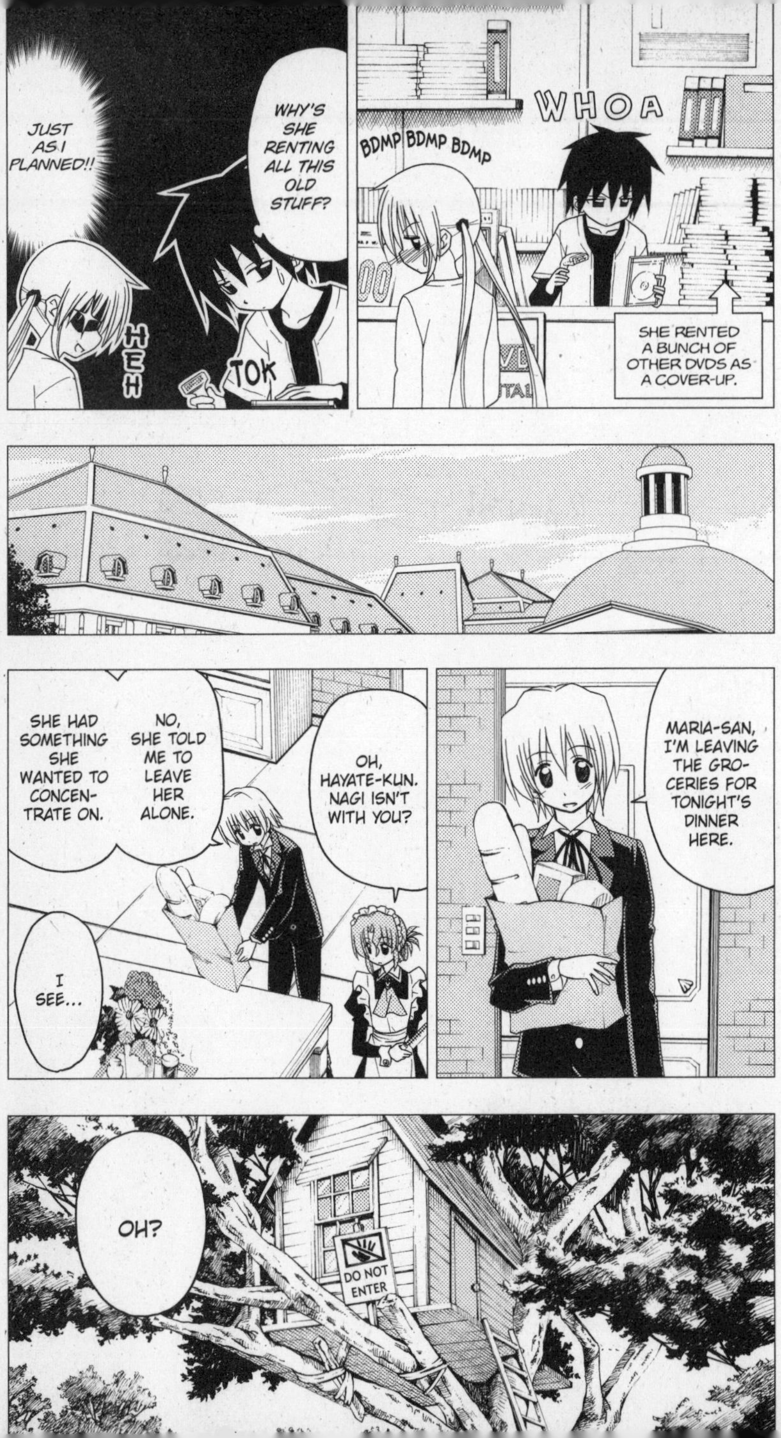
WHOA
BDMP BDMP BDMP
SHE RENTED A BUNCH OF OTHER DVDS AS A COVER-UP.
WHY'S SHE RENTING ALL THIS OLD STUFF?
JUST AS I PLANNED!!
TOK
HEH
MARIA-SAN, I'M LEAVING THE GROCERIES FOR TONIGHT'S DINNER HERE.
OH, HAYATE-KUN. NAGI ISN'T WITH YOU?
NO, SHE TOLD ME TO LEAVE HER ALONE.
SHE HAD SOMETHING SHE WANTED TO CONCENTRATE ON.
I SEE...
OH?
DO NOT ENTER

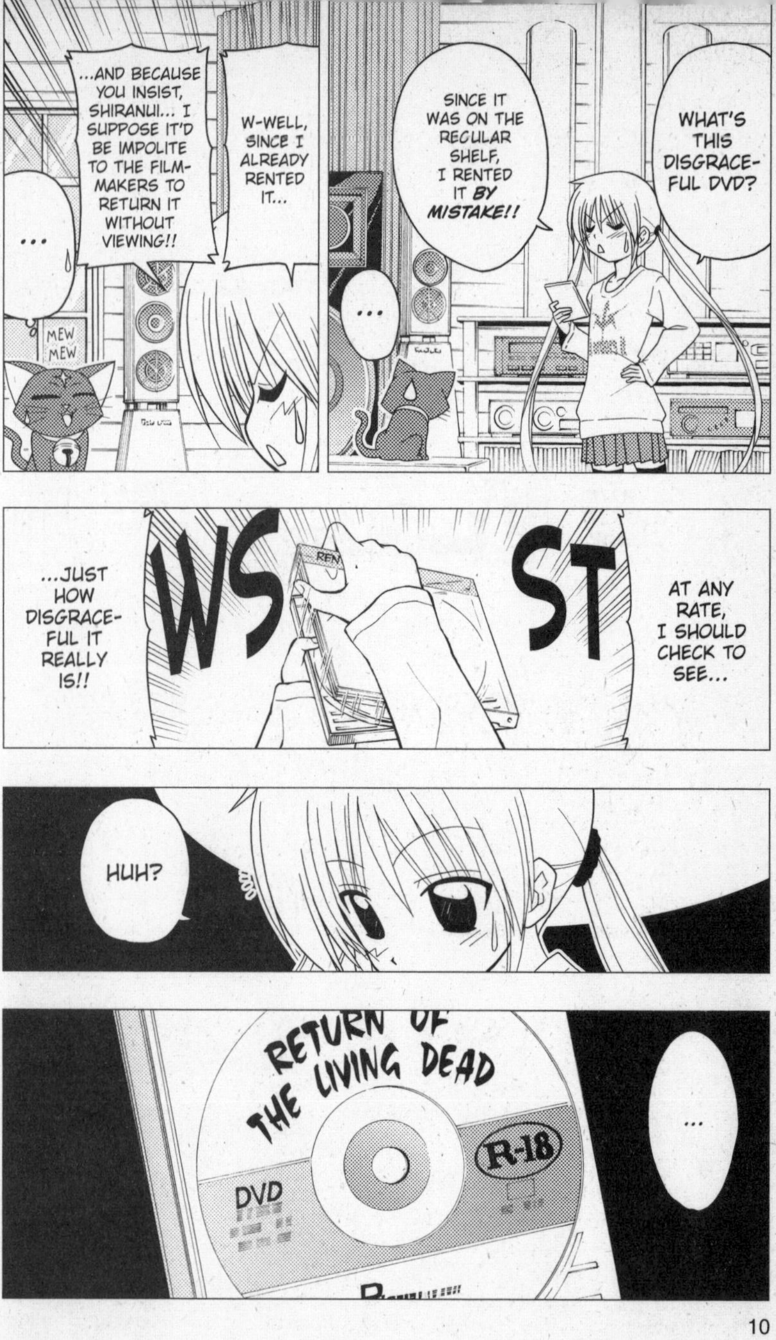
WHAT'S THIS DISGRACEFUL DVD?
SINCE IT WAS ON THE REGULAR SHELF, I RENTED IT *BY MISTAKE!!*
...
W-WELL, SINCE I ALREADY RENTED IT...
...AND BECAUSE YOU INSIST, SHIRANUI... I SUPPOSE IT'D BE IMPOLITE TO THE FILMMAKERS TO RETURN IT WITHOUT VIEWING!!
...
MEW MEW
AT ANY RATE, I SHOULD CHECK TO SEE...
WS
ST
REN
...JUST HOW DISGRACEFUL IT REALLY IS!!
HUH?
...
RETURN OF THE LIVING DEAD
R-18
DVD

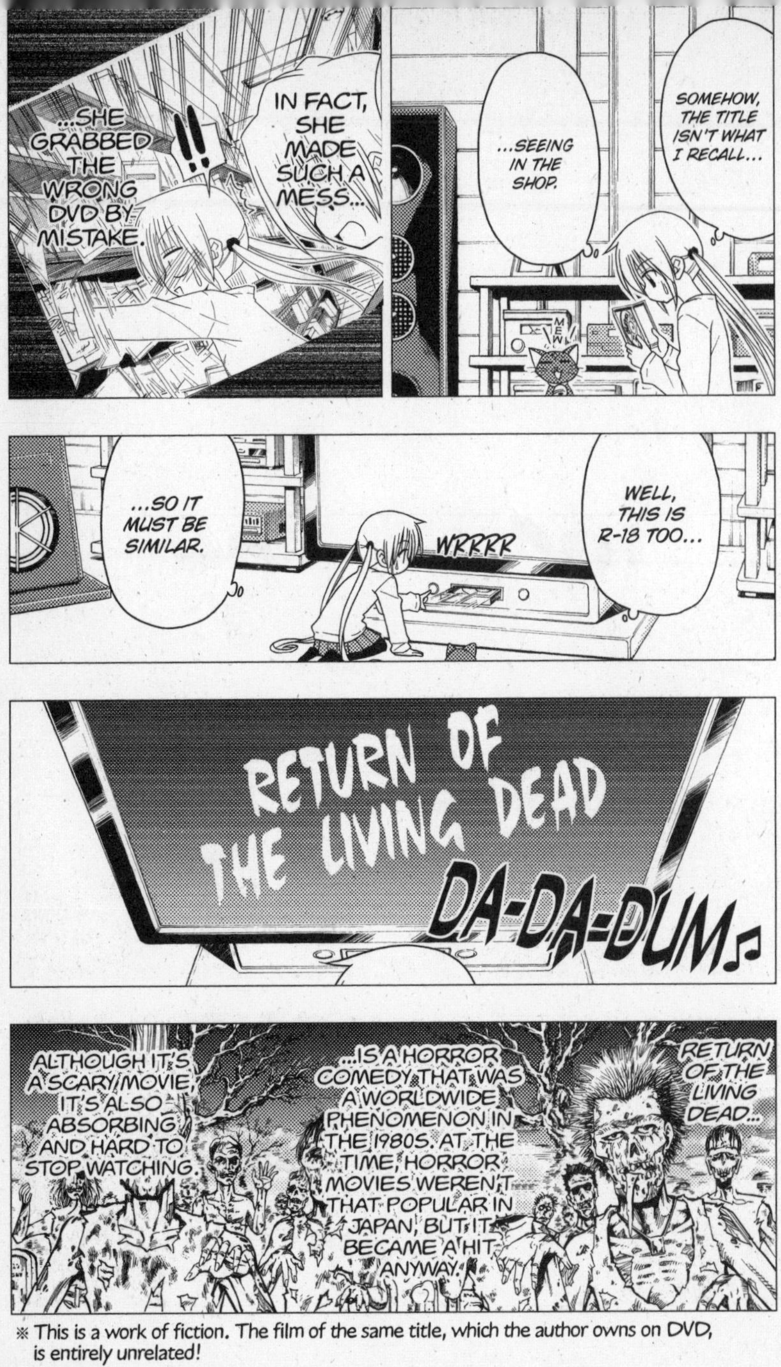
SOMEHOW, THE TITLE ISN'T WHAT I RECALL...
...SEEING IN THE SHOP.
MEW
IN FACT, SHE MADE SUCH A MESS...
!!
...SHE GRABBED THE WRONG DVD BY MISTAKE.
WELL, THIS IS R-18 TOO...
WRRRR
...SO IT MUST BE SIMILAR.
RETURN OF THE LIVING DEAD
DA-DA-DUM♫
RETURN OF THE LIVING DEAD...
...IS A HORROR COMEDY THAT WAS A WORLDWIDE PHENOMENON IN THE 1980S. AT THE TIME, HORROR MOVIES WEREN'T THAT POPULAR IN JAPAN, BUT IT BECAME A HIT ANYWAY.
ALTHOUGH IT'S A SCARY MOVIE, IT'S ALSO ABSORBING AND HARD TO STOP WATCHING.

※ This is a work of fiction. The film of the same title, which the author owns on DVD, is entirely unrelated!

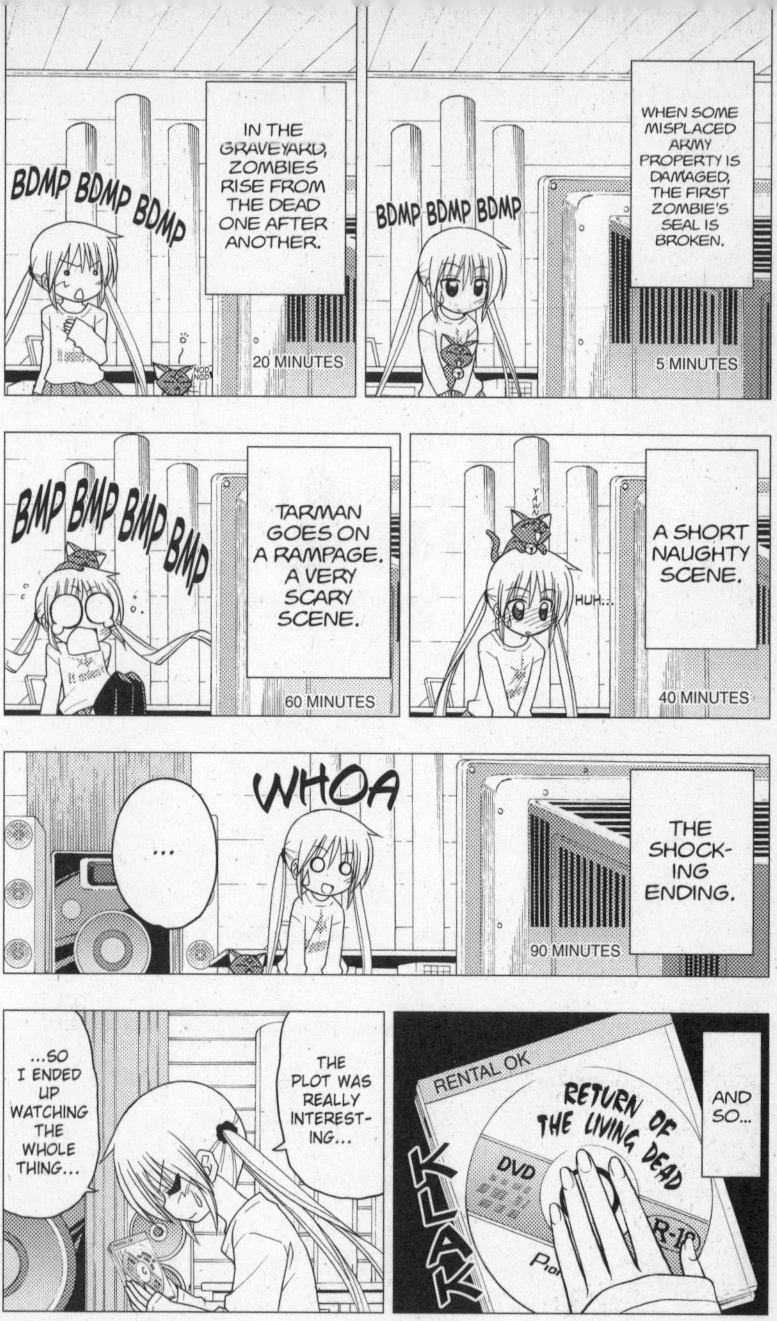
WHEN SOME MISPLACED ARMY PROPERTY IS DAMAGED, THE FIRST ZOMBIE'S SEAL IS BROKEN.
BDMP BDMP BDMP
5 MINUTES
IN THE GRAVEYARD, ZOMBIES RISE FROM THE DEAD ONE AFTER ANOTHER.
BDMP BDMP BDMP
NOD NOD
20 MINUTES
A SHORT NAUGHTY SCENE.
YAWN
HUH...
40 MINUTES
TARMAN GOES ON A RAMPAGE. A VERY SCARY SCENE.
BMP BMP BMP BMP
60 MINUTES
THE SHOCKING ENDING.
90 MINUTES
WHOA
...
AND SO...
RENTAL OK
RETURN OF THE LIVING DEAD
DVD
KLAK
THE PLOT WAS REALLY INTERESTING...
...SO I ENDED UP WATCHING THE WHOLE THING...

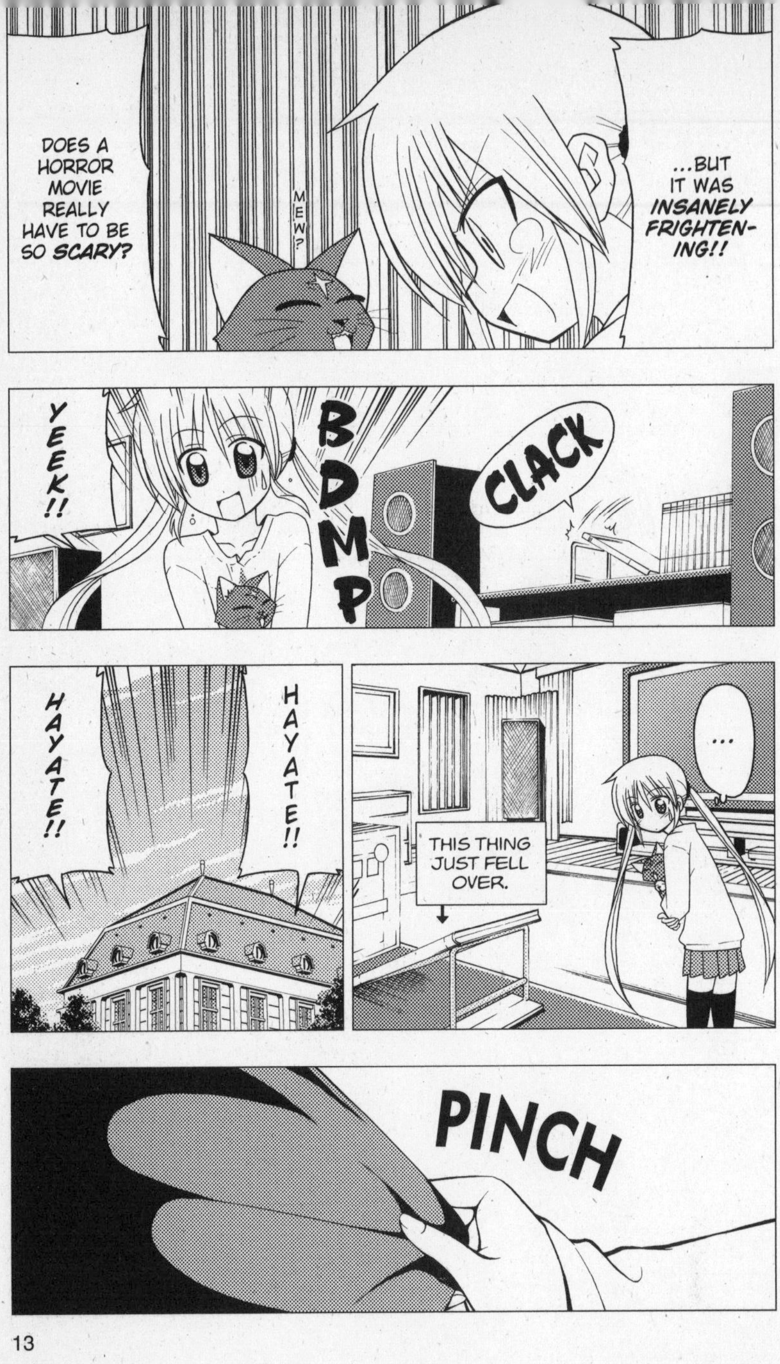
...BUT IT WAS INSANELY FRIGHTEN-ING!!
MEW?
DOES A HORROR MOVIE REALLY HAVE TO BE SO SCARY?
CLACK
BDMP
YEEEK!!
...
THIS THING JUST FELL OVER.
HAYATE!!
HAYATE!!
PINCH

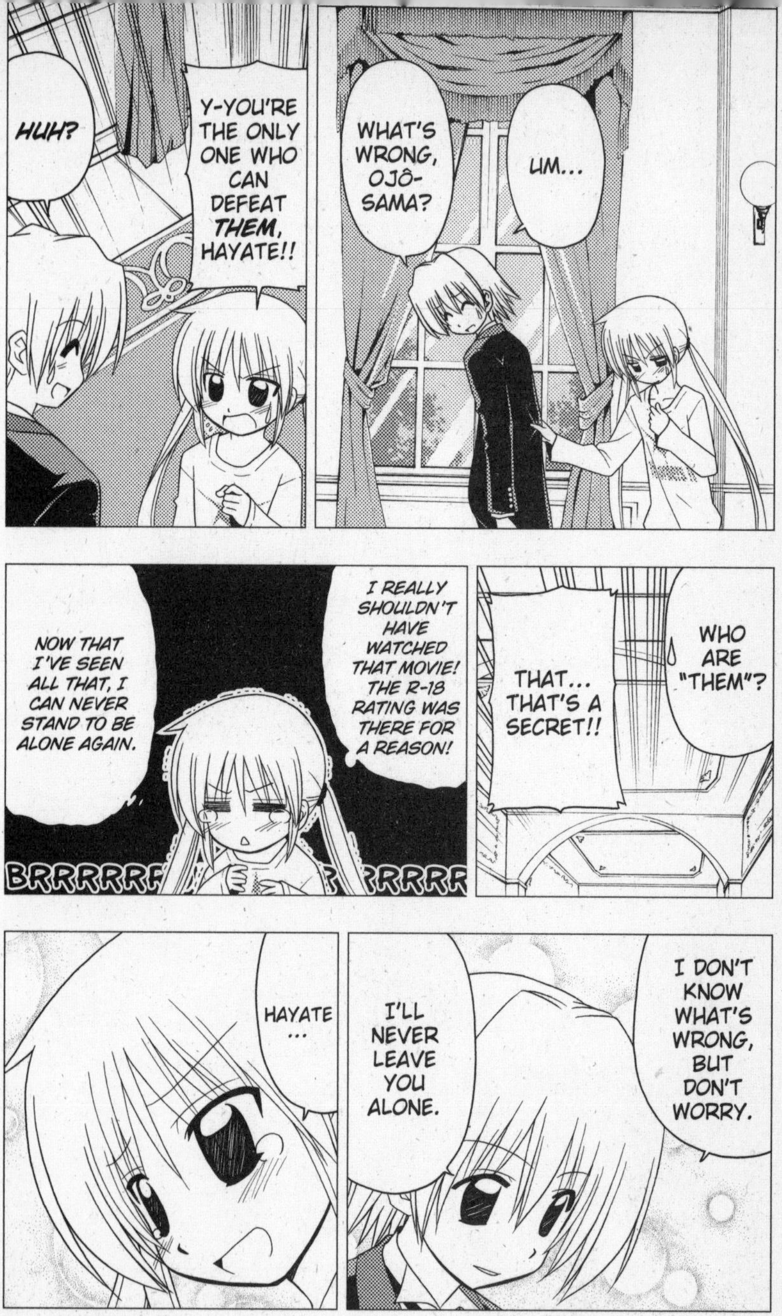
UM...
WHAT'S WRONG, OJÔ-SAMA?
Y-YOU'RE THE ONLY ONE WHO CAN DEFEAT *THEM*, HAYATE!!
HUH?
WHO ARE "THEM"?
THAT... THAT'S A SECRET!!
I REALLY SHOULDN'T HAVE WATCHED THAT MOVIE! THE R-18 RATING WAS THERE FOR A REASON!
NOW THAT I'VE SEEN ALL THAT, I CAN NEVER STAND TO BE ALONE AGAIN.
BRRRRRRRRRRRRRR
I DON'T KNOW WHAT'S WRONG, BUT DON'T WORRY.
I'LL NEVER LEAVE YOU ALONE.
HAYATE...

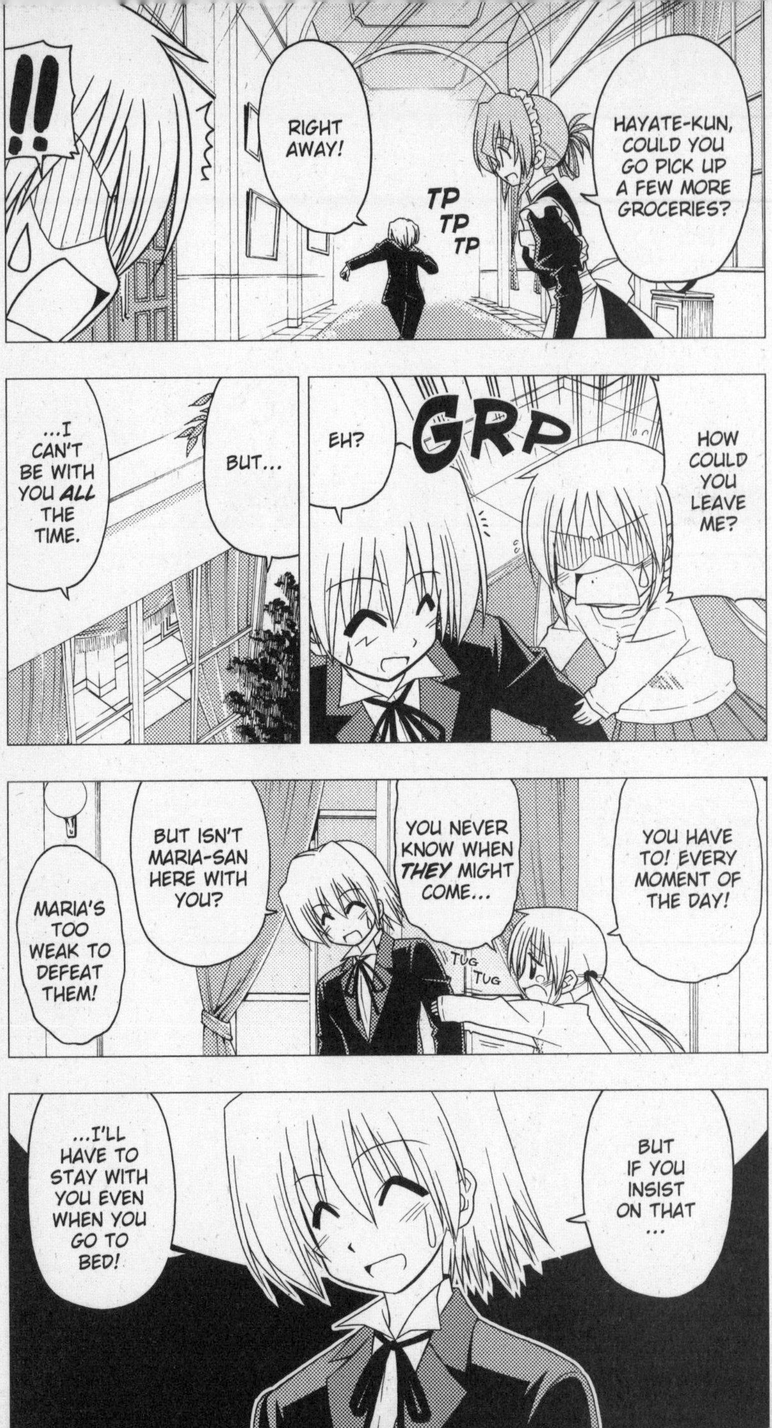
HAYATE-KUN, COULD YOU GO PICK UP A FEW MORE GROCERIES?
RIGHT AWAY!
TP TP TP
!!
HOW COULD YOU LEAVE ME?
GRP
EH?
BUT...
...I CAN'T BE WITH YOU ALL THE TIME.
YOU HAVE TO! EVERY MOMENT OF THE DAY!
YOU NEVER KNOW WHEN THEY MIGHT COME...
TUG TUG
BUT ISN'T MARIA-SAN HERE WITH YOU?
MARIA'S TOO WEAK TO DEFEAT THEM!
BUT IF YOU INSIST ON THAT...
...I'LL HAVE TO STAY WITH YOU EVEN WHEN YOU GO TO BED!

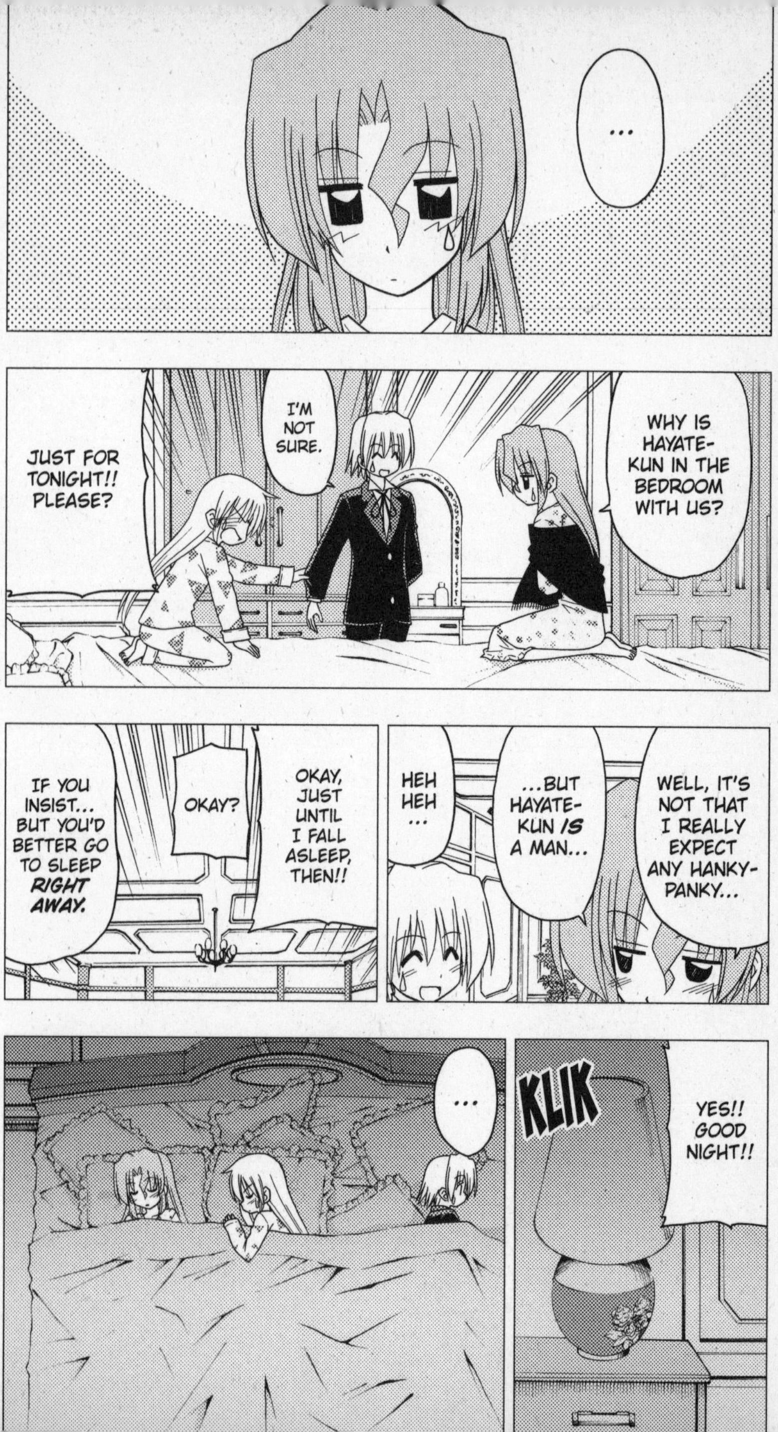
...
WHY IS HAYATE-KUN IN THE BEDROOM WITH US?
I'M NOT SURE.
JUST FOR TONIGHT!! PLEASE?
WELL, IT'S NOT THAT I REALLY EXPECT ANY HANKY-PANKY...
...BUT HAYATE-KUN *IS* A MAN...
HEH HEH ...
OKAY, JUST UNTIL I FALL ASLEEP, THEN!!
OKAY?
IF YOU INSIST... BUT YOU'D BETTER GO TO SLEEP ***RIGHT AWAY.***
YES!! GOOD NIGHT!!
KLIK
...

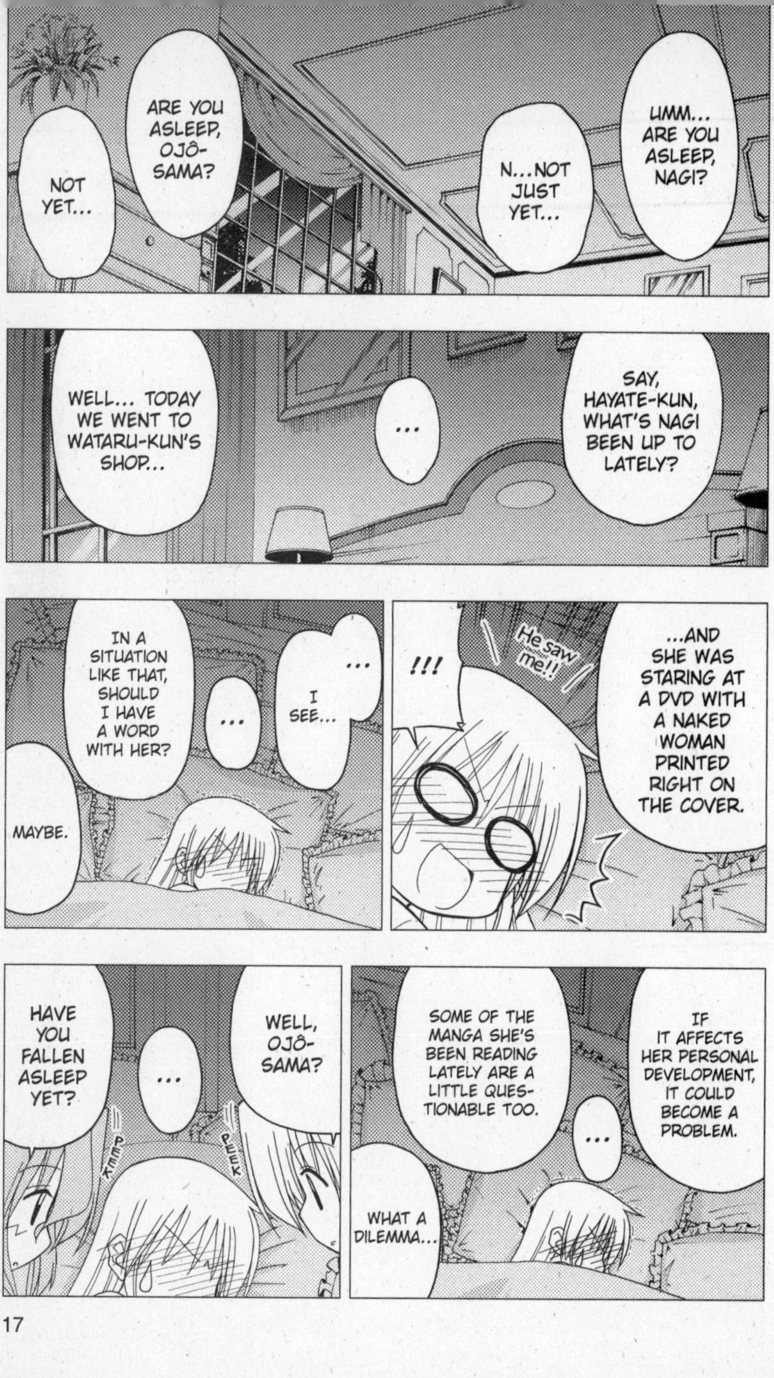
UMM... ARE YOU ASLEEP, NAGI?
N...NOT JUST YET...
ARE YOU ASLEEP, OJÔ-SAMA?
NOT YET...
SAY, HAYATE-KUN, WHAT'S NAGI BEEN UP TO LATELY?
...
WELL... TODAY WE WENT TO WATARU-KUN'S SHOP...
...AND SHE WAS STARING AT A DVD WITH A NAKED WOMAN PRINTED RIGHT ON THE COVER.
He saw me!!
!!!
... I SEE...
...
IN A SITUATION LIKE THAT, SHOULD I HAVE A WORD WITH HER?
MAYBE.
IF IT AFFECTS HER PERSONAL DEVELOPMENT, IT COULD BECOME A PROBLEM.
...
SOME OF THE MANGA SHE'S BEEN READING LATELY ARE A LITTLE QUES-TIONABLE TOO.
WHAT A DILEMMA...
WELL, OJÔ-SAMA?
PEEK
...
HAVE YOU FALLEN ASLEEP YET?
PEEK

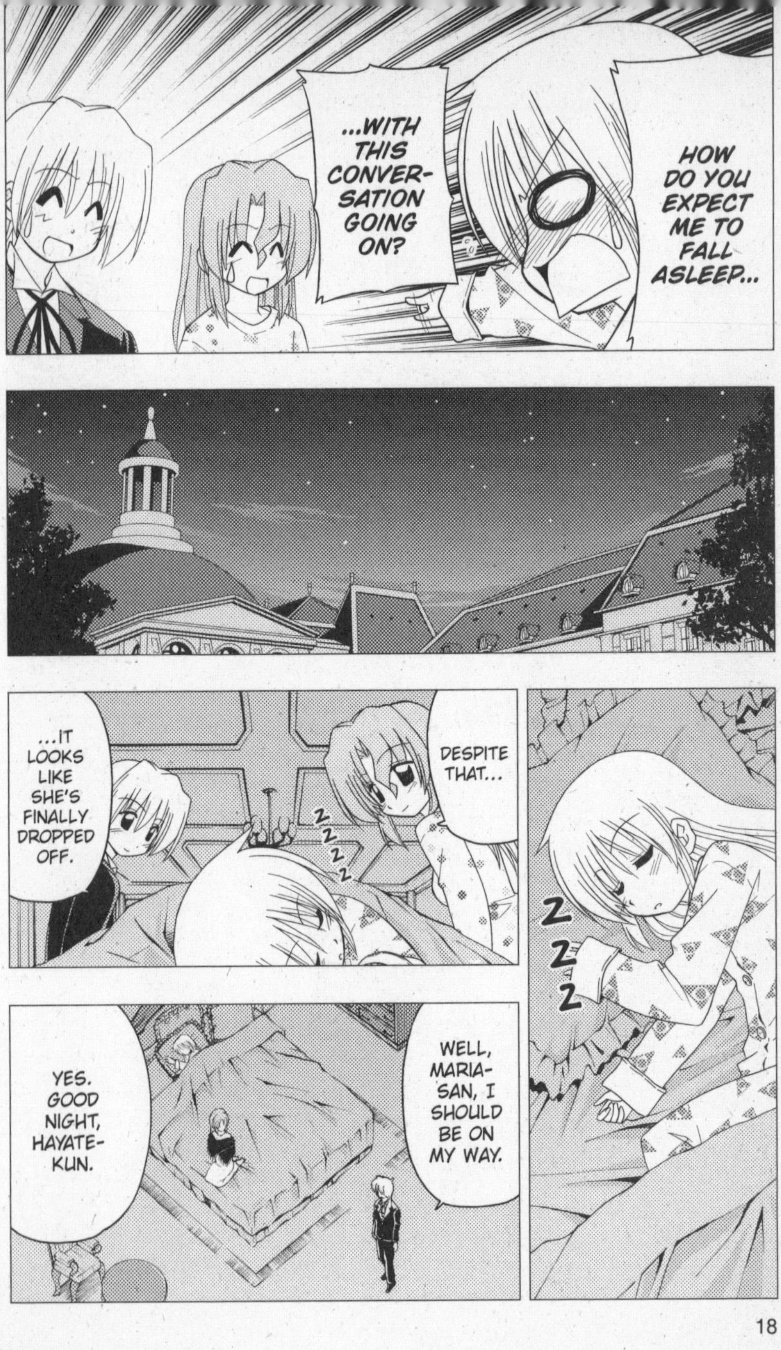
HOW DO YOU EXPECT ME TO FALL ASLEEP...
...WITH THIS CONVER-SATION GOING ON?
Z Z Z
DESPITE THAT...
Z Z Z Z
...IT LOOKS LIKE SHE'S FINALLY DROPPED OFF.
WELL, MARIA-SAN, I SHOULD BE ON MY WAY.
YES. GOOD NIGHT, HAYATE-KUN.

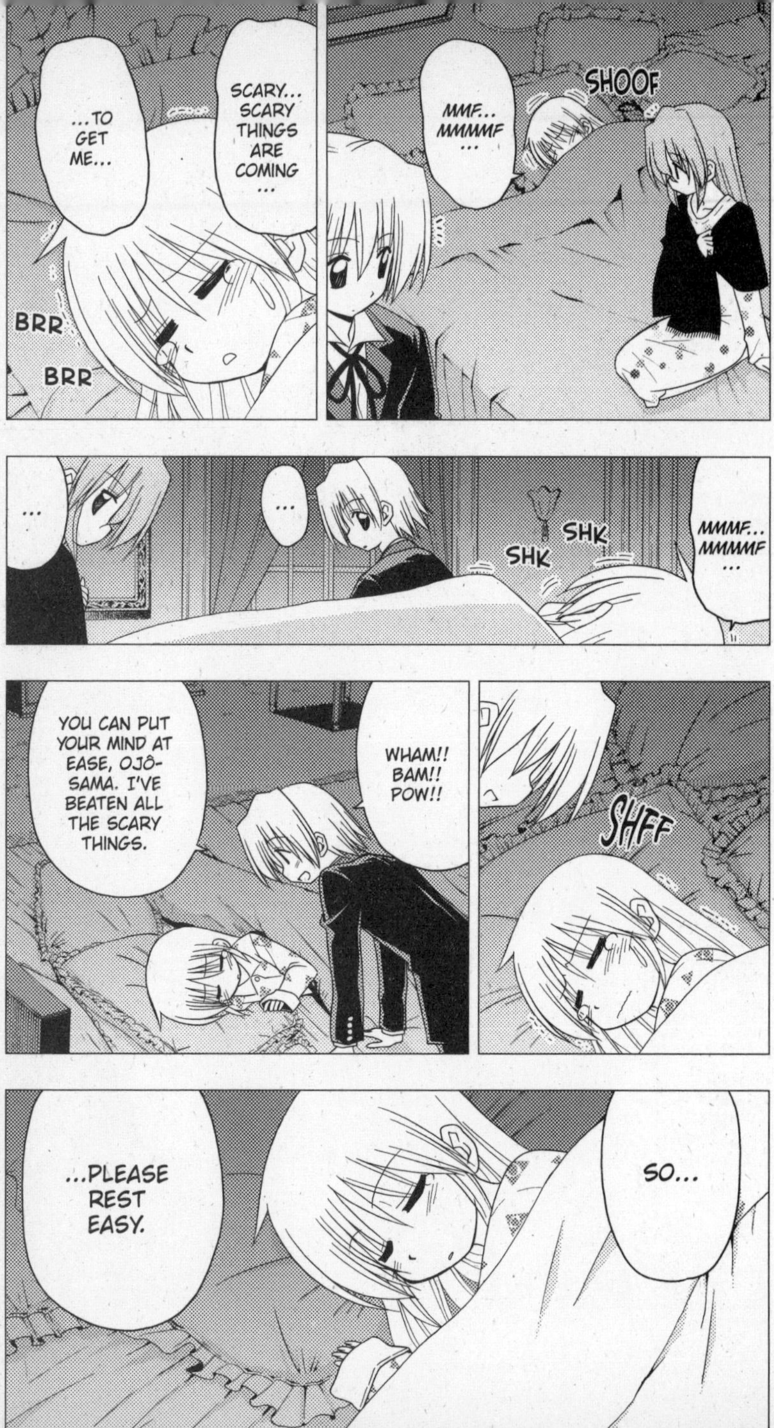
SHOOF
MMF... MMMMF ...
SCARY... SCARY THINGS ARE COMING ...
...TO GET ME...
BRR
BRR
MMMF... MMMMF ...
SHK
SHK
...
...
SHFF
WHAM!! BAM!! POW!!
YOU CAN PUT YOUR MIND AT EASE, OJÔ-SAMA. I'VE BEATEN ALL THE SCARY THINGS.
SO...
...PLEASE REST EASY.

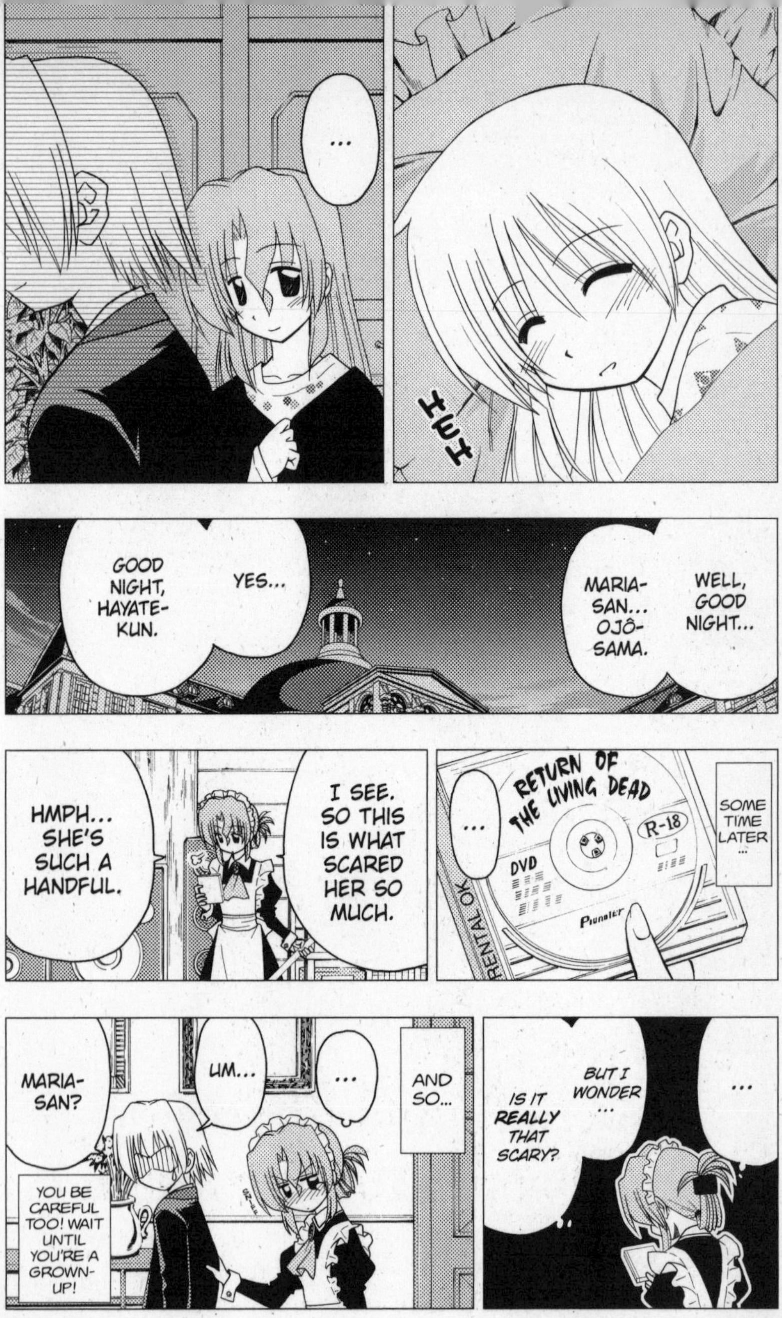
HEH
...
WELL, GOOD NIGHT...
MARIA-SAN... OJÔ-SAMA.
YES...
GOOD NIGHT, HAYATE-KUN.
SOME TIME LATER ...
...
RETURN OF THE LIVING DEAD
R-18
DVD
RENTAL OK
I SEE. SO THIS IS WHAT SCARED HER SO MUCH.
HMPH... SHE'S SUCH A HANDFUL.
...
BUT I WONDER ...
IS IT REALLY THAT SCARY?
AND SO...
...
UM...
MARIA-SAN?
YOU BE CAREFUL TOO! WAIT UNTIL YOU'RE A GROWN-UP!

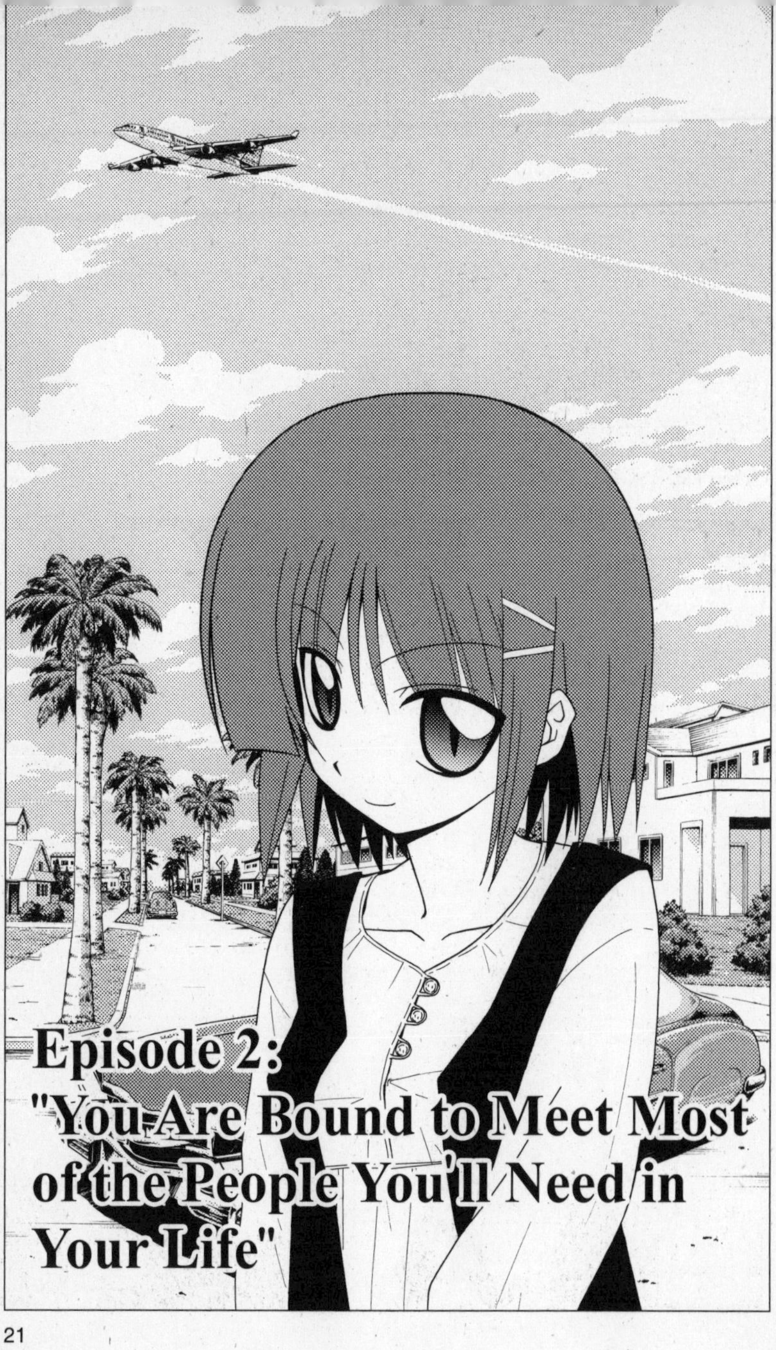
Episode 2:
"You Are Bound to Meet Most of the People You'll Need in Your Life"

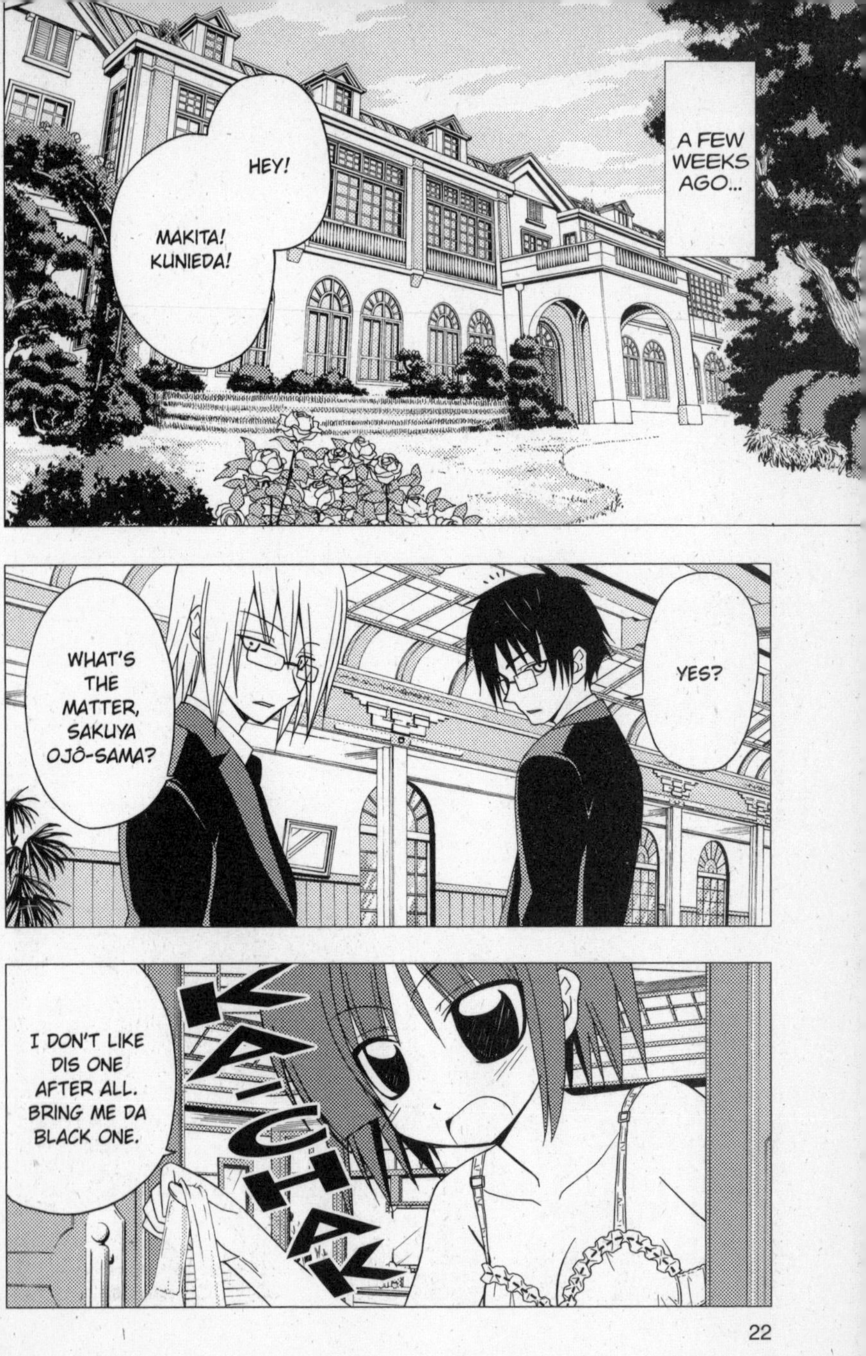
A FEW WEEKS AGO...
HEY!
MAKITA! KUNIEDA!
YES?
WHAT'S THE MATTER, SAKUYA OJÔ-SAMA?
KA-CHAK
I DON'T LIKE DIS ONE AFTER ALL. BRING ME DA BLACK ONE.

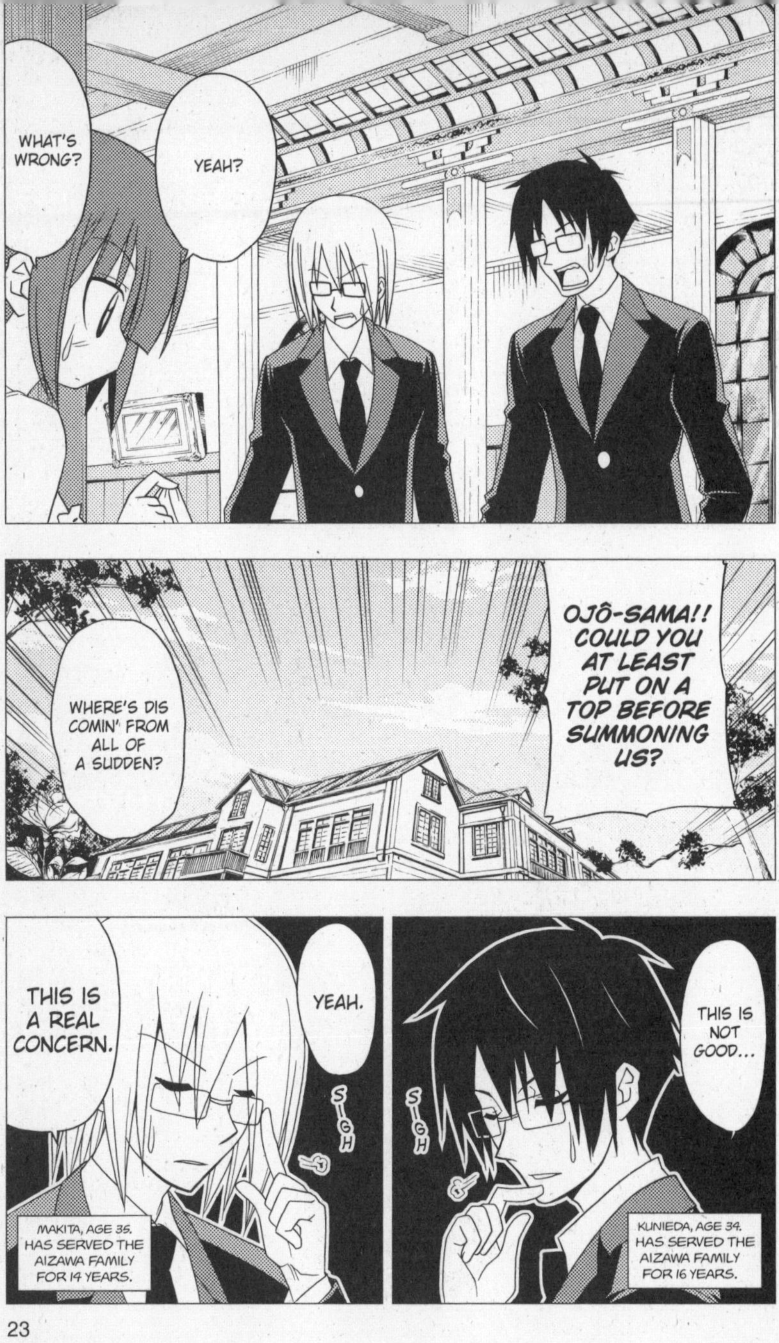
YEAH?
WHAT'S WRONG?
OJÔ-SAMA!! COULD YOU AT LEAST PUT ON A TOP BEFORE SUMMONING US?
WHERE'S DIS COMIN' FROM ALL OF A SUDDEN?
THIS IS NOT GOOD...
SIGH
KUNIEDA, AGE 34. HAS SERVED THE AIZAWA FAMILY FOR 16 YEARS.
YEAH.
THIS IS A REAL CONCERN.
SIGH
MAKITA, AGE 35. HAS SERVED THE AIZAWA FAMILY FOR 14 YEARS.

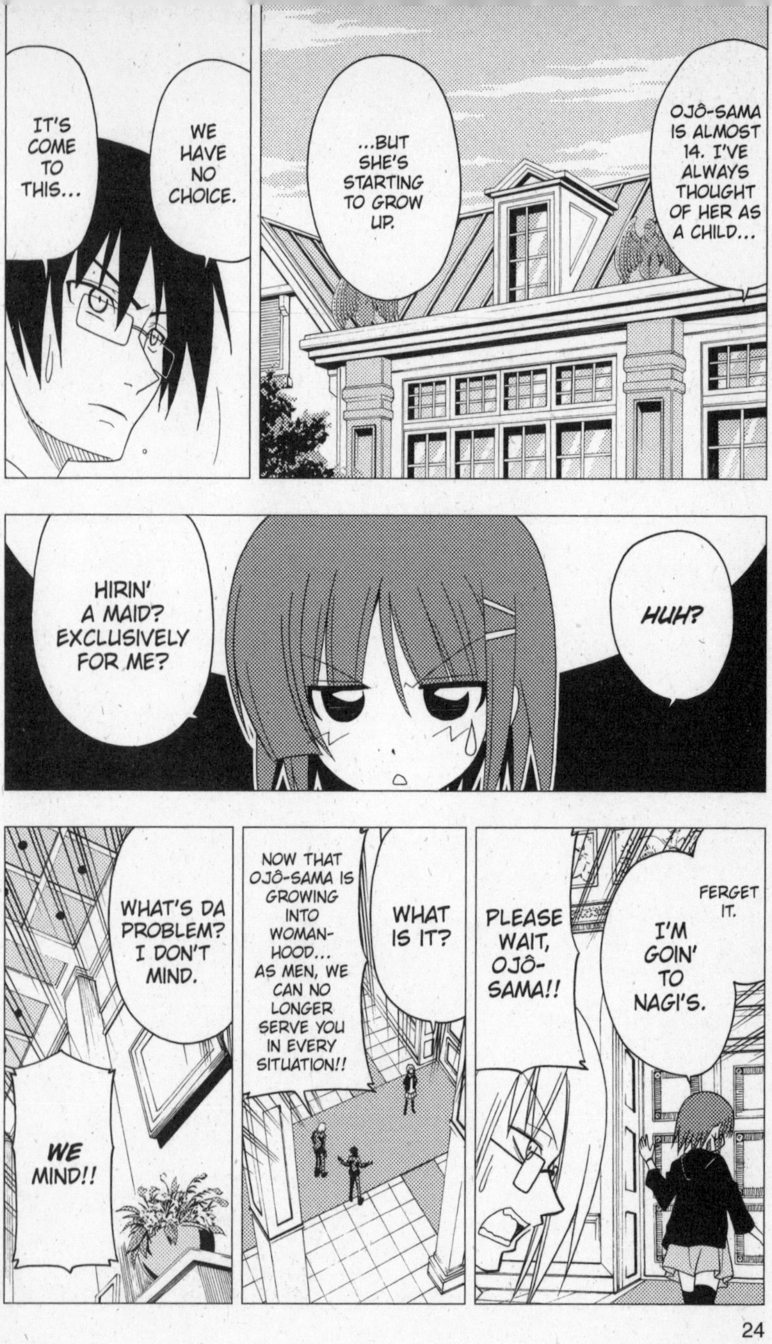
OJÔ-SAMA IS ALMOST 14. I'VE ALWAYS THOUGHT OF HER AS A CHILD...
...BUT SHE'S STARTING TO GROW UP.
WE HAVE NO CHOICE.
IT'S COME TO THIS...
HUH?
HIRIN' A MAID? EXCLUSIVELY FOR ME?
FERGET IT.
I'M GOIN' TO NAGI'S.
PLEASE WAIT, OJÔ-SAMA!!
WHAT IS IT?
NOW THAT OJÔ-SAMA IS GROWING INTO WOMAN-HOOD... AS MEN, WE CAN NO LONGER SERVE YOU IN EVERY SITUATION!!
WHAT'S DA PROBLEM? I DON'T MIND.
WE MIND!!

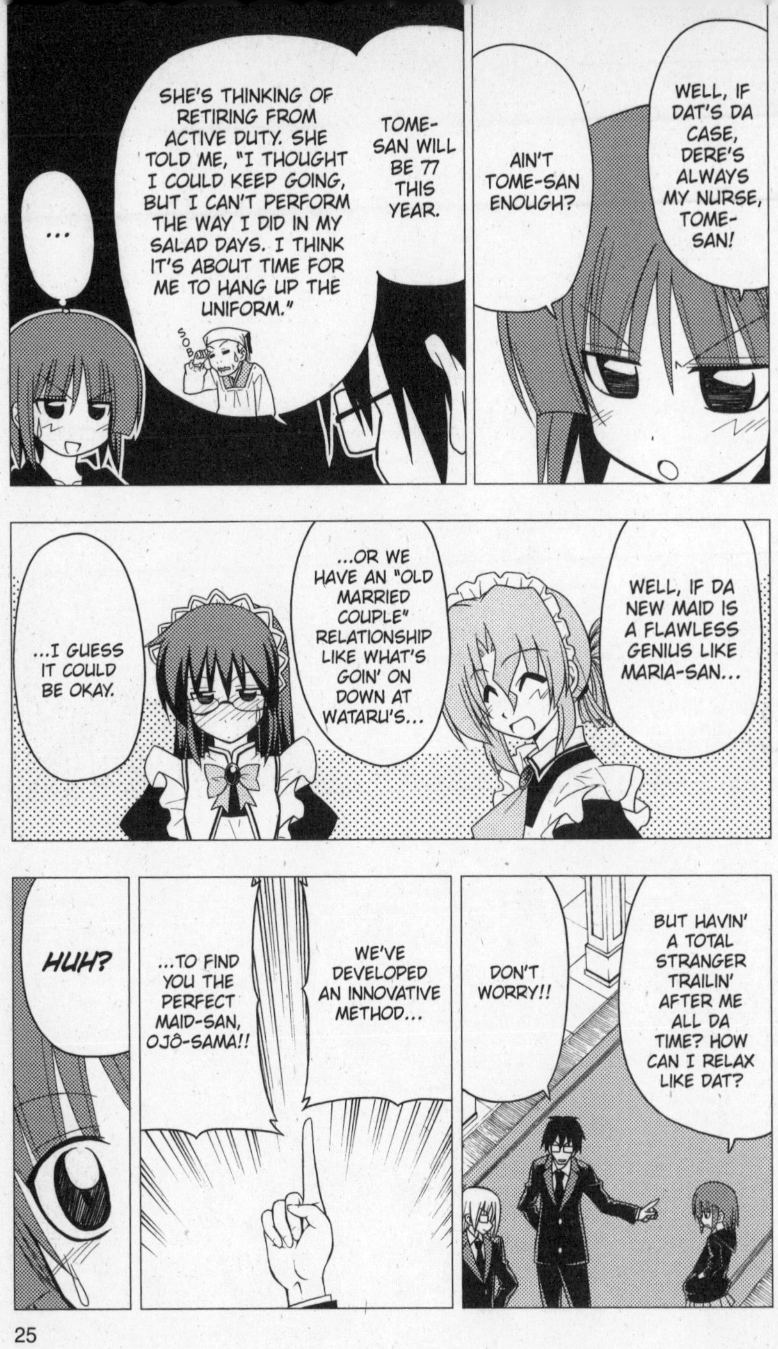
WELL, IF DAT'S DA CASE, DERE'S ALWAYS MY NURSE, TOME-SAN!
AIN'T TOME-SAN ENOUGH?
TOME-SAN WILL BE 77 THIS YEAR.
SHE'S THINKING OF RETIRING FROM ACTIVE DUTY. SHE TOLD ME, "I THOUGHT I COULD KEEP GOING, BUT I CAN'T PERFORM THE WAY I DID IN MY SALAD DAYS. I THINK IT'S ABOUT TIME FOR ME TO HANG UP THE UNIFORM."
SOB
...
WELL, IF DA NEW MAID IS A FLAWLESS GENIUS LIKE MARIA-SAN...
...OR WE HAVE AN "OLD MARRIED COUPLE" RELATIONSHIP LIKE WHAT'S GOIN' ON DOWN AT WATARU'S...
...I GUESS IT COULD BE OKAY.
BUT HAVIN' A TOTAL STRANGER TRAILIN' AFTER ME ALL DA TIME? HOW CAN I RELAX LIKE DAT?
DON'T WORRY!!
WE'VE DEVELOPED AN INNOVATIVE METHOD...
...TO FIND YOU THE PERFECT MAID-SAN, OJÔ-SAMA!!
HUH?

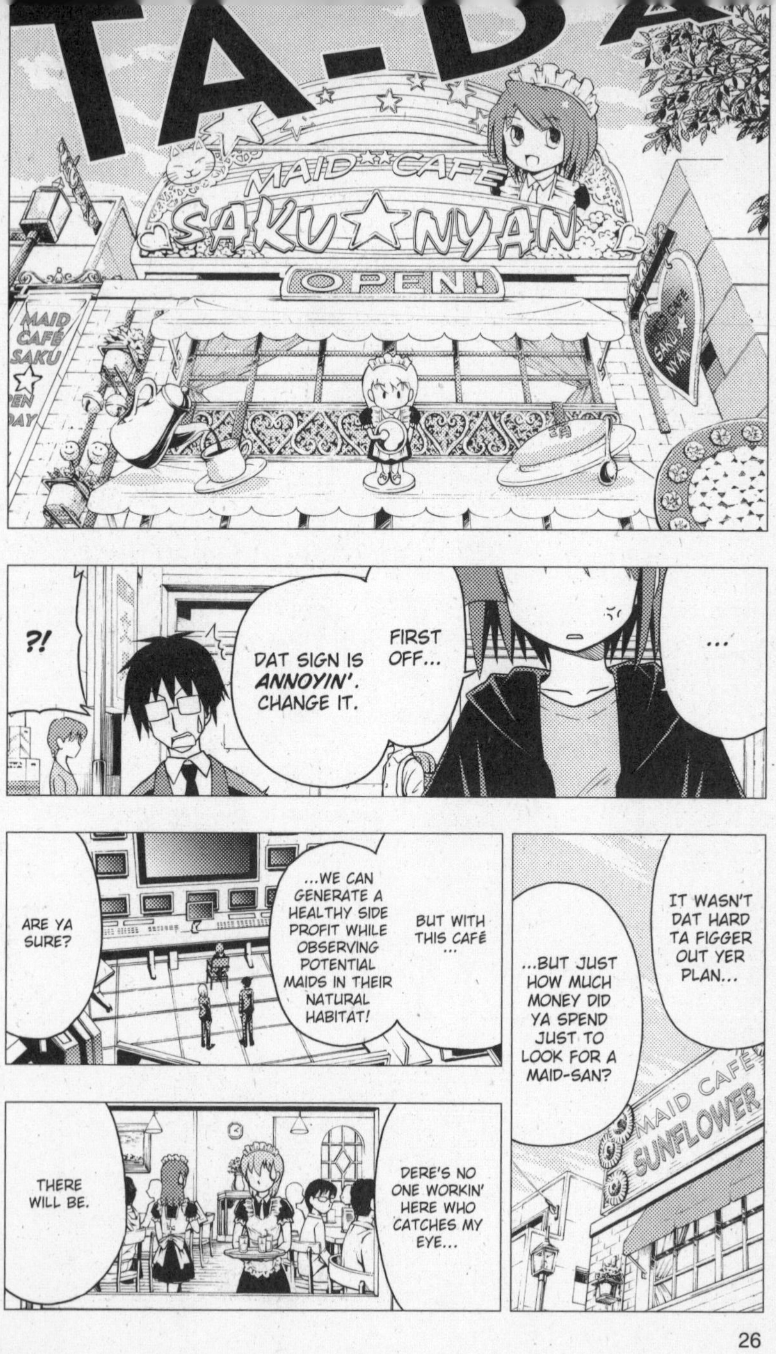
TA-DA
MAID☆☆CAFE
SAKU☆NYAN
OPEN!
MAID CAFÉ SAKU☆
...
FIRST OFF...
DAT SIGN IS ANNOYIN'. CHANGE IT.
?!
IT WASN'T DAT HARD TA FIGGER OUT YER PLAN...
...BUT JUST HOW MUCH MONEY DID YA SPEND JUST TO LOOK FOR A MAID-SAN?
MAID CAFÉ
SUNFLOWER
BUT WITH THIS CAFÉ ...
...WE CAN GENERATE A HEALTHY SIDE PROFIT WHILE OBSERVING POTENTIAL MAIDS IN THEIR NATURAL HABITAT!
ARE YA SURE?
DERE'S NO ONE WORKIN' HERE WHO CATCHES MY EYE...
THERE WILL BE.

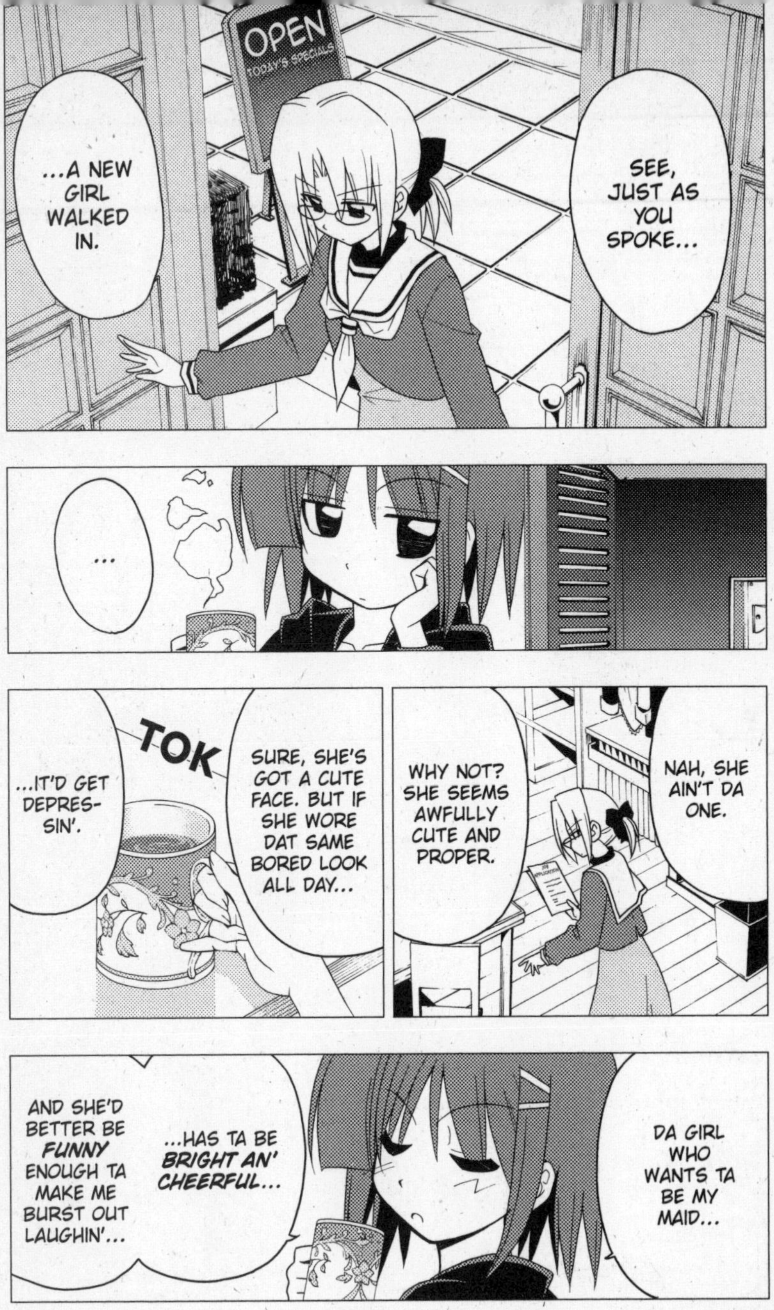
OPEN
TODAY'S SPECIALS
SEE, JUST AS YOU SPOKE...
...A NEW GIRL WALKED IN.
...
NAH, SHE AIN'T DA ONE.
WHY NOT? SHE SEEMS AWFULLY CUTE AND PROPER.
SURE, SHE'S GOT A CUTE FACE. BUT IF SHE WORE DAT SAME BORED LOOK ALL DAY...
TOK
...IT'D GET DEPRES-SIN'.
DA GIRL WHO WANTS TA BE MY MAID...
...HAS TA BE *BRIGHT AN' CHEERFUL*...
AND SHE'D BETTER BE *FUNNY* ENOUGH TA MAKE ME BURST OUT LAUGHIN'...

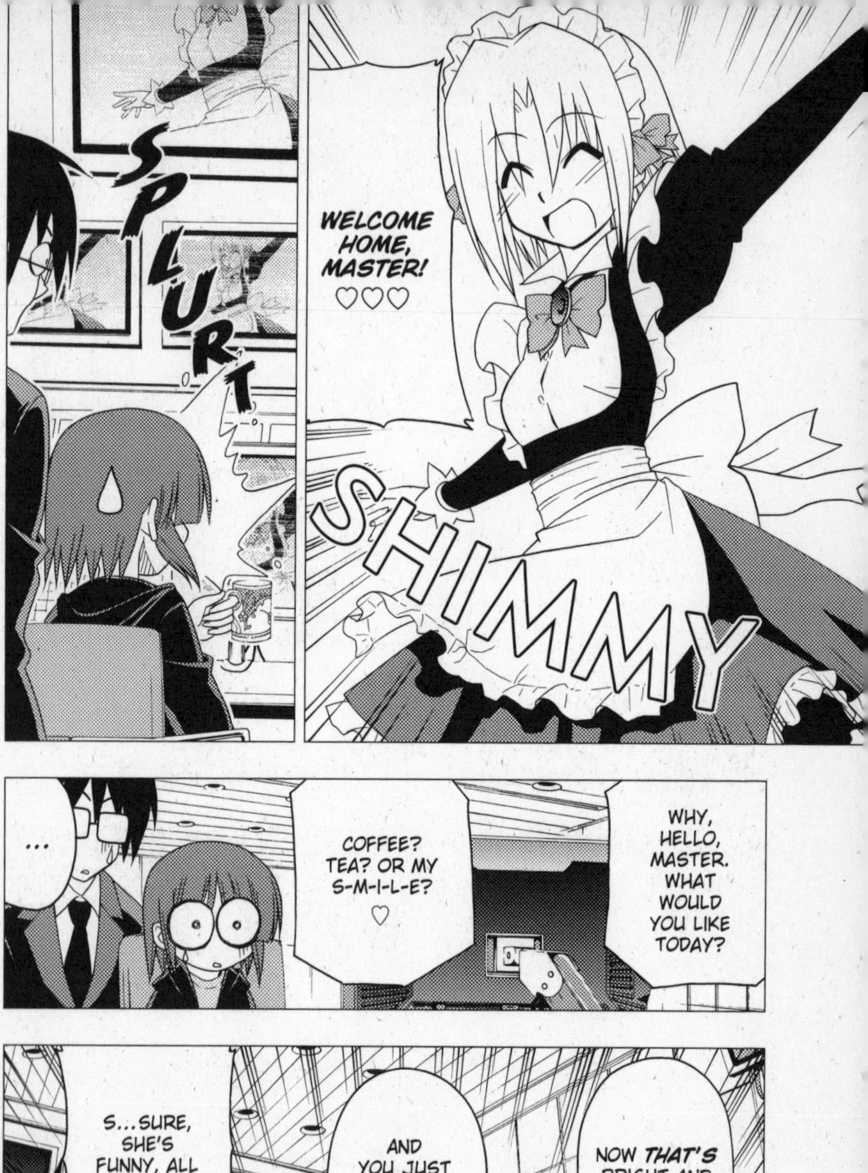
WELCOME HOME, MASTER! ♡♡♡
SHIMMY
SPLURT
WHY, HELLO, MASTER. WHAT WOULD YOU LIKE TODAY?
COFFEE? TEA? OR MY S-M-I-L-E? ♡
...
NOW *THAT'S* BRIGHT AND CHEERFUL.
AND YOU JUST BURST OUT LAUGHING!
S...SURE, SHE'S FUNNY, ALL RIGHT...

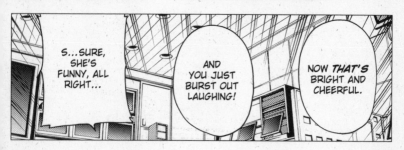

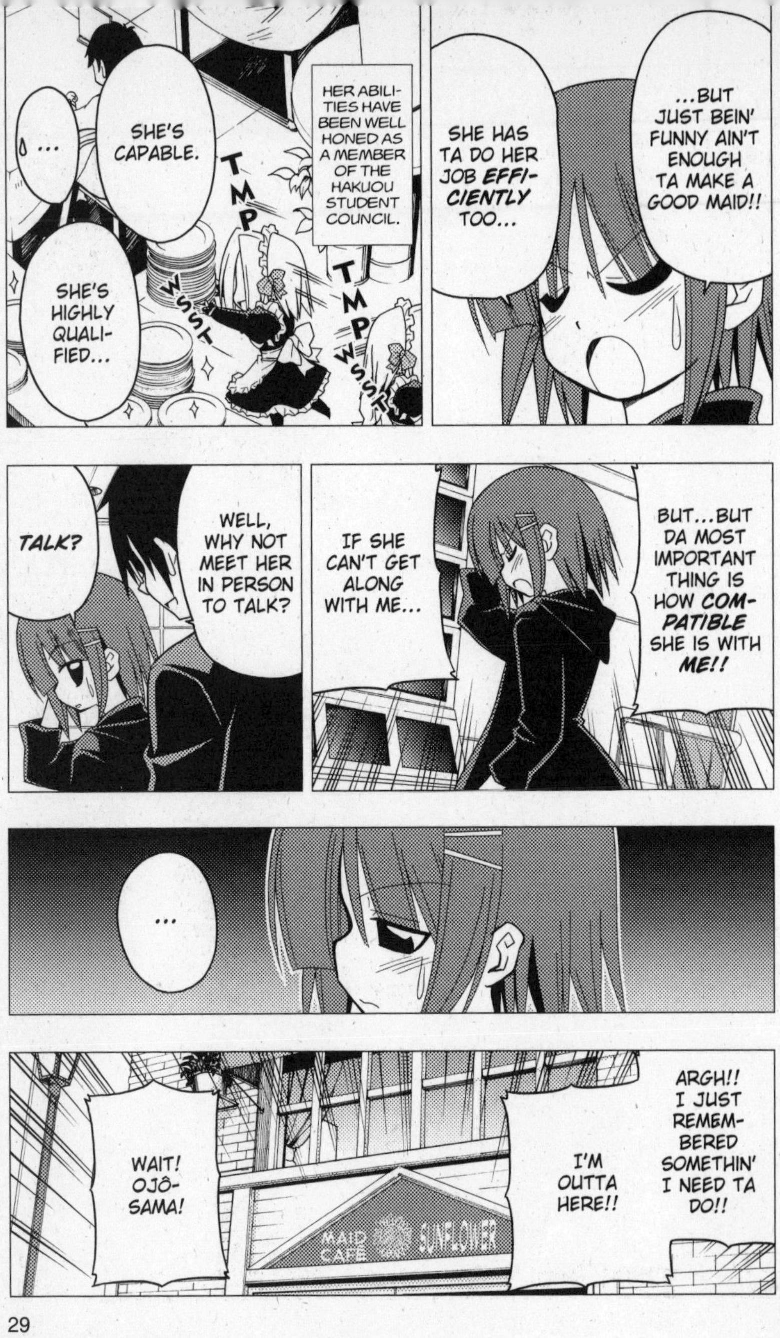
...BUT JUST BEIN' FUNNY AIN'T ENOUGH TA MAKE A GOOD MAID!!
SHE HAS TA DO HER JOB *EFFICIENTLY* TOO...
HER ABILITIES HAVE BEEN WELL HONED AS A MEMBER OF THE HAKUOU STUDENT COUNCIL.
SHE'S CAPABLE.
...
TMP
TMP
WSSST
WSSST
SHE'S HIGHLY QUALIFIED...
BUT...BUT DA MOST IMPORTANT THING IS HOW *COMPATIBLE* SHE IS WITH *ME!!*
IF SHE CAN'T GET ALONG WITH ME...
WELL, WHY NOT MEET HER IN PERSON TO TALK?
TALK?
...
ARGH!! I JUST REMEMBERED SOMETHIN' I NEED TA DO!!
I'M OUTTA HERE!!
MAID CAFE SUNFLOWER
WAIT! OJÔ-SAMA!

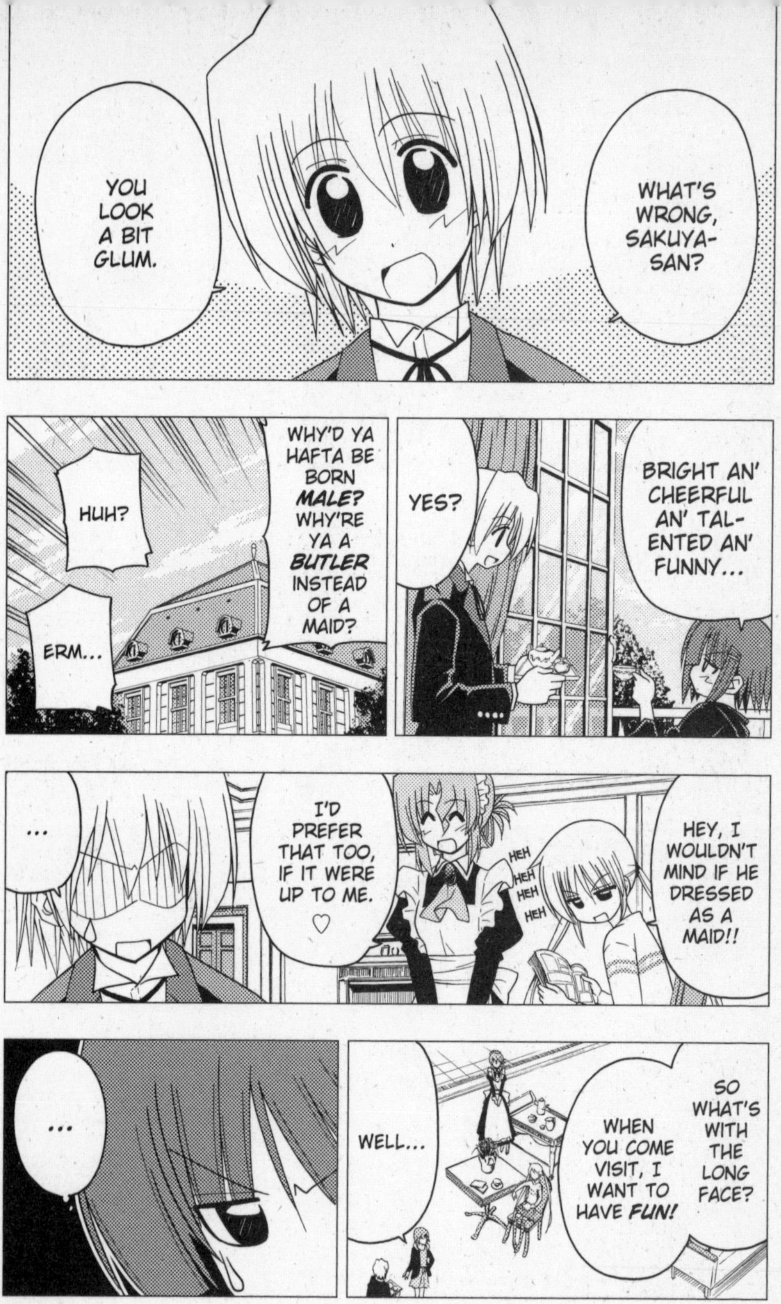
WHAT'S WRONG, SAKUYA-SAN?
YOU LOOK A BIT GLUM.
BRIGHT AN' CHEERFUL AN' TAL-ENTED AN' FUNNY...
YES?
WHY'D YA HAFTA BE BORN *MALE?* WHY'RE YA A *BUTLER* INSTEAD OF A MAID?
HUH?
ERM...
HEY, I WOULDN'T MIND IF HE DRESSED AS A MAID!!
HEH HEH HEH HEH
I'D PREFER THAT TOO, IF IT WERE UP TO ME. ♡
...
SO WHAT'S WITH THE LONG FACE?
WHEN YOU COME VISIT, I WANT TO HAVE *FUN!*
WELL...
...

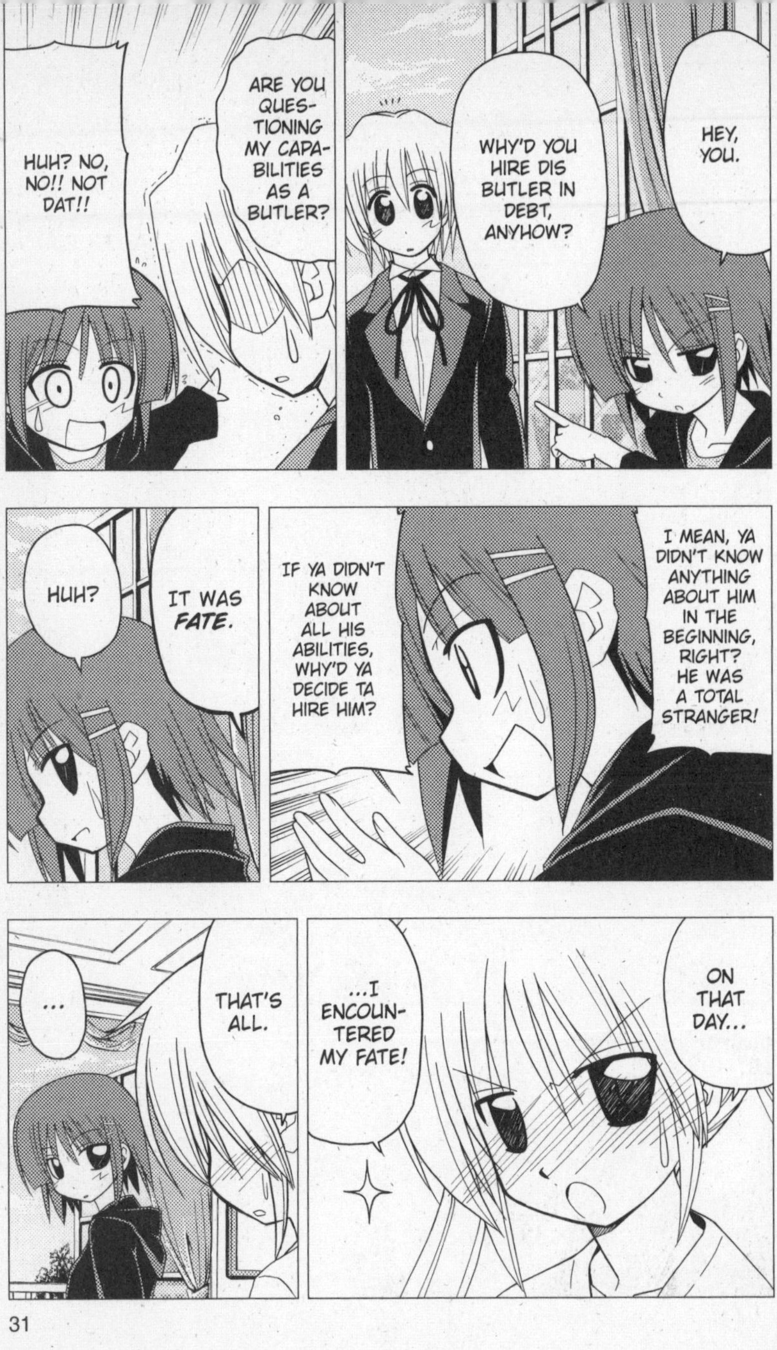
HEY, YOU.
WHY'D YOU HIRE DIS BUTLER IN DEBT, ANYHOW?
ARE YOU QUES-TIONING MY CAPA-BILITIES AS A BUTLER?
HUH? NO, NO!! NOT DAT!!
I MEAN, YA DIDN'T KNOW ANYTHING ABOUT HIM IN THE BEGINNING, RIGHT? HE WAS A TOTAL STRANGER!
IF YA DIDN'T KNOW ABOUT ALL HIS ABILITIES, WHY'D YA DECIDE TA HIRE HIM?
IT WAS *FATE.*
HUH?
ON THAT DAY...
...I ENCOUN-TERED MY FATE!
THAT'S ALL.
...

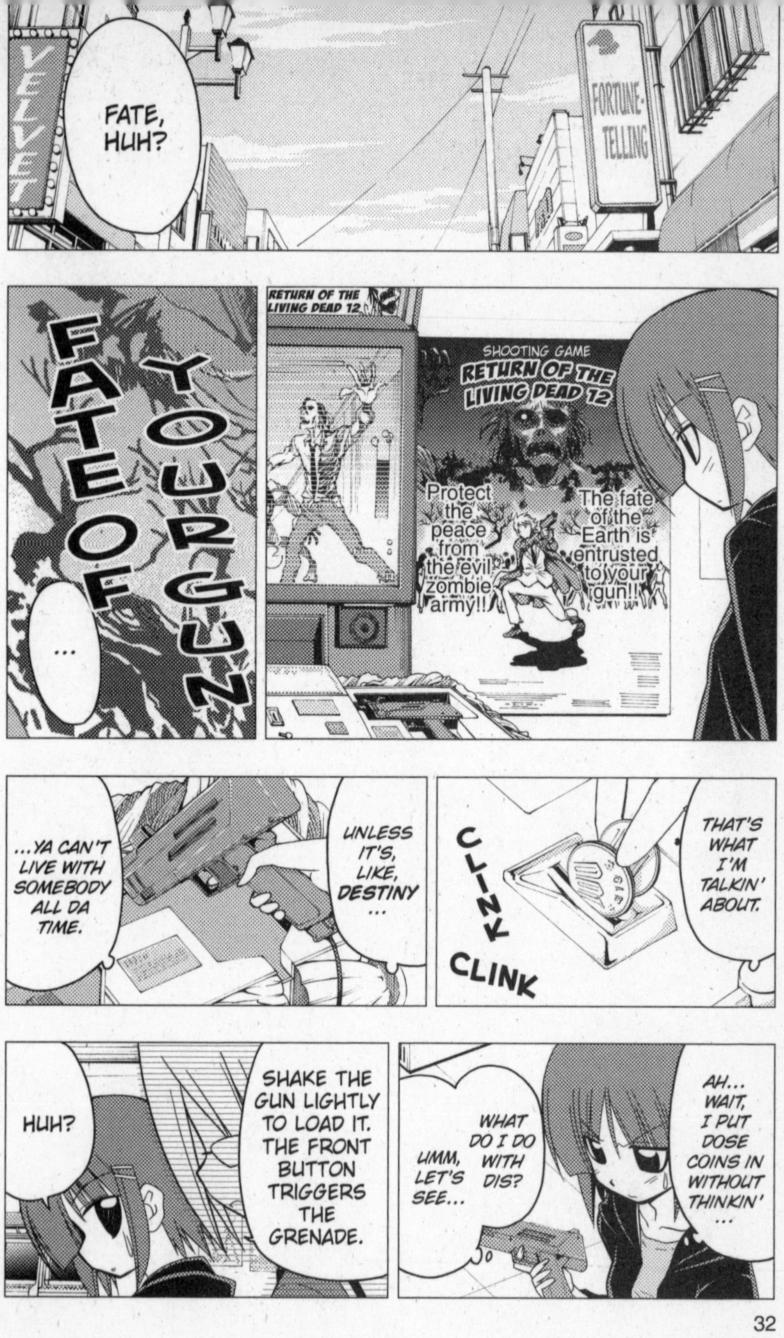
VELVET
FORTUNE-TELLING
FATE, HUH?
RETURN OF THE LIVING DEAD 12
SHOOTING GAME
RETURN OF THE LIVING DEAD 12
The fate of the Earth is entrusted to your gun!!
Protect the peace from the evil zombie army!!
FATE OF YOUR GUN
...
THAT'S WHAT I'M TALKIN' ABOUT.
CLINK
CLINK
UNLESS IT'S, LIKE, DESTINY...
...YA CAN'T LIVE WITH SOMEBODY ALL DA TIME.
AH... WAIT, I PUT DOSE COINS IN WITHOUT THINKIN'...
WHAT DO I DO WITH DIS?
UMM, LET'S SEE...
SHAKE THE GUN LIGHTLY TO LOAD IT. THE FRONT BUTTON TRIGGERS THE GRENADE.
HUH?

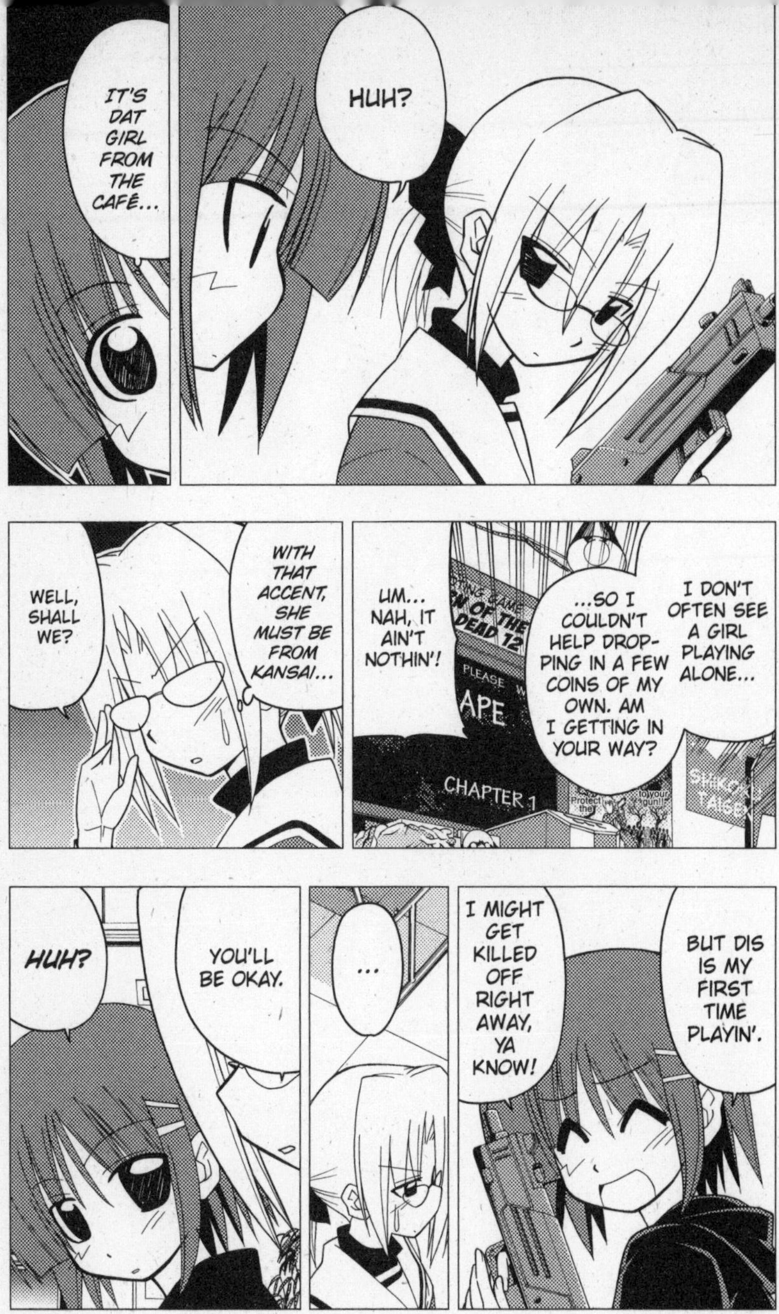
HUH?
IT'S DAT GIRL FROM THE CAFÉ...
I DON'T OFTEN SEE A GIRL PLAYING ALONE...
...SO I COULDN'T HELP DROPPING IN A FEW COINS OF MY OWN. AM I GETTING IN YOUR WAY?
UM... NAH, IT AIN'T NOTHIN'!
CHAPTER 1
WITH THAT ACCENT, SHE MUST BE FROM KANSAI...
WELL, SHALL WE?
BUT DIS IS MY FIRST TIME PLAYIN'.
I MIGHT GET KILLED OFF RIGHT AWAY, YA KNOW!
...
YOU'LL BE OKAY.
HUH?

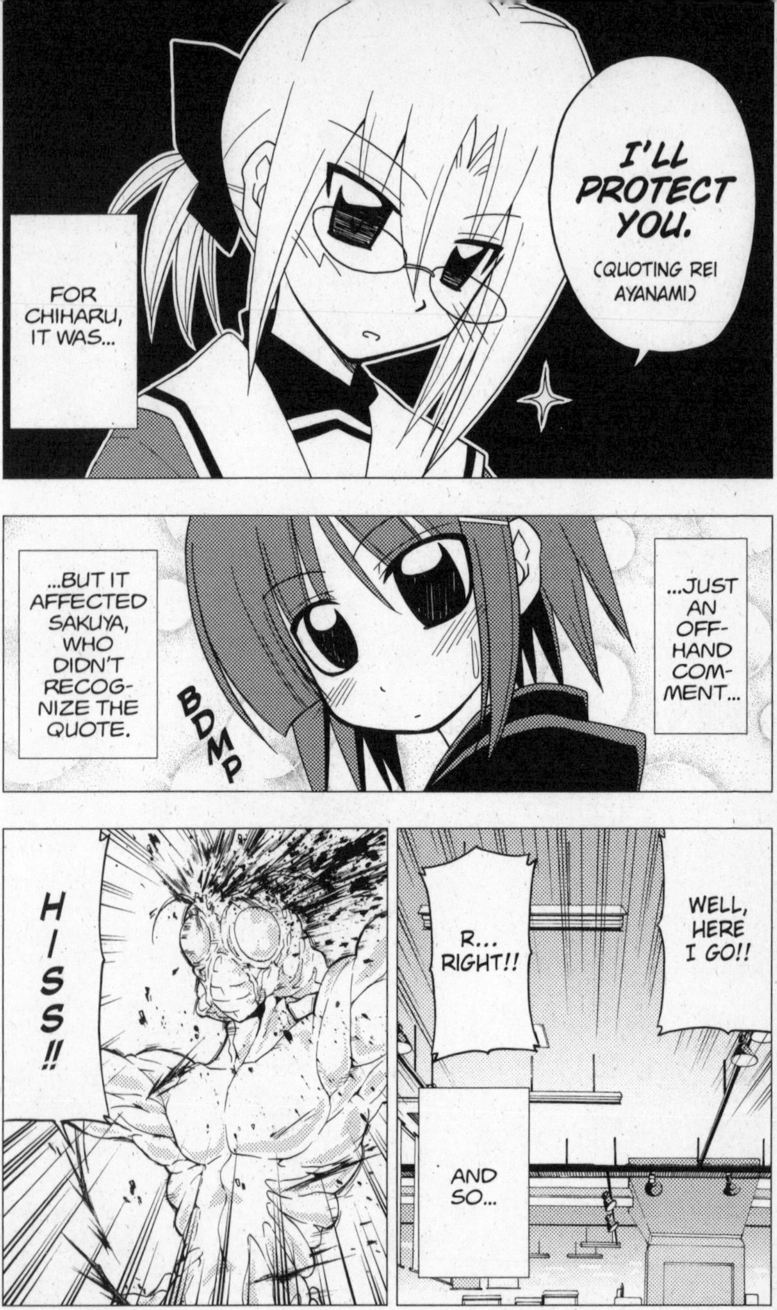
I'LL PROTECT YOU.
(QUOTING REI AYANAMI)
FOR CHIHARU, IT WAS...
...JUST AN OFF-HAND COMMENT...
BDMP
...BUT IT AFFECTED SAKUYA, WHO DIDN'T RECOGNIZE THE QUOTE.
WELL, HERE I GO!!
R... RIGHT!!
AND SO...
HISS!!

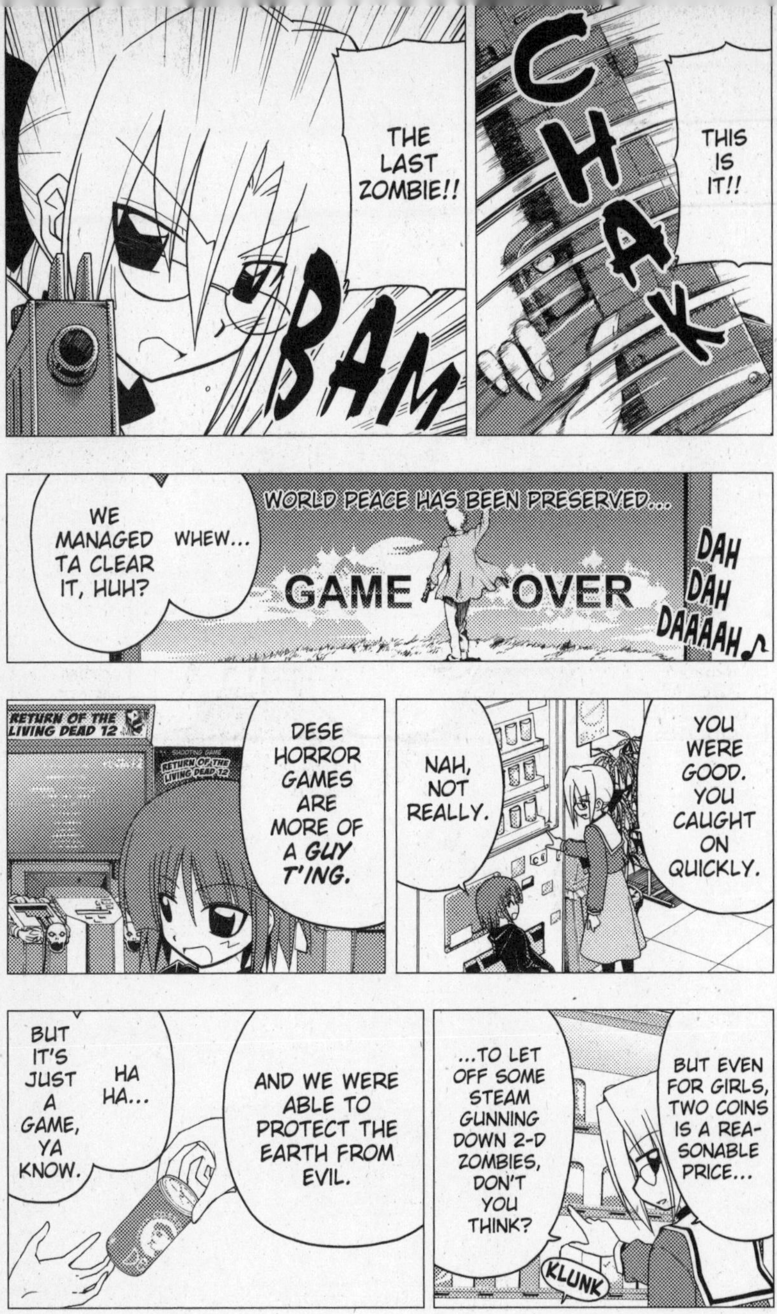
CHAK
THIS IS IT!!
THE LAST ZOMBIE!!
BAM
DAH DAH DAAAAH♪
WORLD PEACE HAS BEEN PRESERVED...
GAME OVER
WHEW...
WE MANAGED TA CLEAR IT, HUH?
YOU WERE GOOD. YOU CAUGHT ON QUICKLY.
NAH, NOT REALLY.
RETURN OF THE LIVING DEAD 12
SHOOTING GAME
RETURN OF THE LIVING DEAD 12
DESE HORROR GAMES ARE MORE OF A *GUY T'ING.*
BUT EVEN FOR GIRLS, TWO COINS IS A REA-SONABLE PRICE...
...TO LET OFF SOME STEAM GUNNING DOWN 2-D ZOMBIES, DON'T YOU THINK?
KLUNK
AND WE WERE ABLE TO PROTECT THE EARTH FROM EVIL.
HA HA...
BUT IT'S JUST A GAME, YA KNOW.

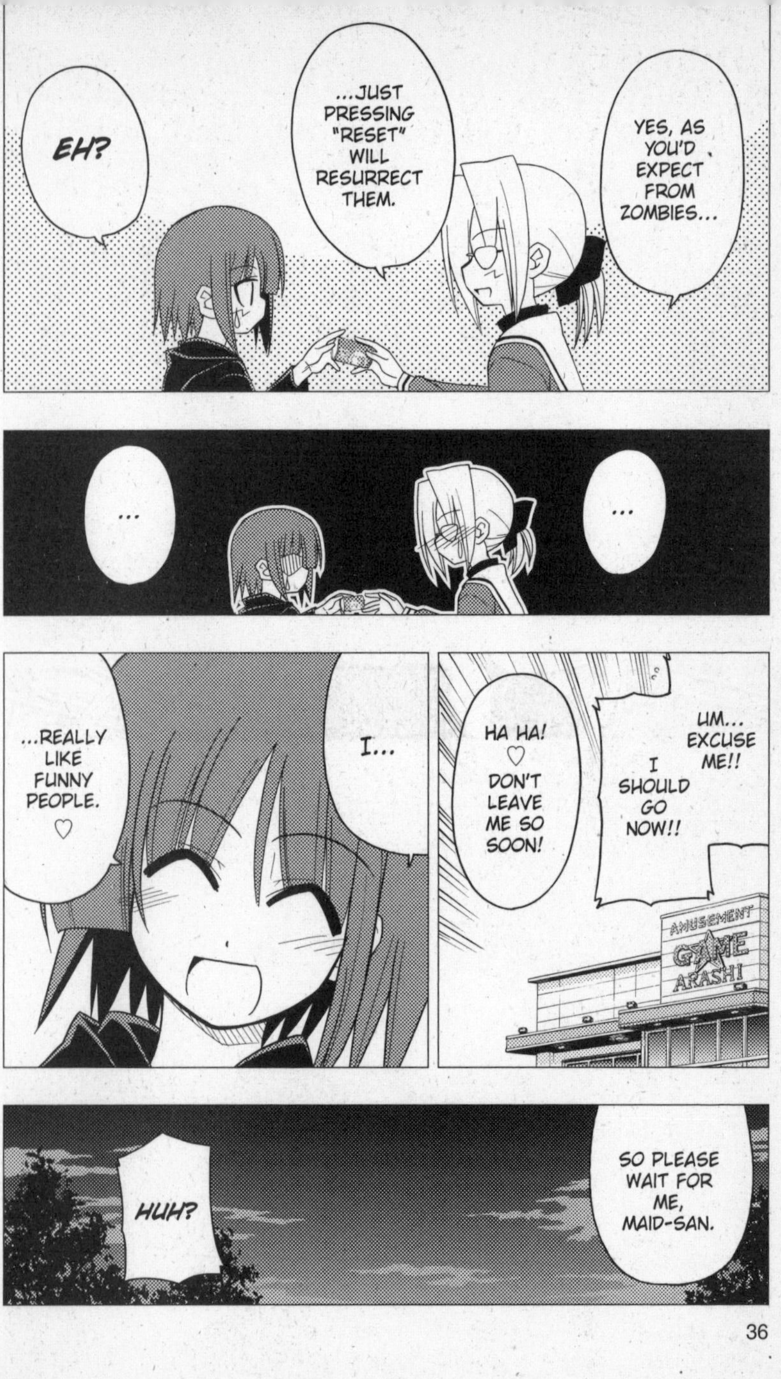
YES, AS YOU'D EXPECT FROM ZOMBIES...
...JUST PRESSING "RESET" WILL RESURRECT THEM.
EH?
...
...
UM... EXCUSE ME!!
I SHOULD GO NOW!!
HA HA! ♡ DON'T LEAVE ME SO SOON!
AMUSEMENT GAME ARASHI
I...
...REALLY LIKE FUNNY PEOPLE. ♡
SO PLEASE WAIT FOR ME, MAID-SAN.
HUH?

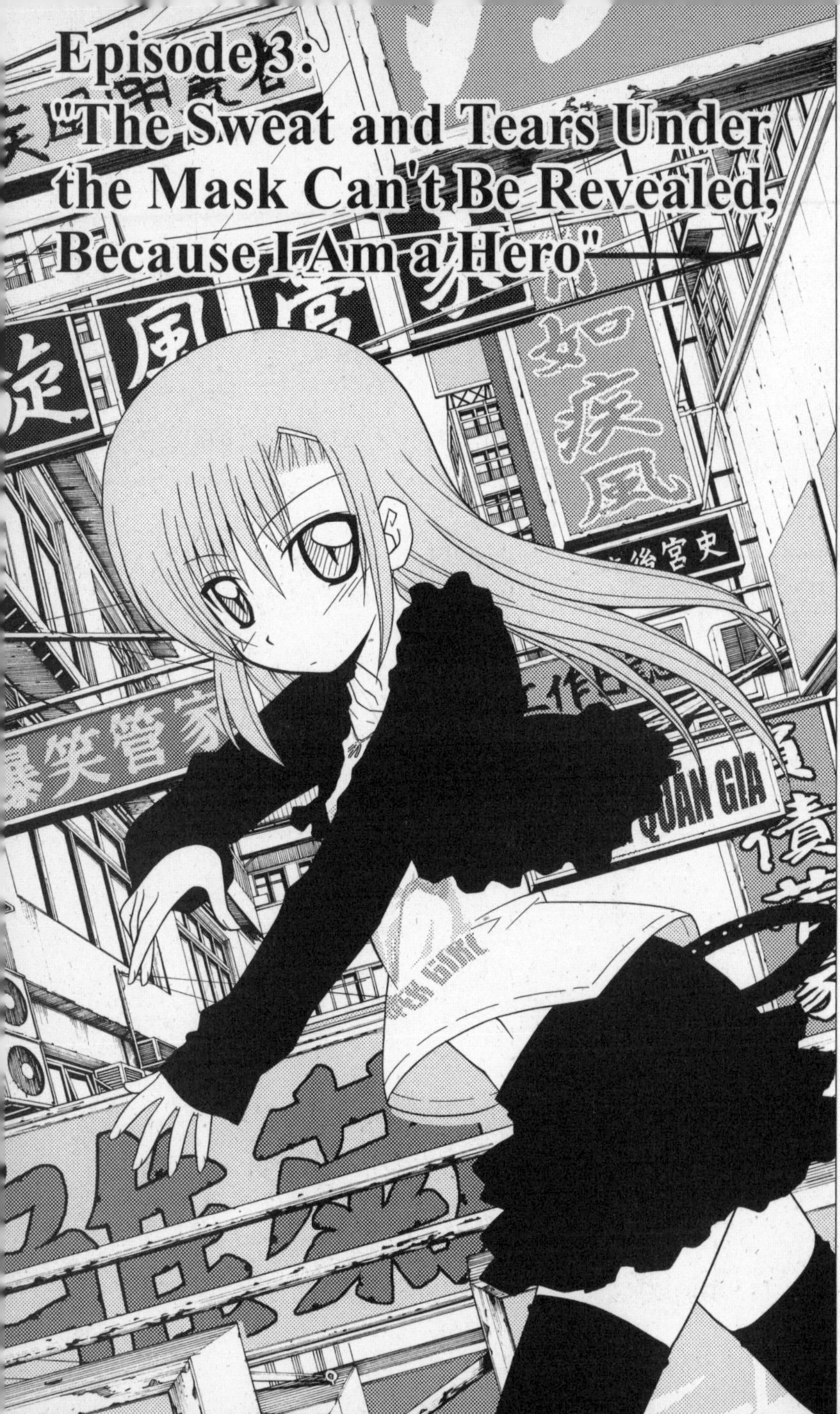
Episode 3:
"The Sweat and Tears Under the Mask Can't Be Revealed, Because I Am a Hero"
如疾風
爆笑管家
QUAN GIA

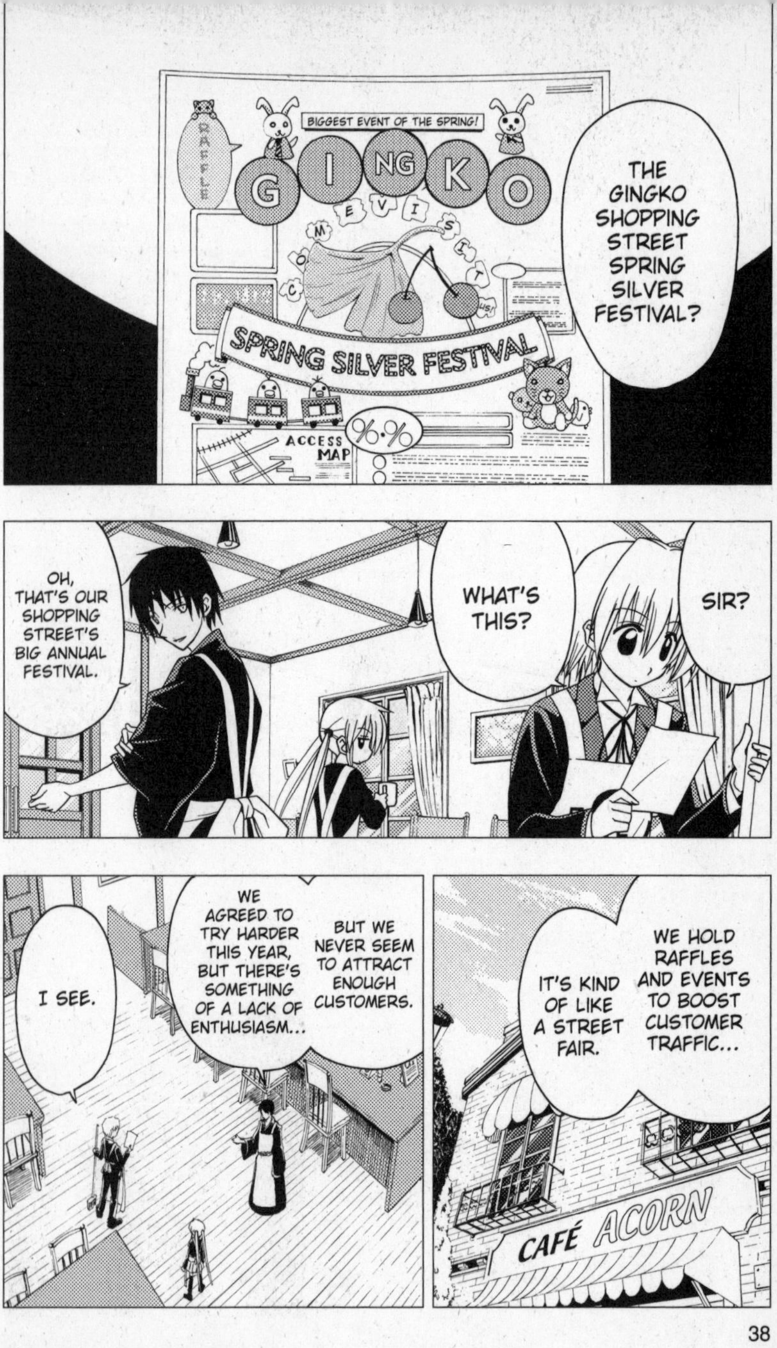
BIGGEST EVENT OF THE SPRING!
RAFFLE
GINGKO
COME VISIT US!
SPRING SILVER FESTIVAL
ACCESS MAP
THE GINGKO SHOPPING STREET SPRING SILVER FESTIVAL?
SIR?
WHAT'S THIS?
OH, THAT'S OUR SHOPPING STREET'S BIG ANNUAL FESTIVAL.
WE HOLD RAFFLES AND EVENTS TO BOOST CUSTOMER TRAFFIC...
IT'S KIND OF LIKE A STREET FAIR.
CAFÉ ACORN
BUT WE NEVER SEEM TO ATTRACT ENOUGH CUSTOMERS.
WE AGREED TO TRY HARDER THIS YEAR, BUT THERE'S SOMETHING OF A LACK OF ENTHUSIASM...
I SEE.

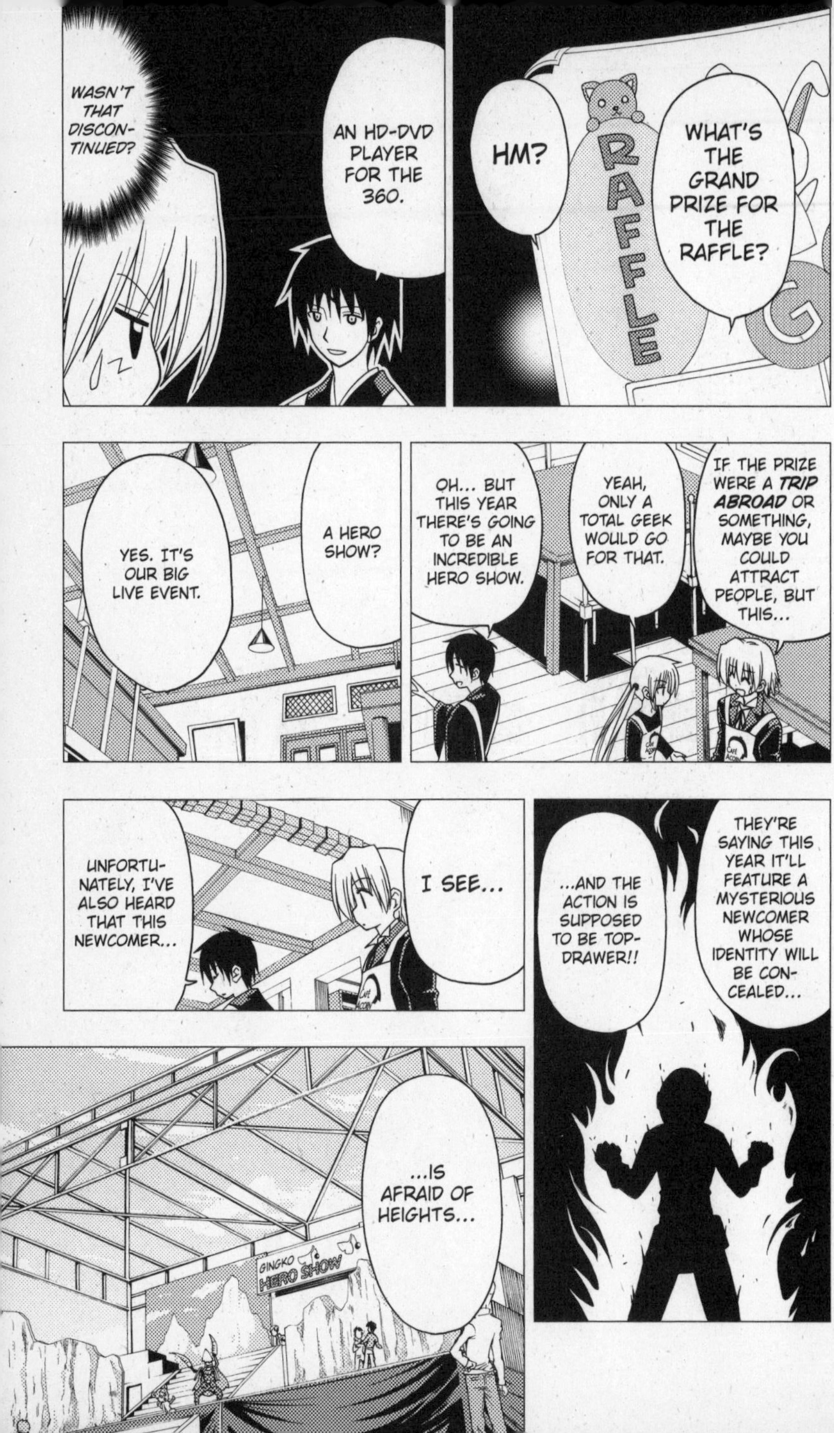
WHAT'S THE GRAND PRIZE FOR THE RAFFLE?
RAFFLE
HM?
AN HD-DVD PLAYER FOR THE 360.
WASN'T THAT DISCONTINUED?
IF THE PRIZE WERE A *TRIP ABROAD* OR SOMETHING, MAYBE YOU COULD ATTRACT PEOPLE, BUT THIS...
YEAH, ONLY A TOTAL GEEK WOULD GO FOR THAT.
OH... BUT THIS YEAR THERE'S GOING TO BE AN INCREDIBLE HERO SHOW.
A HERO SHOW?
YES. IT'S OUR BIG LIVE EVENT.
THEY'RE SAYING THIS YEAR IT'LL FEATURE A MYSTERIOUS NEWCOMER WHOSE IDENTITY WILL BE CONCEALED...
...AND THE ACTION IS SUPPOSED TO BE TOP-DRAWER!!
I SEE...
UNFORTUNATELY, I'VE ALSO HEARD THAT THIS NEWCOMER...
...IS AFRAID OF HEIGHTS...
GINGKO HERO SHOW

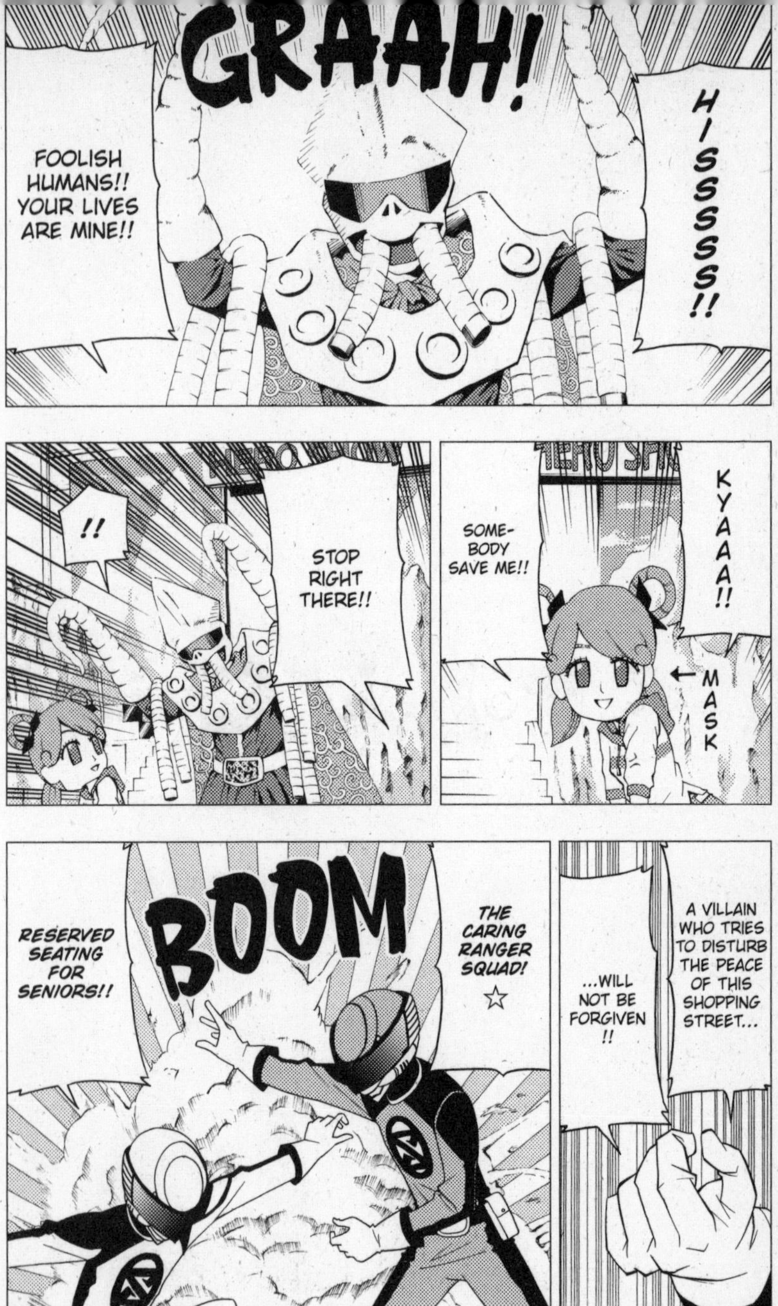
GRAAH!
HISSSSSS!!
FOOLISH HUMANS!! YOUR LIVES ARE MINE!!
KYAAAA!!
SOME-BODY SAVE ME!!
← MASK
STOP RIGHT THERE!!
!!
A VILLAIN WHO TRIES TO DISTURB THE PEACE OF THIS SHOPPING STREET...
...WILL NOT BE FORGIVEN !!
THE CARING RANGER SQUAD! ☆
BOOM
RESERVED SEATING FOR SENIORS!!

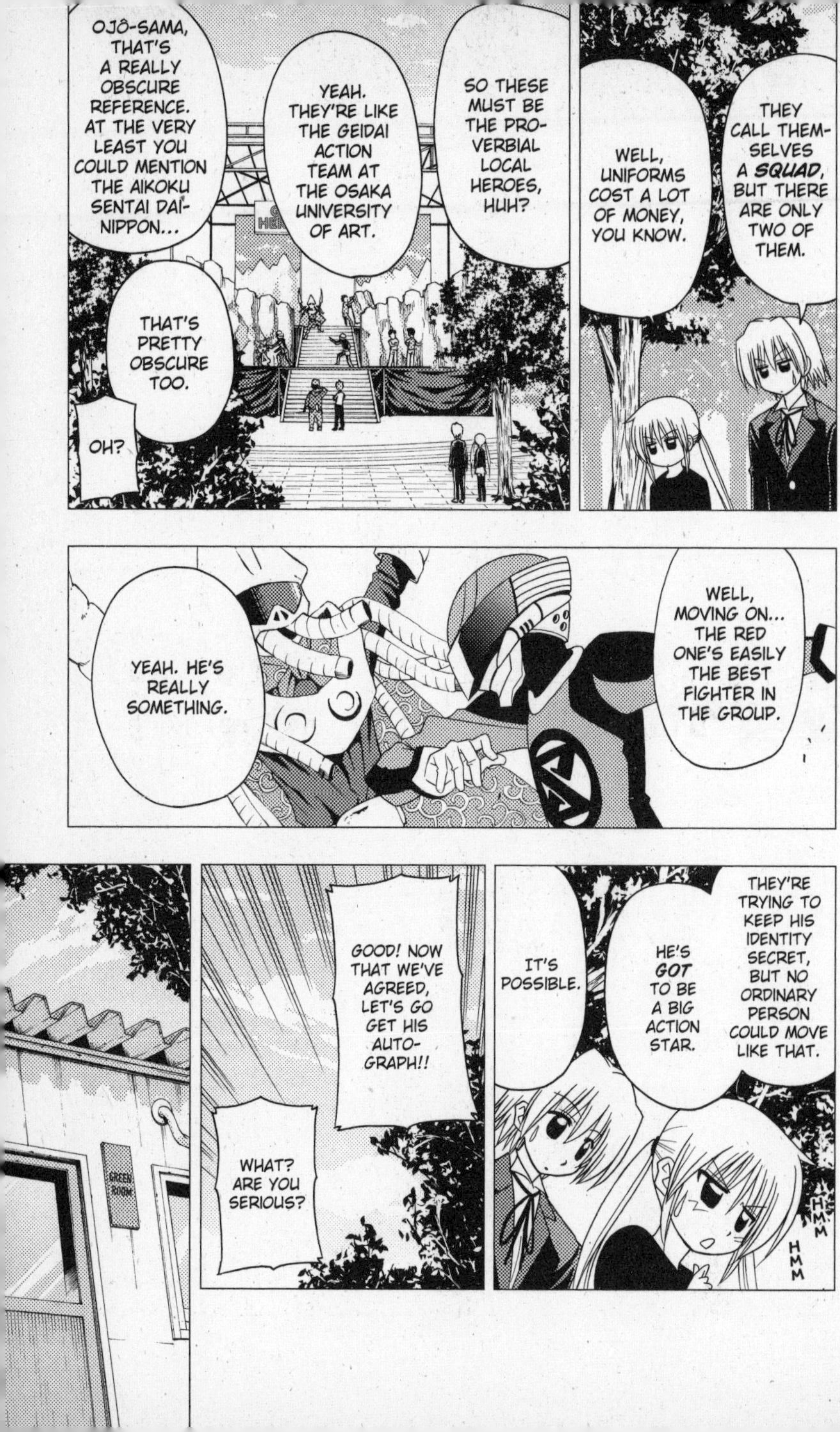
THEY CALL THEMSELVES A ***SQUAD***, BUT THERE ARE ONLY TWO OF THEM.
WELL, UNIFORMS COST A LOT OF MONEY, YOU KNOW.
SO THESE MUST BE THE PROVERBIAL LOCAL HEROES, HUH?
YEAH. THEY'RE LIKE THE GEIDAI ACTION TEAM AT THE OSAKA UNIVERSITY OF ART.
OJÔ-SAMA, THAT'S A REALLY OBSCURE REFERENCE. AT THE VERY LEAST YOU COULD MENTION THE AIKOKU SENTAI DAI-NIPPON...
THAT'S PRETTY OBSCURE TOO.
OH?
WELL, MOVING ON... THE RED ONE'S EASILY THE BEST FIGHTER IN THE GROUP.
YEAH. HE'S REALLY SOMETHING.
THEY'RE TRYING TO KEEP HIS IDENTITY SECRET, BUT NO ORDINARY PERSON COULD MOVE LIKE THAT.
HE'S ***GOT*** TO BE A BIG ACTION STAR.
IT'S POSSIBLE.
HMM
HMM
GOOD! NOW THAT WE'VE AGREED, LET'S GO GET HIS AUTOGRAPH!!
WHAT? ARE YOU SERIOUS?
GREEN ROOM

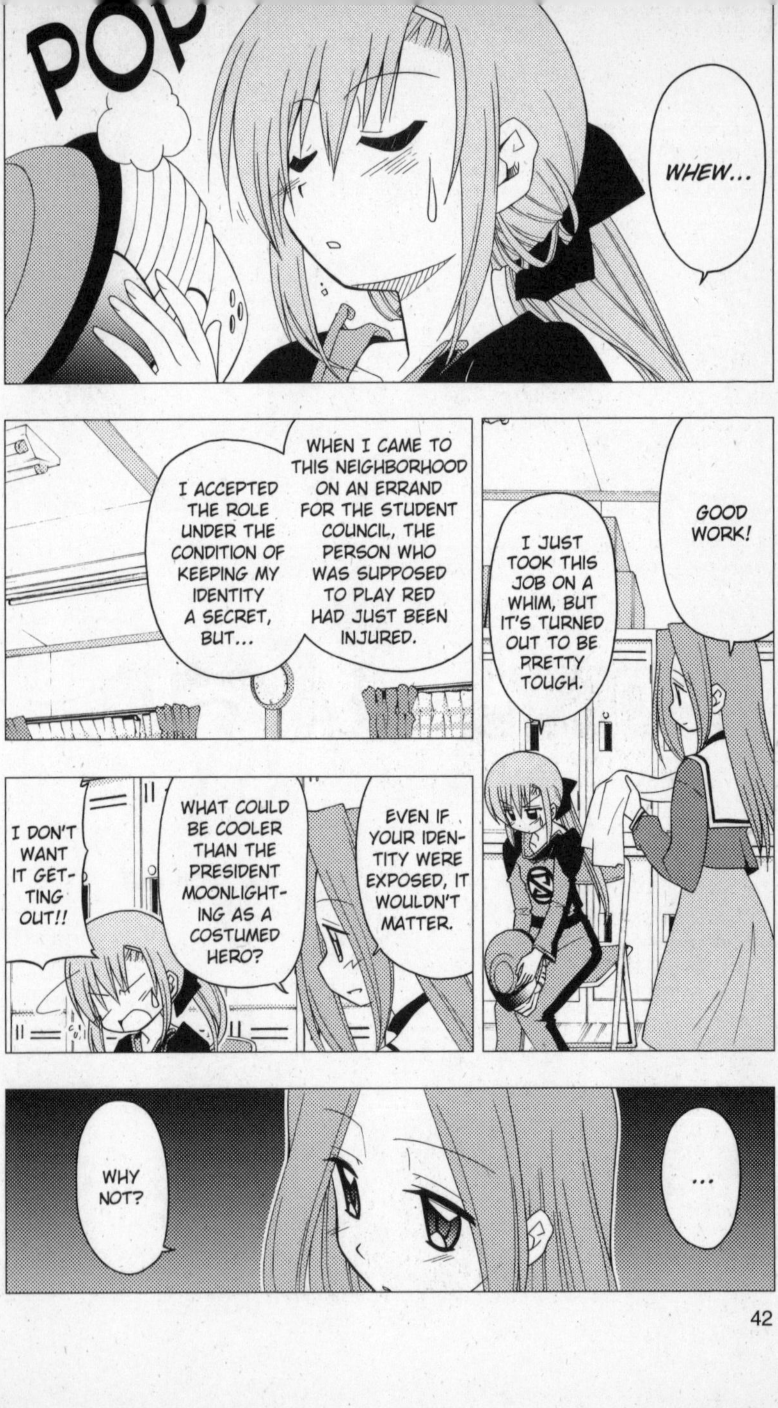
POP
WHEW...
GOOD WORK!
I JUST TOOK THIS JOB ON A WHIM, BUT IT'S TURNED OUT TO BE PRETTY TOUGH.
WHEN I CAME TO THIS NEIGHBORHOOD ON AN ERRAND FOR THE STUDENT COUNCIL, THE PERSON WHO WAS SUPPOSED TO PLAY RED HAD JUST BEEN INJURED.
I ACCEPTED THE ROLE UNDER THE CONDITION OF KEEPING MY IDENTITY A SECRET, BUT...
EVEN IF YOUR IDEN-TITY WERE EXPOSED, IT WOULDN'T MATTER.
WHAT COULD BE COOLER THAN THE PRESIDENT MOONLIGHT-ING AS A COSTUMED HERO?
I DON'T WANT IT GET-TING OUT!!
...
WHY NOT?

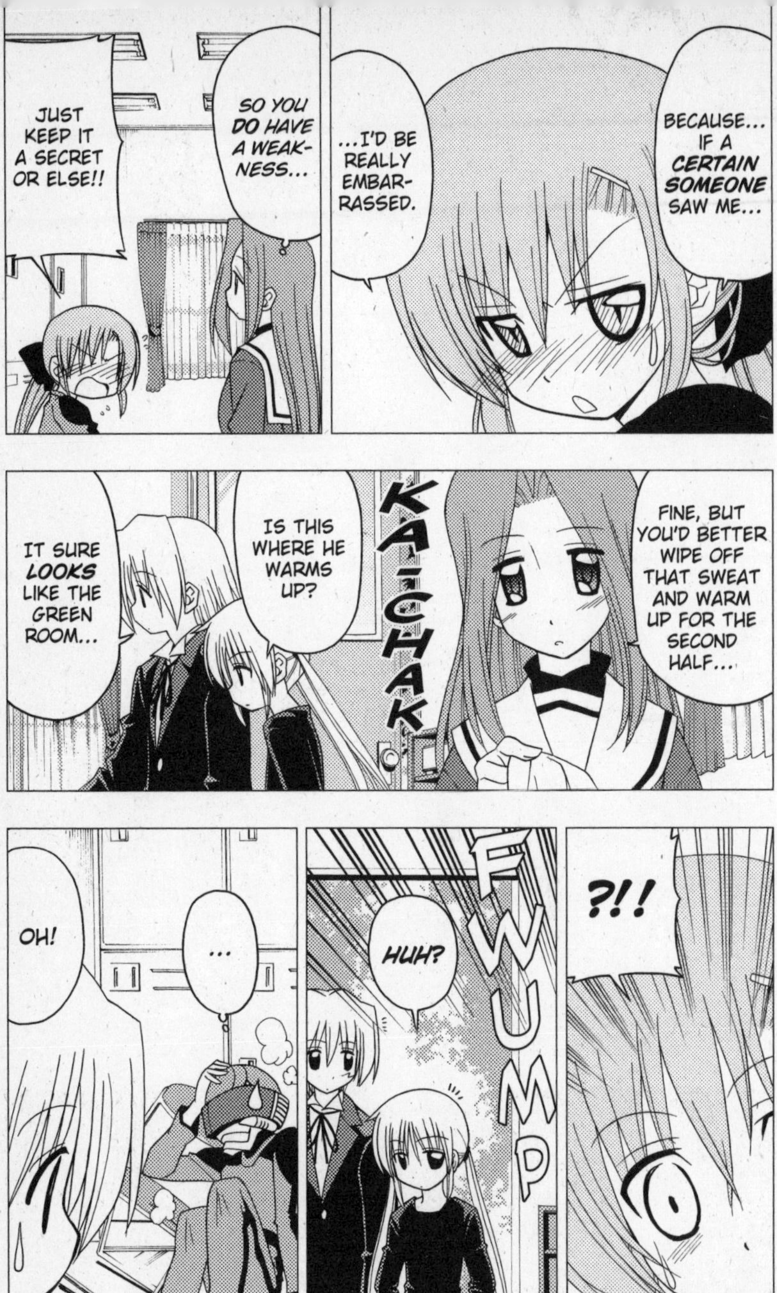
BECAUSE... IF A CERTAIN SOMEONE SAW ME...
...I'D BE REALLY EMBARRASSED.
SO YOU DO HAVE A WEAKNESS...
JUST KEEP IT A SECRET OR ELSE!!
FINE, BUT YOU'D BETTER WIPE OFF THAT SWEAT AND WARM UP FOR THE SECOND HALF...
KA-CHAK
IS THIS WHERE HE WARMS UP?
IT SURE LOOKS LIKE THE GREEN ROOM...
?!!
FWUMP
HUH?
...
OH!

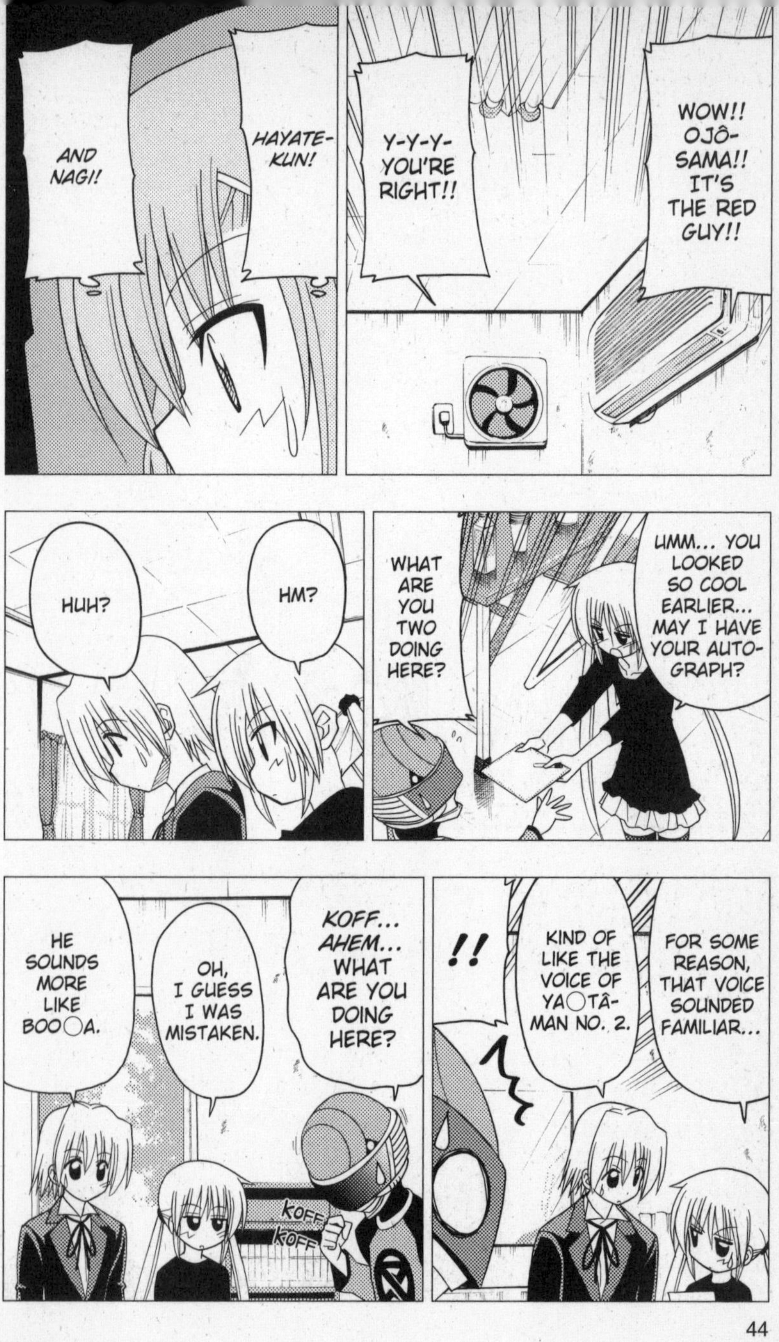
WOW!! OJÔ-SAMA!! IT'S THE RED GUY!!
Y-Y-Y-YOU'RE RIGHT!!
HAYATE-KUN!
AND NAGI!
UMM... YOU LOOKED SO COOL EARLIER... MAY I HAVE YOUR AUTOGRAPH?
WHAT ARE YOU TWO DOING HERE?
HM?
HUH?
FOR SOME REASON, THAT VOICE SOUNDED FAMILIAR...
KIND OF LIKE THE VOICE OF YA○TÂ-MAN NO. 2.
!!
KOFF... AHEM... WHAT ARE YOU DOING HERE?
KOFF KOFF
OH, I GUESS I WAS MISTAKEN.
HE SOUNDS MORE LIKE BOO○A.

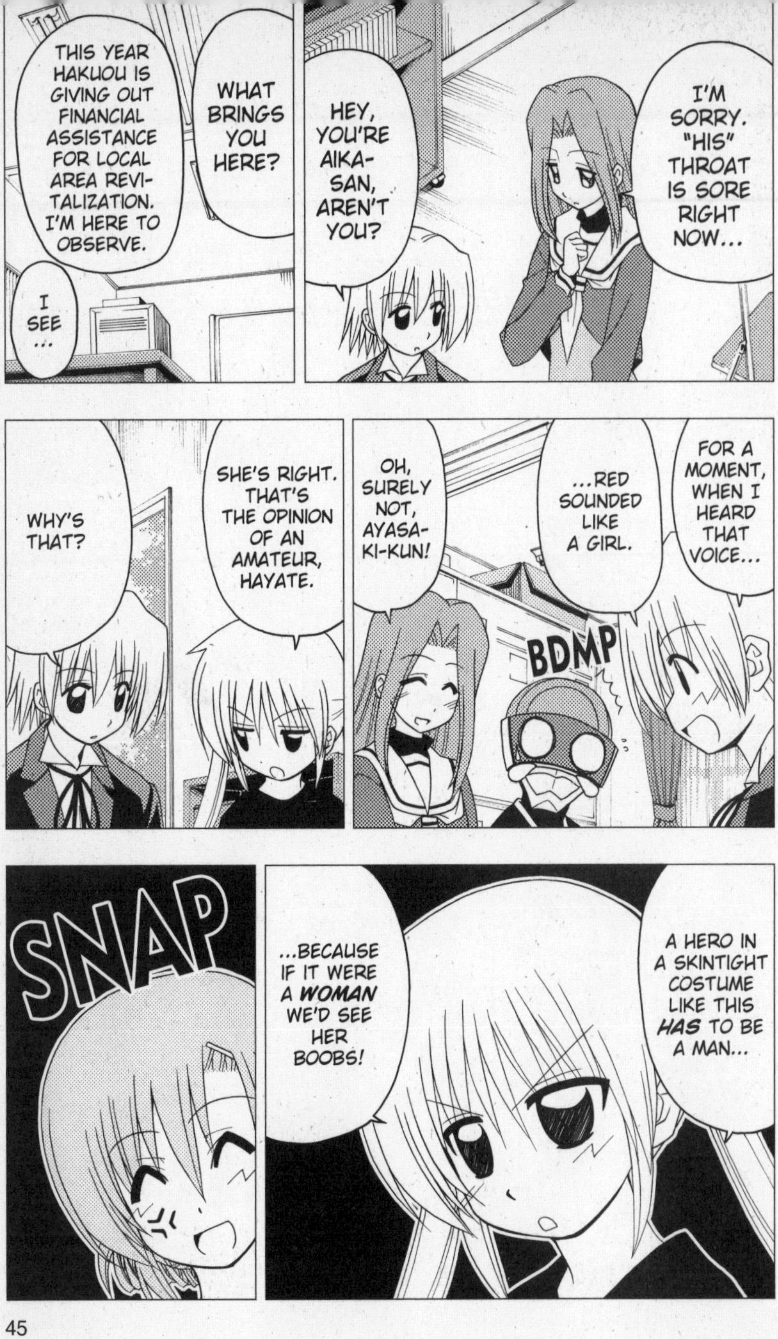
I'M SORRY. "HIS" THROAT IS SORE RIGHT NOW...
HEY, YOU'RE AIKA-SAN, AREN'T YOU?
WHAT BRINGS YOU HERE?
THIS YEAR HAKUOU IS GIVING OUT FINANCIAL ASSISTANCE FOR LOCAL AREA REVI-TALIZATION. I'M HERE TO OBSERVE.
I SEE ...
FOR A MOMENT, WHEN I HEARD THAT VOICE...
...RED SOUNDED LIKE A GIRL.
BDMP
OH, SURELY NOT, AYASA-KI-KUN!
SHE'S RIGHT. THAT'S THE OPINION OF AN AMATEUR, HAYATE.
WHY'S THAT?
A HERO IN A SKINTIGHT COSTUME LIKE THIS *HAS* TO BE A MAN...
...BECAUSE IF IT WERE A *WOMAN* WE'D SEE HER BOOBS!
SNAP

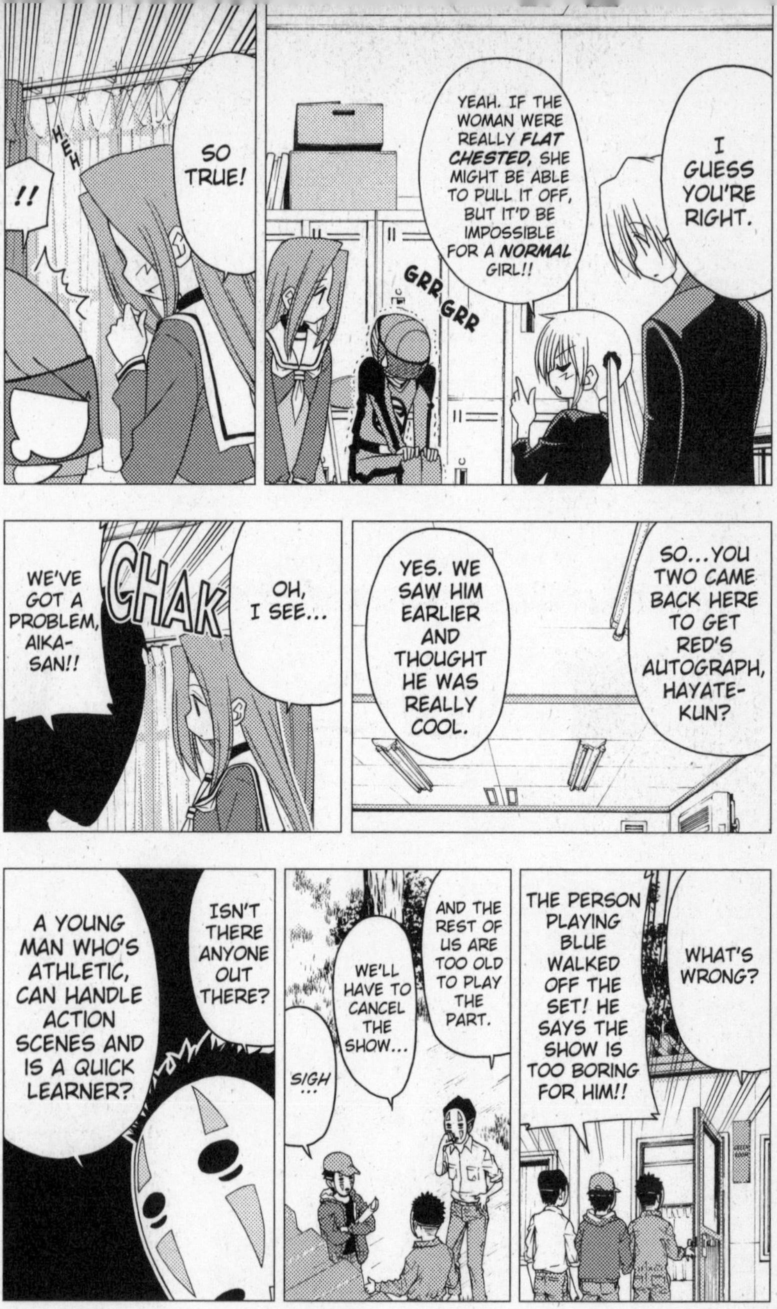
I GUESS YOU'RE RIGHT.
YEAH. IF THE WOMAN WERE REALLY **FLAT CHESTED,** SHE MIGHT BE ABLE TO PULL IT OFF, BUT IT'D BE IMPOSSIBLE FOR A **NORMAL** GIRL!!
GRR GRR
SO TRUE!
HEH
!!
SO...YOU TWO CAME BACK HERE TO GET RED'S AUTOGRAPH, HAYATE-KUN?
YES. WE SAW HIM EARLIER AND THOUGHT HE WAS REALLY COOL.
OH, I SEE...
CHAK
WE'VE GOT A PROBLEM, AIKA-SAN!!
WHAT'S WRONG?
THE PERSON PLAYING BLUE WALKED OFF THE SET! HE SAYS THE SHOW IS TOO BORING FOR HIM!!
AND THE REST OF US ARE TOO OLD TO PLAY THE PART.
WE'LL HAVE TO CANCEL THE SHOW...
SIGH...
ISN'T THERE ANYONE OUT THERE?
A YOUNG MAN WHO'S ATHLETIC, CAN HANDLE ACTION SCENES AND IS A QUICK LEARNER?

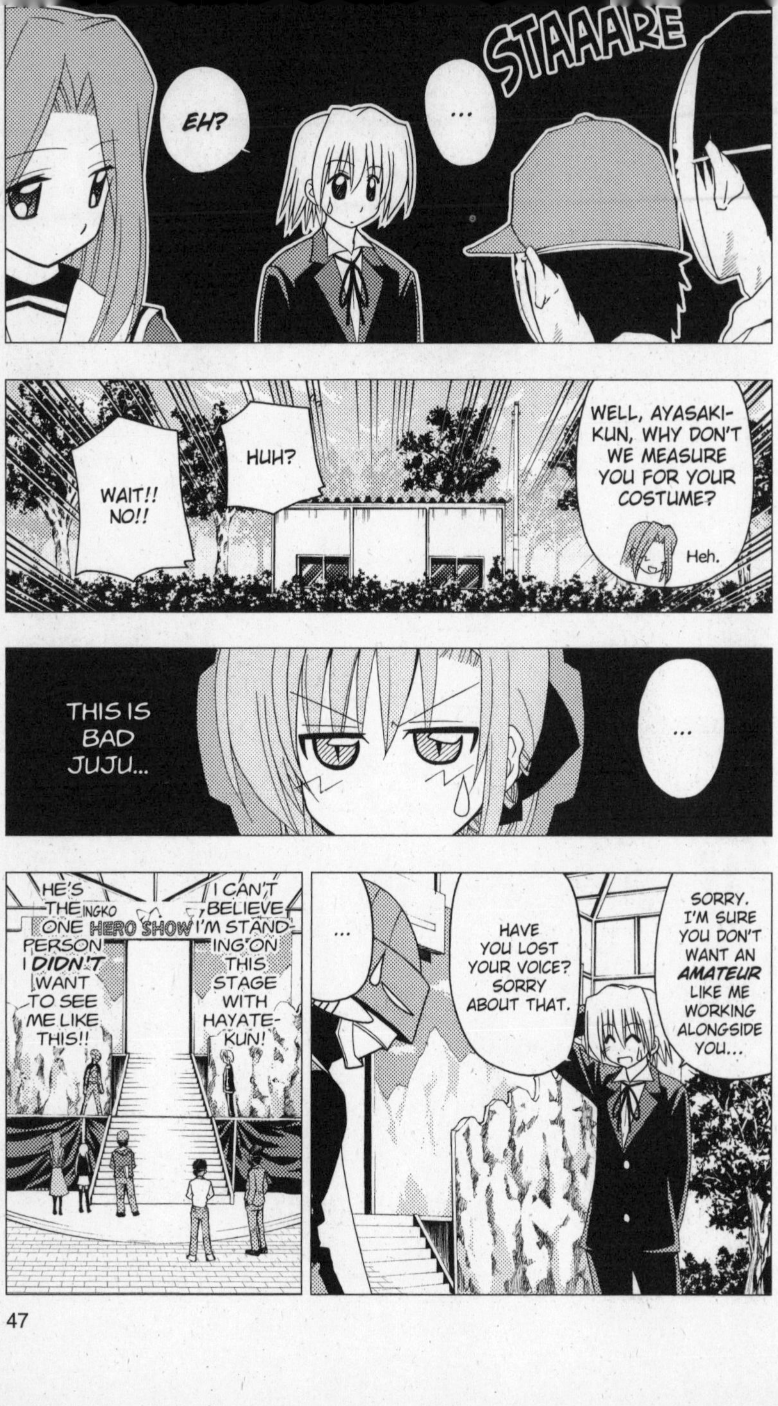
STAAARE
...
EH?
WELL, AYASAKI-KUN, WHY DON'T WE MEASURE YOU FOR YOUR COSTUME?
Heh.
HUH?
WAIT!! NO!!
...
THIS IS BAD JUJU...
SORRY. I'M SURE YOU DON'T WANT AN **AMATEUR** LIKE ME WORKING ALONGSIDE YOU...
HAVE YOU LOST YOUR VOICE? SORRY ABOUT THAT.
...
I CAN'T BELIEVE I'M STANDING ON THIS STAGE WITH HAYATE-KUN!
INGKO HERO SHOW
HE'S THE ONE PERSON I **DIDN'T** WANT TO SEE ME LIKE THIS!!

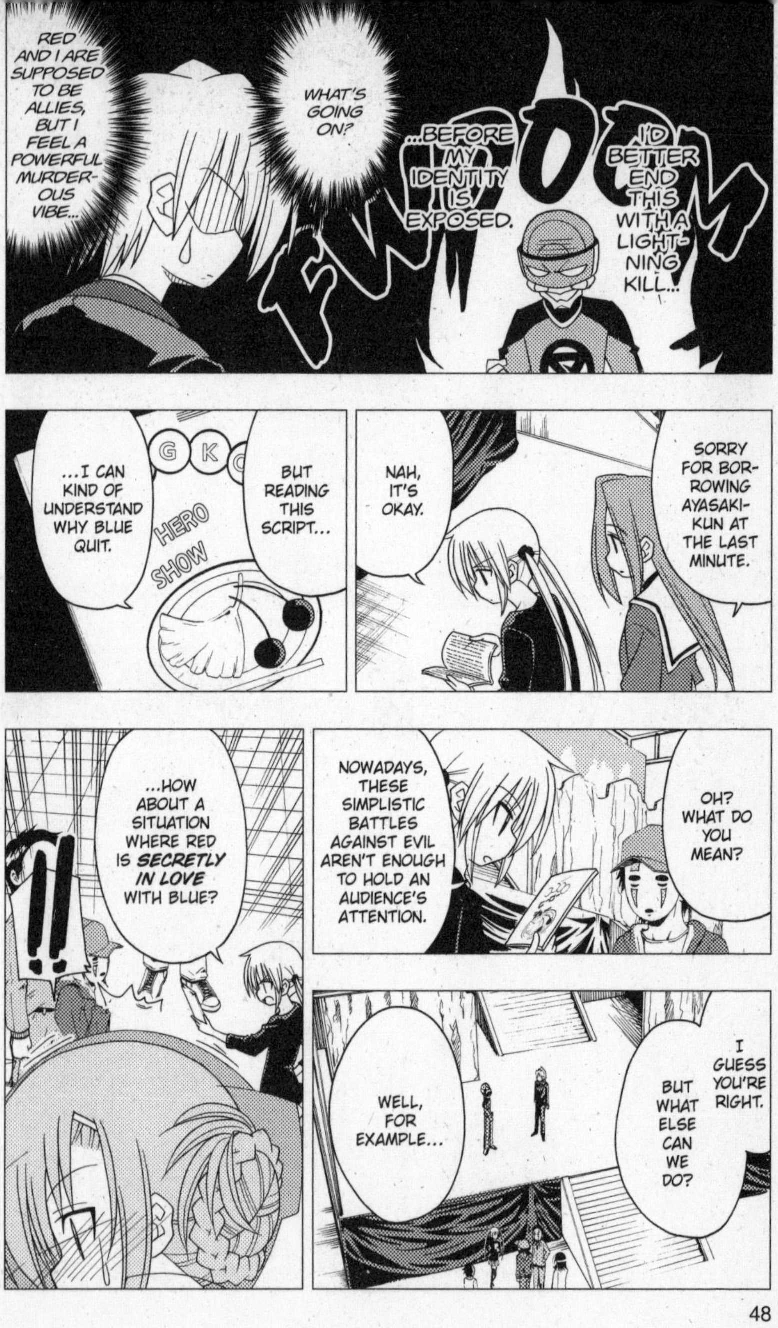
I'D BETTER END THIS WITH A LIGHTNING KILL...
...BEFORE MY IDENTITY IS EXPOSED.
FWOOOM
WHAT'S GOING ON?
RED AND I ARE SUPPOSED TO BE ALLIES, BUT I FEEL A POWERFUL MURDEROUS VIBE...
SORRY FOR BORROWING AYASAKI-KUN AT THE LAST MINUTE.
NAH, IT'S OKAY.
BUT READING THIS SCRIPT...
G K C
HERO SHOW
...I CAN KIND OF UNDERSTAND WHY BLUE QUIT.
OH? WHAT DO YOU MEAN?
NOWADAYS, THESE SIMPLISTIC BATTLES AGAINST EVIL AREN'T ENOUGH TO HOLD AN AUDIENCE'S ATTENTION.
I GUESS YOU'RE RIGHT.
BUT WHAT ELSE CAN WE DO?
WELL, FOR EXAMPLE...
...HOW ABOUT A SITUATION WHERE RED IS ***SECRETLY IN LOVE*** WITH BLUE?
!!

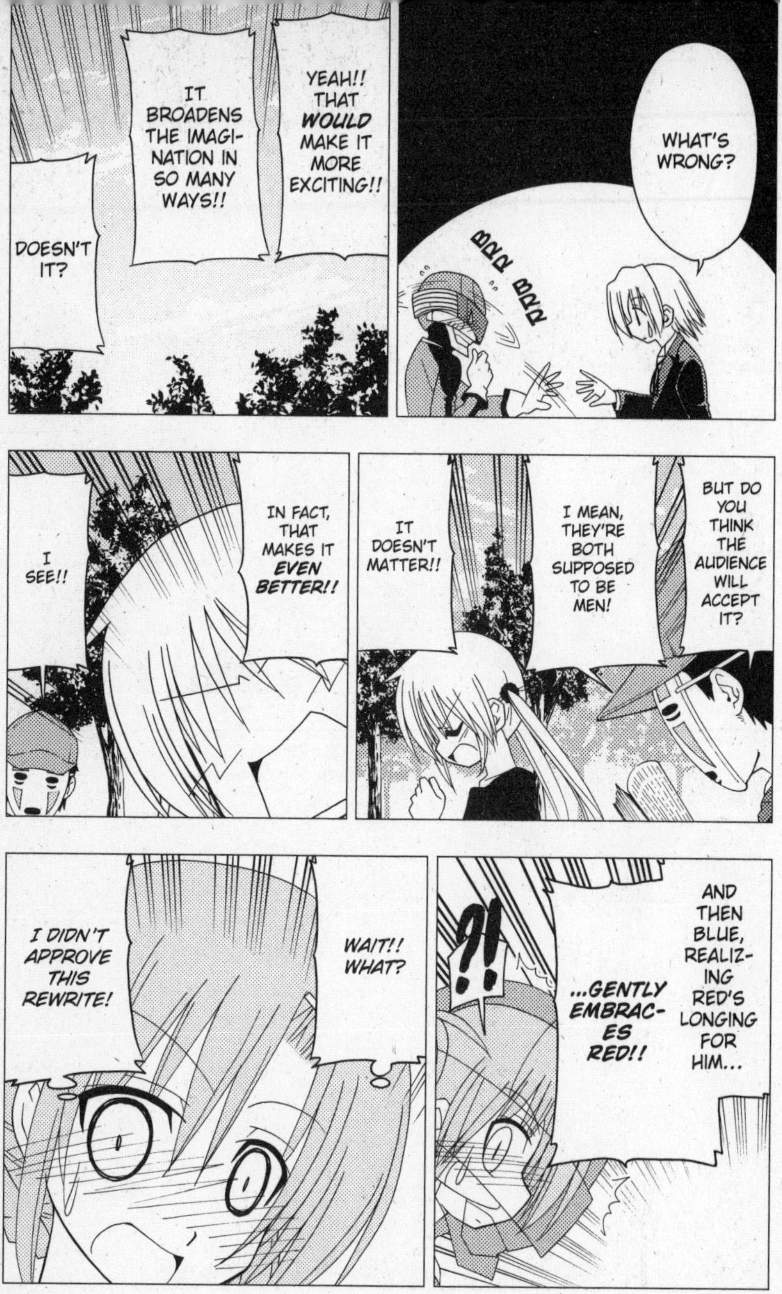
WHAT'S WRONG?
YEAH!! THAT WOULD MAKE IT MORE EXCITING!!
IT BROADENS THE IMAGINATION IN SO MANY WAYS!!
DOESN'T IT?
BUT DO YOU THINK THE AUDIENCE WILL ACCEPT IT?
I MEAN, THEY'RE BOTH SUPPOSED TO BE MEN!
IT DOESN'T MATTER!!
IN FACT, THAT MAKES IT EVEN BETTER!!
I SEE!!
AND THEN BLUE, REALIZING RED'S LONGING FOR HIM...
...GENTLY EMBRACES RED!!
?!
WAIT!! WHAT?
I DIDN'T APPROVE THIS REWRITE!

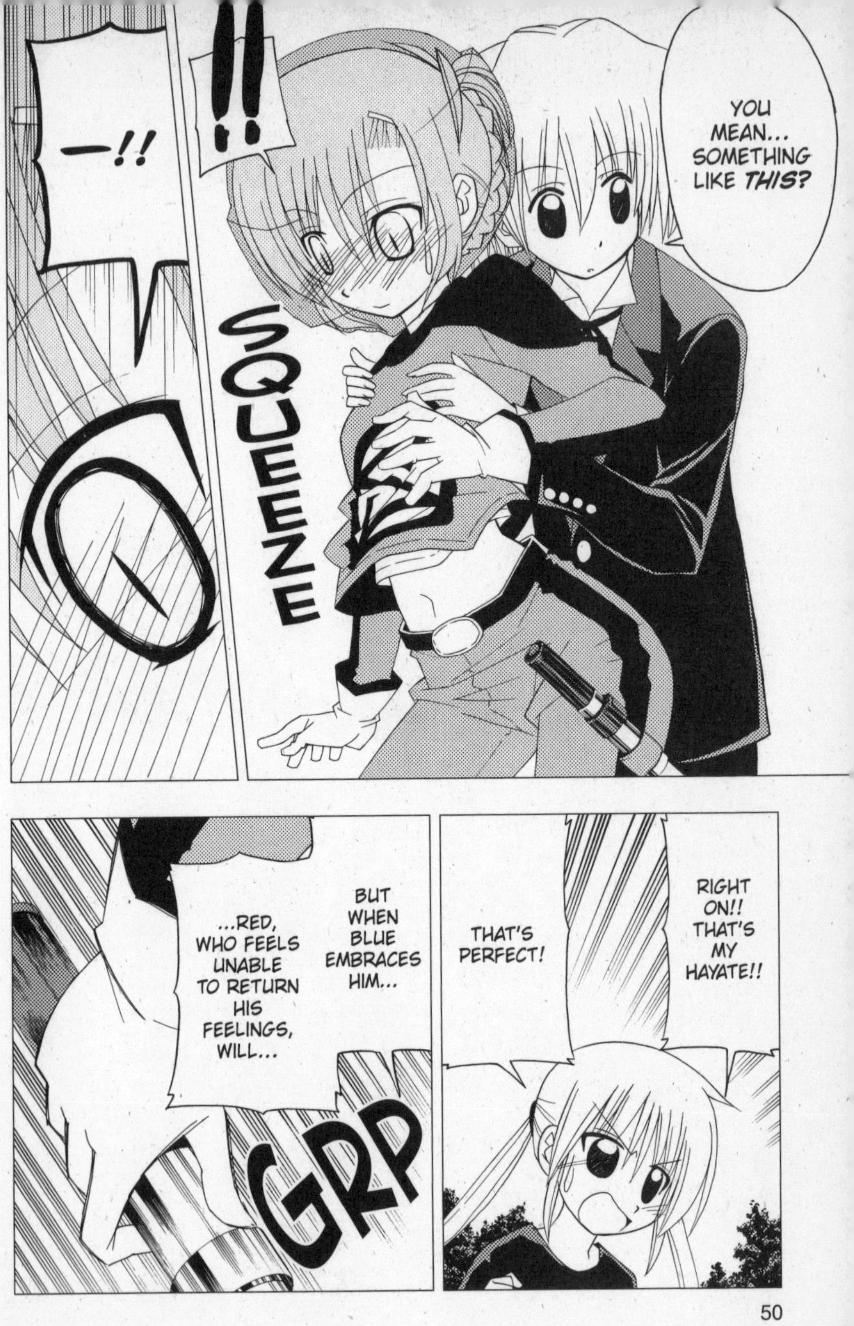
YOU MEAN... SOMETHING LIKE THIS?
!!
—!!
SQUEEZE
RIGHT ON!! THAT'S MY HAYATE!!
THAT'S PERFECT!
BUT WHEN BLUE EMBRACES HIM...
...RED, WHO FEELS UNABLE TO RETURN HIS FEELINGS, WILL...
GRP

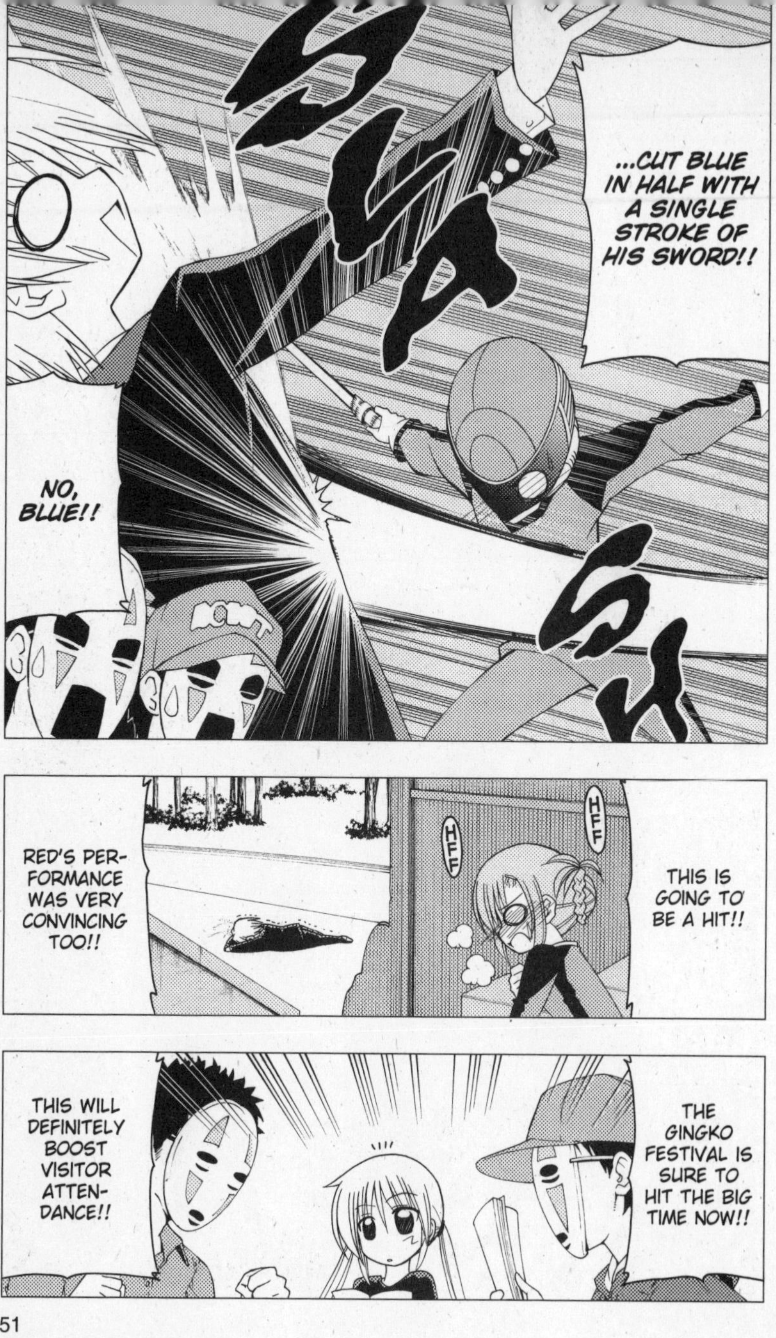
...CUT BLUE IN HALF WITH A SINGLE STROKE OF HIS SWORD!!
NO, BLUE!!
HFF
HFF
THIS IS GOING TO BE A HIT!!
RED'S PER-FORMANCE WAS VERY CONVINCING TOO!!
THE GINGKO FESTIVAL IS SURE TO HIT THE BIG TIME NOW!!
THIS WILL DEFINITELY BOOST VISITOR ATTEN-DANCE!!

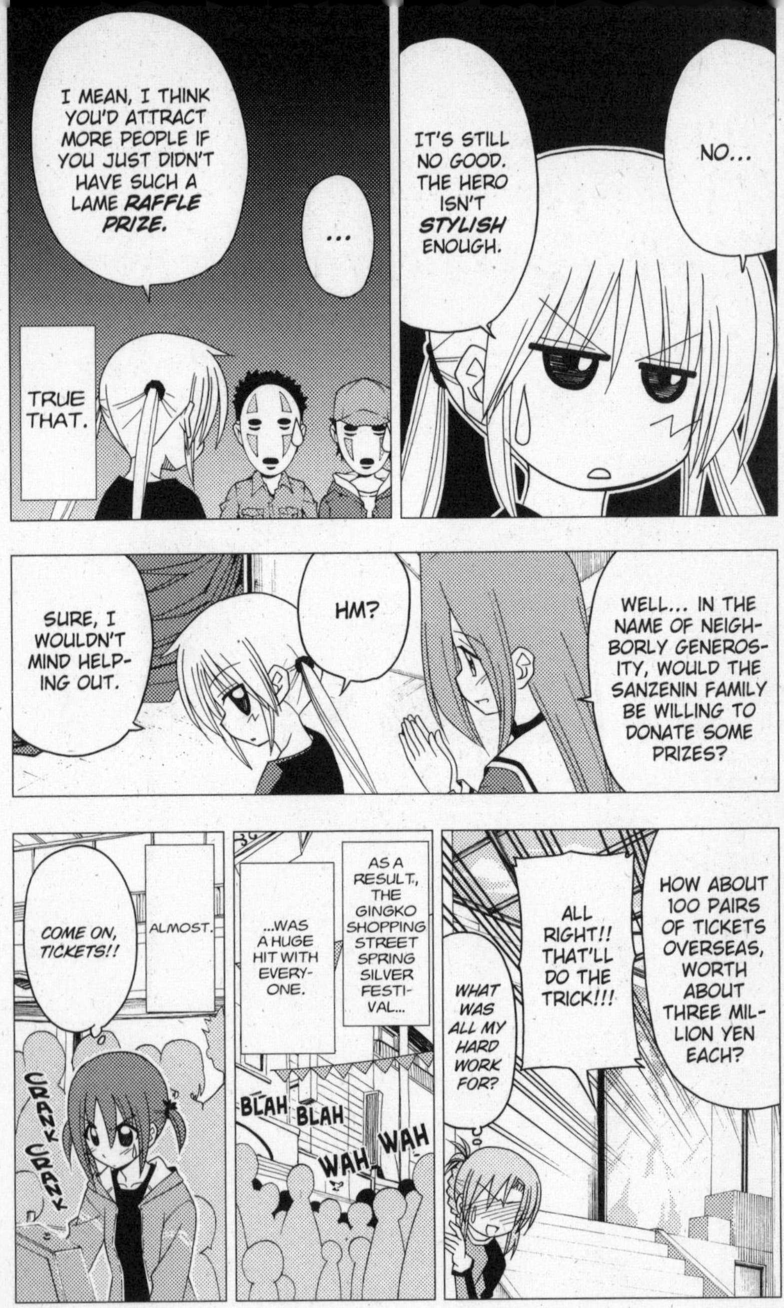
NO...
IT'S STILL NO GOOD. THE HERO ISN'T STYLISH ENOUGH.
I MEAN, I THINK YOU'D ATTRACT MORE PEOPLE IF YOU JUST DIDN'T HAVE SUCH A LAME RAFFLE PRIZE.
...
TRUE THAT.
WELL... IN THE NAME OF NEIGHBORLY GENEROSITY, WOULD THE SANZENIN FAMILY BE WILLING TO DONATE SOME PRIZES?
HM?
SURE, I WOULDN'T MIND HELPING OUT.
HOW ABOUT 100 PAIRS OF TICKETS OVERSEAS, WORTH ABOUT THREE MILLION YEN EACH?
ALL RIGHT!! THAT'LL DO THE TRICK!!!
WHAT WAS ALL MY HARD WORK FOR?
AS A RESULT, THE GINGKO SHOPPING STREET SPRING SILVER FESTIVAL...
...WAS A HUGE HIT WITH EVERYONE.
BLAH BLAH
WAH WAH
ALMOST.
COME ON, TICKETS!!
CRANK CRANK

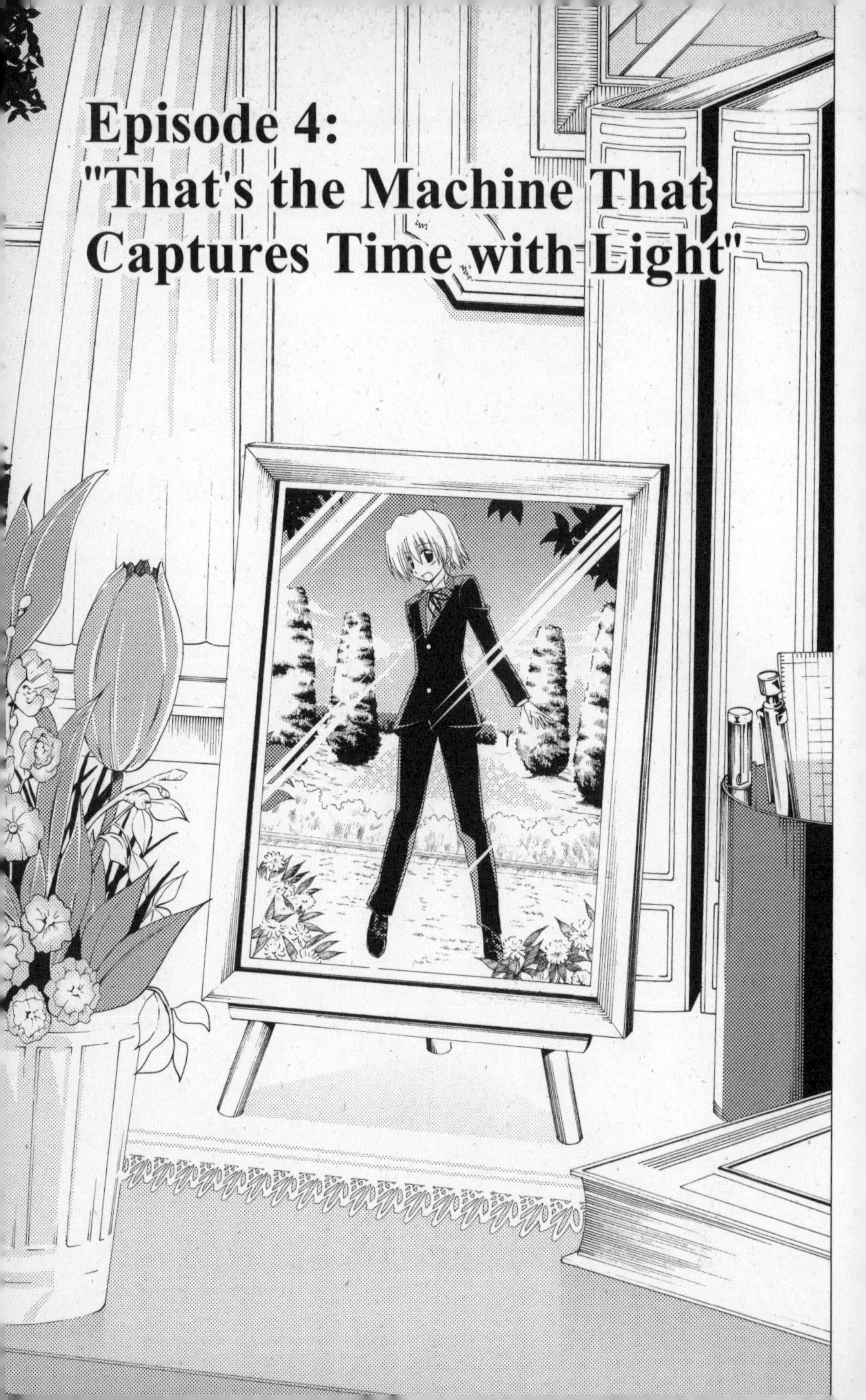
Episode 4:
"That's the Machine That Captures Time with Light"

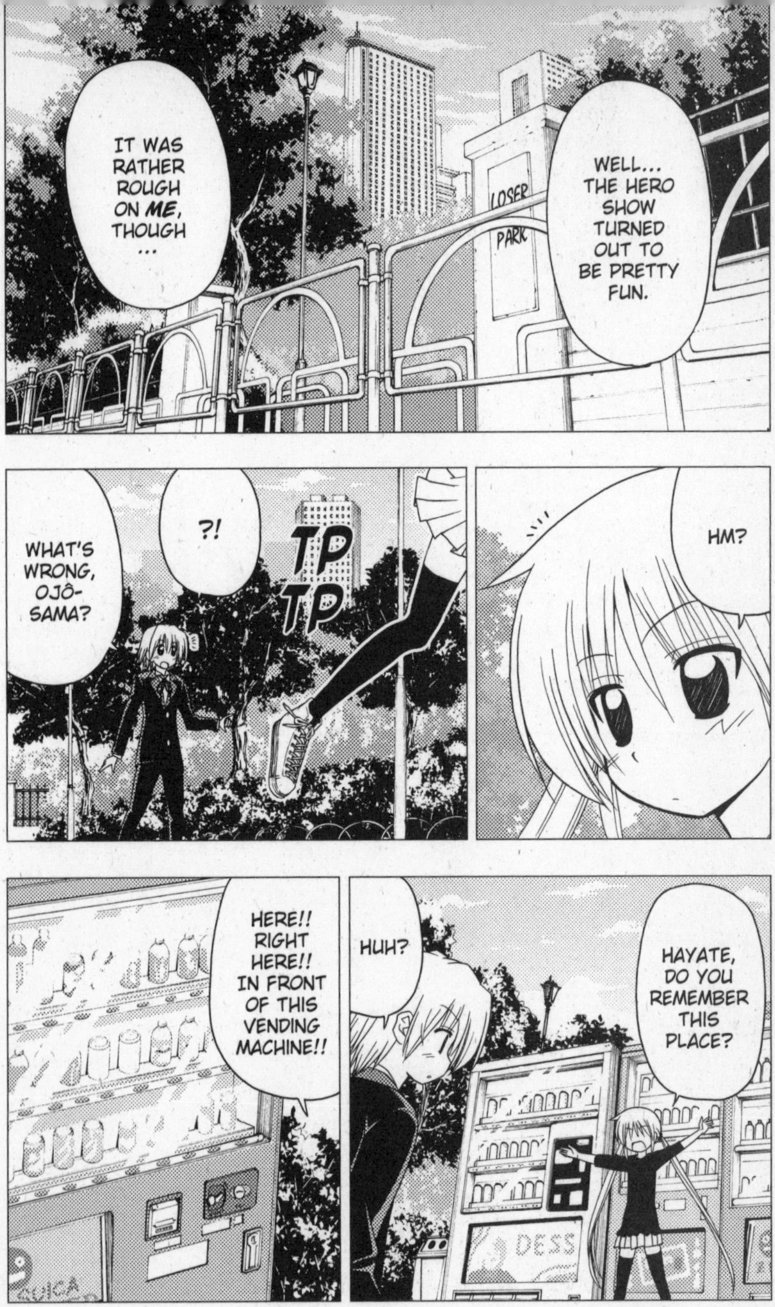
WELL... THE HERO SHOW TURNED OUT TO BE PRETTY FUN.
LOSER
PARK
IT WAS RATHER ROUGH ON *ME*, THOUGH...
HM?
TP TP
?!
WHAT'S WRONG, OJÔ-SAMA?
HAYATE, DO YOU REMEMBER THIS PLACE?
HUH?
DESS
HERE!! RIGHT HERE!! IN FRONT OF THIS VENDING MACHINE!!

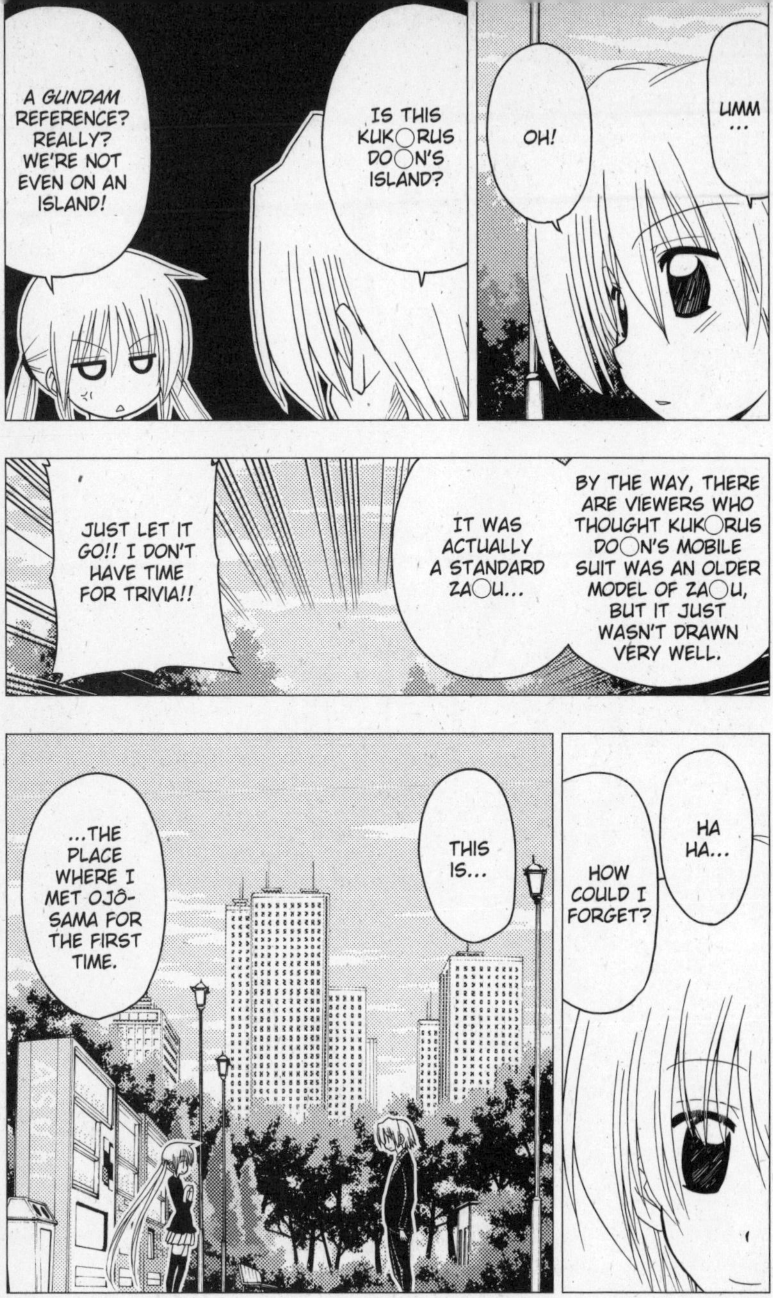
UMM...
OH!
IS THIS KUK◯RUS DO◯N'S ISLAND?
A *GUNDAM* REFERENCE? REALLY? WE'RE NOT EVEN ON AN ISLAND!
BY THE WAY, THERE ARE VIEWERS WHO THOUGHT KUK◯RUS DO◯N'S MOBILE SUIT WAS AN OLDER MODEL OF ZA◯U, BUT IT JUST WASN'T DRAWN VERY WELL.
IT WAS ACTUALLY A STANDARD ZA◯U...
JUST LET IT GO!! I DON'T HAVE TIME FOR TRIVIA!!
HA HA...
HOW COULD I FORGET?
THIS IS...
...THE PLACE WHERE I MET OJÔ-SAMA FOR THE FIRST TIME.

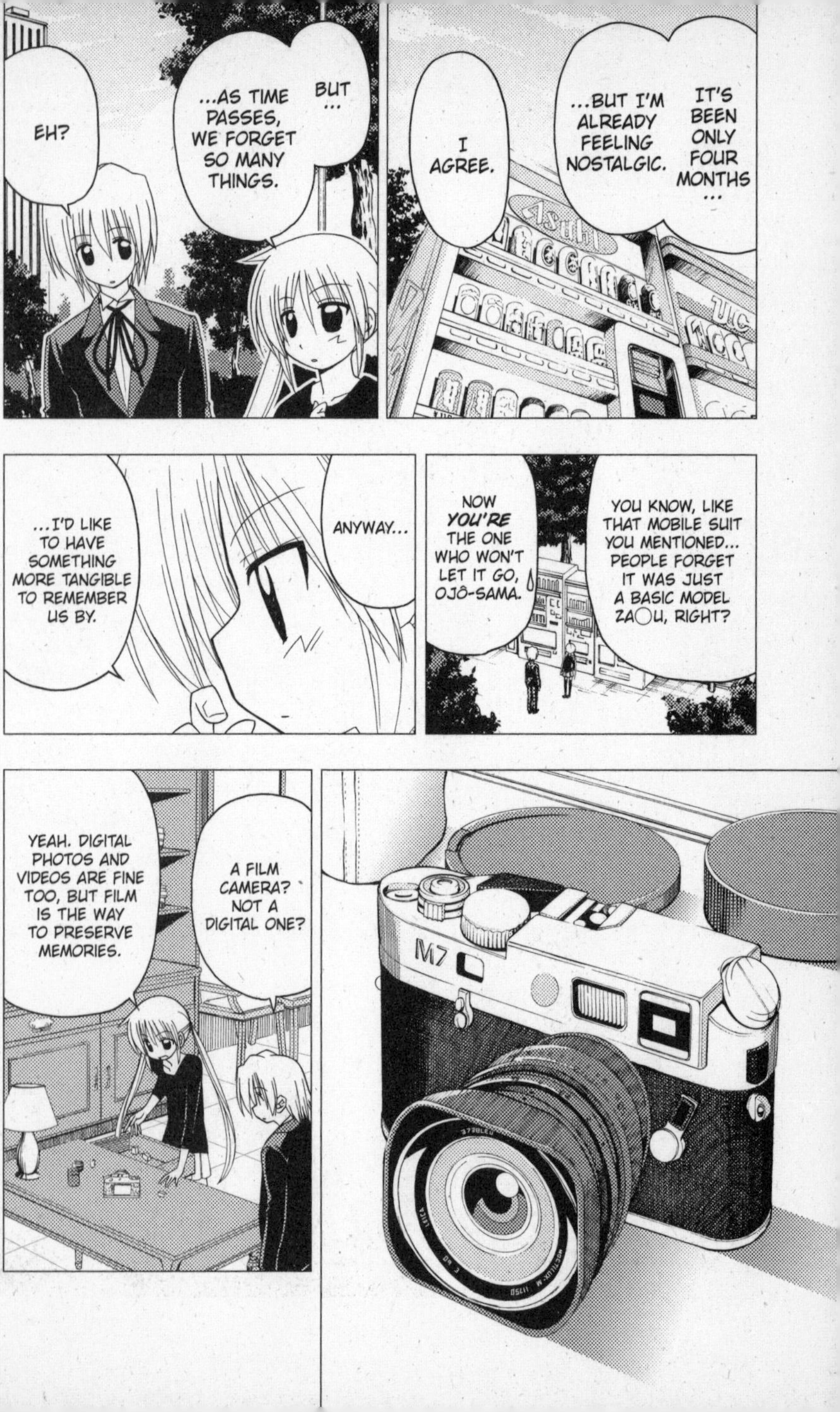
IT'S BEEN ONLY FOUR MONTHS...
...BUT I'M ALREADY FEELING NOSTALGIC.
I AGREE.
BUT...
...AS TIME PASSES, WE FORGET SO MANY THINGS.
EH?
YOU KNOW, LIKE THAT MOBILE SUIT YOU MENTIONED... PEOPLE FORGET IT WAS JUST A BASIC MODEL ZA◯U, RIGHT?
NOW *YOU'RE* THE ONE WHO WON'T LET IT GO, OJÔ-SAMA.
ANYWAY...
...I'D LIKE TO HAVE SOMETHING MORE TANGIBLE TO REMEMBER US BY.
M7
A FILM CAMERA? NOT A DIGITAL ONE?
YEAH. DIGITAL PHOTOS AND VIDEOS ARE FINE TOO, BUT FILM IS THE WAY TO PRESERVE MEMORIES.

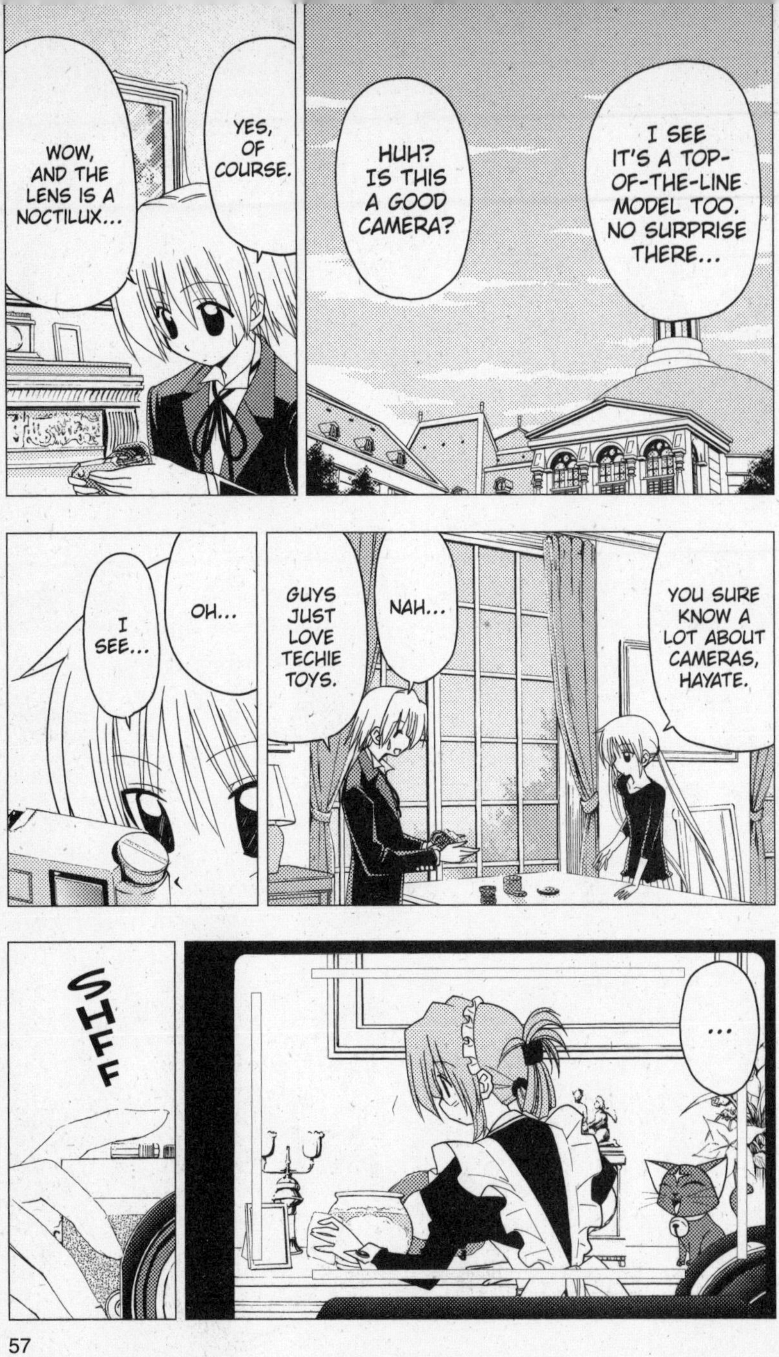
I SEE IT'S A TOP-OF-THE-LINE MODEL TOO. NO SURPRISE THERE...
HUH? IS THIS A GOOD CAMERA?
YES, OF COURSE.
WOW, AND THE LENS IS A NOCTILUX...
YOU SURE KNOW A LOT ABOUT CAMERAS, HAYATE.
NAH...
GUYS JUST LOVE TECHIE TOYS.
OH...
I SEE...
...
SHFF

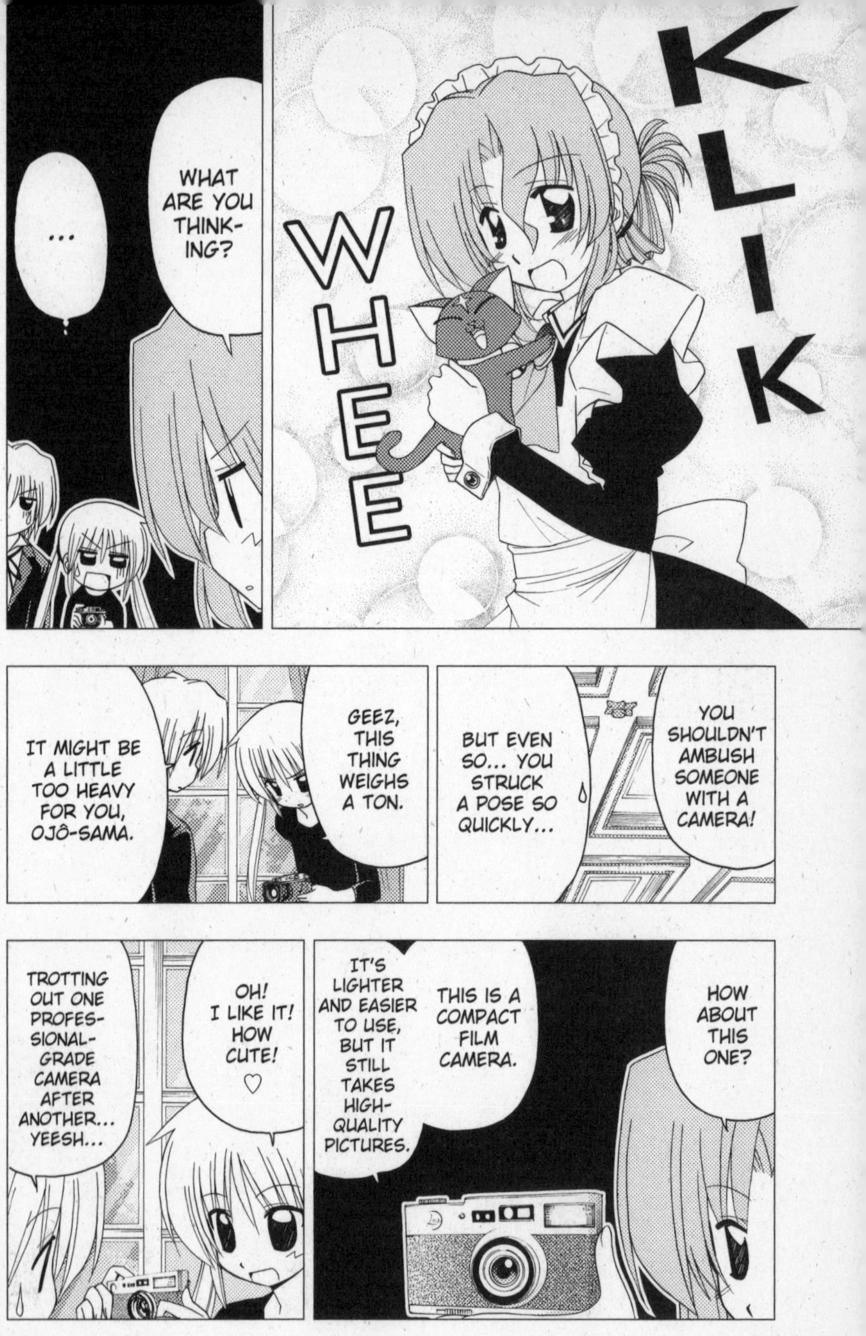
KLIK
WHEE
WHAT ARE YOU THINKING?
...
YOU SHOULDN'T AMBUSH SOMEONE WITH A CAMERA!
BUT EVEN SO... YOU STRUCK A POSE SO QUICKLY...
GEEZ, THIS THING WEIGHS A TON.
IT MIGHT BE A LITTLE TOO HEAVY FOR YOU, OJÔ-SAMA.
HOW ABOUT THIS ONE?
THIS IS A COMPACT FILM CAMERA.
IT'S LIGHTER AND EASIER TO USE, BUT IT STILL TAKES HIGH-QUALITY PICTURES.
OH! I LIKE IT! HOW CUTE! ♡
TROTTING OUT ONE PROFESSIONAL-GRADE CAMERA AFTER ANOTHER... YEESH...

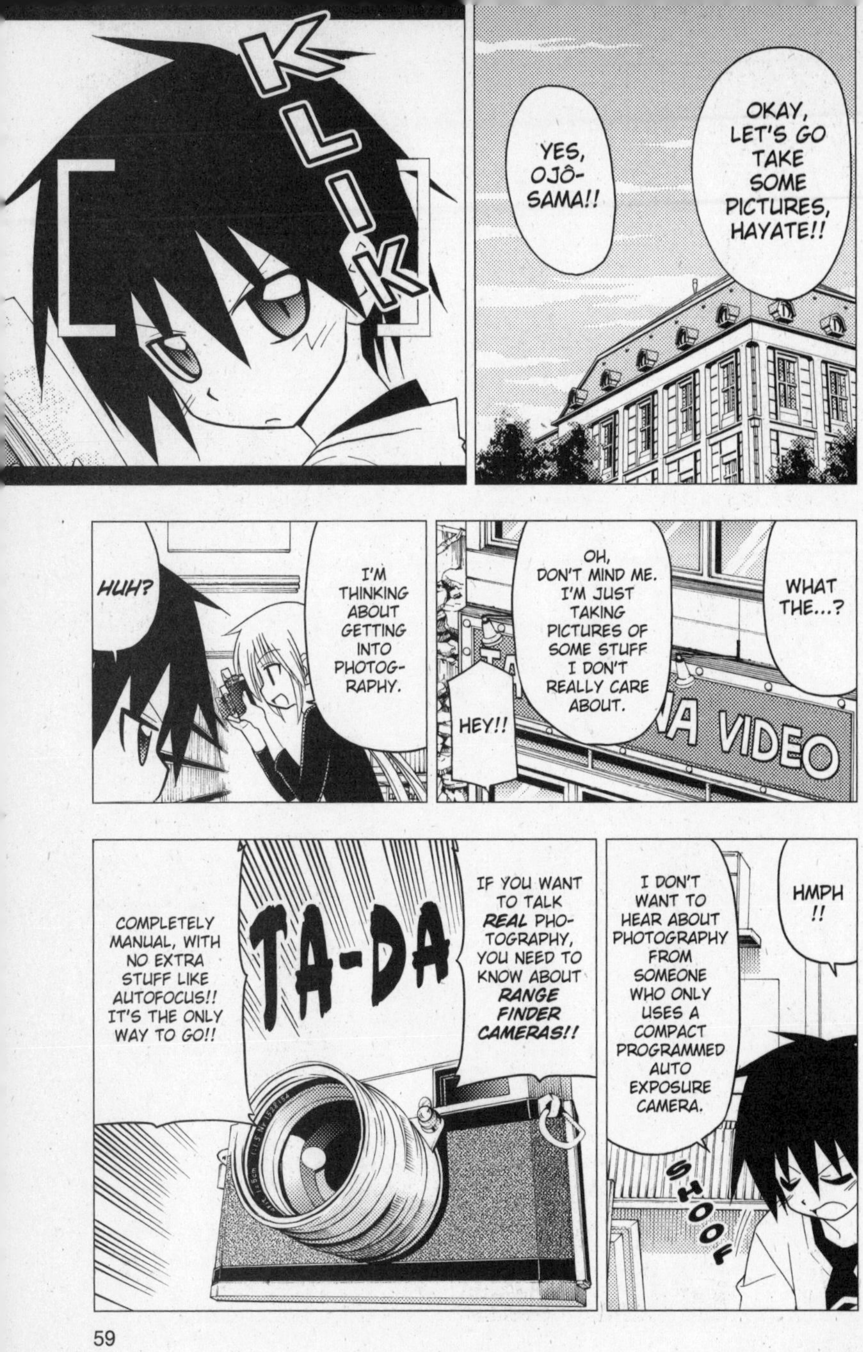
OKAY, LET'S GO TAKE SOME PICTURES, HAYATE!!
YES, OJÔ-SAMA!!
KLIK
WHAT THE...?
OH, DON'T MIND ME. I'M JUST TAKING PICTURES OF SOME STUFF I DON'T REALLY CARE ABOUT.
HEY!!
VIDEO
I'M THINKING ABOUT GETTING INTO PHOTOG-RAPHY.
HUH?
HMPH!!
I DON'T WANT TO HEAR ABOUT PHOTOGRAPHY FROM SOMEONE WHO ONLY USES A COMPACT PROGRAMMED AUTO EXPOSURE CAMERA.
SHOOF
IF YOU WANT TO TALK REAL PHO-TOGRAPHY, YOU NEED TO KNOW ABOUT RANGE FINDER CAMERAS!!
TA-DA
COMPLETELY MANUAL, WITH NO EXTRA STUFF LIKE AUTOFOCUS!! IT'S THE ONLY WAY TO GO!!

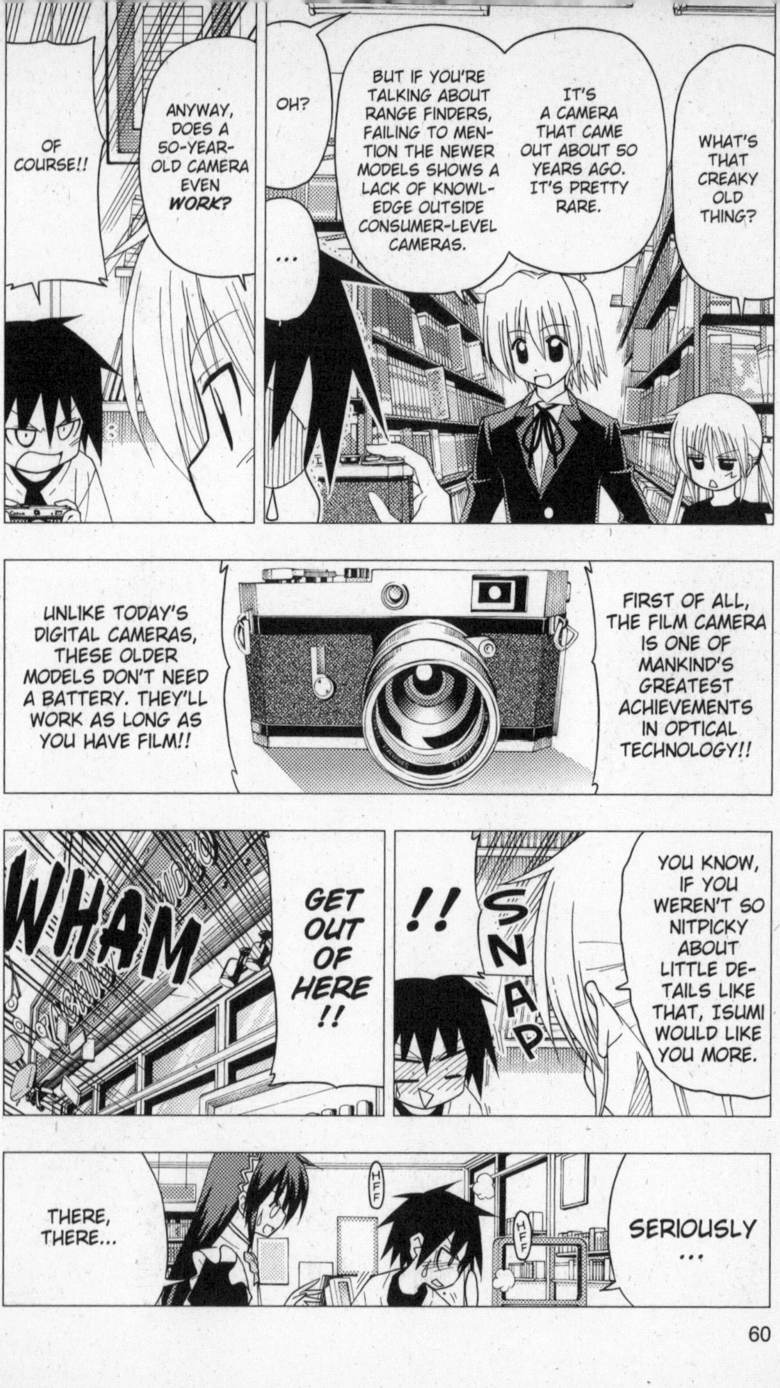
WHAT'S THAT CREAKY OLD THING?
IT'S A CAMERA THAT CAME OUT ABOUT 50 YEARS AGO. IT'S PRETTY RARE.
BUT IF YOU'RE TALKING ABOUT RANGE FINDERS, FAILING TO MENTION THE NEWER MODELS SHOWS A LACK OF KNOWLEDGE OUTSIDE CONSUMER-LEVEL CAMERAS.
OH?
...
ANYWAY, DOES A 50-YEAR-OLD CAMERA EVEN WORK?
OF COURSE!!
FIRST OF ALL, THE FILM CAMERA IS ONE OF MANKIND'S GREATEST ACHIEVEMENTS IN OPTICAL TECHNOLOGY!!
UNLIKE TODAY'S DIGITAL CAMERAS, THESE OLDER MODELS DON'T NEED A BATTERY. THEY'LL WORK AS LONG AS YOU HAVE FILM!!
YOU KNOW, IF YOU WEREN'T SO NITPICKY ABOUT LITTLE DETAILS LIKE THAT, ISUMI WOULD LIKE YOU MORE.
SNAP
!!
GET OUT OF HERE!!
WHAM
SERIOUSLY...
HFF
HFF
THERE, THERE...

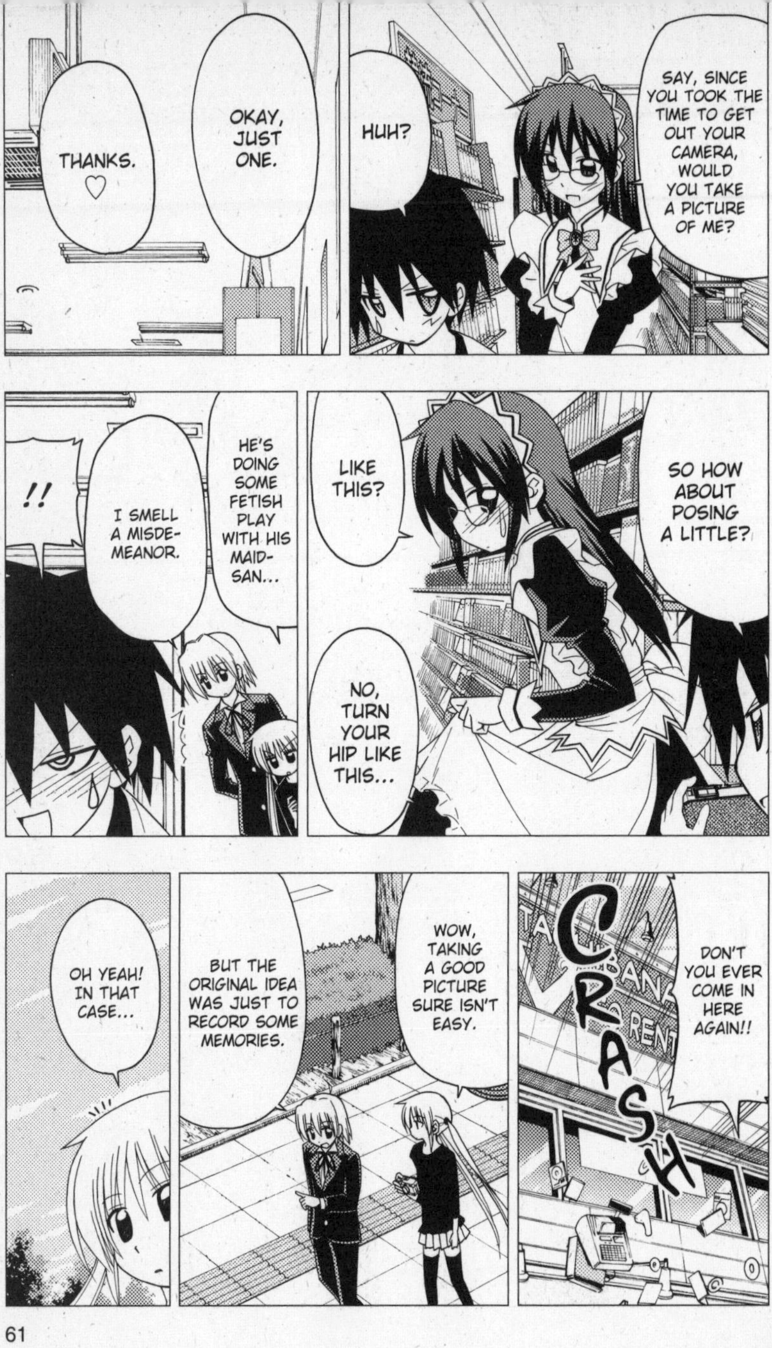
SAY, SINCE YOU TOOK THE TIME TO GET OUT YOUR CAMERA, WOULD YOU TAKE A PICTURE OF ME?
HUH?
OKAY, JUST ONE.
THANKS. ♡
SO HOW ABOUT POSING A LITTLE?
LIKE THIS?
NO, TURN YOUR HIP LIKE THIS...
HE'S DOING SOME FETISH PLAY WITH HIS MAID-SAN...
I SMELL A MISDE-MEANOR.
!!
CRASH
DON'T YOU EVER COME IN HERE AGAIN!!
WOW, TAKING A GOOD PICTURE SURE ISN'T EASY.
BUT THE ORIGINAL IDEA WAS JUST TO RECORD SOME MEMORIES.
OH YEAH! IN THAT CASE...

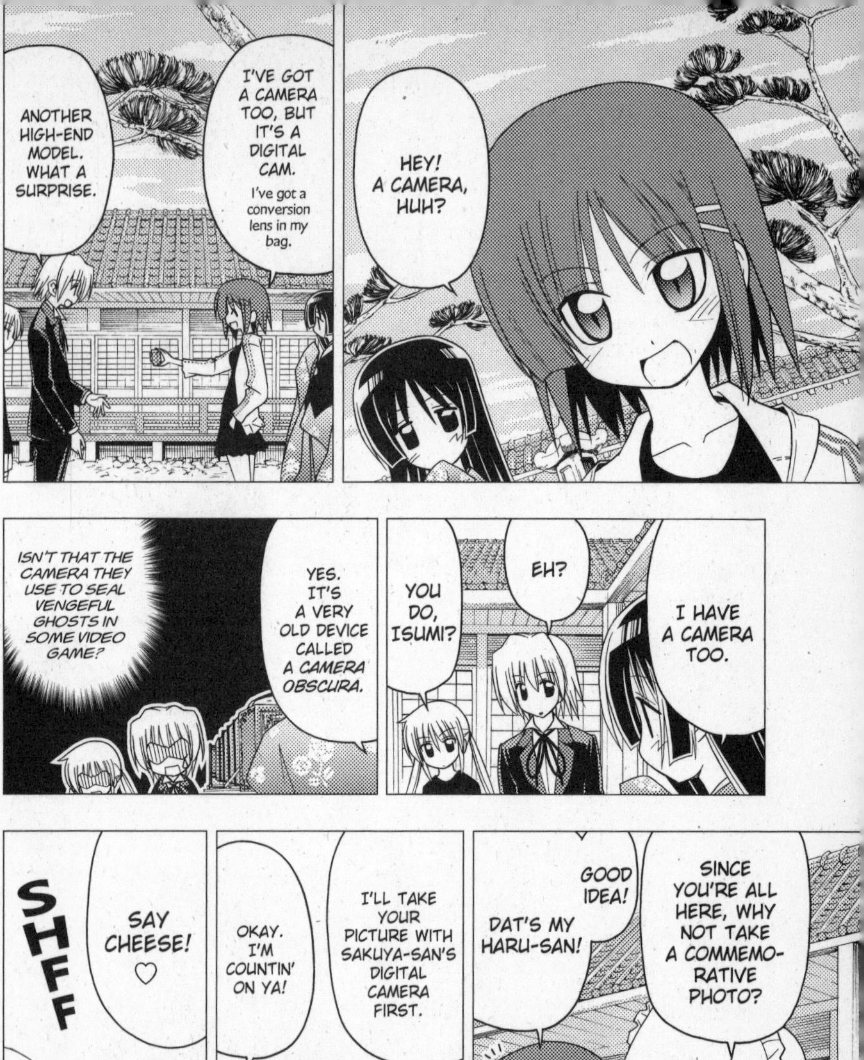
HEY! A CAMERA, HUH?
I'VE GOT A CAMERA TOO, BUT IT'S A DIGITAL CAM.
I've got a conversion lens in my bag.
ANOTHER HIGH-END MODEL. WHAT A SURPRISE.
I HAVE A CAMERA TOO.
EH?
YOU DO, ISUMI?
YES. IT'S A VERY OLD DEVICE CALLED A *CAMERA OBSCURA*.
ISN'T THAT THE CAMERA THEY USE TO SEAL VENGEFUL GHOSTS IN SOME VIDEO GAME?
SINCE YOU'RE ALL HERE, WHY NOT TAKE A COMMEMO-RATIVE PHOTO?
GOOD IDEA!
DAT'S MY HARU-SAN!
I'LL TAKE YOUR PICTURE WITH SAKUYA-SAN'S DIGITAL CAMERA FIRST.
OKAY. I'M COUNTIN' ON YA!
SAY CHEESE! ♡
SHFF

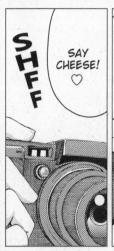

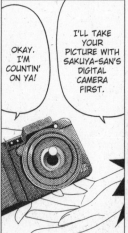

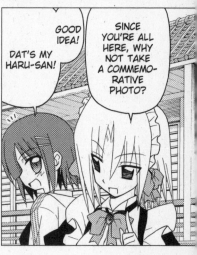

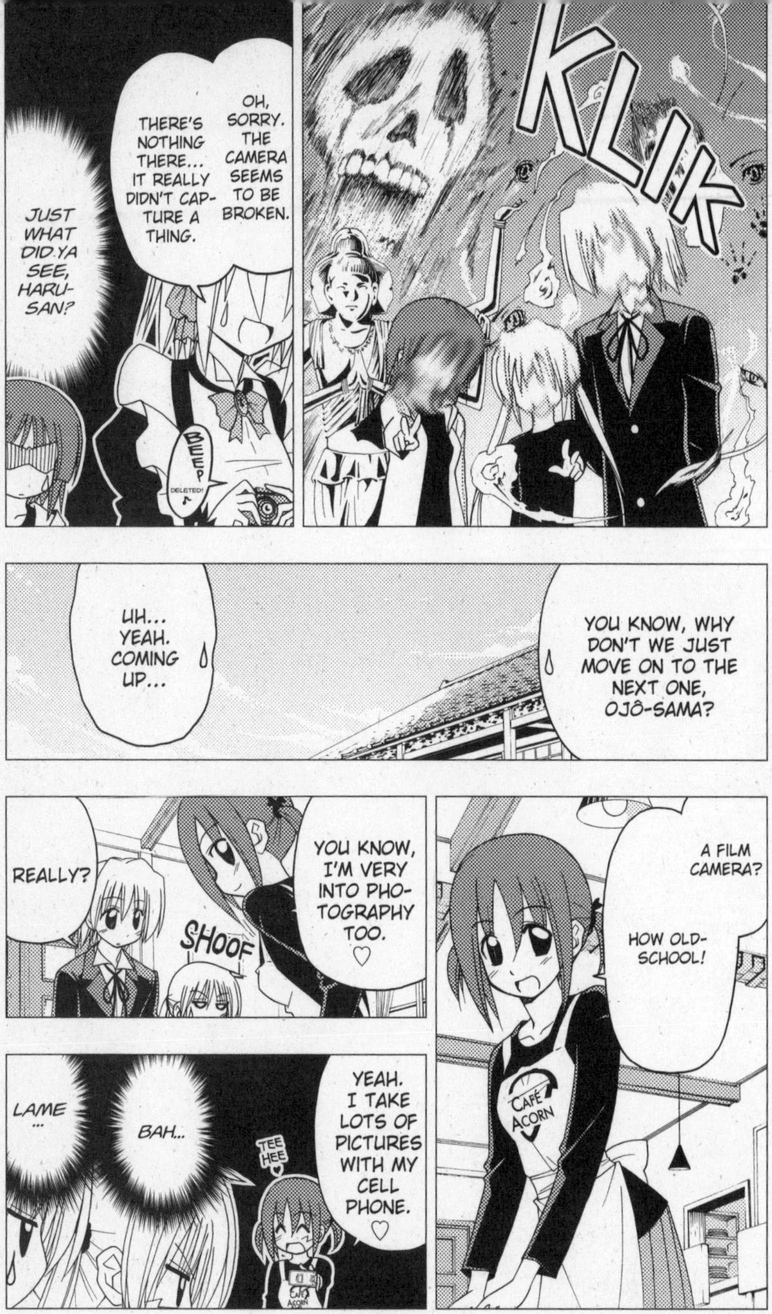
KLIK
OH, SORRY. THE CAMERA SEEMS TO BE BROKEN.
THERE'S NOTHING THERE... IT REALLY DIDN'T CAPTURE A THING.
JUST WHAT DID YA SEE, HARU-SAN?
BEEP
DELETED! ♪
YOU KNOW, WHY DON'T WE JUST MOVE ON TO THE NEXT ONE, OJÔ-SAMA?
UH... YEAH. COMING UP...
A FILM CAMERA?
HOW OLD-SCHOOL!
YOU KNOW, I'M VERY INTO PHOTOGRAPHY TOO. ♡
SHOOF
REALLY?
YEAH. I TAKE LOTS OF PICTURES WITH MY CELL PHONE. ♡
TEE HEE ♡
BAH...
LAME ...

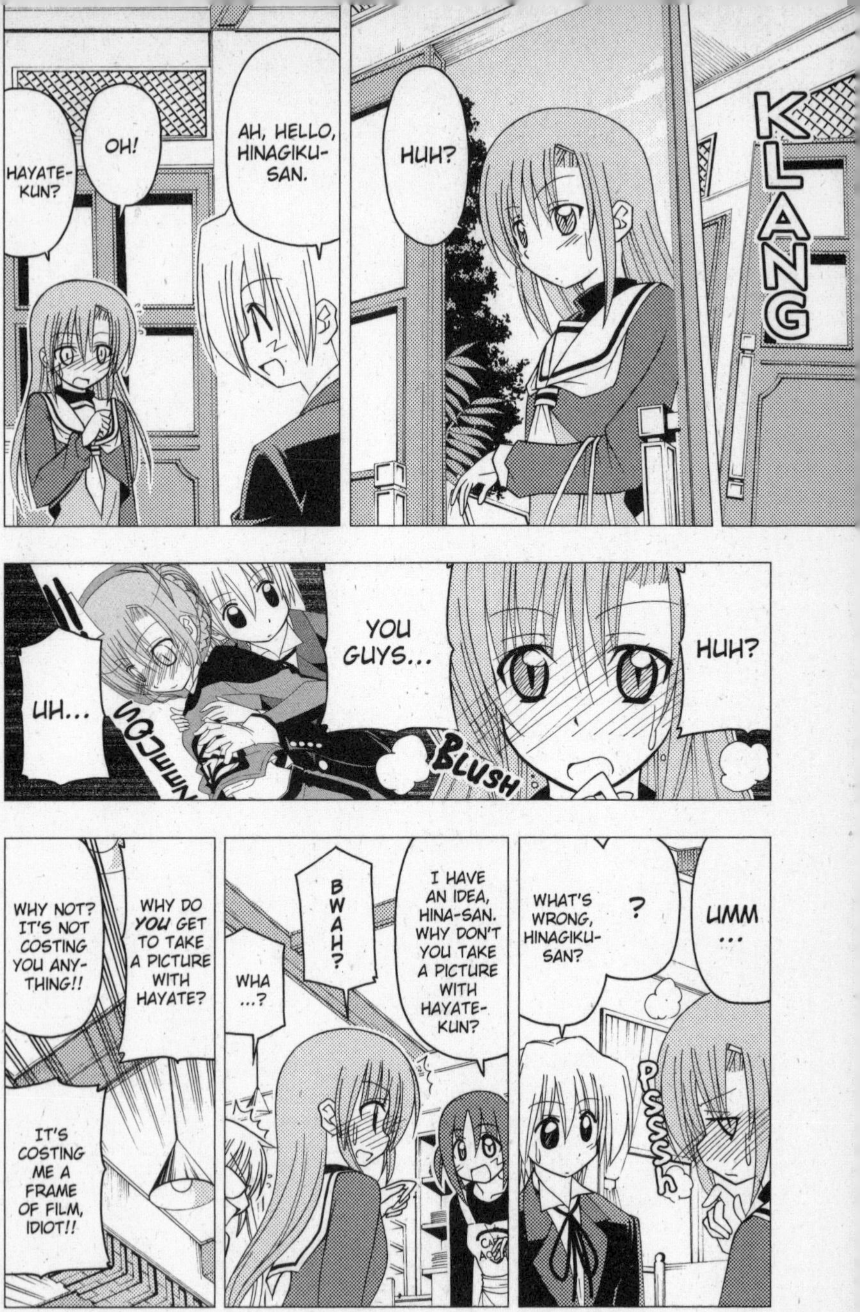
KLANG
HUH?
AH, HELLO, HINAGIKU-SAN.
OH!
HAYATE-KUN?
HUH?
YOU GUYS...
BLUSH
SQUEEEN
UH...
UMM...
?
WHAT'S WRONG, HINAGIKU-SAN?
PSSSH
I HAVE AN IDEA, HINA-SAN. WHY DON'T YOU TAKE A PICTURE WITH HAYATE-KUN?
BWAH?
WHA...?
WHY DO *YOU* GET TO TAKE A PICTURE WITH HAYATE?
WHY NOT? IT'S NOT COSTING YOU ANYTHING!!
IT'S COSTING ME A FRAME OF FILM, IDIOT!!

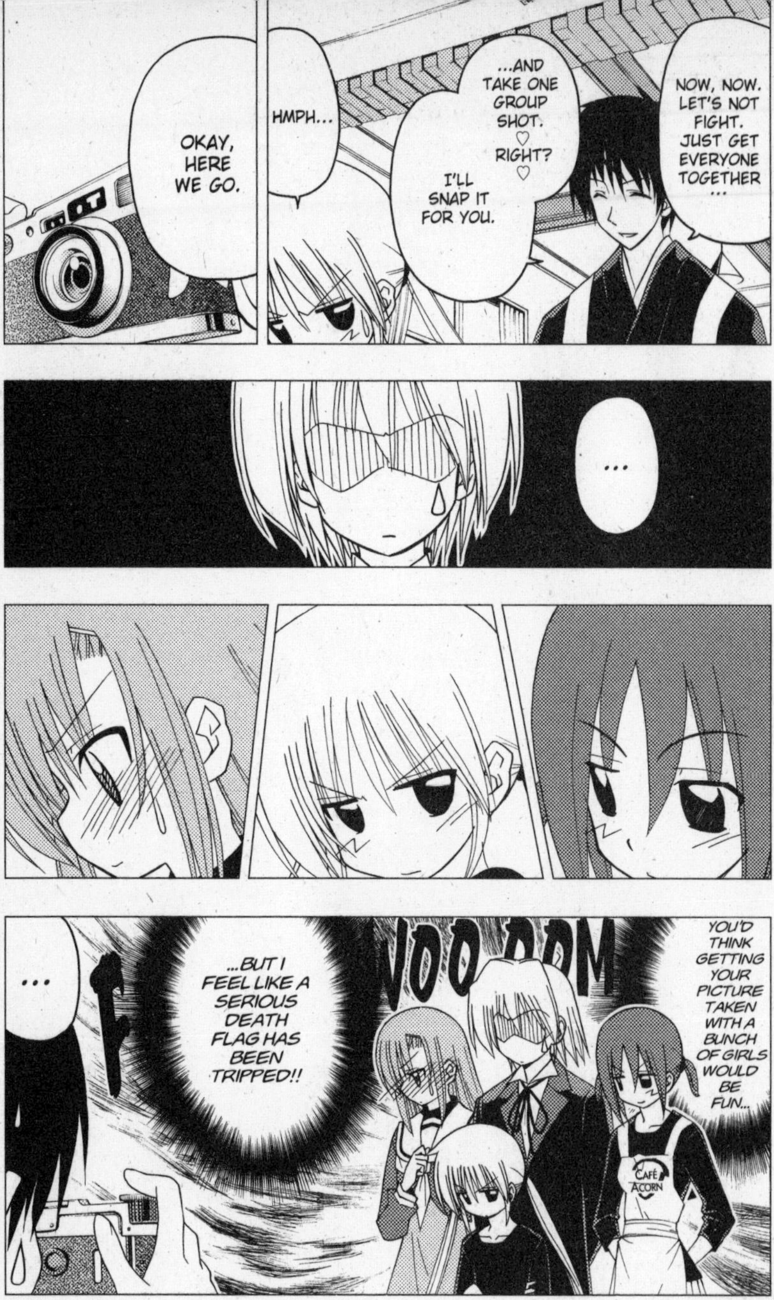
NOW, NOW. LET'S NOT FIGHT. JUST GET EVERYONE TOGETHER...
...AND TAKE ONE GROUP SHOT. ♡ RIGHT? ♡
I'LL SNAP IT FOR YOU.
HMPH...
OKAY, HERE WE GO.
...
YOU'D THINK GETTING YOUR PICTURE TAKEN WITH A BUNCH OF GIRLS WOULD BE FUN...
...BUT I FEEL LIKE A SERIOUS DEATH FLAG HAS BEEN TRIPPED!!
...
CAFÉ ACORN

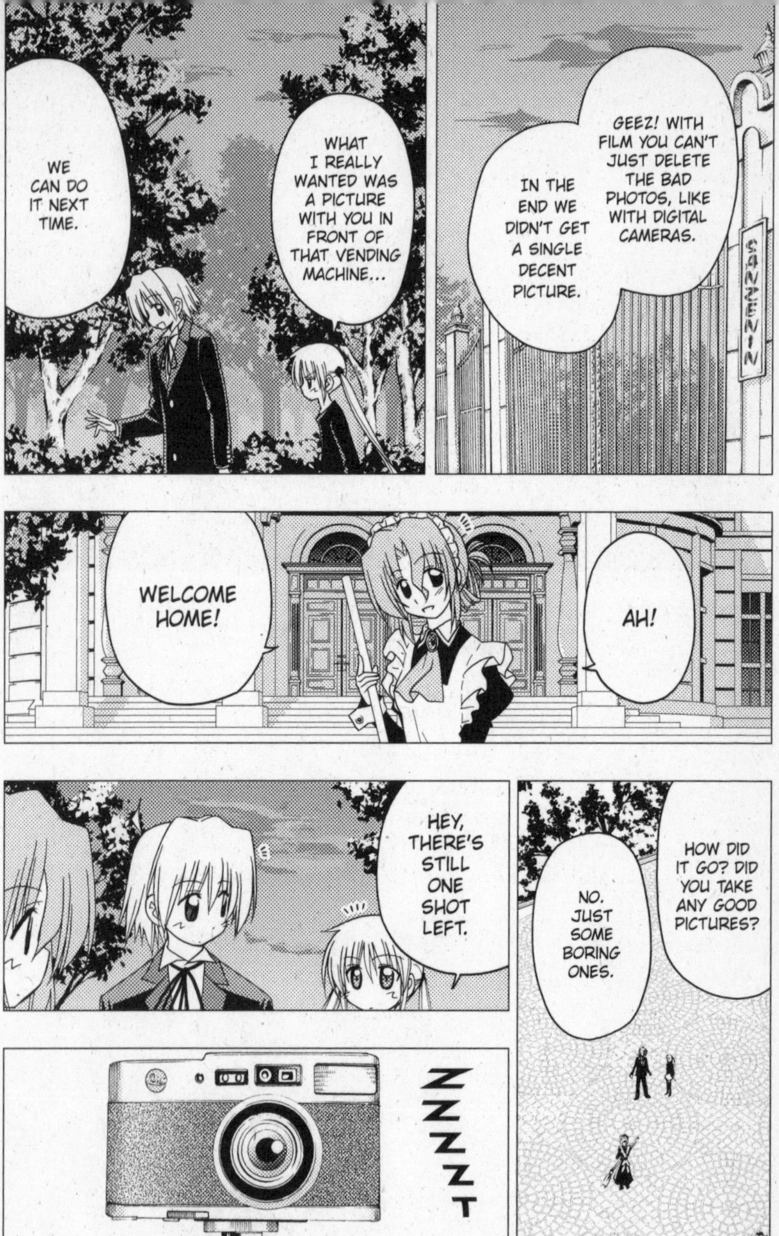
SANZENIN
GEEZ! WITH FILM YOU CAN'T JUST DELETE THE BAD PHOTOS, LIKE WITH DIGITAL CAMERAS.
IN THE END WE DIDN'T GET A SINGLE DECENT PICTURE.
WHAT I REALLY WANTED WAS A PICTURE WITH YOU IN FRONT OF THAT VENDING MACHINE...
WE CAN DO IT NEXT TIME.
AH!
WELCOME HOME!
HOW DID IT GO? DID YOU TAKE ANY GOOD PICTURES?
NO. JUST SOME BORING ONES.
HEY, THERE'S STILL ONE SHOT LEFT.
ZZZZT

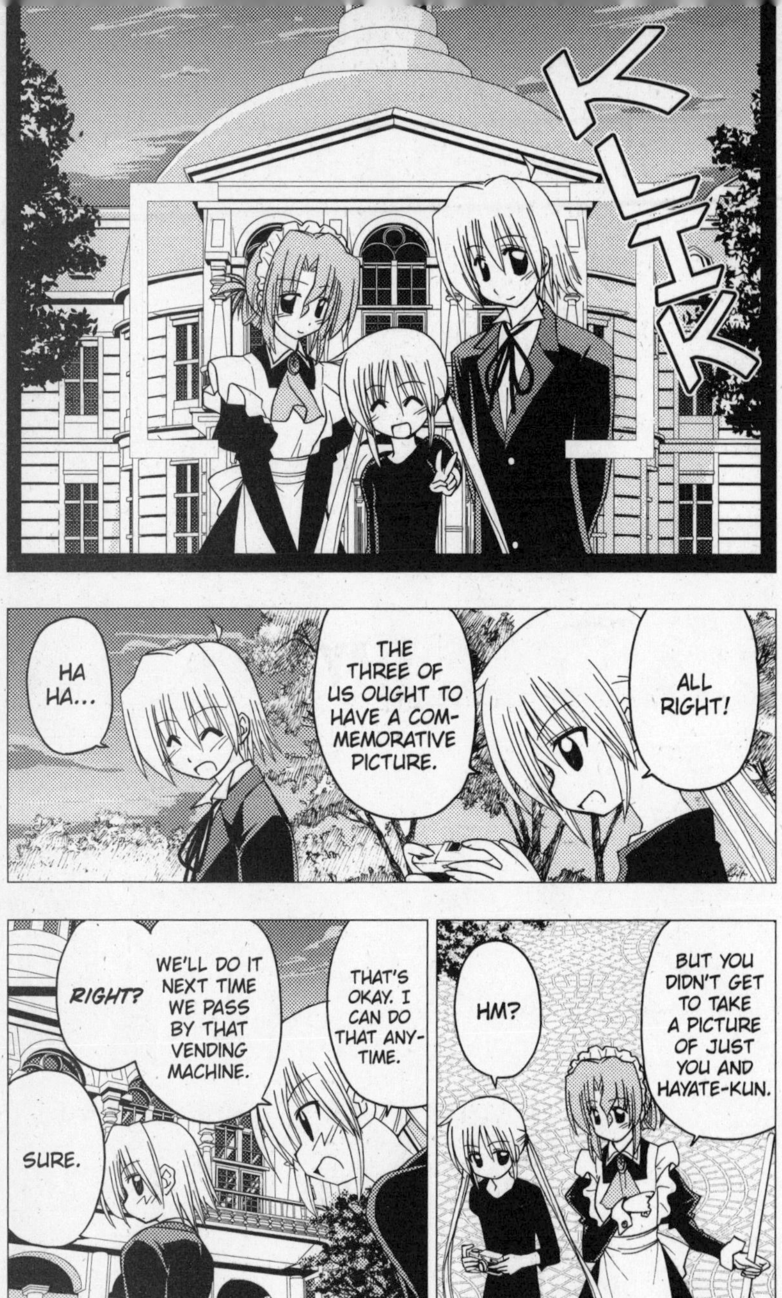
KLIK
ALL RIGHT!
THE THREE OF US OUGHT TO HAVE A COM-MEMORATIVE PICTURE.
HA HA...
BUT YOU DIDN'T GET TO TAKE A PICTURE OF JUST YOU AND HAYATE-KUN.
HM?
THAT'S OKAY. I CAN DO THAT ANY-TIME.
WE'LL DO IT NEXT TIME WE PASS BY THAT VENDING MACHINE.
RIGHT?
SURE.

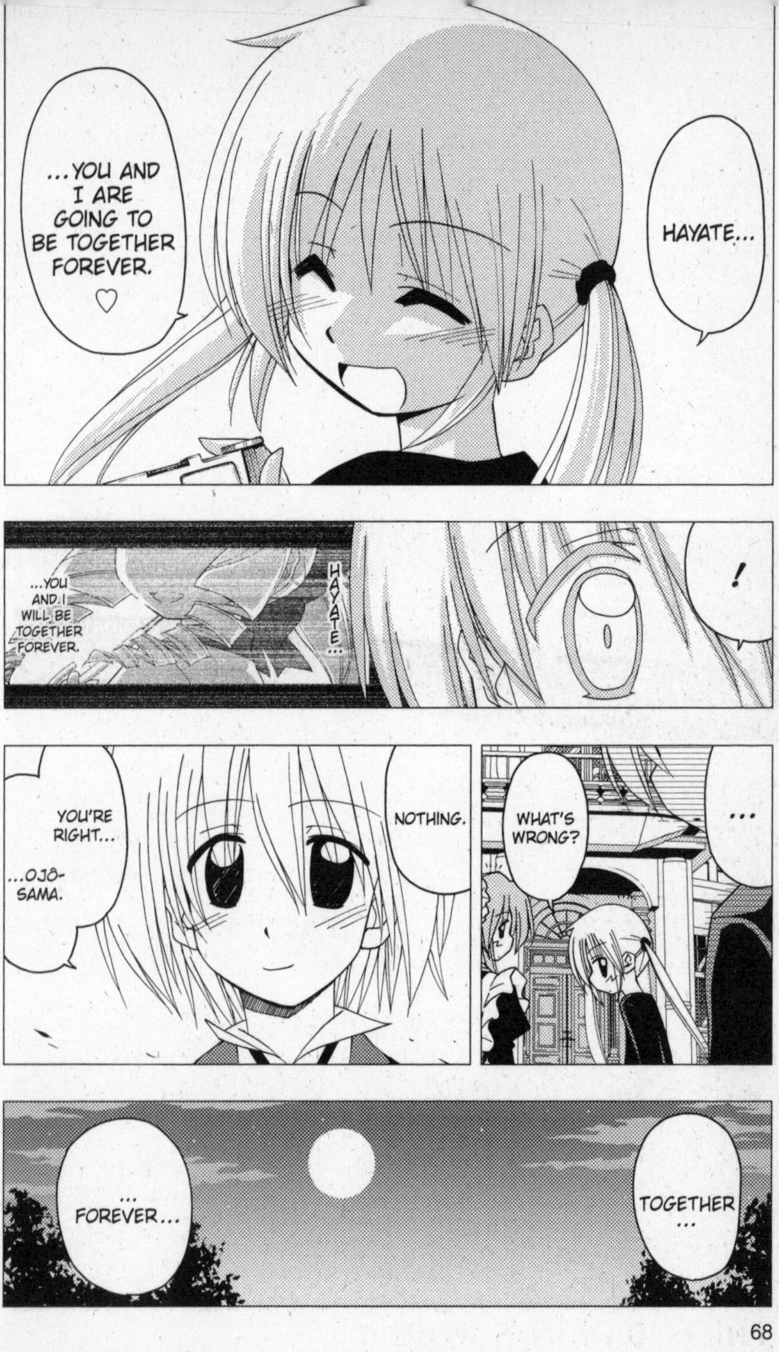
HAYATE...
...YOU AND I ARE GOING TO BE TOGETHER FOREVER. ♡
!
HAYATE...
...YOU AND I WILL BE TOGETHER FOREVER.
...
WHAT'S WRONG?
NOTHING.
YOU'RE RIGHT...
...OJÔ-SAMA.
TOGETHER...
...FOREVER...

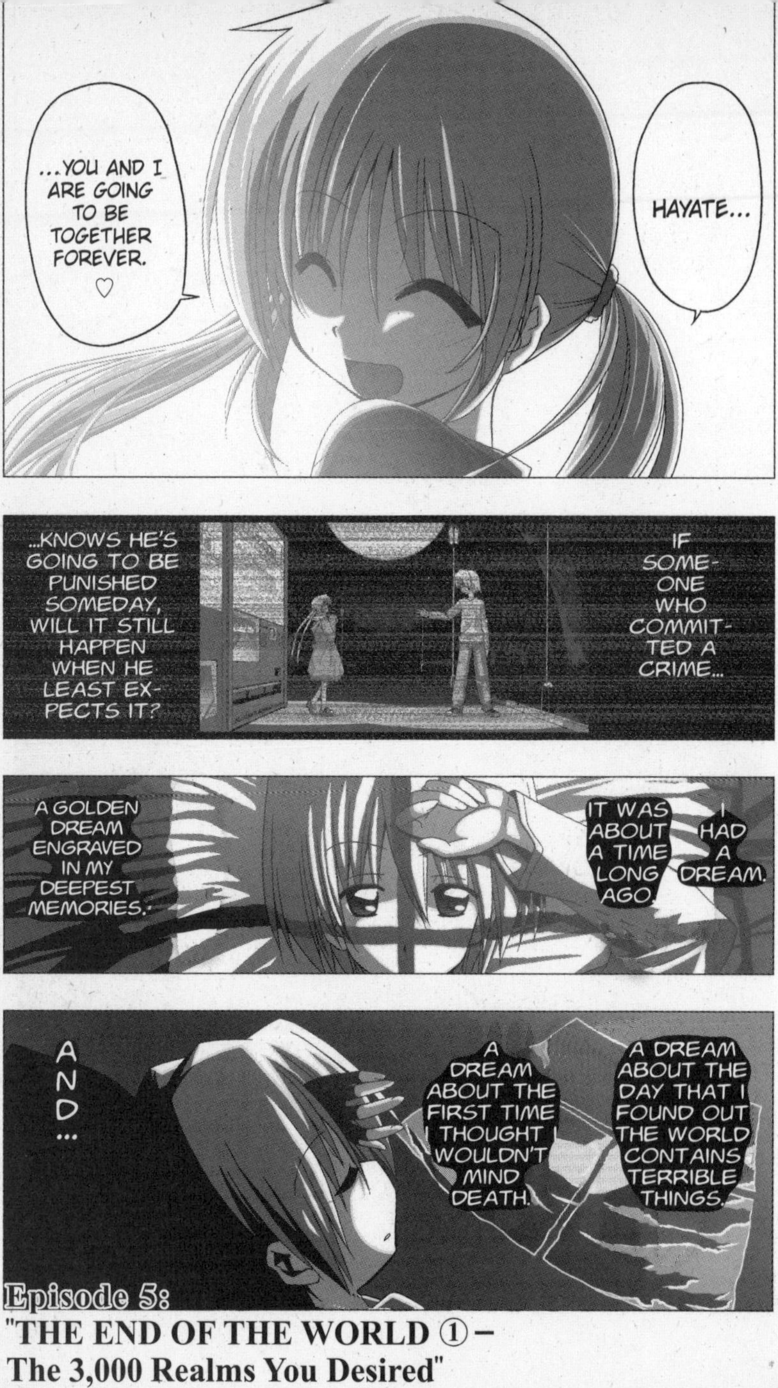
HAYATE...
...YOU AND I ARE GOING TO BE TOGETHER FOREVER. ♡
IF SOME-ONE WHO COMMIT-TED A CRIME...
...KNOWS HE'S GOING TO BE PUNISHED SOMEDAY, WILL IT STILL HAPPEN WHEN HE LEAST EX-PECTS IT?
I HAD A DREAM.
IT WAS ABOUT A TIME LONG AGO.
A GOLDEN DREAM ENGRAVED IN MY DEEPEST MEMORIES.
A DREAM ABOUT THE DAY THAT I FOUND OUT THE WORLD CONTAINS TERRIBLE THINGS.
A DREAM ABOUT THE FIRST TIME I THOUGHT I WOULDN'T MIND DEATH.
AND...

Episode 5:
"THE END OF THE WORLD ① – The 3,000 Realms You Desired"

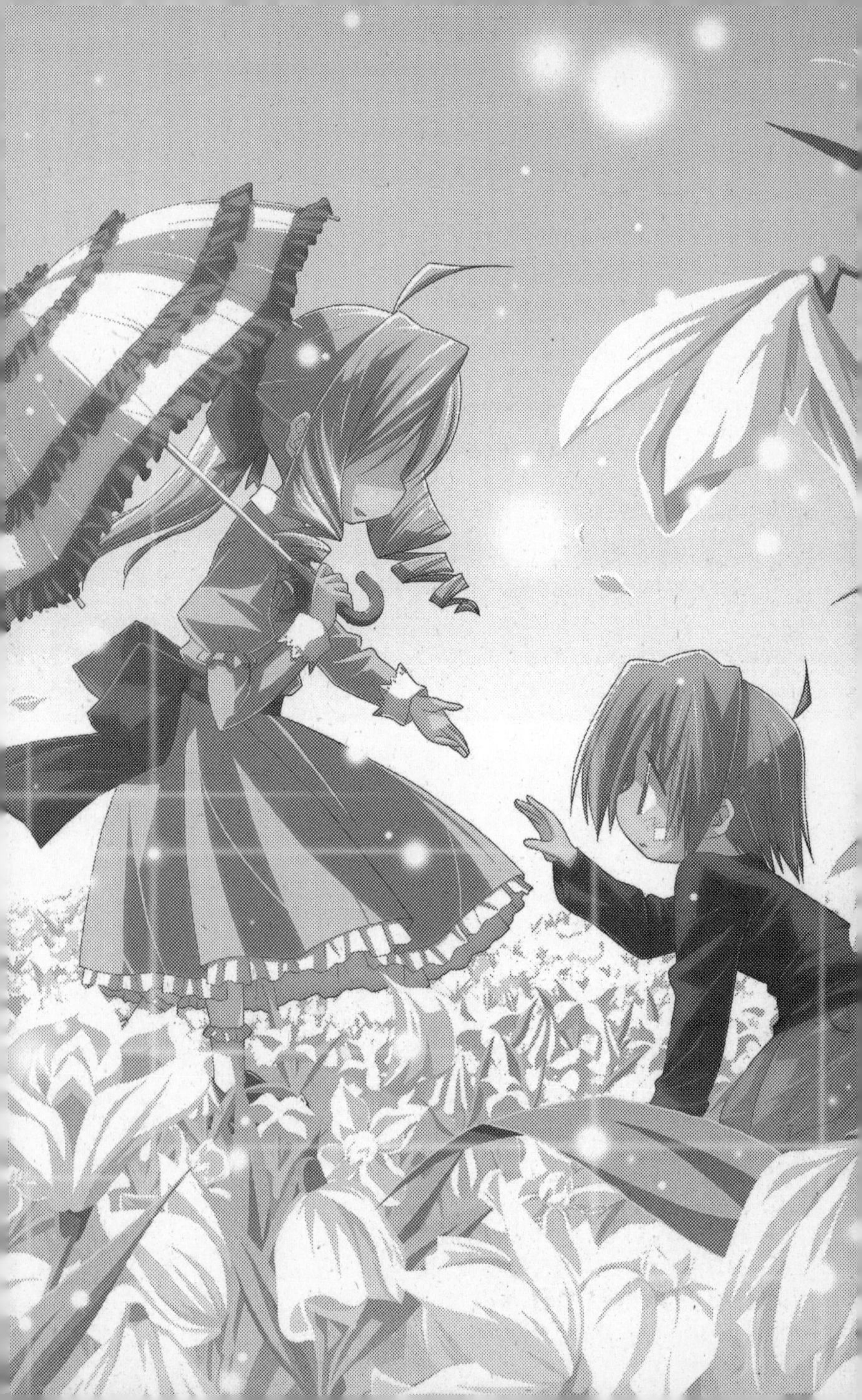

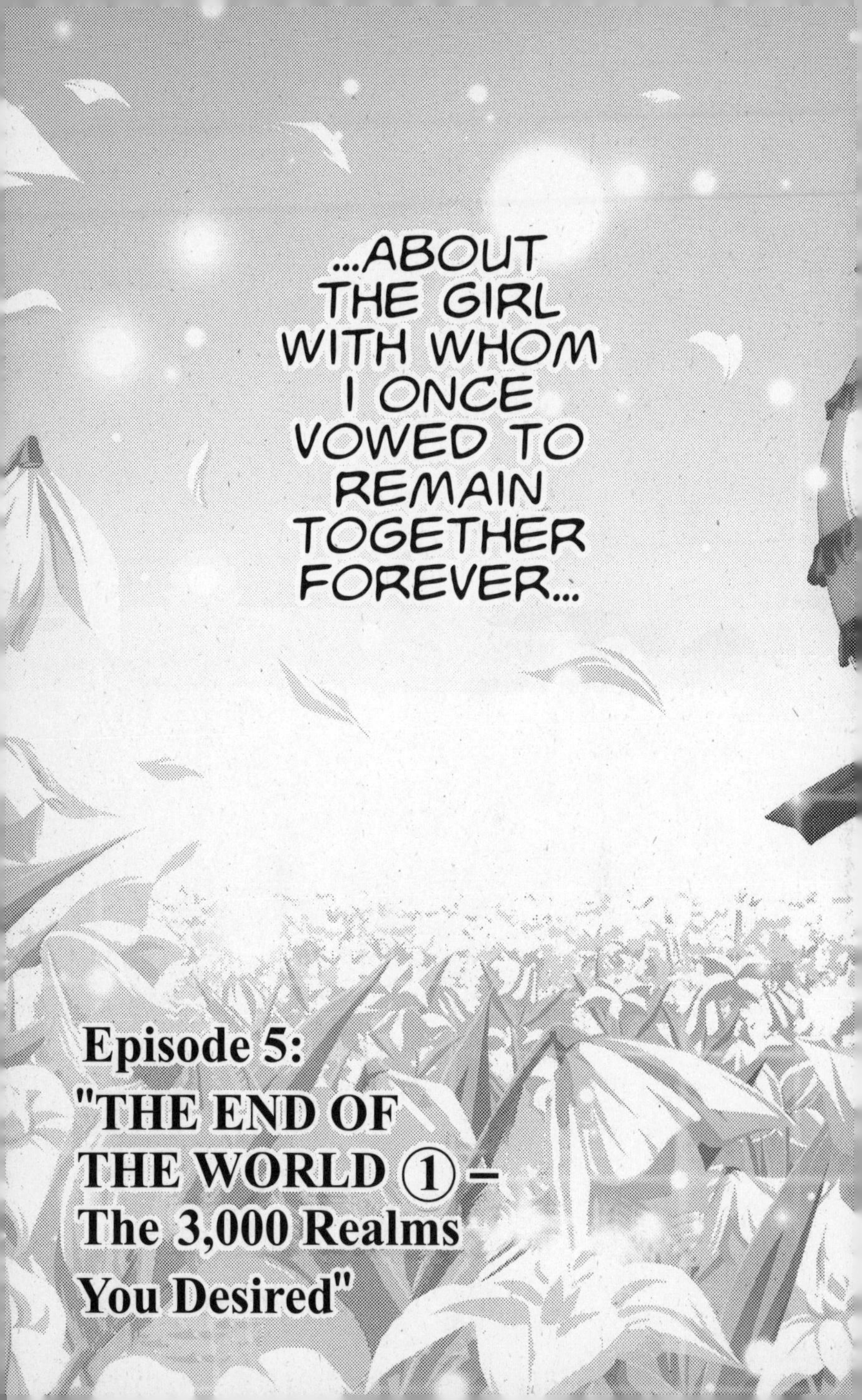
...ABOUT THE GIRL WITH WHOM I ONCE VOWED TO REMAIN TOGETHER FOREVER...
Episode 5:
"THE END OF THE WORLD ① – The 3,000 Realms You Desired"

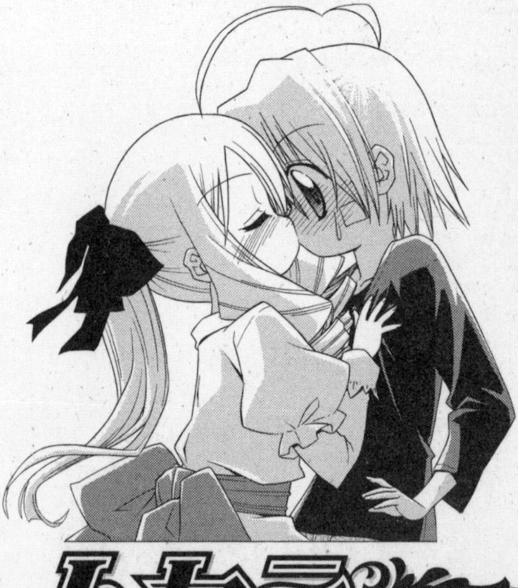

ハヤテのごとく!
Hayate the combat butler

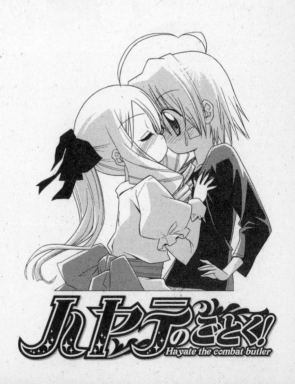

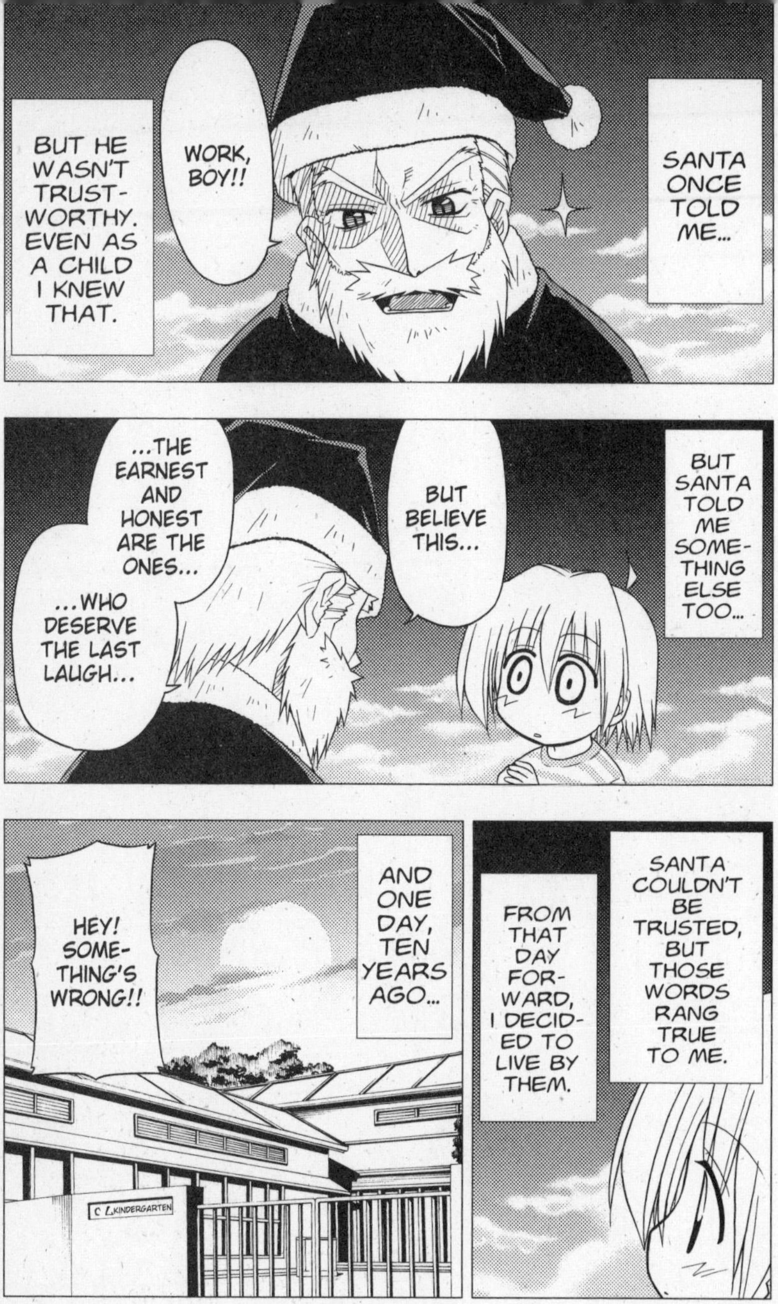
SANTA ONCE TOLD ME...
WORK, BOY!!
BUT HE WASN'T TRUST-WORTHY. EVEN AS A CHILD I KNEW THAT.
BUT SANTA TOLD ME SOME-THING ELSE TOO...
BUT BELIEVE THIS...
...THE EARNEST AND HONEST ARE THE ONES...
...WHO DESERVE THE LAST LAUGH...
SANTA COULDN'T BE TRUSTED, BUT THOSE WORDS RANG TRUE TO ME.
FROM THAT DAY FOR-WARD, I DECID-ED TO LIVE BY THEM.
AND ONE DAY, TEN YEARS AGO...
HEY! SOME-THING'S WRONG!!

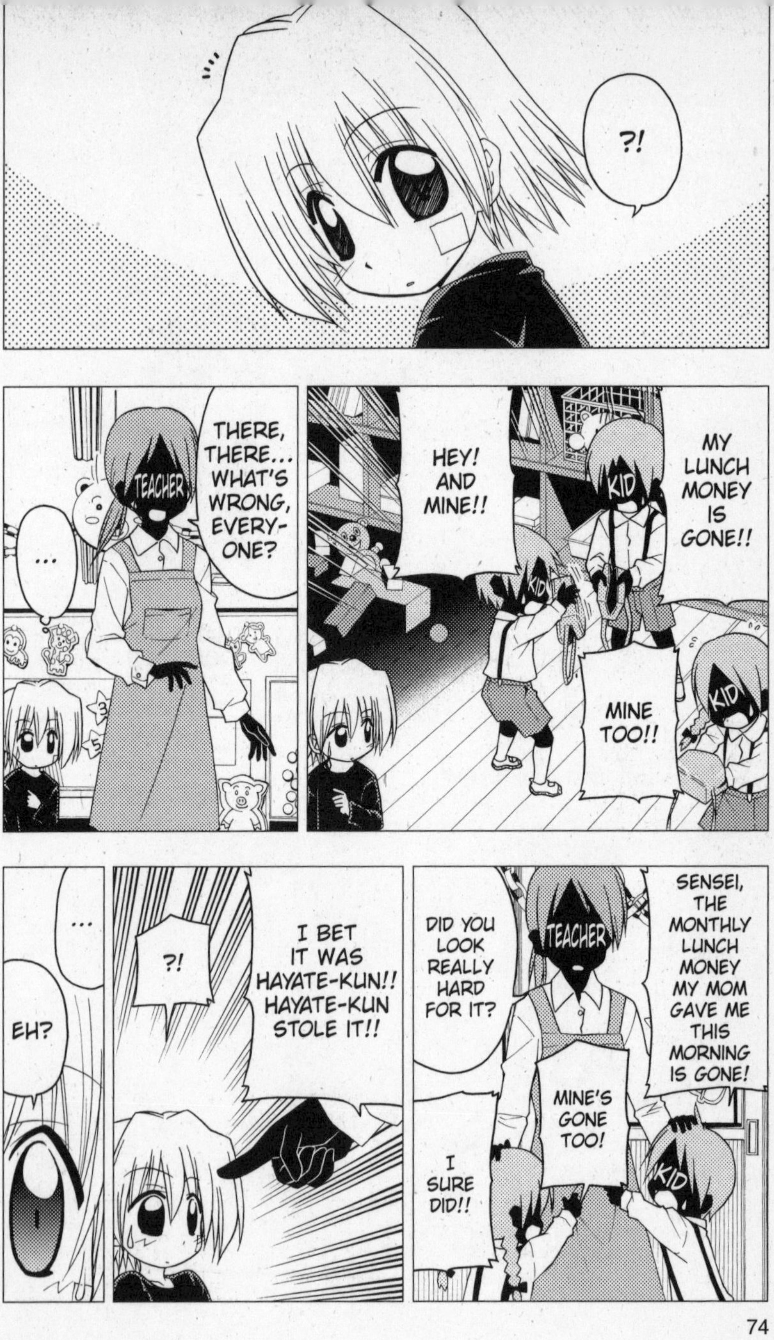
?!
MY LUNCH MONEY IS GONE!!
KID
HEY! AND MINE!!
KID
MINE TOO!!
KID
TEACHER
THERE, THERE... WHAT'S WRONG, EVERY-ONE?
...
SENSEI, THE MONTHLY LUNCH MONEY MY MOM GAVE ME THIS MORNING IS GONE!
TEACHER
DID YOU LOOK REALLY HARD FOR IT?
MINE'S GONE TOO!
KID
I SURE DID!!
I BET IT WAS HAYATE-KUN!! HAYATE-KUN STOLE IT!!
?!
...
EH?

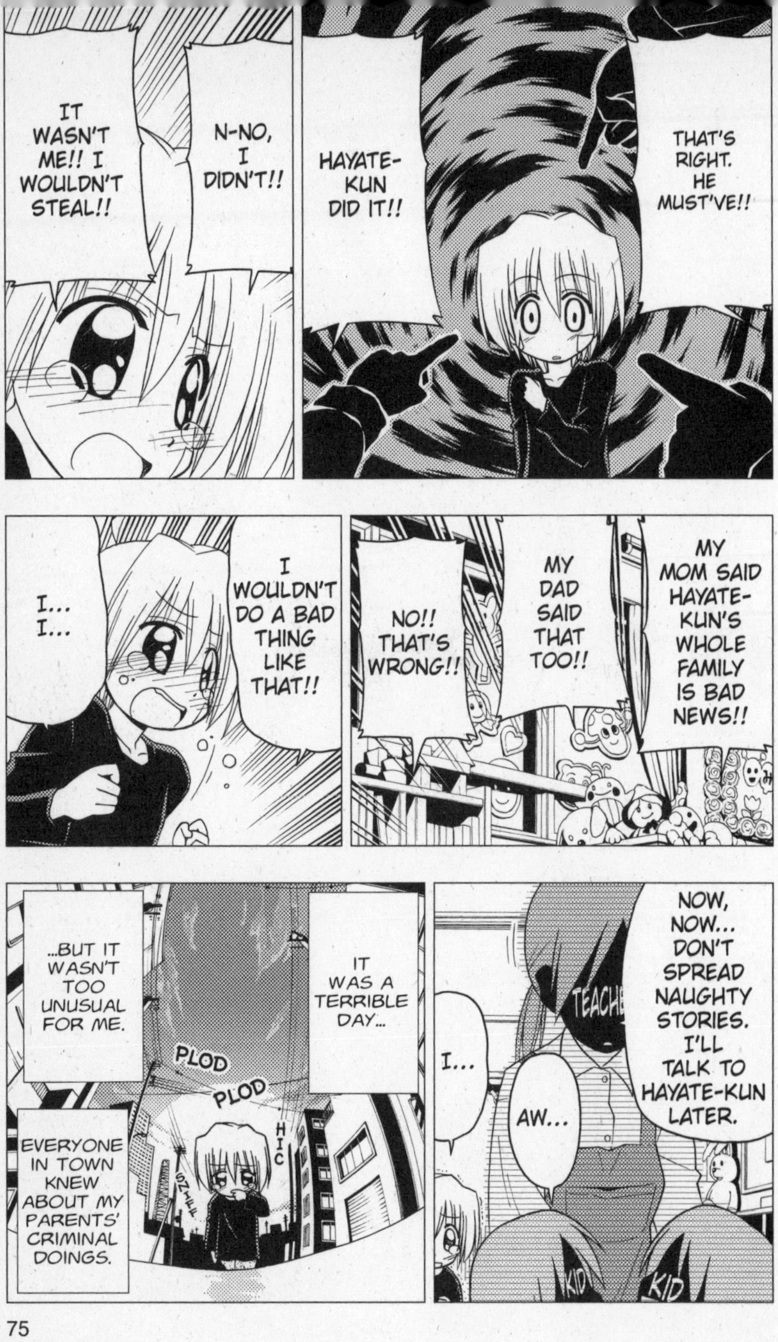
THAT'S RIGHT. HE MUST'VE!!
HAYATE-KUN DID IT!!
N-NO, I DIDN'T!!
IT WASN'T ME!! I WOULDN'T STEAL!!
MY MOM SAID HAYATE-KUN'S WHOLE FAMILY IS BAD NEWS!!
MY DAD SAID THAT TOO!!
NO!! THAT'S WRONG!!
I WOULDN'T DO A BAD THING LIKE THAT!!
I... I...
NOW, NOW... DON'T SPREAD NAUGHTY STORIES. I'LL TALK TO HAYATE-KUN LATER.
I...
AW...
KID
KID
IT WAS A TERRIBLE DAY...
...BUT IT WASN'T TOO UNUSUAL FOR ME.
PLOD
PLOD
HIC
SNIFF
EVERYONE IN TOWN KNEW ABOUT MY PARENTS' CRIMINAL DOINGS.

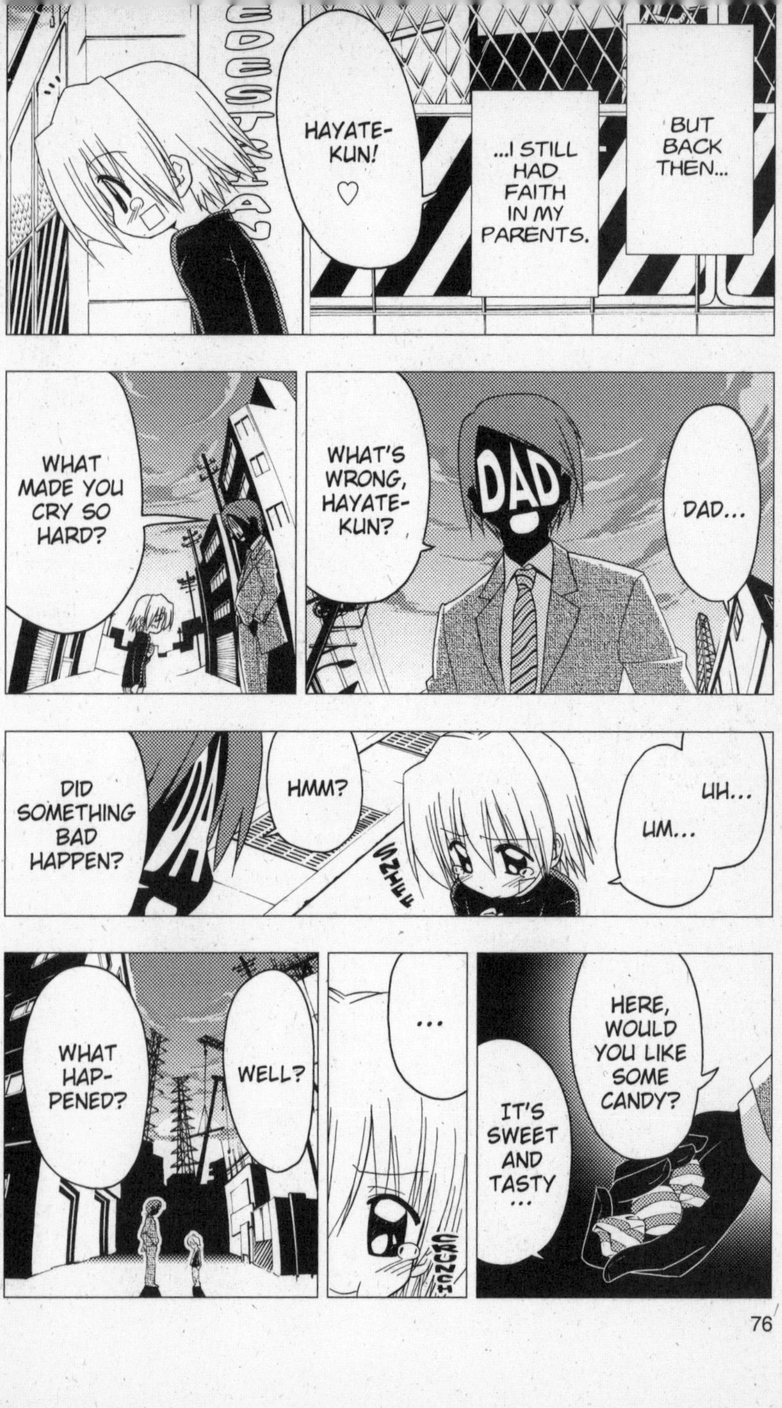
BUT BACK THEN...
...I STILL HAD FAITH IN MY PARENTS.
HAYATE-KUN! ♡
DAD...
WHAT'S WRONG, HAYATE-KUN?
WHAT MADE YOU CRY SO HARD?
UH... UM...
HMM?
SNIFF
DID SOMETHING BAD HAPPEN?
HERE, WOULD YOU LIKE SOME CANDY?
IT'S SWEET AND TASTY...
...
CRUNCH
WELL?
WHAT HAPPENED?

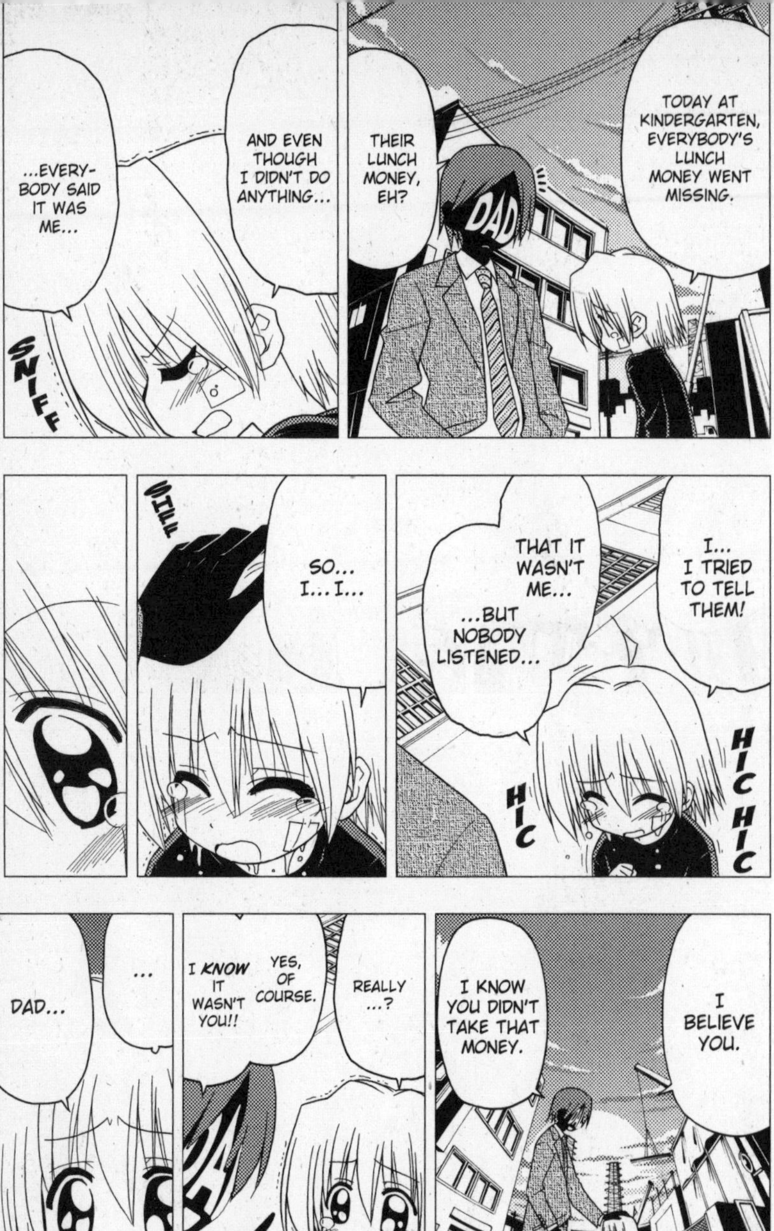
TODAY AT KINDERGARTEN, EVERYBODY'S LUNCH MONEY WENT MISSING.
THEIR LUNCH MONEY, EH?
DAD
AND EVEN THOUGH I DIDN'T DO ANYTHING...
...EVERYBODY SAID IT WAS ME...
SNIFF
I... I TRIED TO TELL THEM!
THAT IT WASN'T ME...
...BUT NOBODY LISTENED...
HIC HIC
HIC
SO... I... I...
I BELIEVE YOU.
I KNOW YOU DIDN'T TAKE THAT MONEY.
REALLY ...?
YES, OF COURSE.
I *KNOW* IT WASN'T YOU!!
...
DAD...

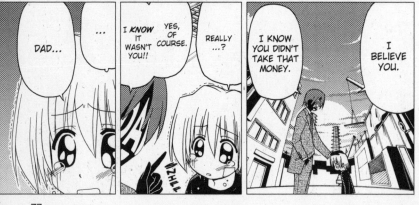

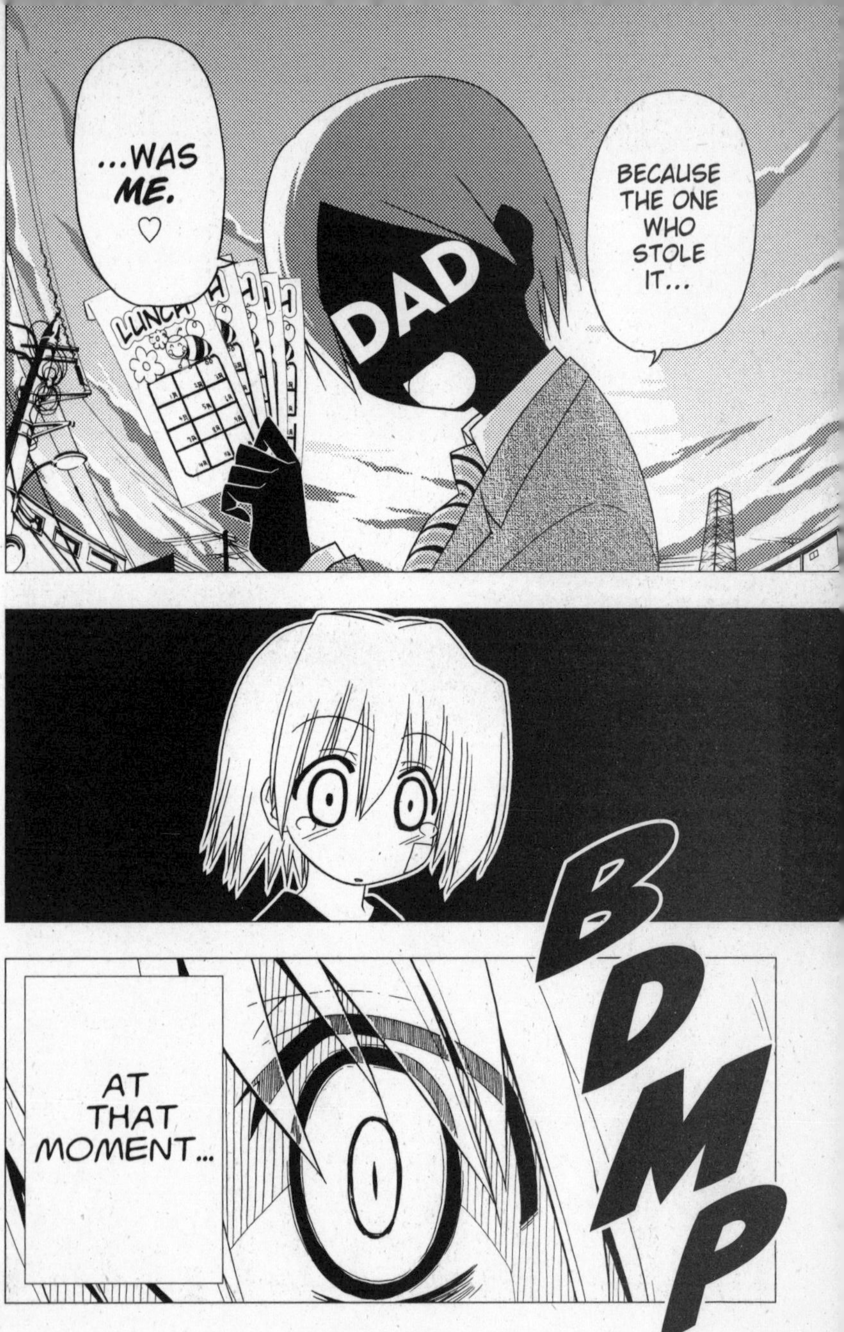
BECAUSE THE ONE WHO STOLE IT...
...WAS ME. ♡
DAD
BDMP
AT THAT MOMENT...

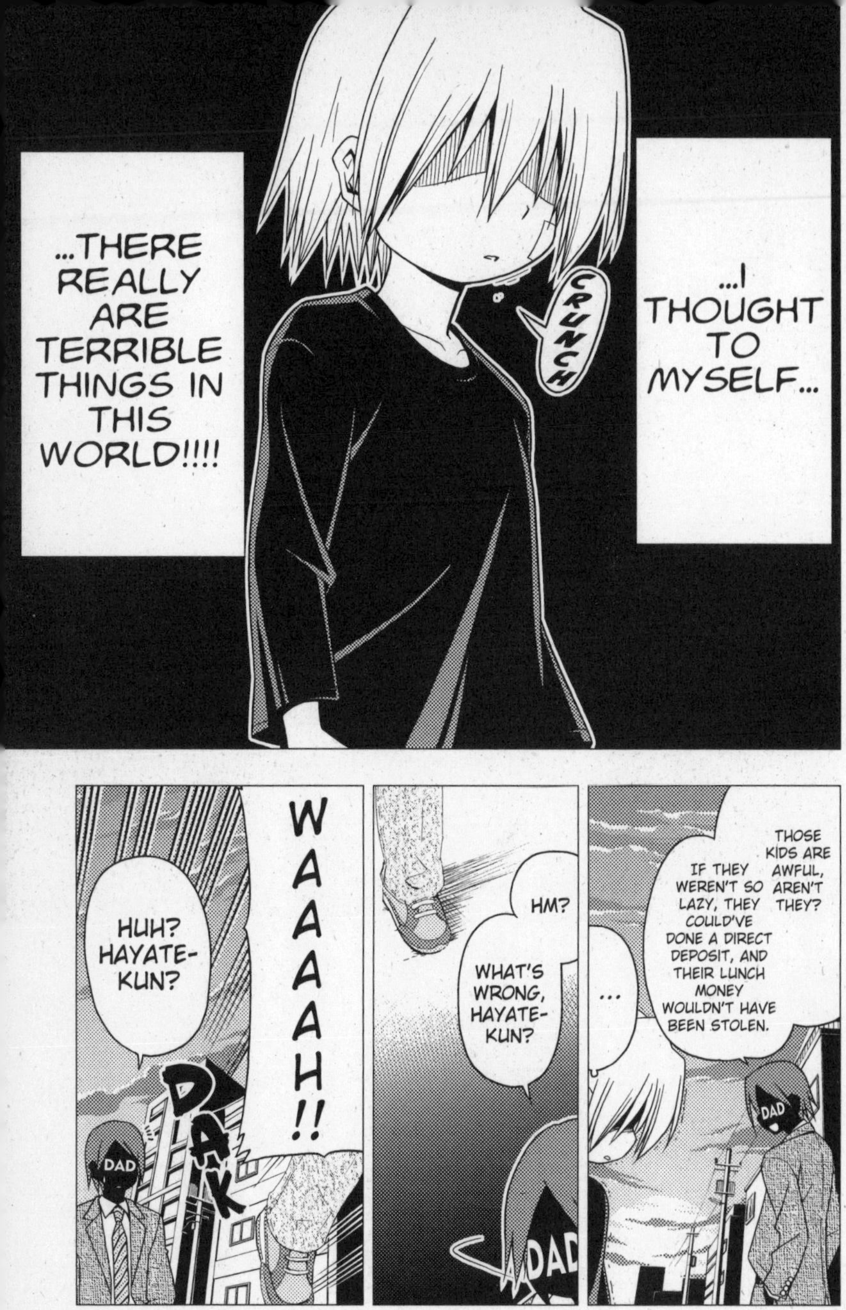

...I THOUGHT TO MYSELF...
CRUNCH
...THERE REALLY ARE TERRIBLE THINGS IN THIS WORLD!!!!
THOSE KIDS ARE AWFUL, AREN'T THEY?
IF THEY WEREN'T SO LAZY, THEY COULD'VE DONE A DIRECT DEPOSIT, AND THEIR LUNCH MONEY WOULDN'T HAVE BEEN STOLEN.
...
DAD
HM?
WHAT'S WRONG, HAYATE-KUN?
DAD
WAAAAAH!!
HUH? HAYATE-KUN?
DAK
DAD

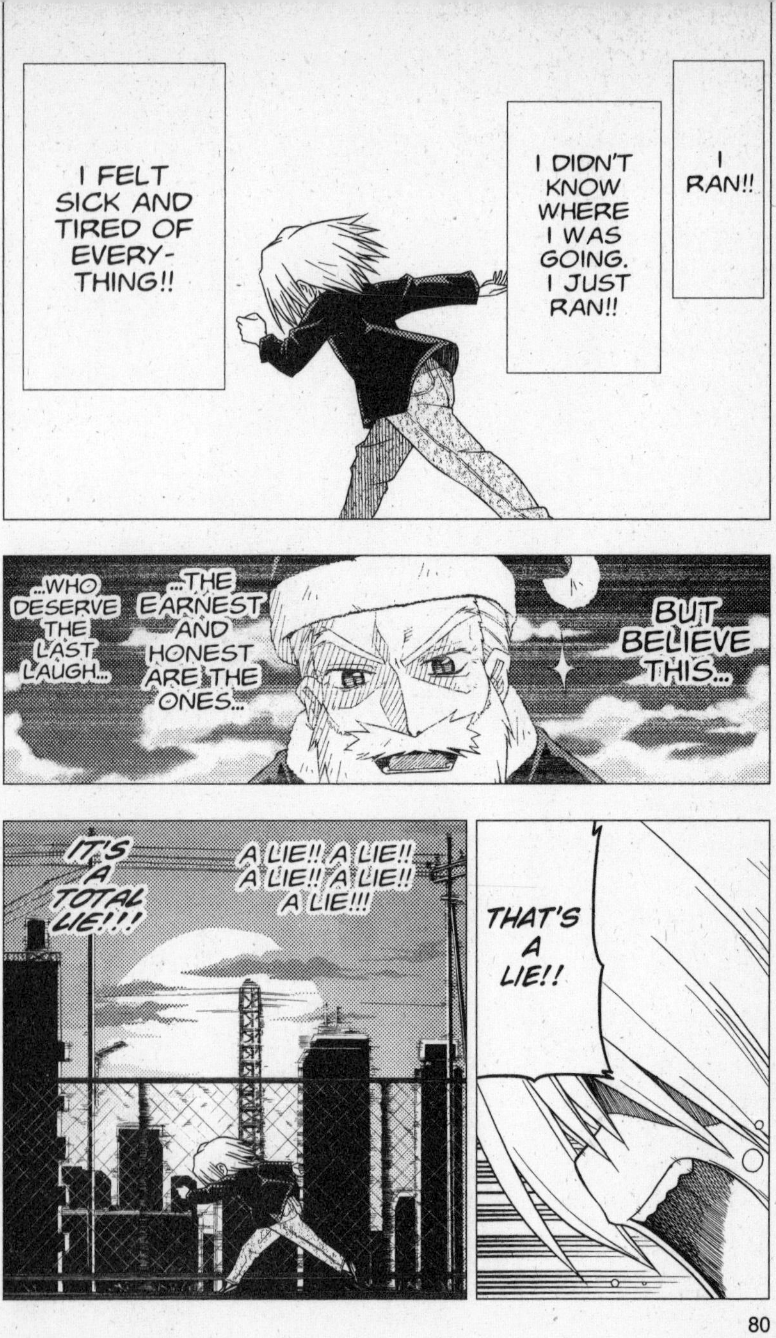
I RAN!!
I DIDN'T KNOW WHERE I WAS GOING. I JUST RAN!!
I FELT SICK AND TIRED OF EVERY-THING!!
BUT BELIEVE THIS...
...THE EARNEST AND HONEST ARE THE ONES...
...WHO DESERVE THE LAST LAUGH...
THAT'S A LIE!!
A LIE!! A LIE!! A LIE!! A LIE!! A LIE!!!
IT'S A TOTAL LIE!!!

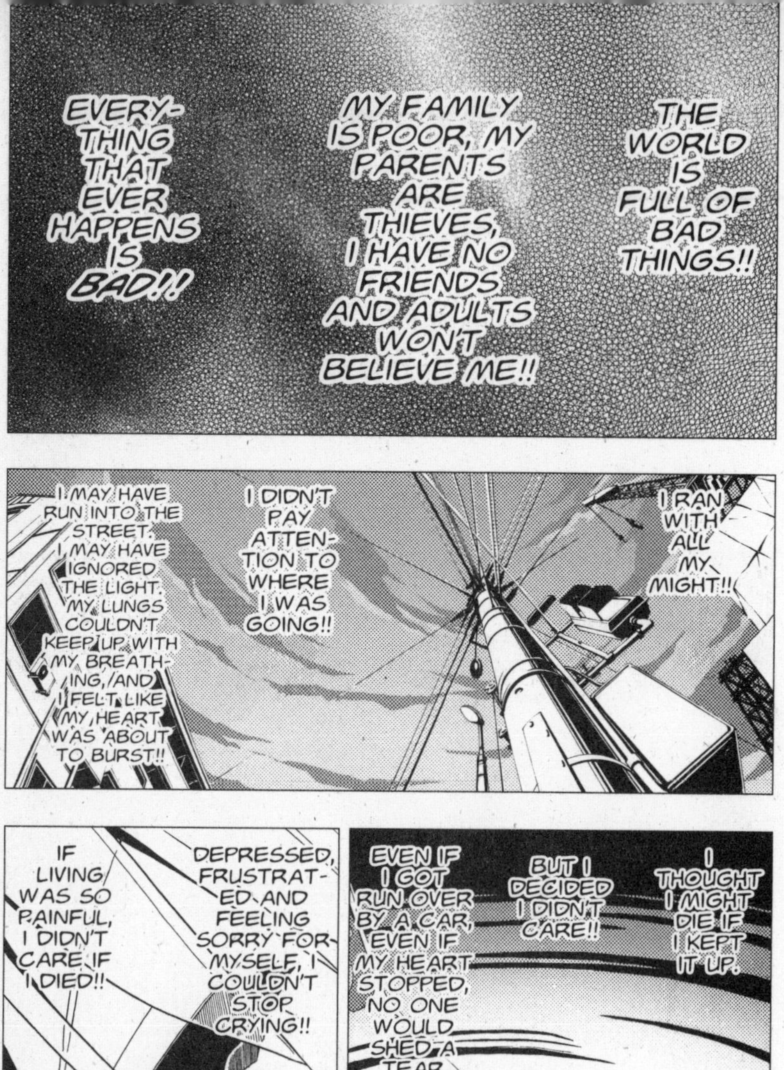
THE WORLD IS FULL OF BAD THINGS!!
MY FAMILY IS POOR, MY PARENTS ARE THIEVES, I HAVE NO FRIENDS AND ADULTS WON'T BELIEVE ME!!
EVERYTHING THAT EVER HAPPENS IS BAD!!
I RAN WITH ALL MY MIGHT!!
I DIDN'T PAY ATTENTION TO WHERE I WAS GOING!!
I MAY HAVE RUN INTO THE STREET. I MAY HAVE IGNORED THE LIGHT. MY LUNGS COULDN'T KEEP UP WITH MY BREATHING, AND I FELT LIKE MY HEART WAS ABOUT TO BURST!!
I THOUGHT I MIGHT DIE IF I KEPT IT UP.
BUT I DECIDED I DIDN'T CARE!!
EVEN IF I GOT RUN OVER BY A CAR, EVEN IF MY HEART STOPPED, NO ONE WOULD SHED A TEAR FOR ME!!
DEPRESSED, FRUSTRATED AND FEELING SORRY FOR MYSELF, I COULDN'T STOP CRYING!!
IF LIVING WAS SO PAINFUL, I DIDN'T CARE IF I DIED!!

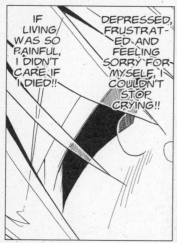

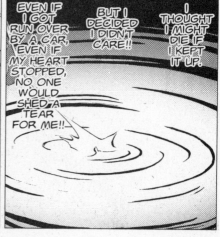

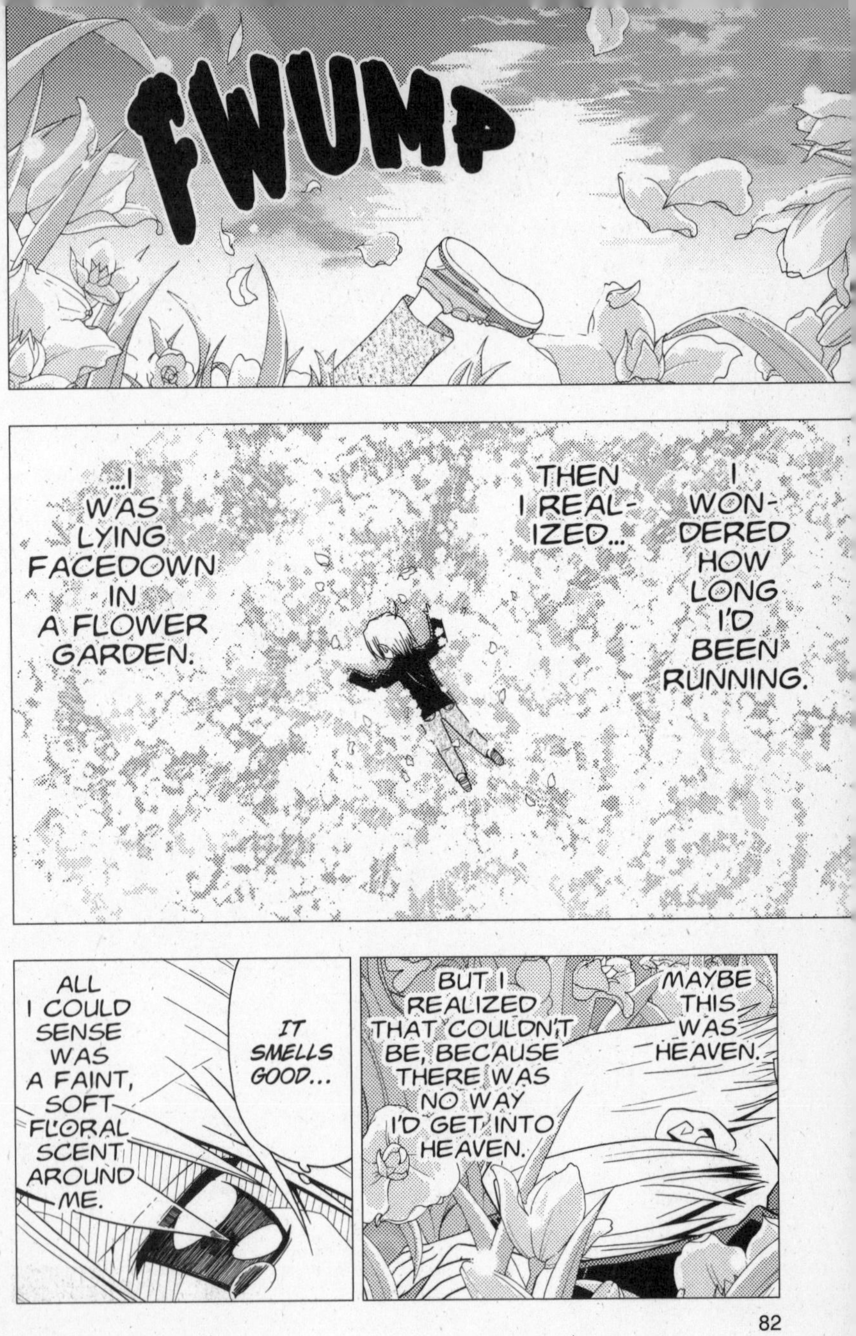
FWUMP
I WONDERED HOW LONG I'D BEEN RUNNING.
THEN I REALIZED...
...I WAS LYING FACEDOWN IN A FLOWER GARDEN.
MAYBE THIS WAS HEAVEN.
BUT I REALIZED THAT COULDN'T BE, BECAUSE THERE WAS NO WAY I'D GET INTO HEAVEN.
IT SMELLS GOOD...
ALL I COULD SENSE WAS A FAINT, SOFT FLORAL SCENT AROUND ME.

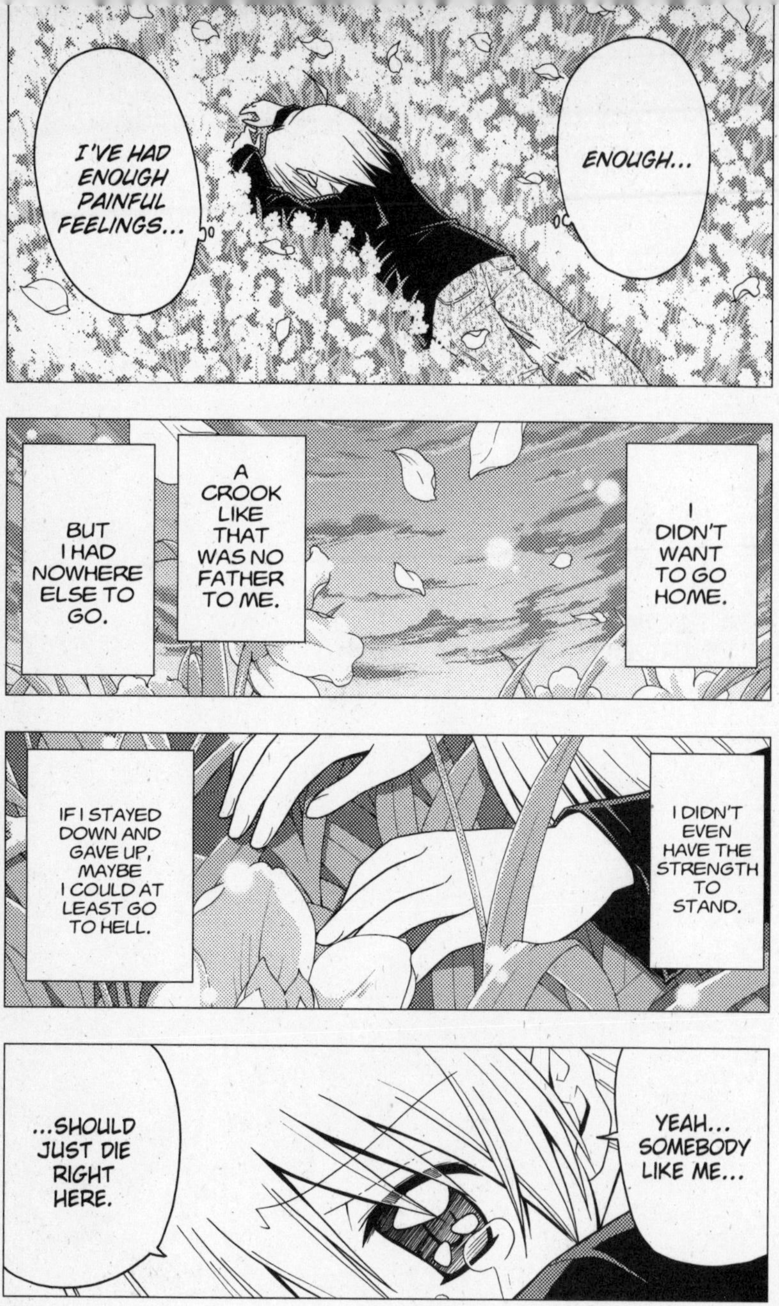
ENOUGH...
I'VE HAD ENOUGH PAINFUL FEELINGS...
I DIDN'T WANT TO GO HOME.
A CROOK LIKE THAT WAS NO FATHER TO ME.
BUT I HAD NOWHERE ELSE TO GO.
I DIDN'T EVEN HAVE THE STRENGTH TO STAND.
IF I STAYED DOWN AND GAVE UP, MAYBE I COULD AT LEAST GO TO HELL.
YEAH... SOMEBODY LIKE ME...
...SHOULD JUST DIE RIGHT HERE.

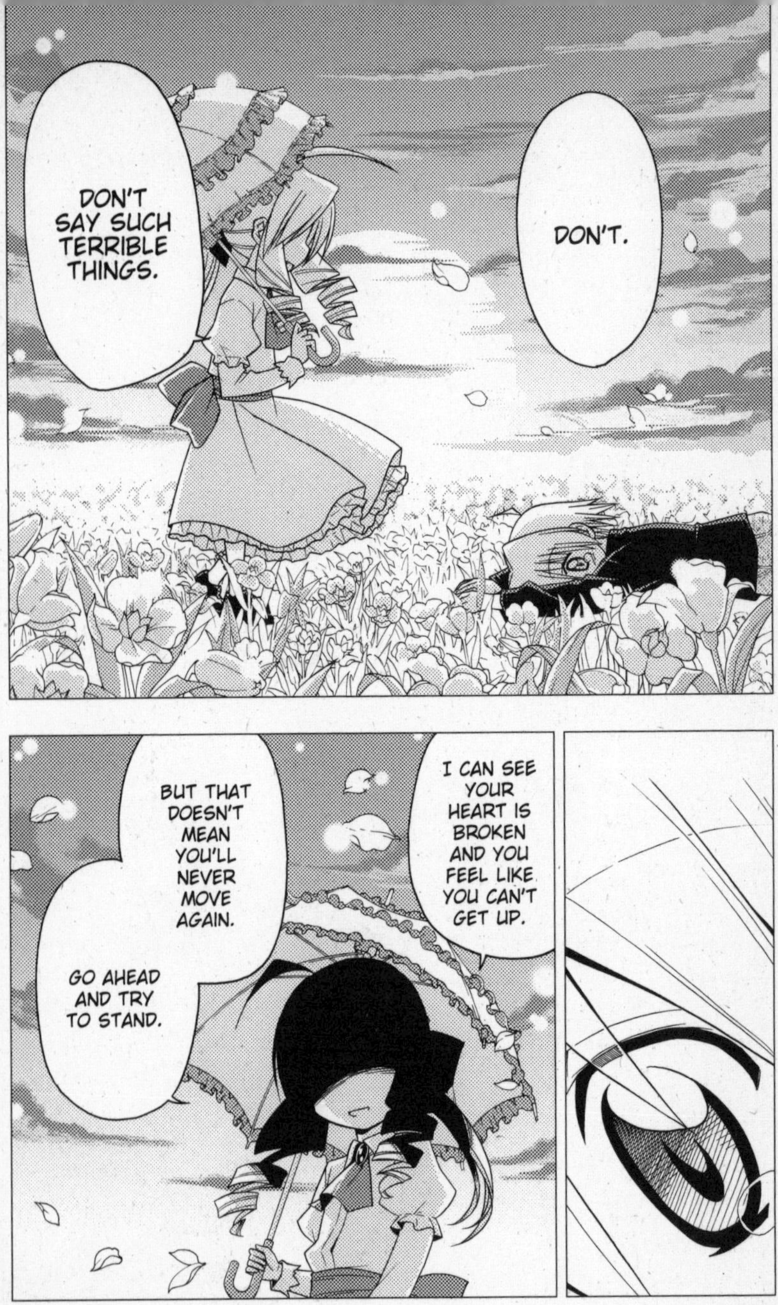
DON'T.
DON'T SAY SUCH TERRIBLE THINGS.
I CAN SEE YOUR HEART IS BROKEN AND YOU FEEL LIKE YOU CAN'T GET UP.
BUT THAT DOESN'T MEAN YOU'LL NEVER MOVE AGAIN.
GO AHEAD AND TRY TO STAND.

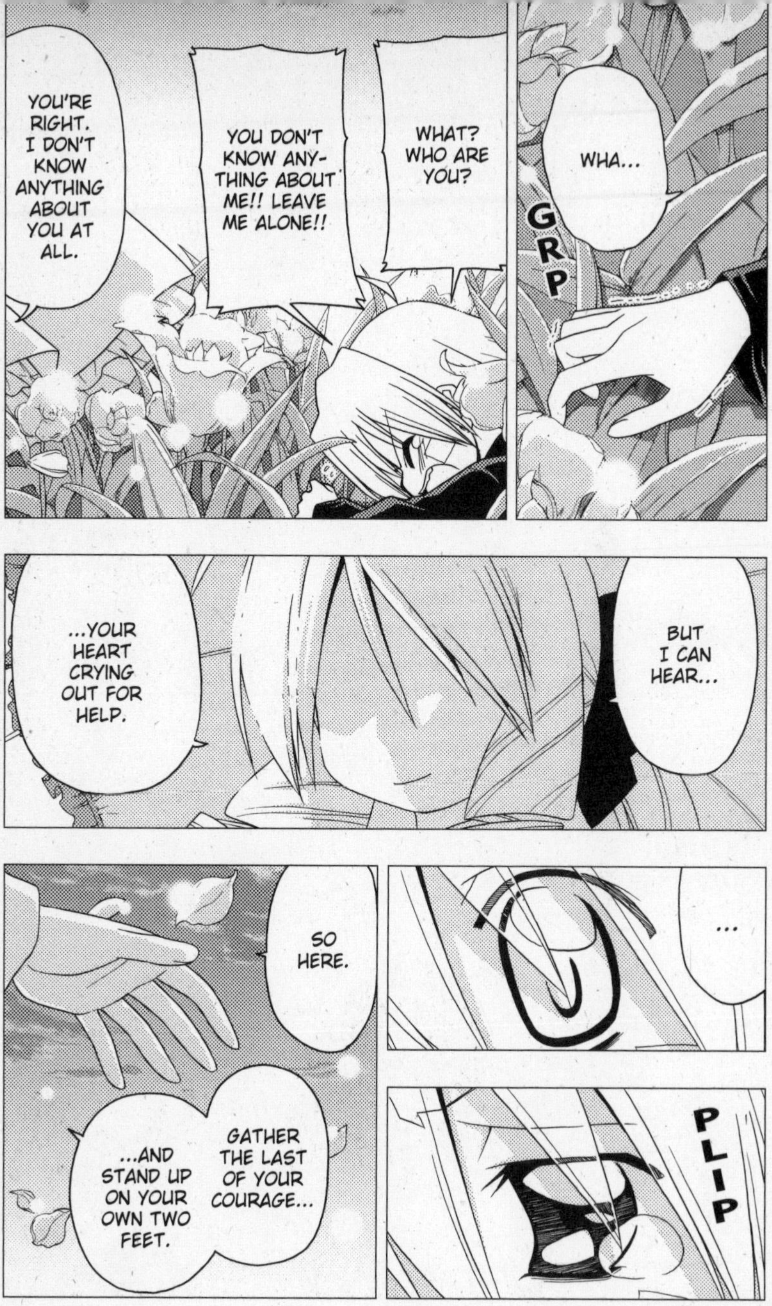
WHA...
GRP
WHAT? WHO ARE YOU?
YOU DON'T KNOW ANY-THING ABOUT ME!! LEAVE ME ALONE!!
YOU'RE RIGHT. I DON'T KNOW ANYTHING ABOUT YOU AT ALL.
BUT I CAN HEAR...
...YOUR HEART CRYING OUT FOR HELP.
...
PLIP
SO HERE.
GATHER THE LAST OF YOUR COURAGE...
...AND STAND UP ON YOUR OWN TWO FEET.

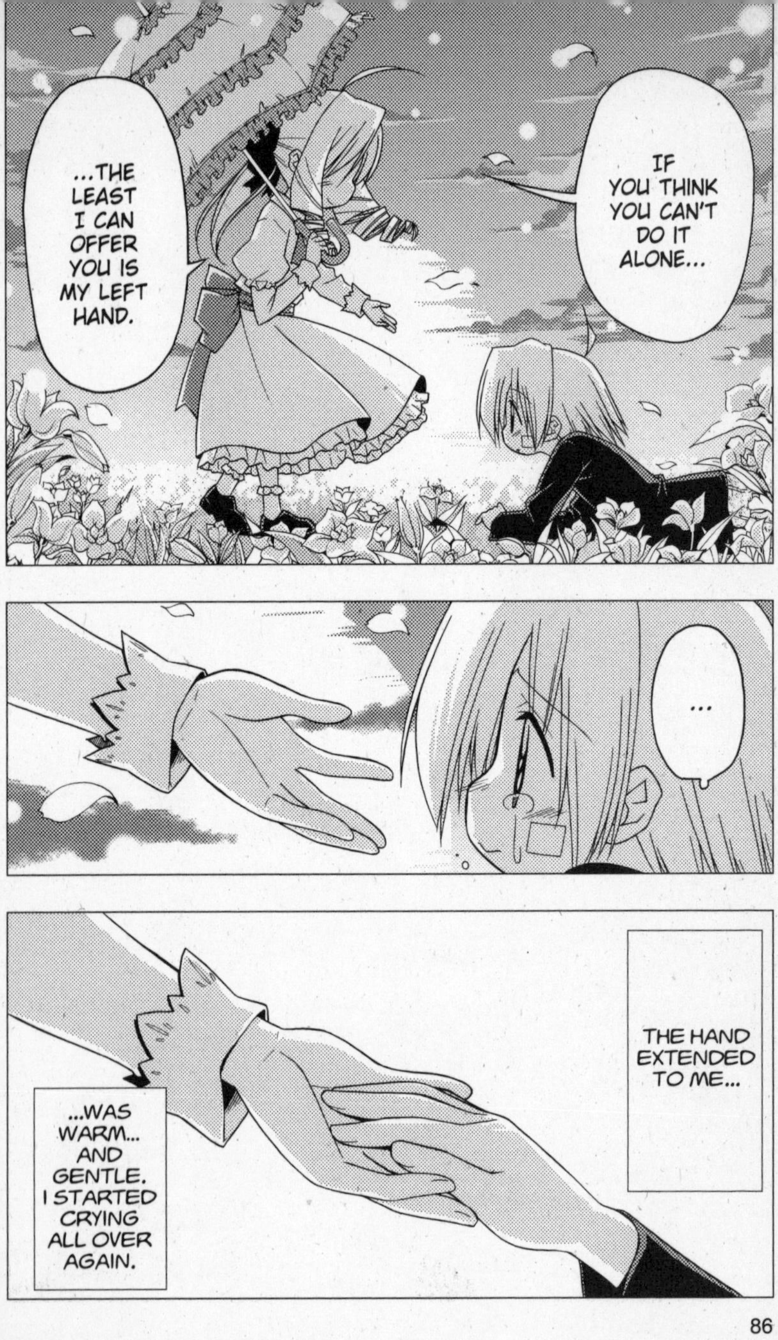
IF YOU THINK YOU CAN'T DO IT ALONE...
...THE LEAST I CAN OFFER YOU IS MY LEFT HAND.
...
THE HAND EXTENDED TO ME...
...WAS WARM... AND GENTLE. I STARTED CRYING ALL OVER AGAIN.

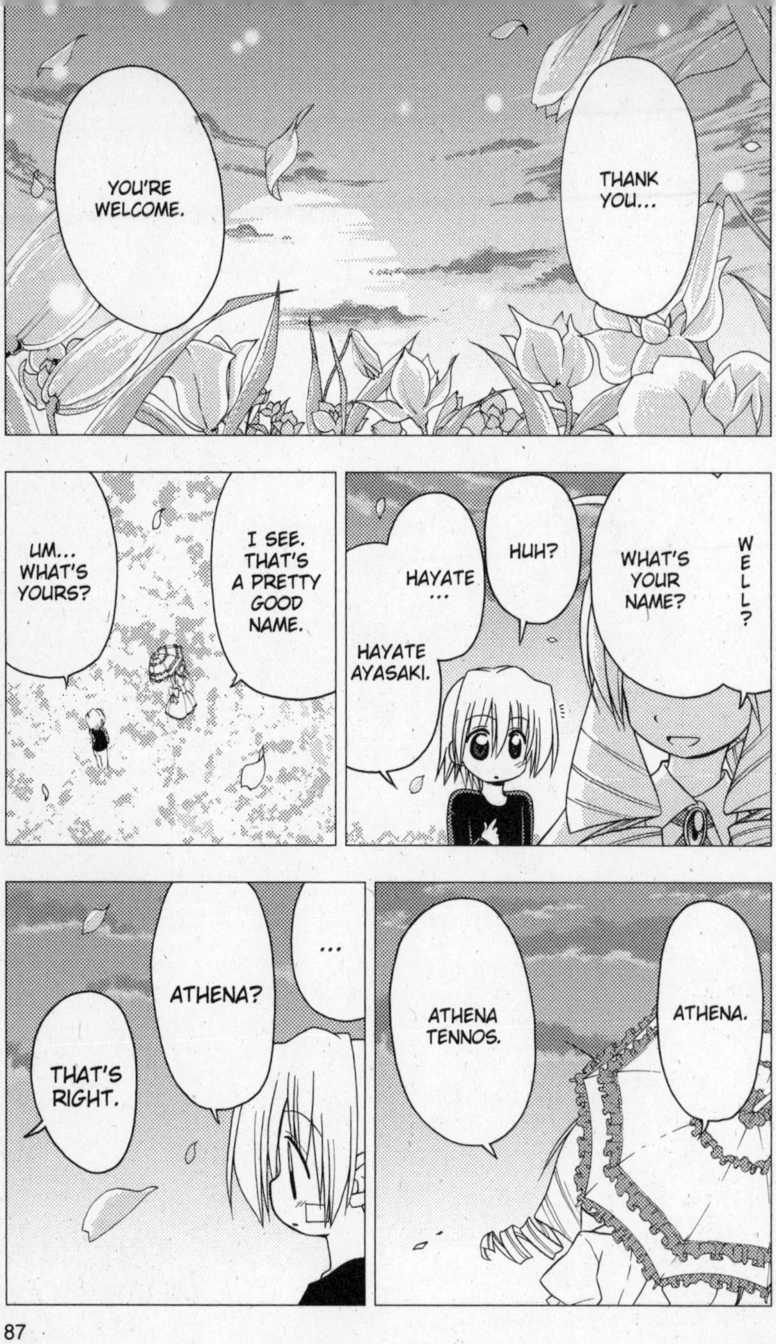
THANK YOU...
YOU'RE WELCOME.
WELL?
WHAT'S YOUR NAME?
HUH?
HAYATE ...
HAYATE AYASAKI.
I SEE. THAT'S A PRETTY GOOD NAME.
UM... WHAT'S YOURS?
ATHENA.
ATHENA TENNOS.
...
ATHENA?
THAT'S RIGHT.

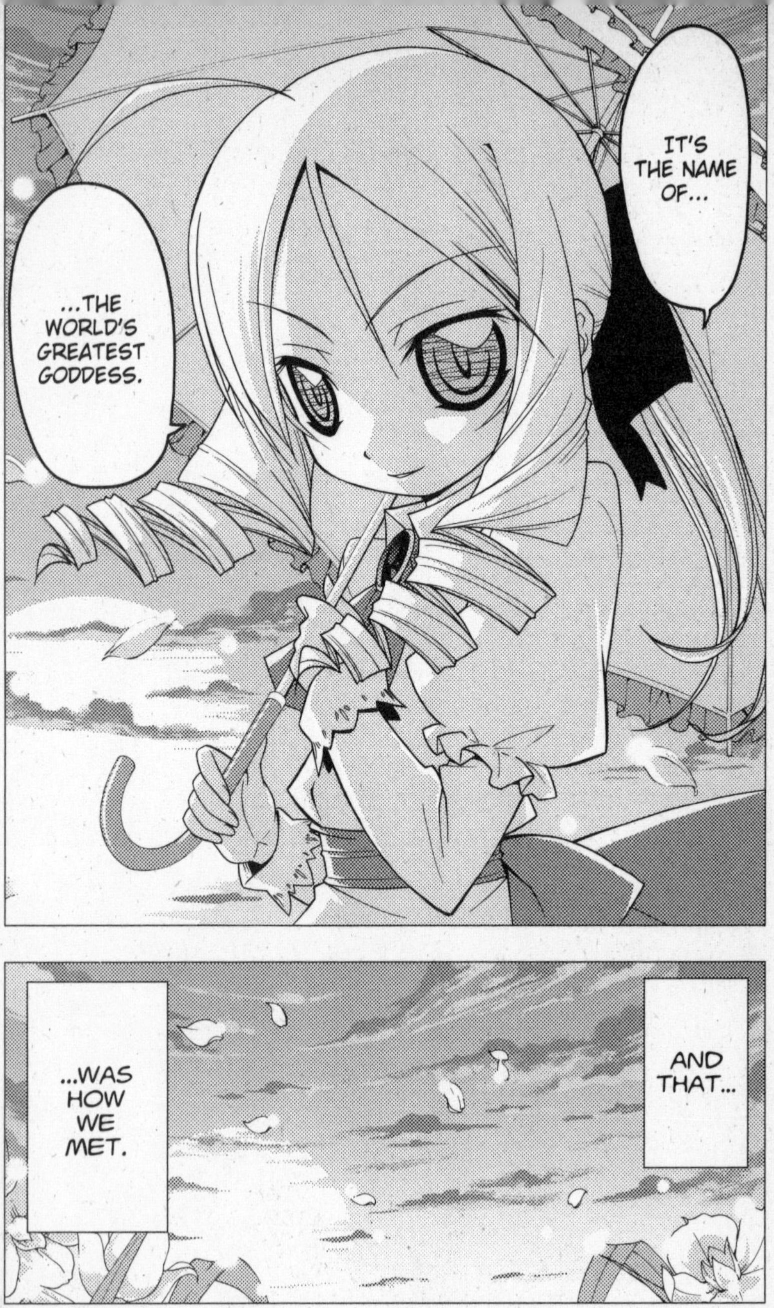
IT'S THE NAME OF...
...THE WORLD'S GREATEST GODDESS.
AND THAT...
...WAS HOW WE MET.

EPISODE 6: "THE END OF THE WORLD ② – The Castle Where God Is Said to Dwell"

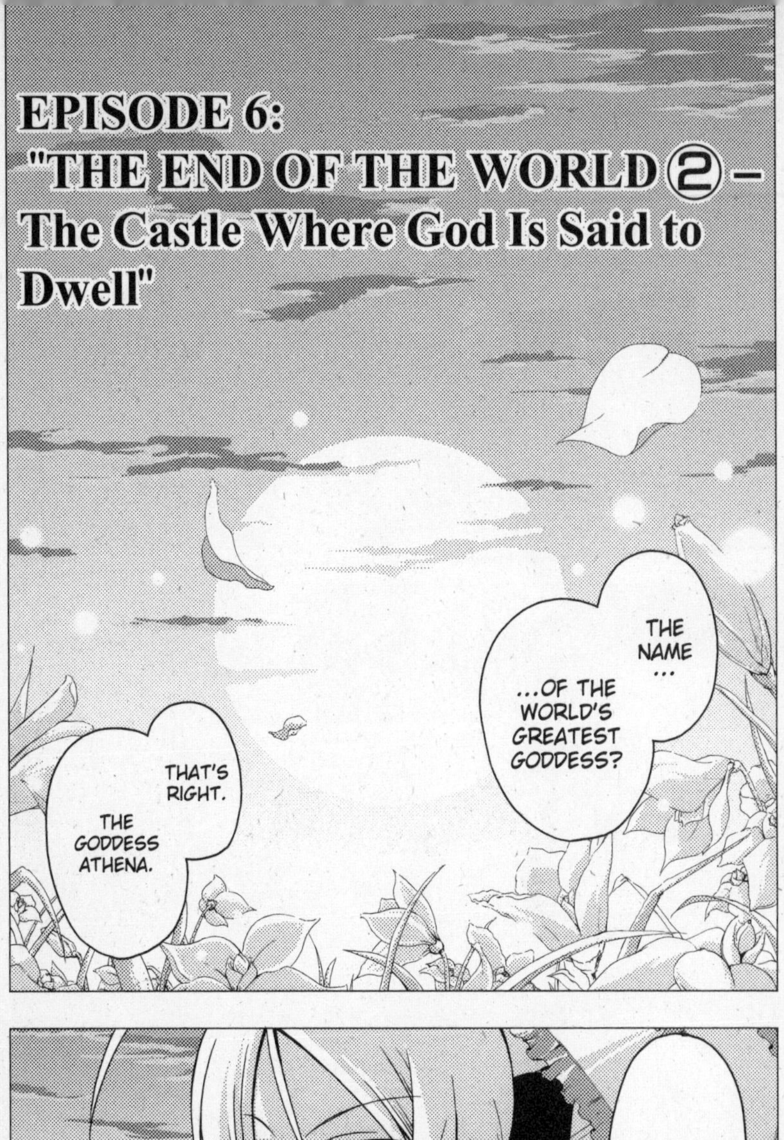
THE NAME...
...OF THE WORLD'S GREATEST GODDESS?
THAT'S RIGHT.
THE GODDESS ATHENA.
THAT'S MY NAME.

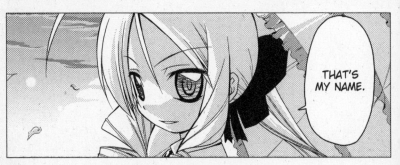

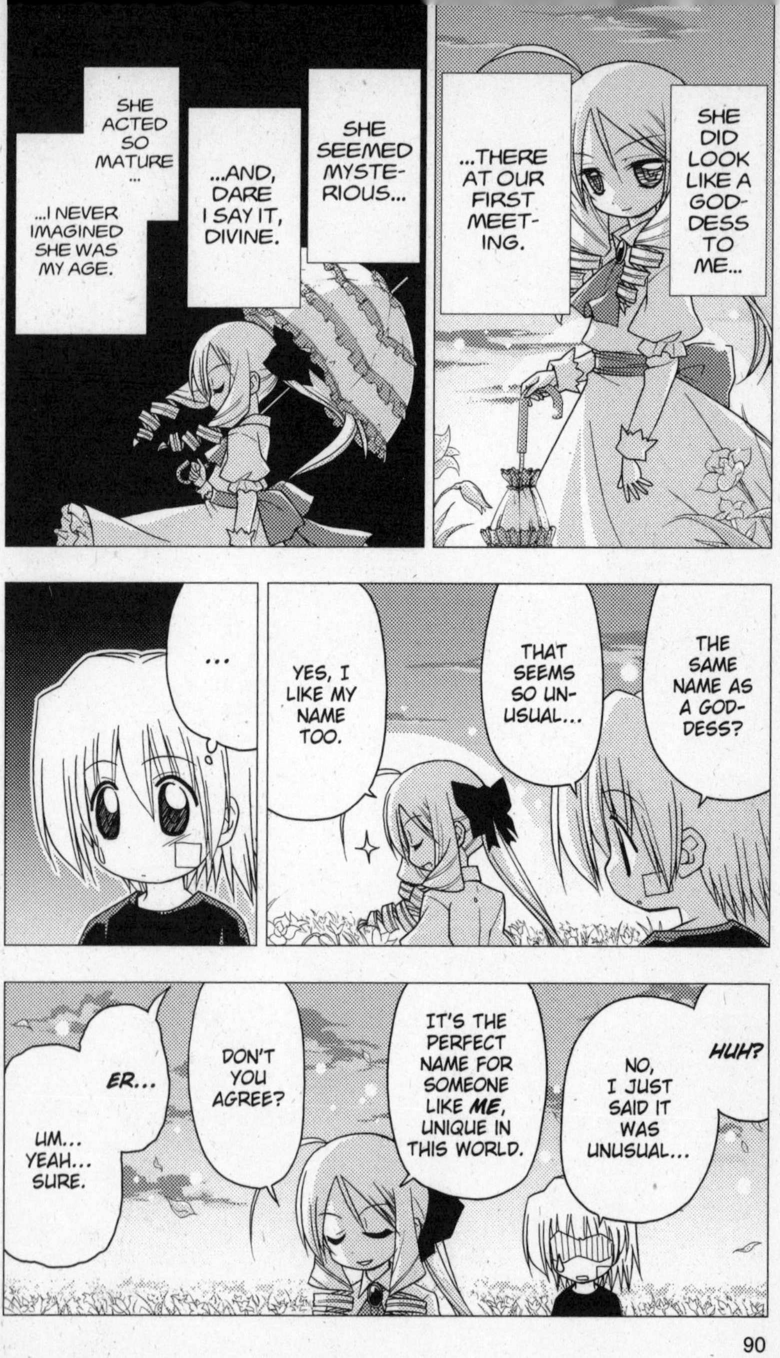
SHE DID LOOK LIKE A GODDESS TO ME...
...THERE AT OUR FIRST MEETING.
SHE SEEMED MYSTERIOUS...
...AND, DARE I SAY IT, DIVINE.
SHE ACTED SO MATURE...
...I NEVER IMAGINED SHE WAS MY AGE.
THE SAME NAME AS A GODDESS?
THAT SEEMS SO UNUSUAL...
YES, I LIKE MY NAME TOO.
...
HUH?
NO, I JUST SAID IT WAS UNUSUAL...
IT'S THE PERFECT NAME FOR SOMEONE LIKE *ME*, UNIQUE IN THIS WORLD.
DON'T YOU AGREE?
ER...
UM... YEAH... SURE.

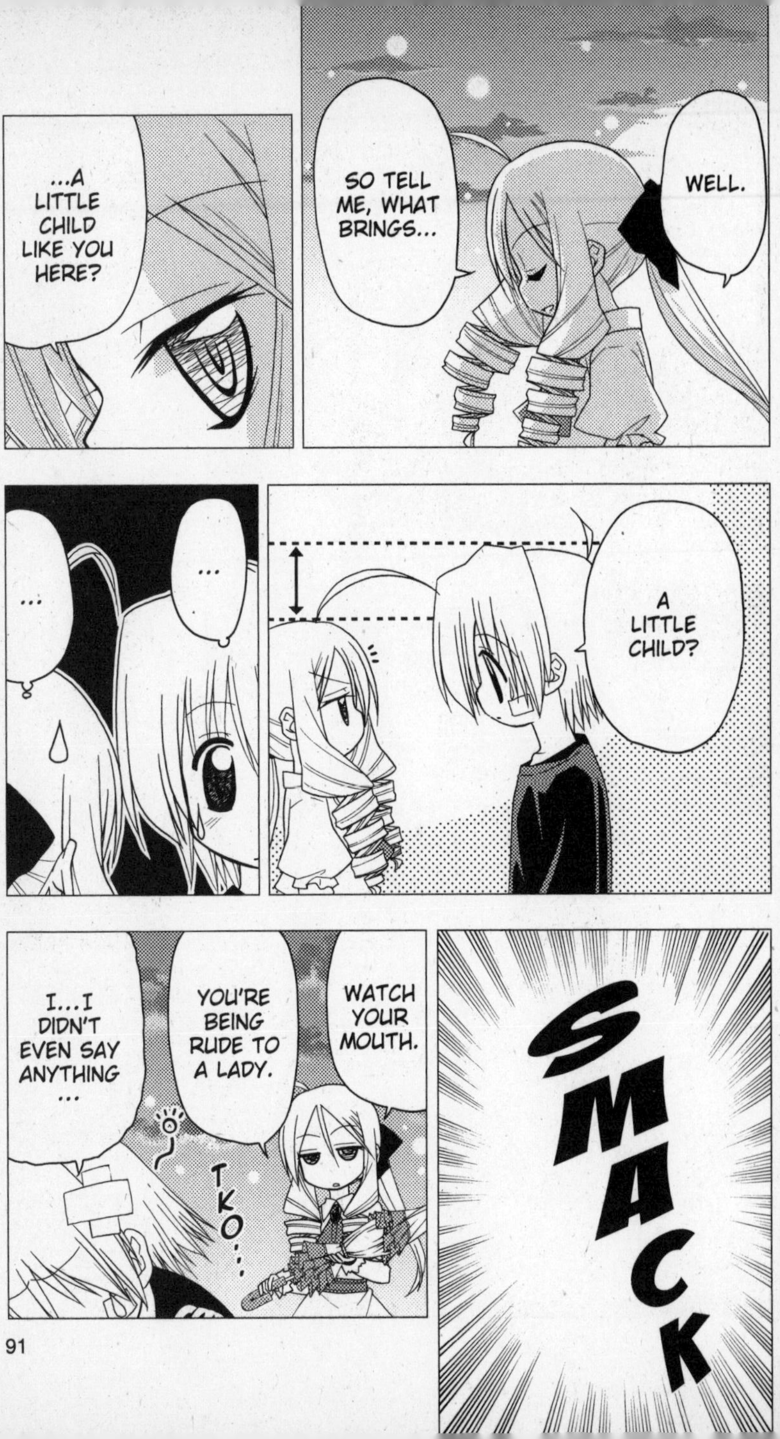
WELL.
SO TELL ME, WHAT BRINGS...
...A LITTLE CHILD LIKE YOU HERE?
A LITTLE CHILD?
...
...
SMACK
WATCH YOUR MOUTH.
YOU'RE BEING RUDE TO A LADY.
TKO...
I...I DIDN'T EVEN SAY ANYTHING...

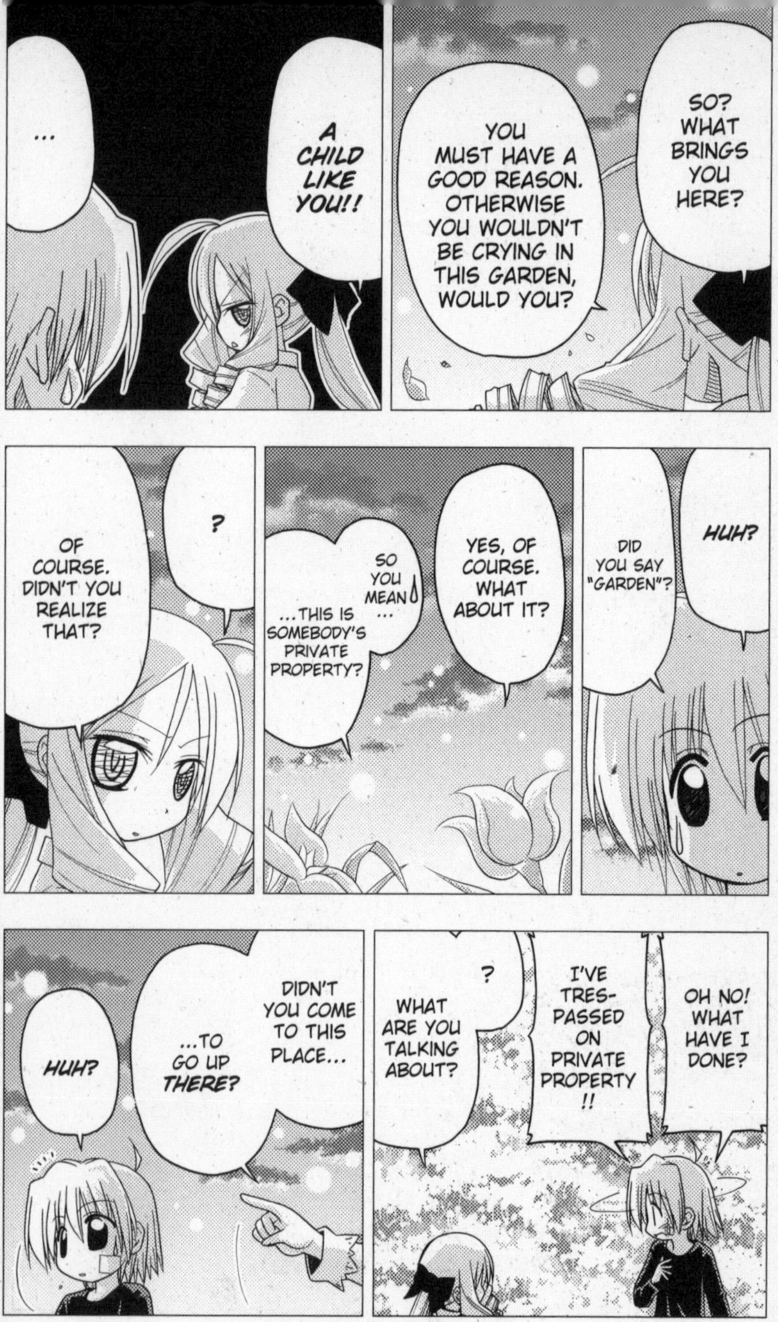
SO? WHAT BRINGS YOU HERE?
YOU MUST HAVE A GOOD REASON. OTHERWISE YOU WOULDN'T BE CRYING IN THIS GARDEN, WOULD YOU?
A CHILD LIKE YOU!!
...
HUH?
DID YOU SAY "GARDEN"?
YES, OF COURSE. WHAT ABOUT IT?
SO YOU MEAN ...
...THIS IS SOMEBODY'S PRIVATE PROPERTY?
?
OF COURSE. DIDN'T YOU REALIZE THAT?
OH NO! WHAT HAVE I DONE?
I'VE TRES-PASSED ON PRIVATE PROPERTY !!
?
WHAT ARE YOU TALKING ABOUT?
DIDN'T YOU COME TO THIS PLACE...
...TO GO UP THERE?
HUH?

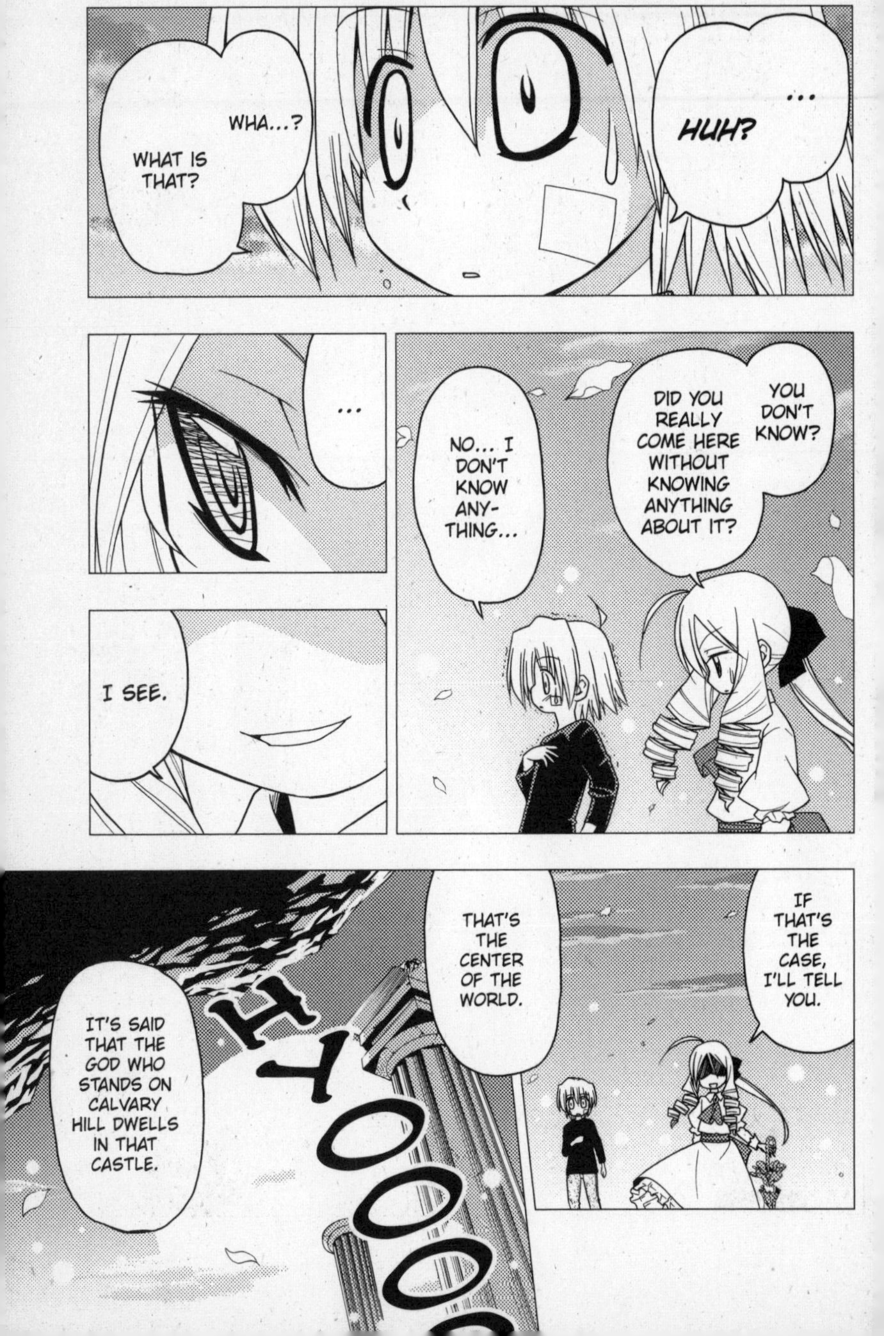
...
HUH?
WHA...?
WHAT IS THAT?
YOU DON'T KNOW?
DID YOU REALLY COME HERE WITHOUT KNOWING ANYTHING ABOUT IT?
NO... I DON'T KNOW ANY-THING...
...
I SEE.
IF THAT'S THE CASE, I'LL TELL YOU.
THAT'S THE CENTER OF THE WORLD.
IT'S SAID THAT THE GOD WHO STANDS ON CALVARY HILL DWELLS IN THAT CASTLE.
HYOOO

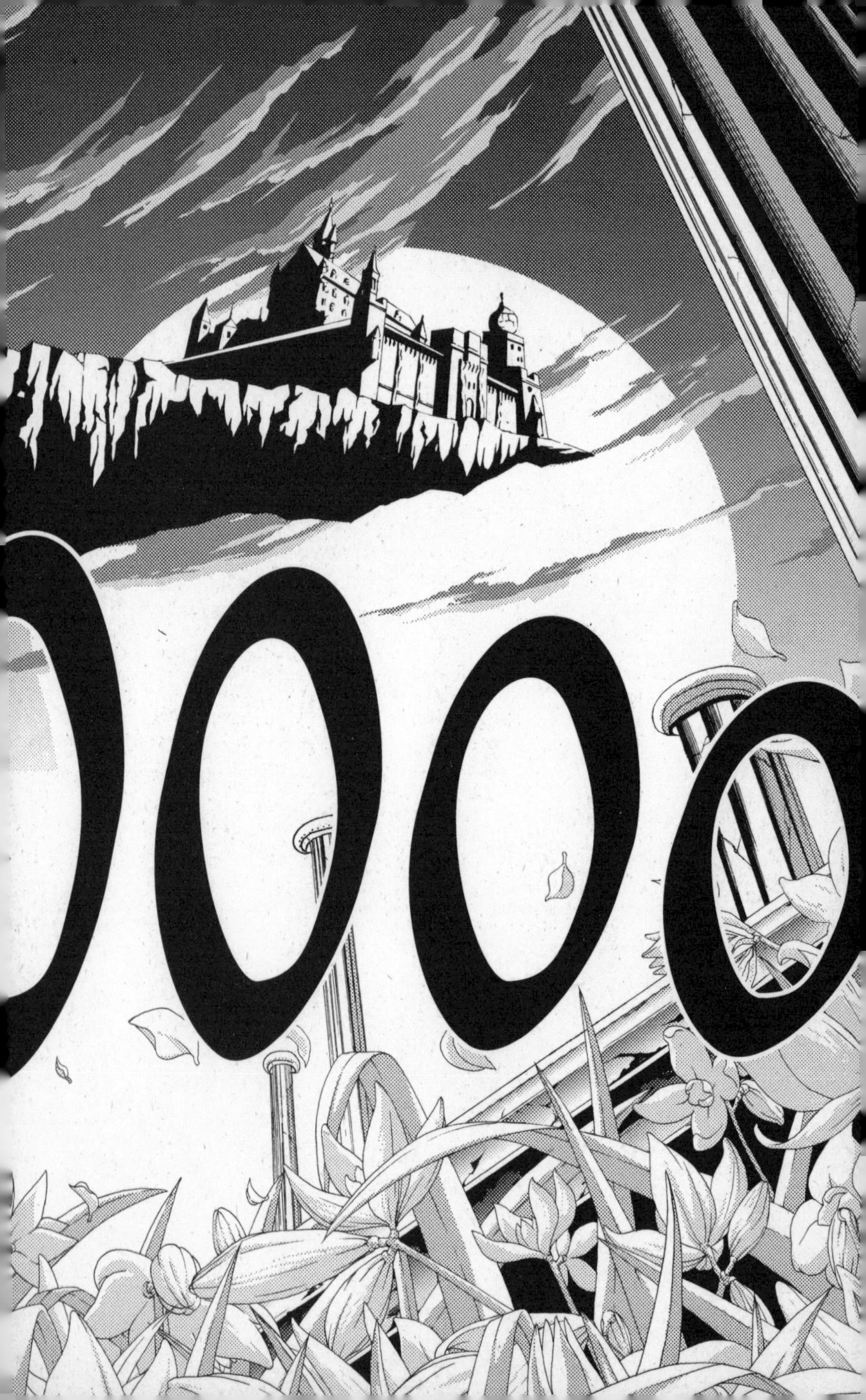
OOOO

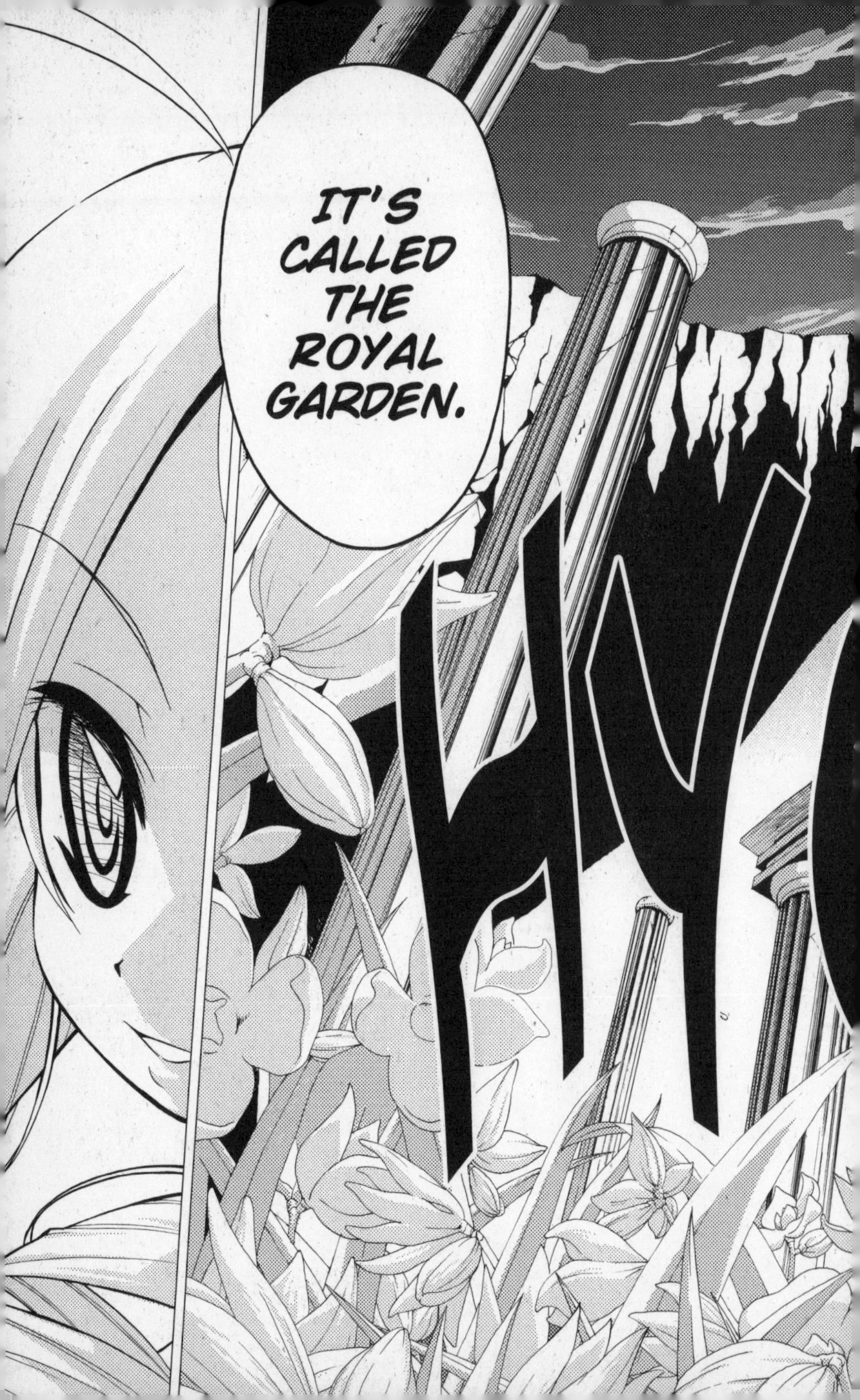
IT'S CALLED THE ROYAL GARDEN.

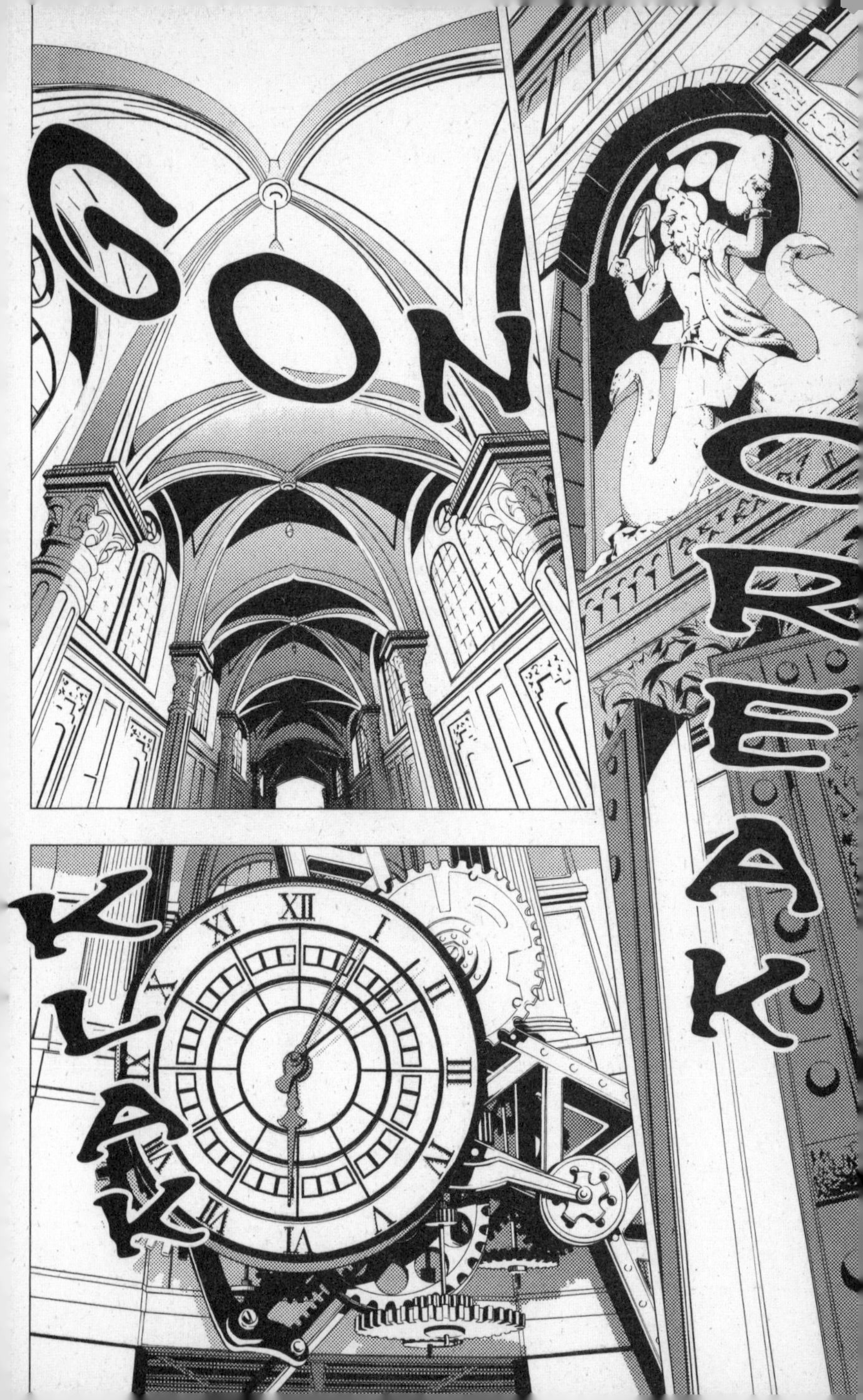
CREAK
GONG
KLAK

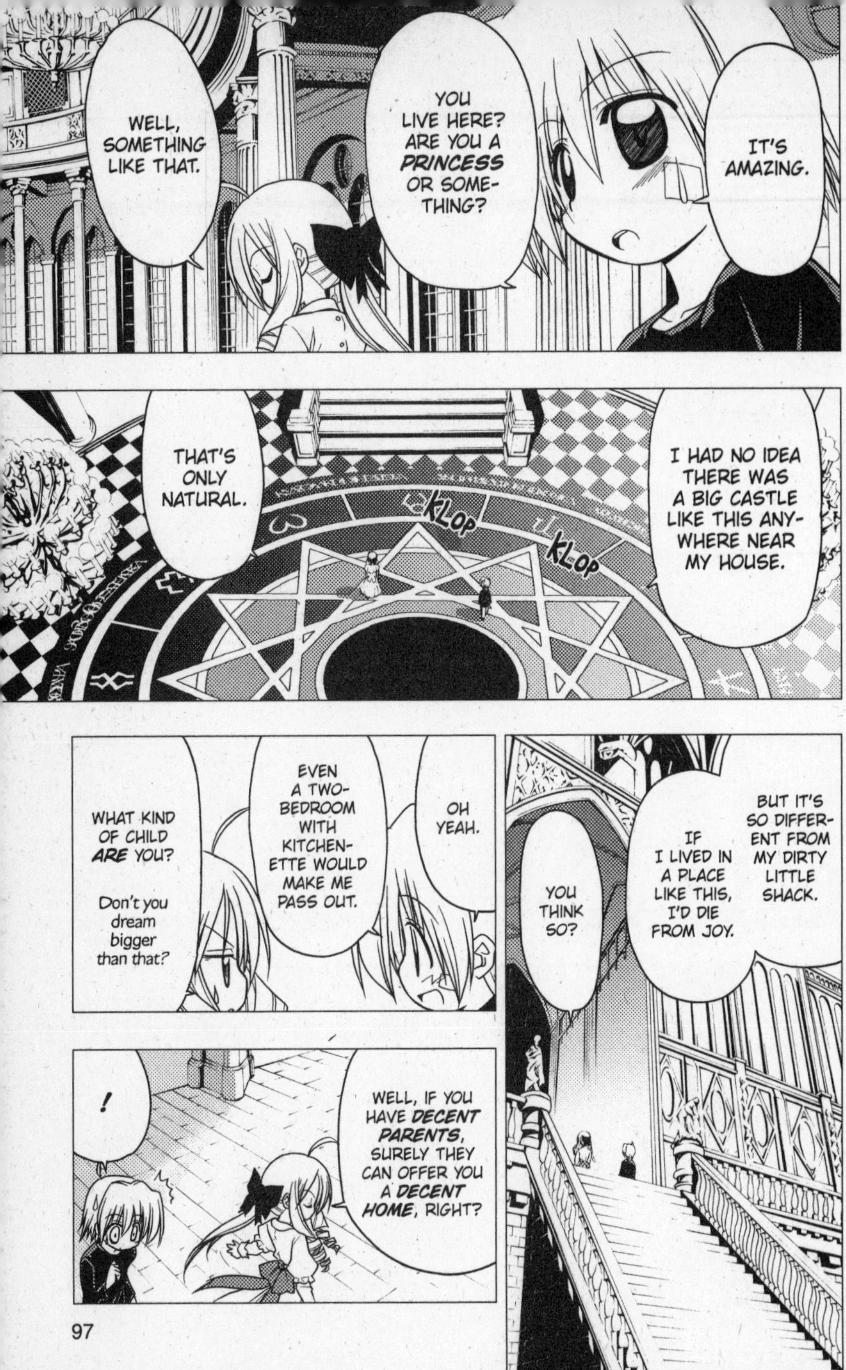
IT'S AMAZING.
YOU LIVE HERE? ARE YOU A PRINCESS OR SOME-THING?
WELL, SOMETHING LIKE THAT.
I HAD NO IDEA THERE WAS A BIG CASTLE LIKE THIS ANY-WHERE NEAR MY HOUSE.
KLOP
KLOP
THAT'S ONLY NATURAL.
BUT IT'S SO DIFFER-ENT FROM MY DIRTY LITTLE SHACK.
IF I LIVED IN A PLACE LIKE THIS, I'D DIE FROM JOY.
YOU THINK SO?
OH YEAH.
EVEN A TWO-BEDROOM WITH KITCHEN-ETTE WOULD MAKE ME PASS OUT.
WHAT KIND OF CHILD ARE YOU?
Don't you dream bigger than that?
WELL, IF YOU HAVE DECENT PARENTS, SURELY THEY CAN OFFER YOU A DECENT HOME, RIGHT?
!

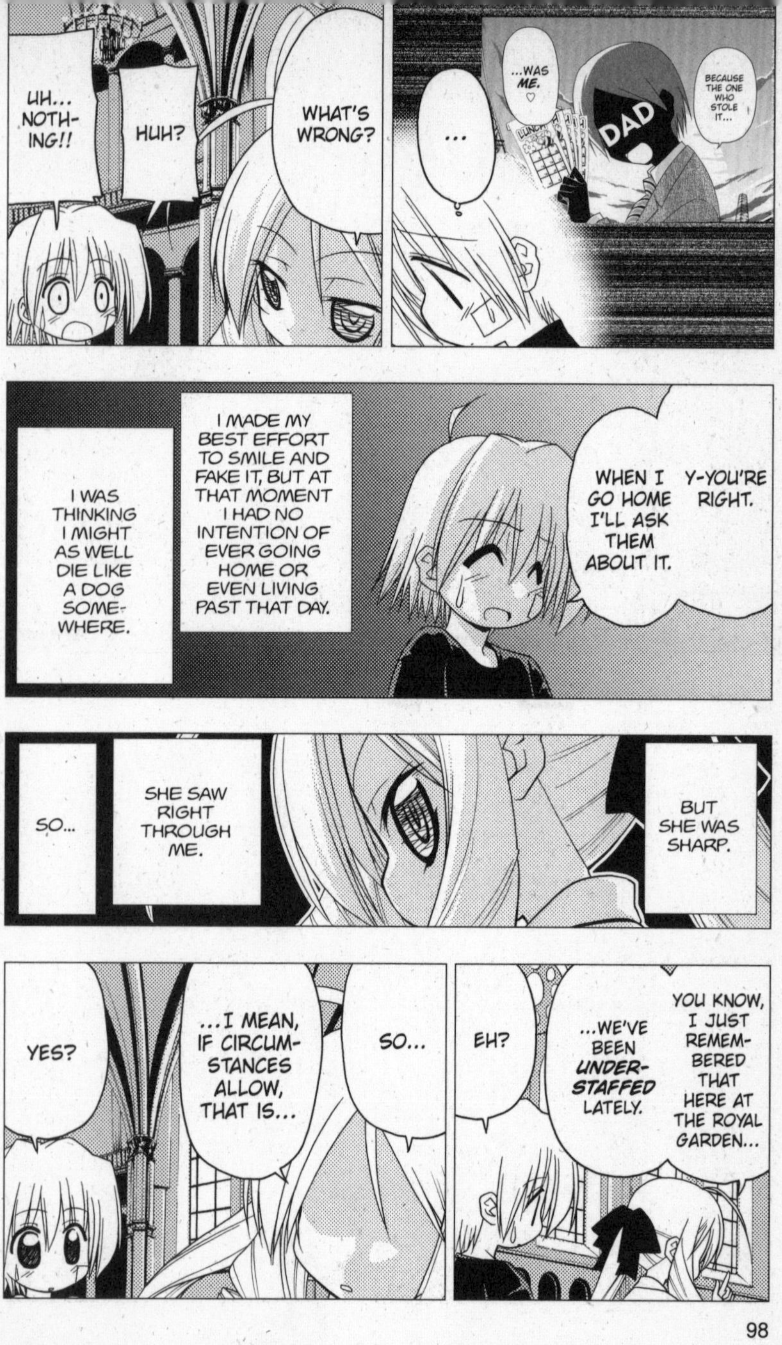
BECAUSE THE ONE WHO STOLE IT...
...WAS ME. ♡
DAD
...
WHAT'S WRONG?
HUH?
UH... NOTHING!!
Y-YOU'RE RIGHT.
WHEN I GO HOME I'LL ASK THEM ABOUT IT.
I MADE MY BEST EFFORT TO SMILE AND FAKE IT, BUT AT THAT MOMENT I HAD NO INTENTION OF EVER GOING HOME OR EVEN LIVING PAST THAT DAY.
I WAS THINKING I MIGHT AS WELL DIE LIKE A DOG SOMEWHERE.
BUT SHE WAS SHARP.
SHE SAW RIGHT THROUGH ME.
SO...
YOU KNOW, I JUST REMEMBERED THAT HERE AT THE ROYAL GARDEN...
...WE'VE BEEN UNDERSTAFFED LATELY.
EH?
SO...
...I MEAN, IF CIRCUMSTANCES ALLOW, THAT IS...
YES?

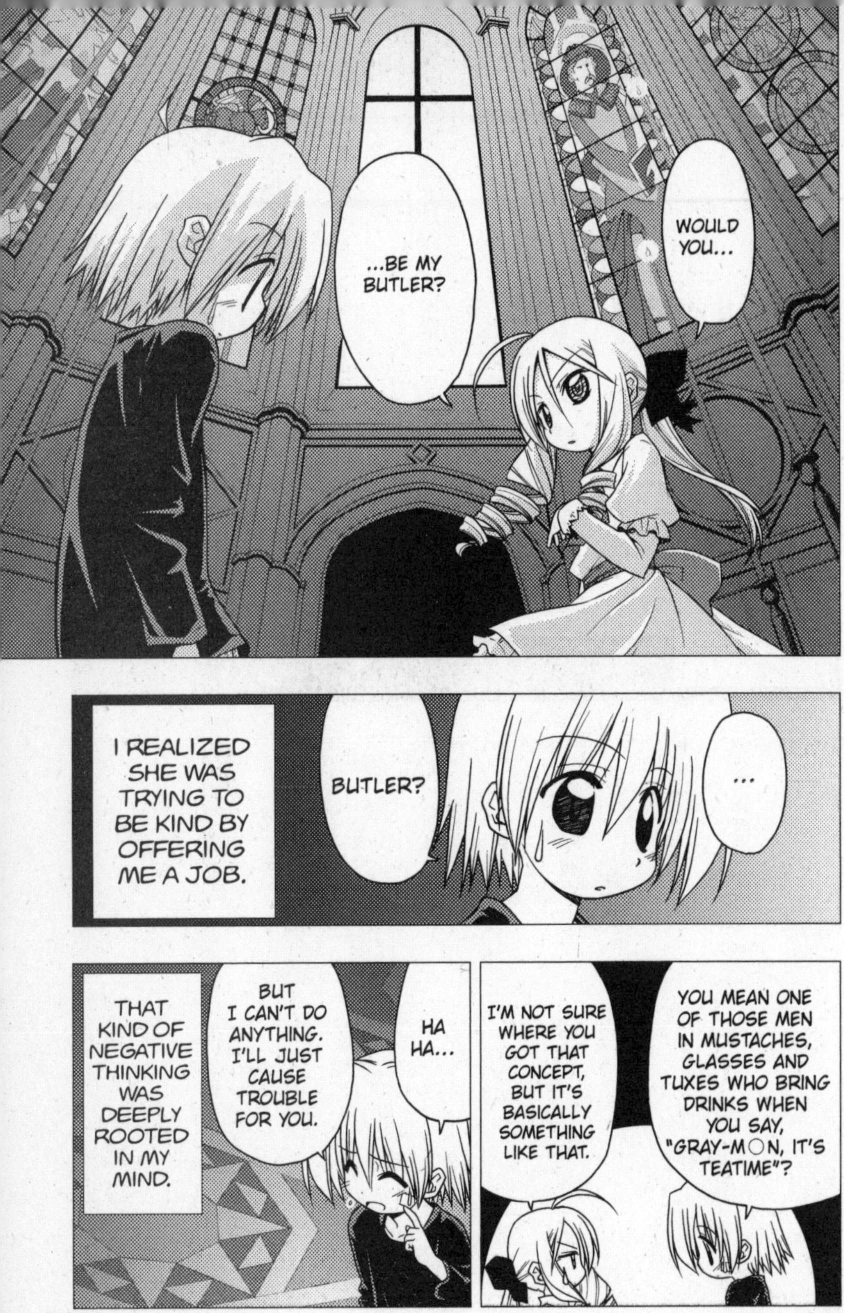
WOULD YOU...
...BE MY BUTLER?
...
BUTLER?
I REALIZED SHE WAS TRYING TO BE KIND BY OFFERING ME A JOB.
YOU MEAN ONE OF THOSE MEN IN MUSTACHES, GLASSES AND TUXES WHO BRING DRINKS WHEN YOU SAY, "GRAY-M○N, IT'S TEATIME"?
I'M NOT SURE WHERE YOU GOT THAT CONCEPT, BUT IT'S BASICALLY SOMETHING LIKE THAT.
HA HA...
BUT I CAN'T DO ANYTHING. I'LL JUST CAUSE TROUBLE FOR YOU.
THAT KIND OF NEGATIVE THINKING WAS DEEPLY ROOTED IN MY MIND.

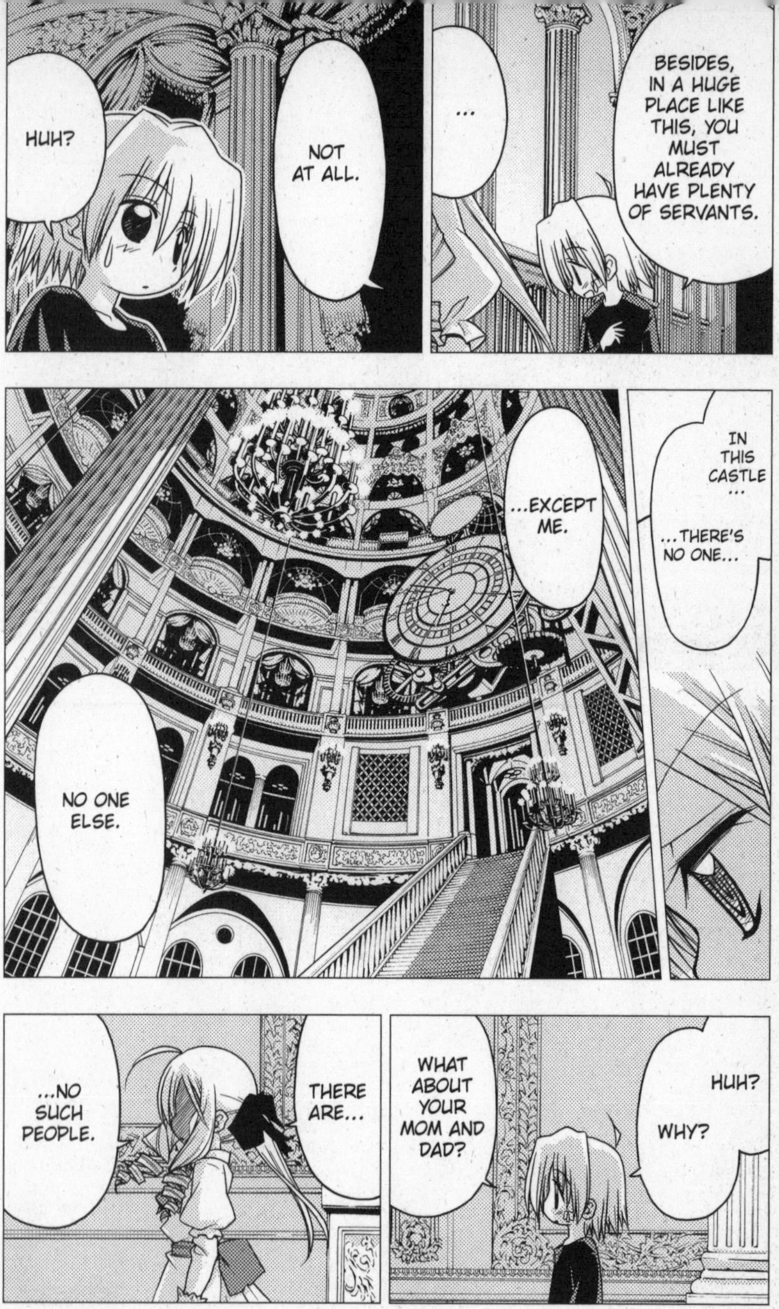
BESIDES, IN A HUGE PLACE LIKE THIS, YOU MUST ALREADY HAVE PLENTY OF SERVANTS.
...
NOT AT ALL.
HUH?
IN THIS CASTLE...
...THERE'S NO ONE...
...EXCEPT ME.
NO ONE ELSE.
HUH?
WHY?
WHAT ABOUT YOUR MOM AND DAD?
THERE ARE...
...NO SUCH PEOPLE.

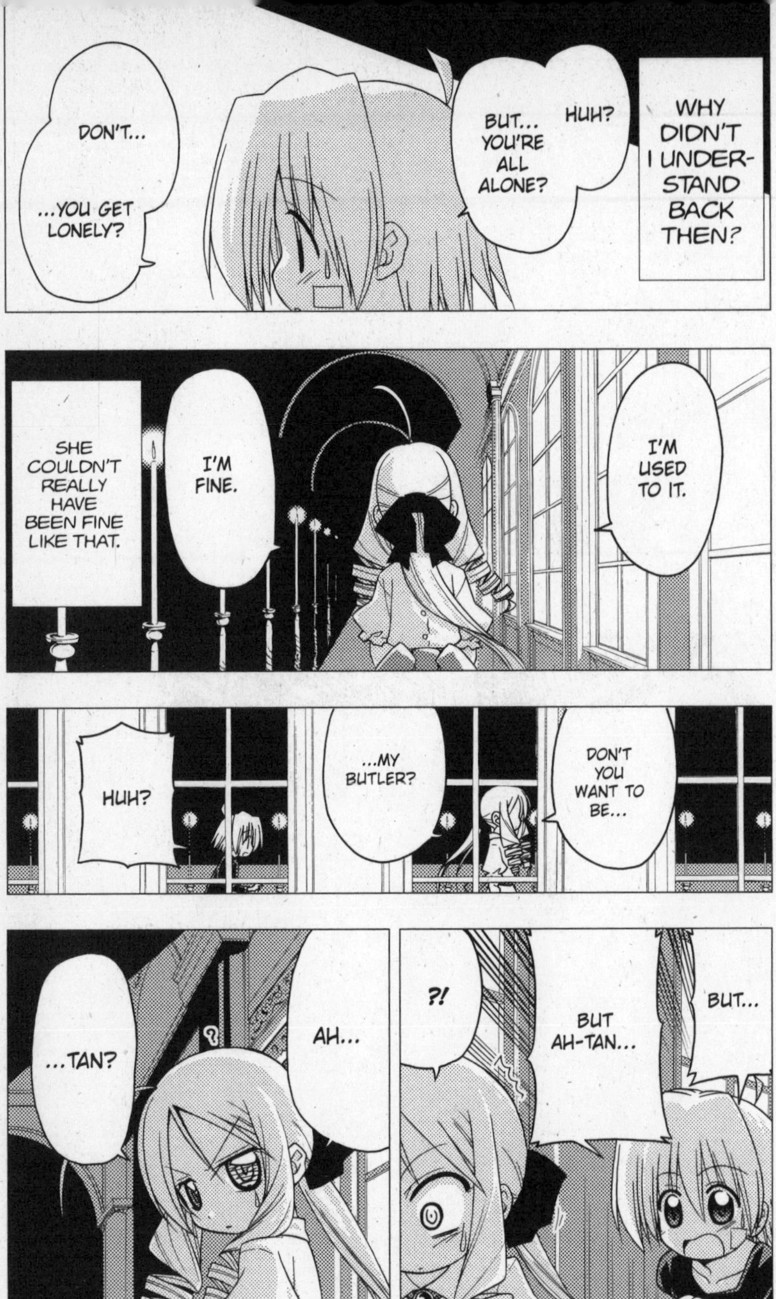
WHY DIDN'T I UNDERSTAND BACK THEN?
HUH?
BUT... YOU'RE ALL ALONE?
DON'T...
...YOU GET LONELY?
I'M USED TO IT.
I'M FINE.
SHE COULDN'T REALLY HAVE BEEN FINE LIKE THAT.
DON'T YOU WANT TO BE...
...MY BUTLER?
HUH?
BUT...
BUT AH-TAN...
?!
AH...
...TAN?
?

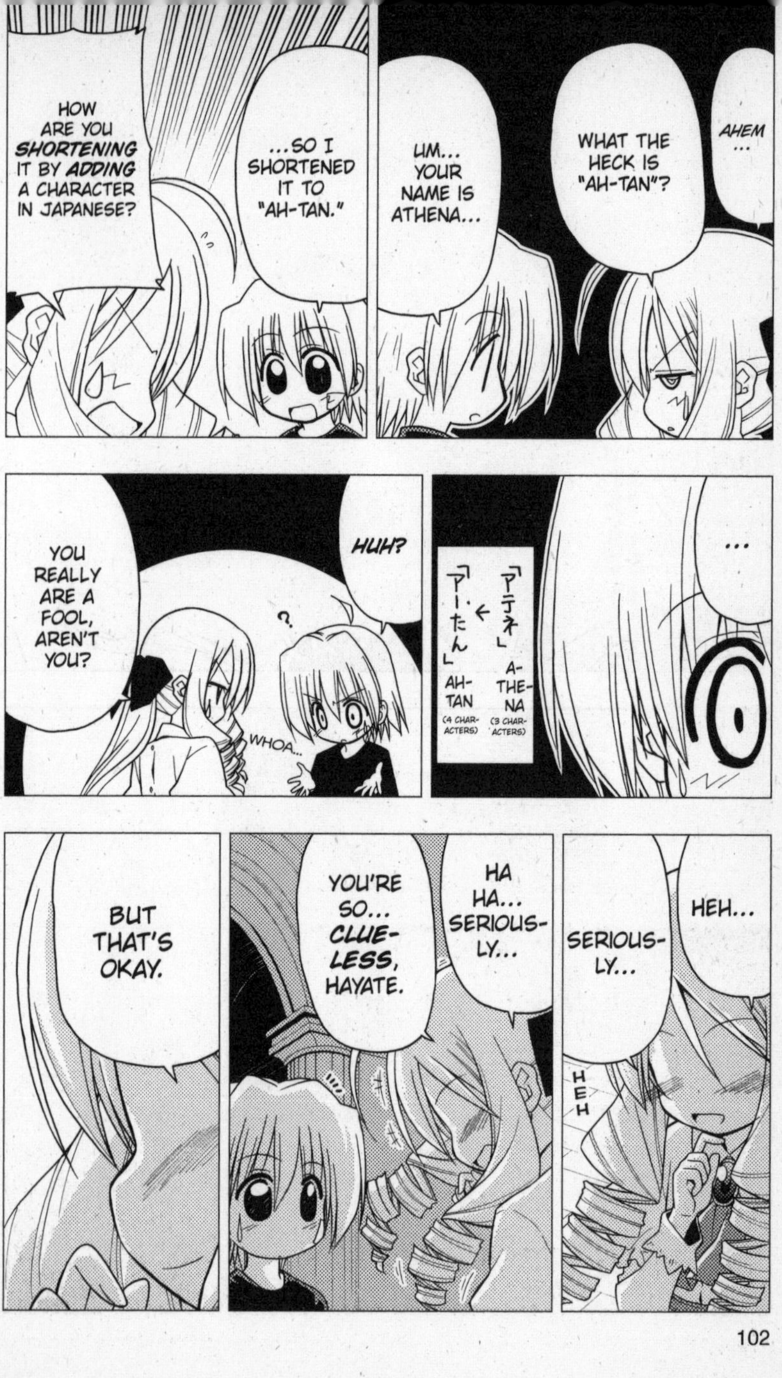
AHEM...
WHAT THE HECK IS "AH-TAN"?
UM... YOUR NAME IS ATHENA...
...SO I SHORTENED IT TO "AH-TAN."
HOW ARE YOU ***SHORTENING*** IT BY ***ADDING*** A CHARACTER IN JAPANESE?
...
「アテネ」 ← 「アーたん」
A-THE-NA (3 CHARACTERS)
AH-TAN (4 CHARACTERS)
HUH?
YOU REALLY ARE A FOOL, AREN'T YOU?
WHOA...
HEH...
SERIOUS-LY...
HEH HEH
HA HA... SERIOUS-LY...
YOU'RE SO... ***CLUE-LESS***, HAYATE.
BUT THAT'S OKAY.

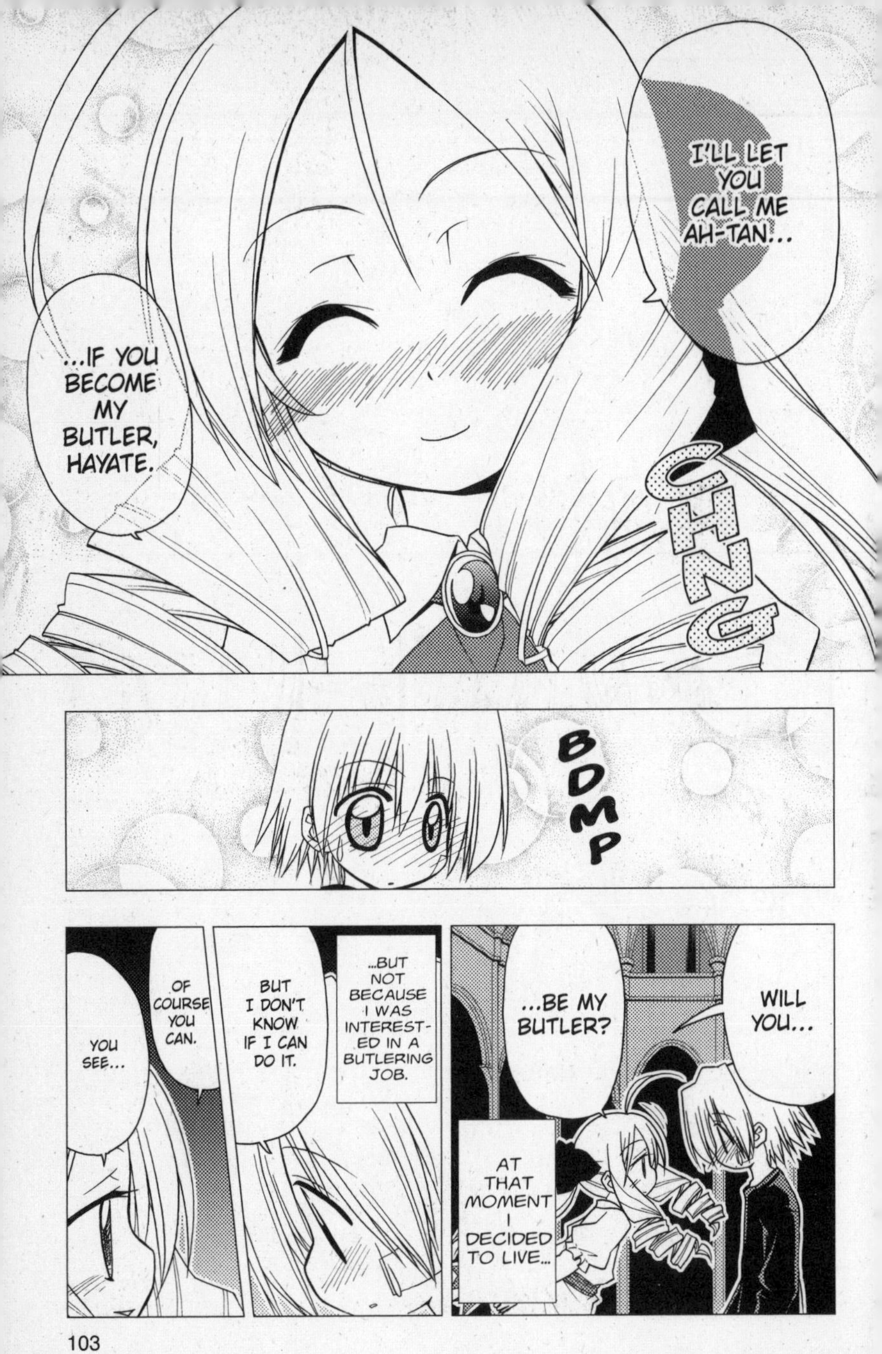
I'LL LET YOU CALL ME AH-TAN...
CHNG
...IF YOU BECOME MY BUTLER, HAYATE.
BDMP
WILL YOU...
...BE MY BUTLER?
AT THAT MOMENT I DECIDED TO LIVE...
...BUT NOT BECAUSE I WAS INTEREST-ED IN A BUTLERING JOB.
BUT I DON'T KNOW IF I CAN DO IT.
OF COURSE YOU CAN.
YOU SEE...

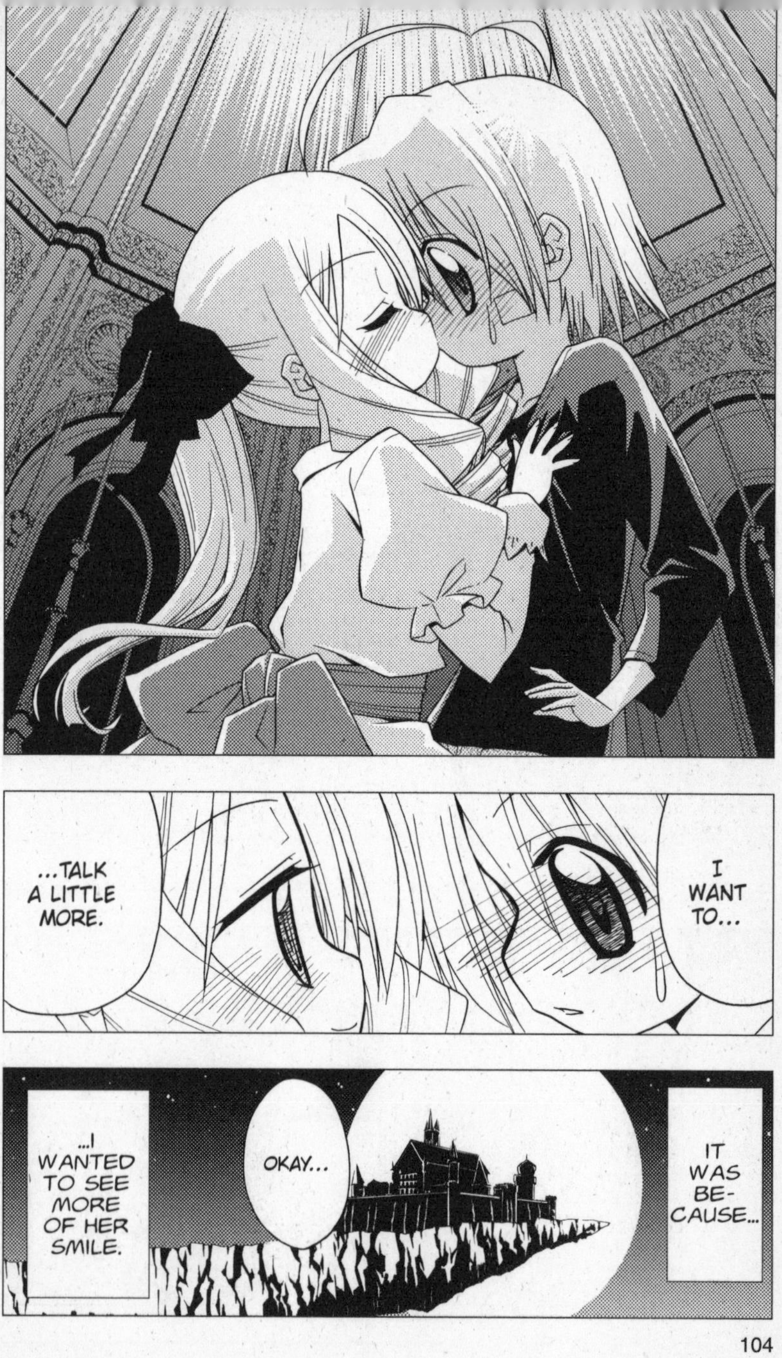
I WANT TO...
...TALK A LITTLE MORE.
IT WAS BE-CAUSE...
OKAY...
...I WANTED TO SEE MORE OF HER SMILE.

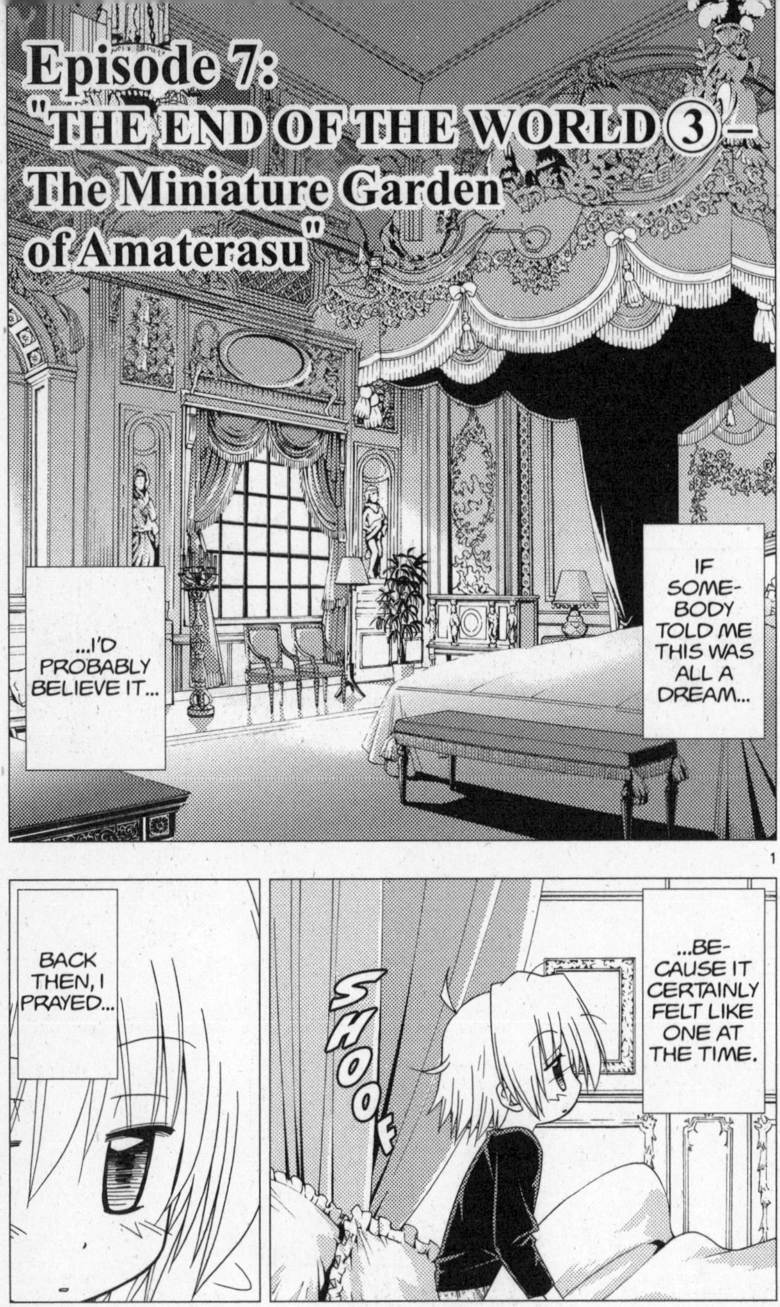
Episode 7:
"THE END OF THE WORLD ③ – The Miniature Garden of Amaterasu"
IF SOMEBODY TOLD ME THIS WAS ALL A DREAM...
...I'D PROBABLY BELIEVE IT...
...BECAUSE IT CERTAINLY FELT LIKE ONE AT THE TIME.
SHOOF
BACK THEN, I PRAYED...

1

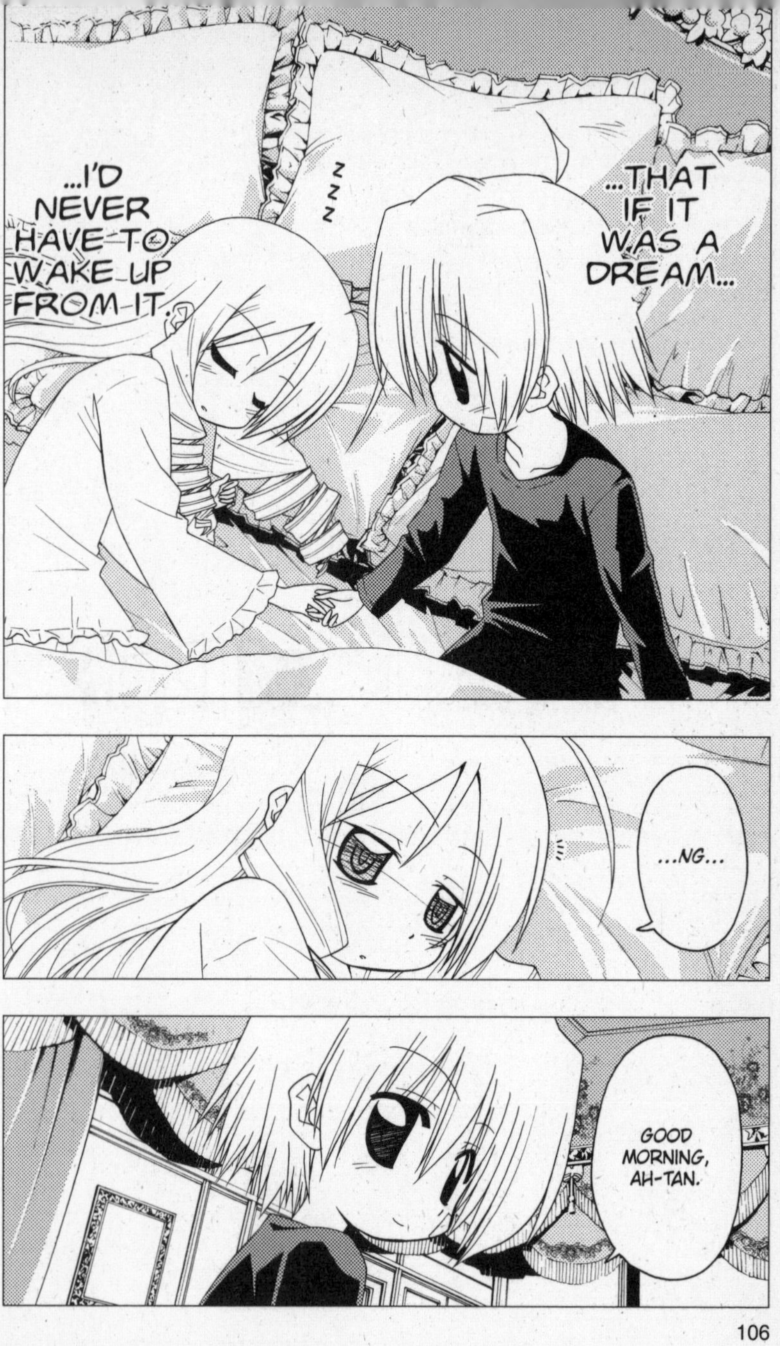
...THAT IF IT WAS A DREAM...
ZZZ
...I'D NEVER HAVE TO WAKE UP FROM IT.
...NG...
GOOD MORNING, AH-TAN.

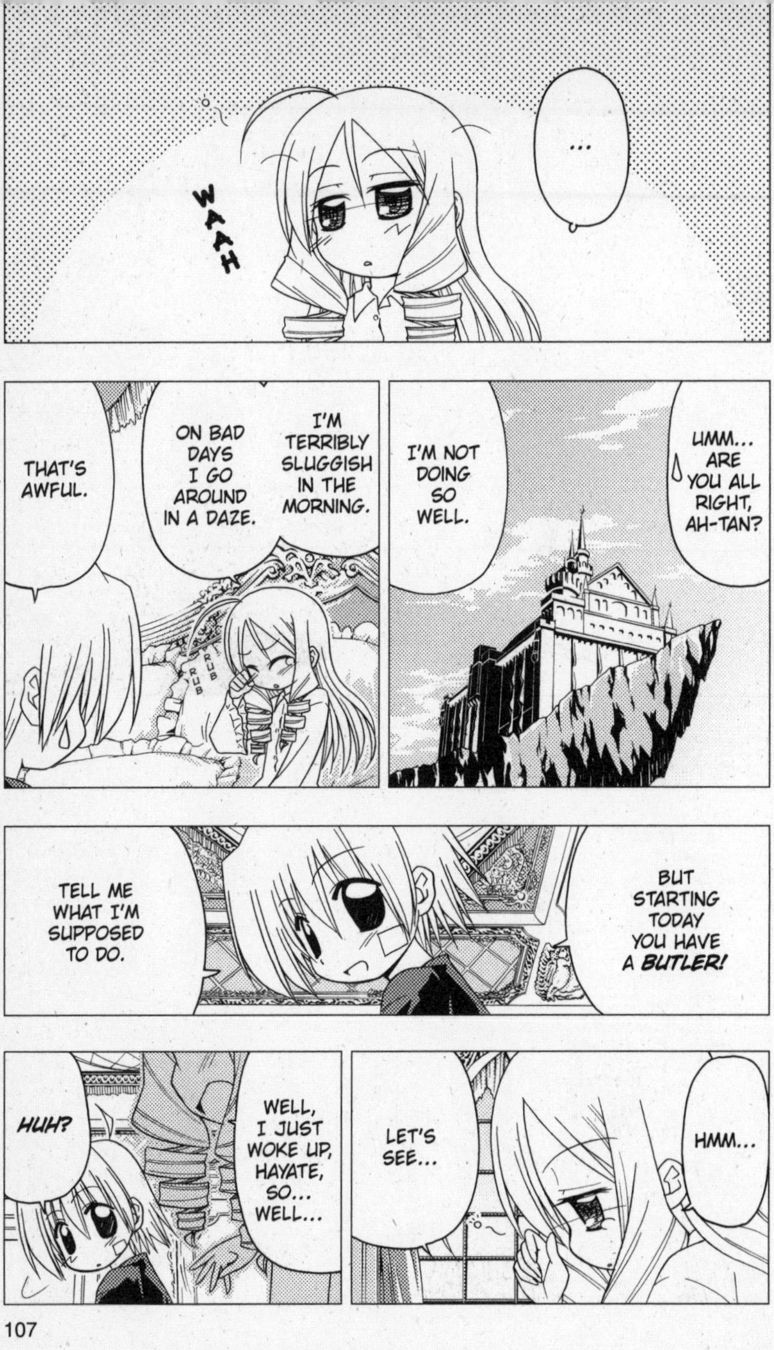
...
WAAH
UMM... ARE YOU ALL RIGHT, AH-TAN?
I'M NOT DOING SO WELL.
I'M TERRIBLY SLUGGISH IN THE MORNING.
ON BAD DAYS I GO AROUND IN A DAZE.
RUB RUB
THAT'S AWFUL.
BUT STARTING TODAY YOU HAVE A *BUTLER!*
TELL ME WHAT I'M SUPPOSED TO DO.
HMM...
LET'S SEE...
WELL, I JUST WOKE UP, HAYATE, SO... WELL...
HUH?

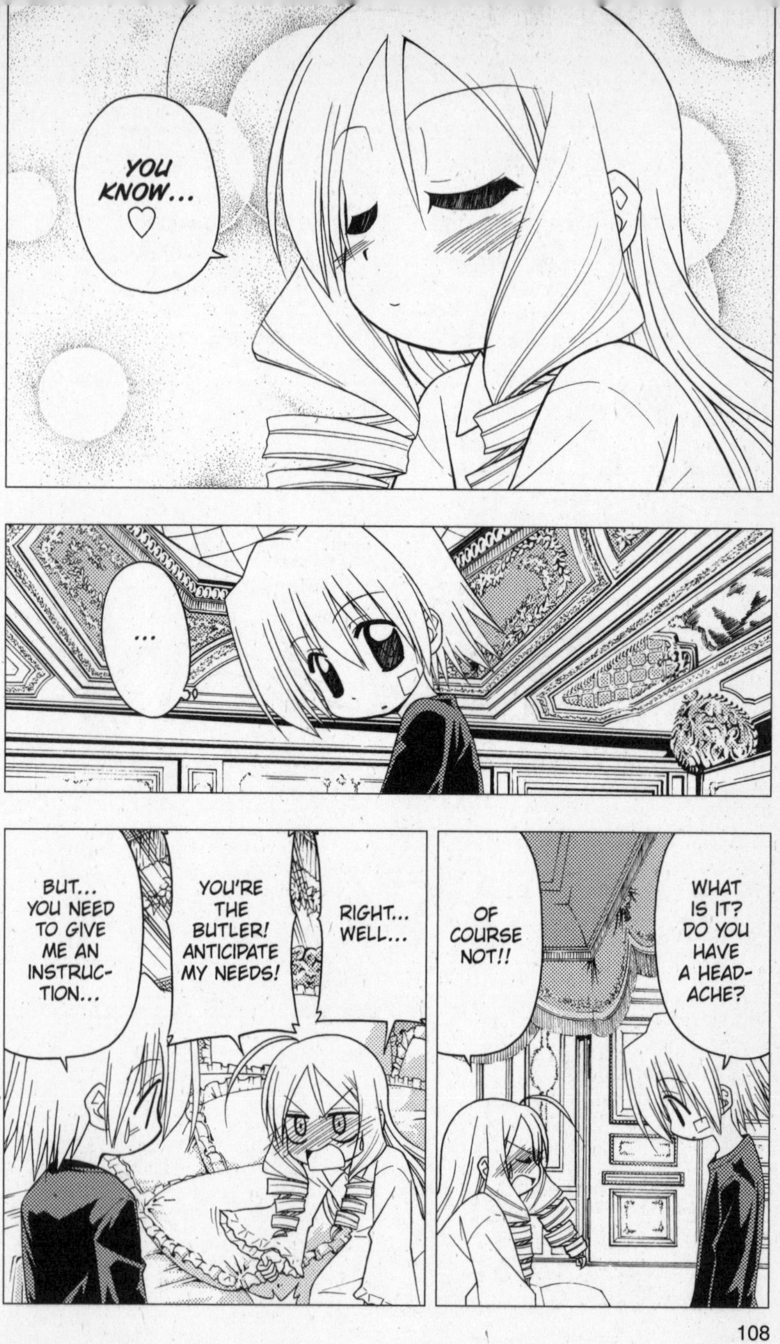
YOU KNOW... ♡
...
WHAT IS IT? DO YOU HAVE A HEADACHE?
OF COURSE NOT!!
RIGHT... WELL...
YOU'RE THE BUTLER! ANTICIPATE MY NEEDS!
BUT... YOU NEED TO GIVE ME AN INSTRUCTION...

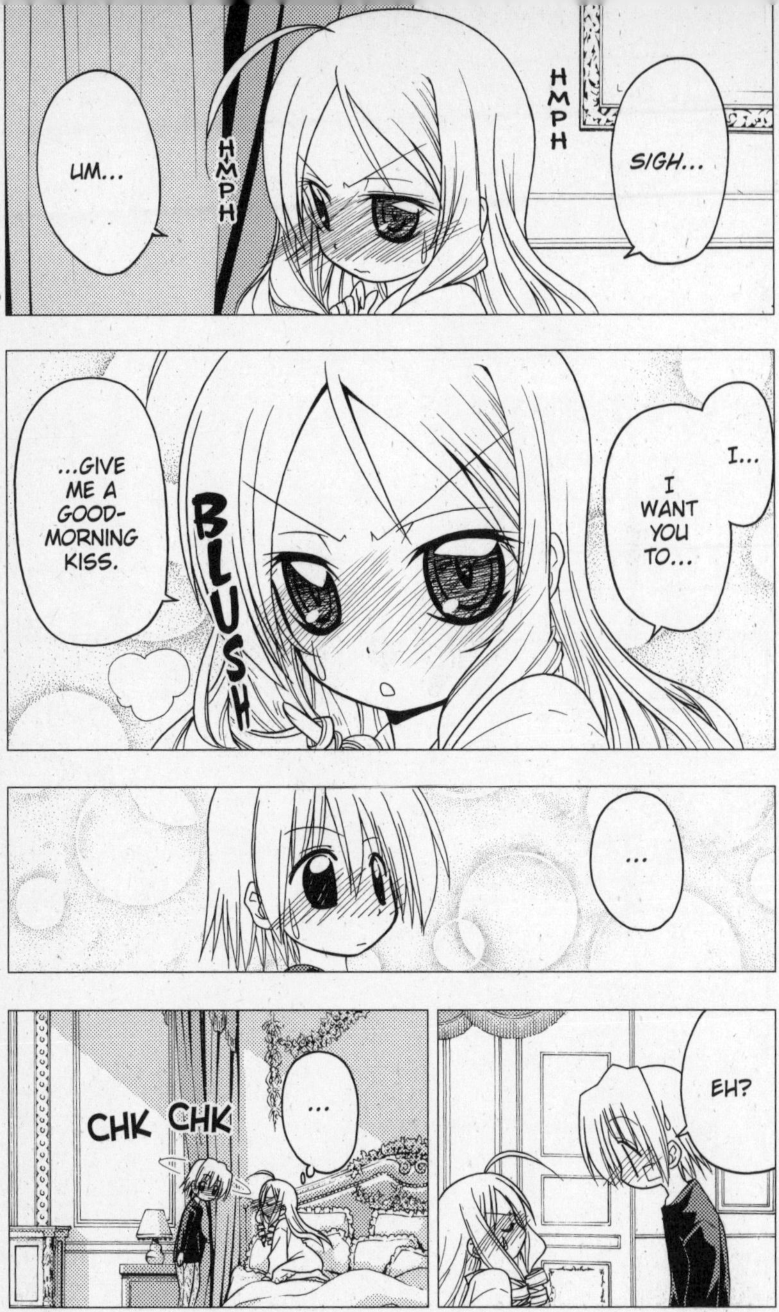
SIGH...
HMPH
HMPH
UM...
I... I WANT YOU TO...
BLUSH
...GIVE ME A GOOD-MORNING KISS.
...
EH?
...
CHK CHK

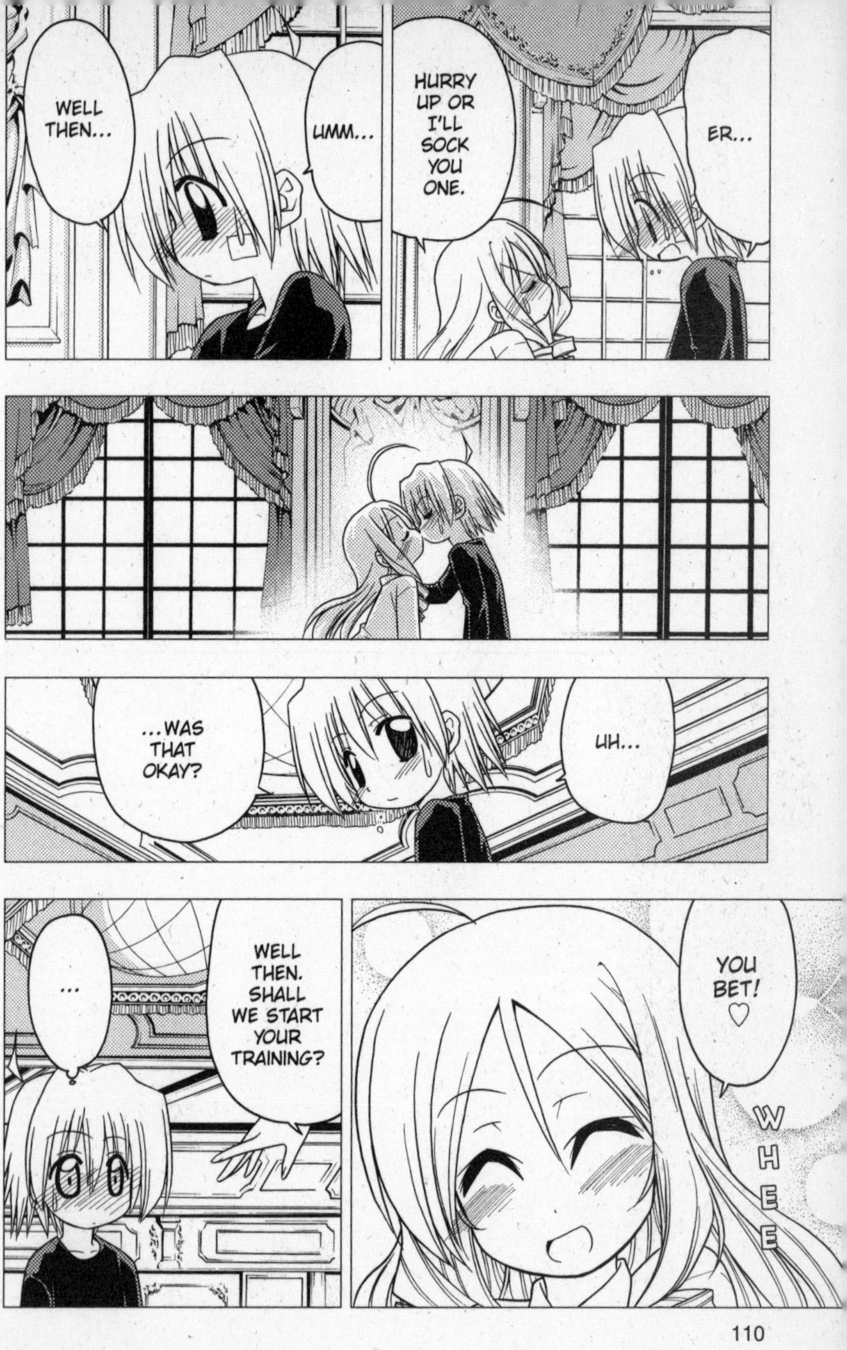
ER...
HURRY UP OR I'LL SOCK YOU ONE.
UMM...
WELL THEN...
UH...
...WAS THAT OKAY?
YOU BET! ♡
WHEE
WELL THEN. SHALL WE START YOUR TRAINING?
...

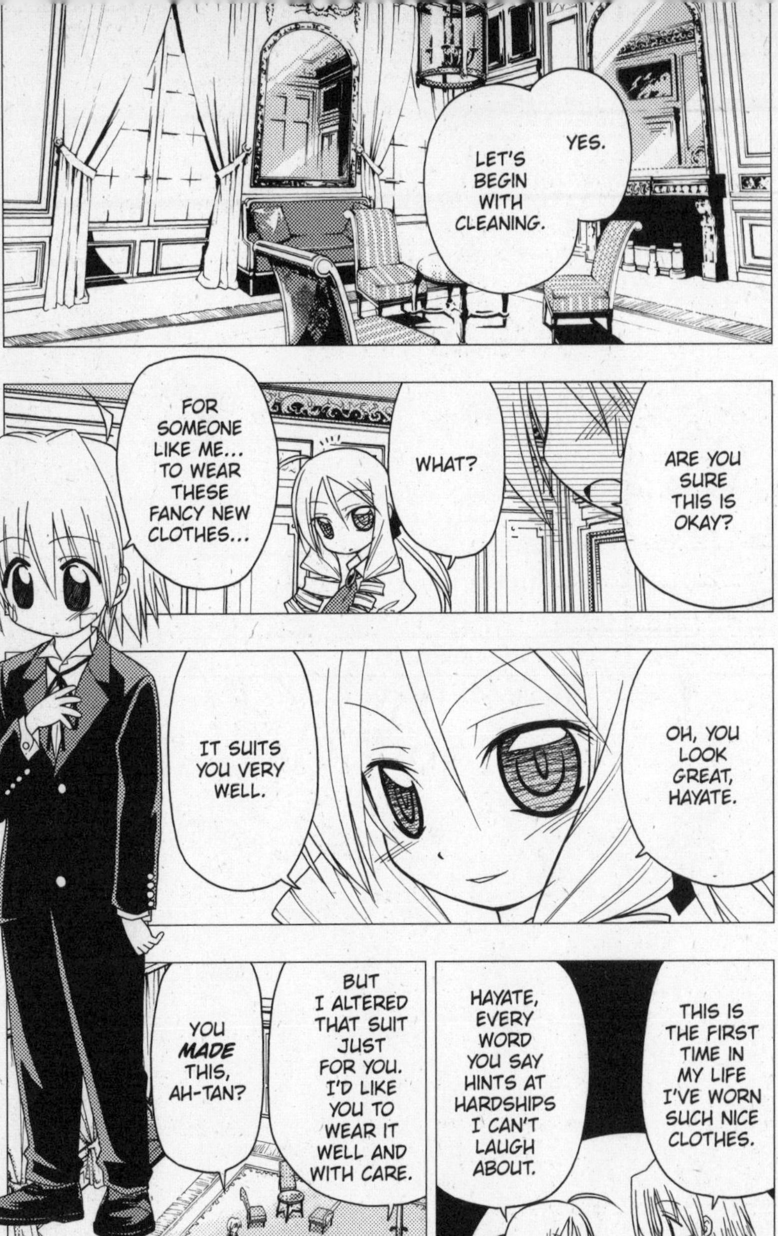
YES.
LET'S BEGIN WITH CLEANING.
ARE YOU SURE THIS IS OKAY?
WHAT?
FOR SOMEONE LIKE ME... TO WEAR THESE FANCY NEW CLOTHES...
OH, YOU LOOK GREAT, HAYATE.
IT SUITS YOU VERY WELL.
THIS IS THE FIRST TIME IN MY LIFE I'VE WORN SUCH NICE CLOTHES.
HAYATE, EVERY WORD YOU SAY HINTS AT HARDSHIPS I CAN'T LAUGH ABOUT.
BUT I ALTERED THAT SUIT JUST FOR YOU. I'D LIKE YOU TO WEAR IT WELL AND WITH CARE.
YOU *MADE* THIS, AH-TAN?

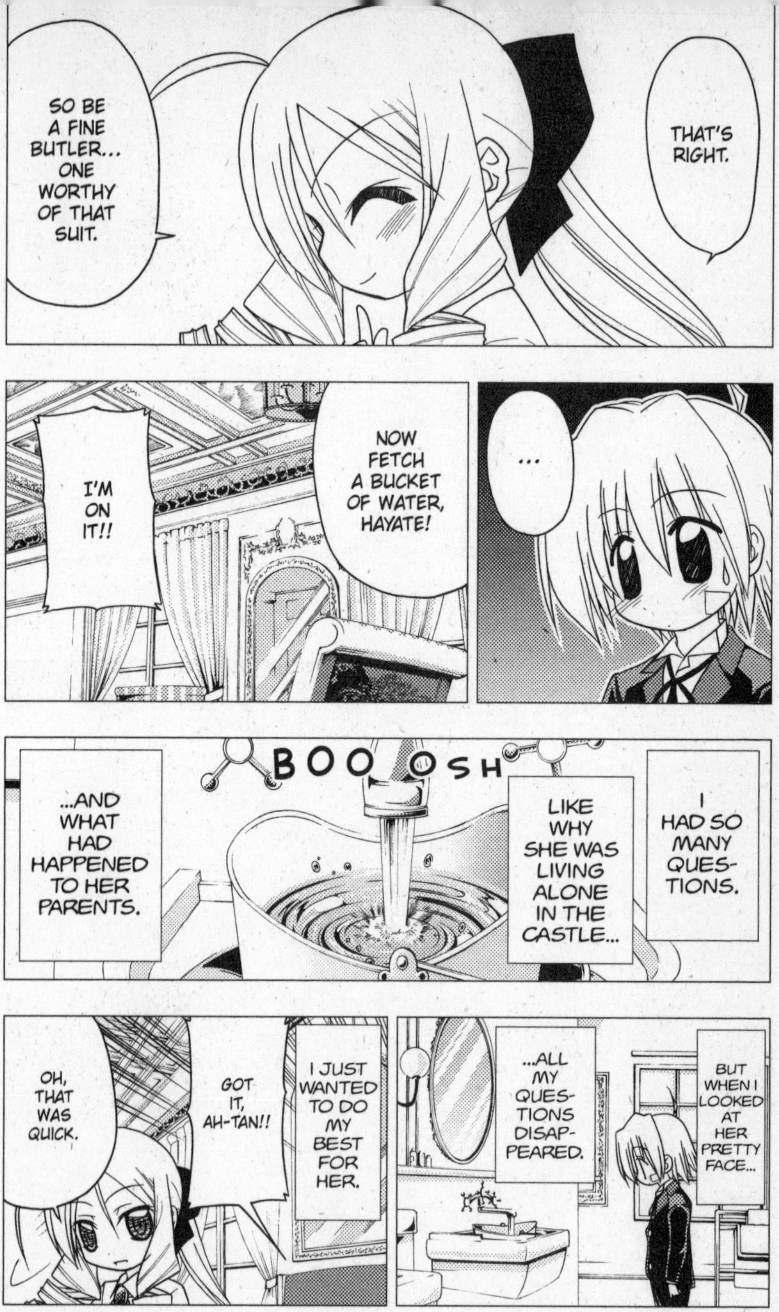
THAT'S RIGHT.
SO BE A FINE BUTLER... ONE WORTHY OF THAT SUIT.
...
NOW FETCH A BUCKET OF WATER, HAYATE!
I'M ON IT!!
I HAD SO MANY QUES-TIONS.
LIKE WHY SHE WAS LIVING ALONE IN THE CASTLE...
BOO OSH
...AND WHAT HAD HAPPENED TO HER PARENTS.
BUT WHEN I LOOKED AT HER PRETTY FACE...
...ALL MY QUES-TIONS DISAP-PEARED.
I JUST WANTED TO DO MY BEST FOR HER.
GOT IT, AH-TAN!!
OH, THAT WAS QUICK.

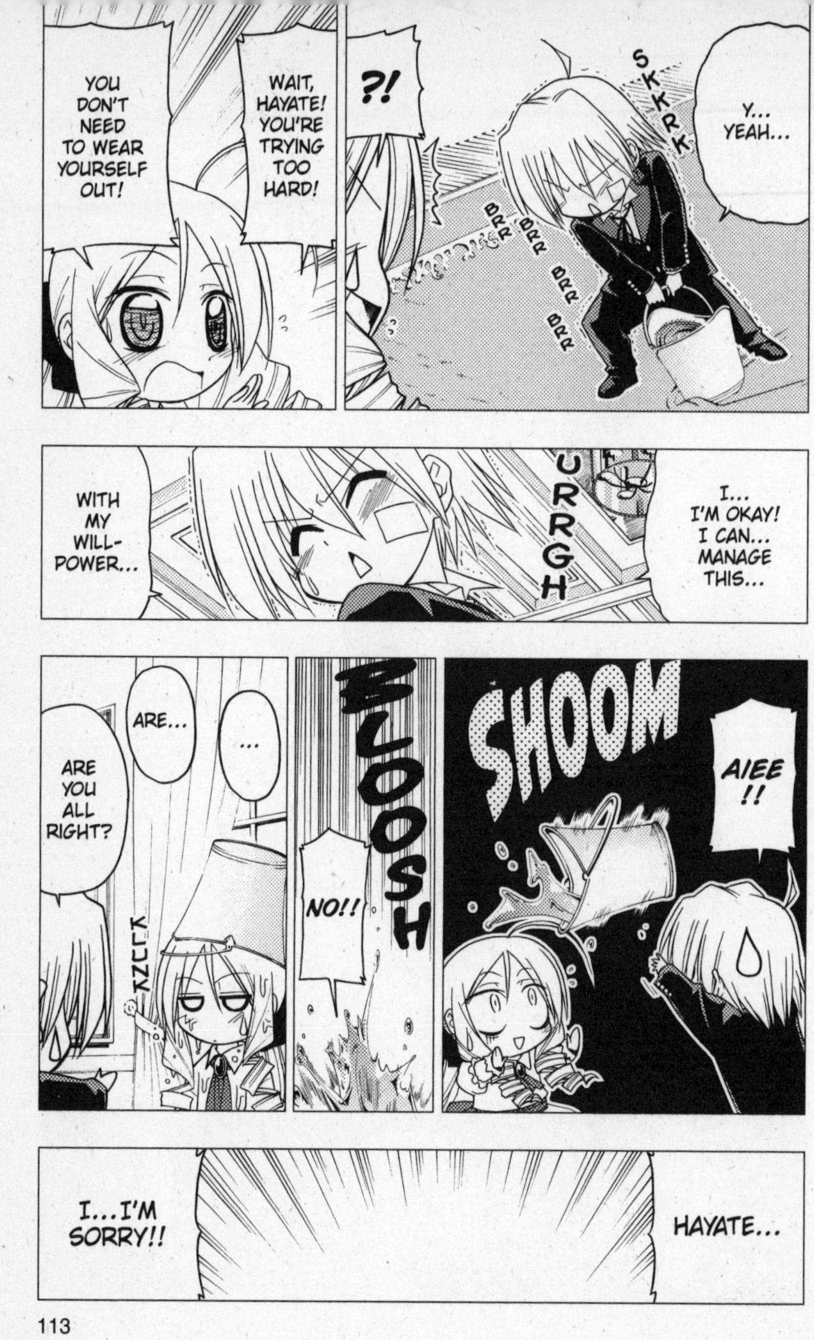

Y... YEAH...
SKKRK
?!
BRR BRR BRR BRR
WAIT, HAYATE! YOU'RE TRYING TOO HARD!
YOU DON'T NEED TO WEAR YOURSELF OUT!
I... I'M OKAY! I CAN... MANAGE THIS...
URRGH
WITH MY WILL-POWER...
AIEE!!
SHOOM
NO!!
BLOOSH
...
ARE...
ARE YOU ALL RIGHT?
KLUNK
HAYATE...
I...I'M SORRY!!

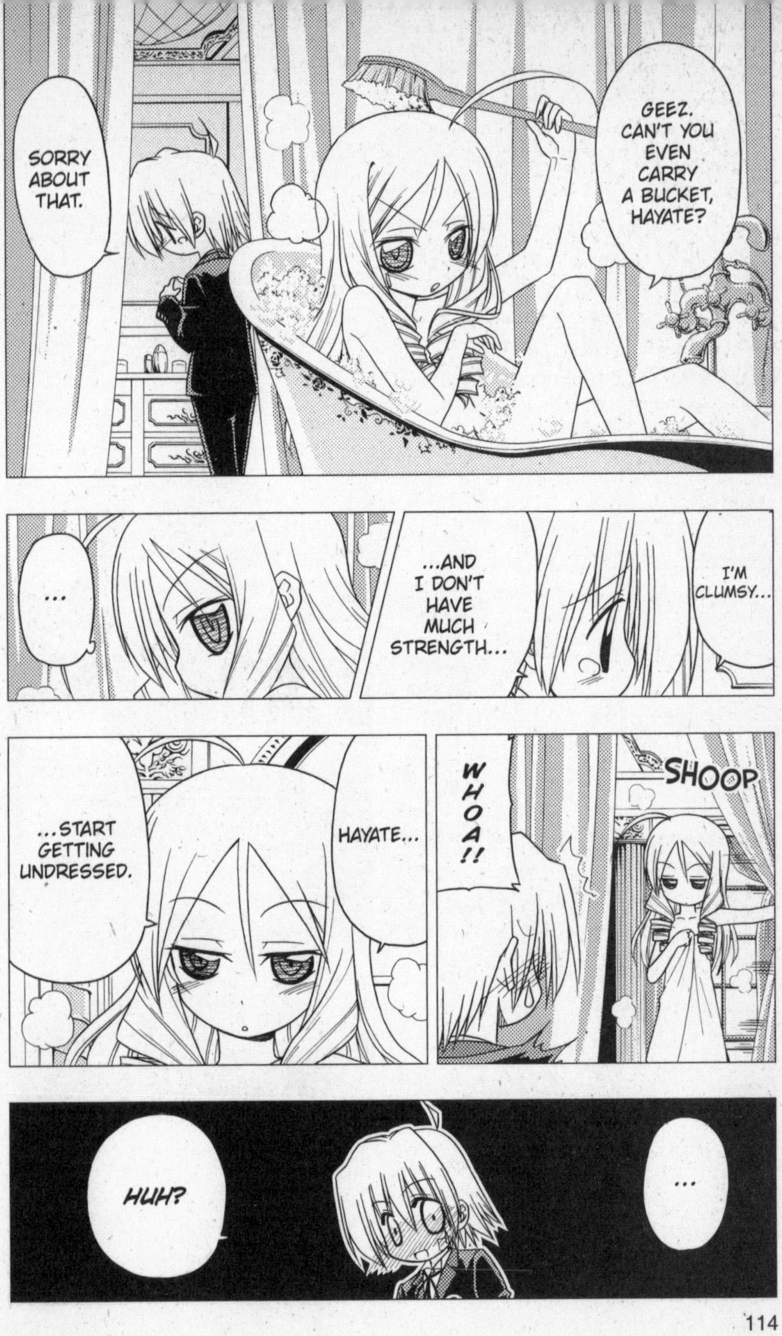
GEEZ. CAN'T YOU EVEN CARRY A BUCKET, HAYATE?
SORRY ABOUT THAT.
I'M CLUMSY...
...AND I DON'T HAVE MUCH STRENGTH...
...
SHOOP
WHOA!!
HAYATE...
...START GETTING UNDRESSED.
...
HUH?

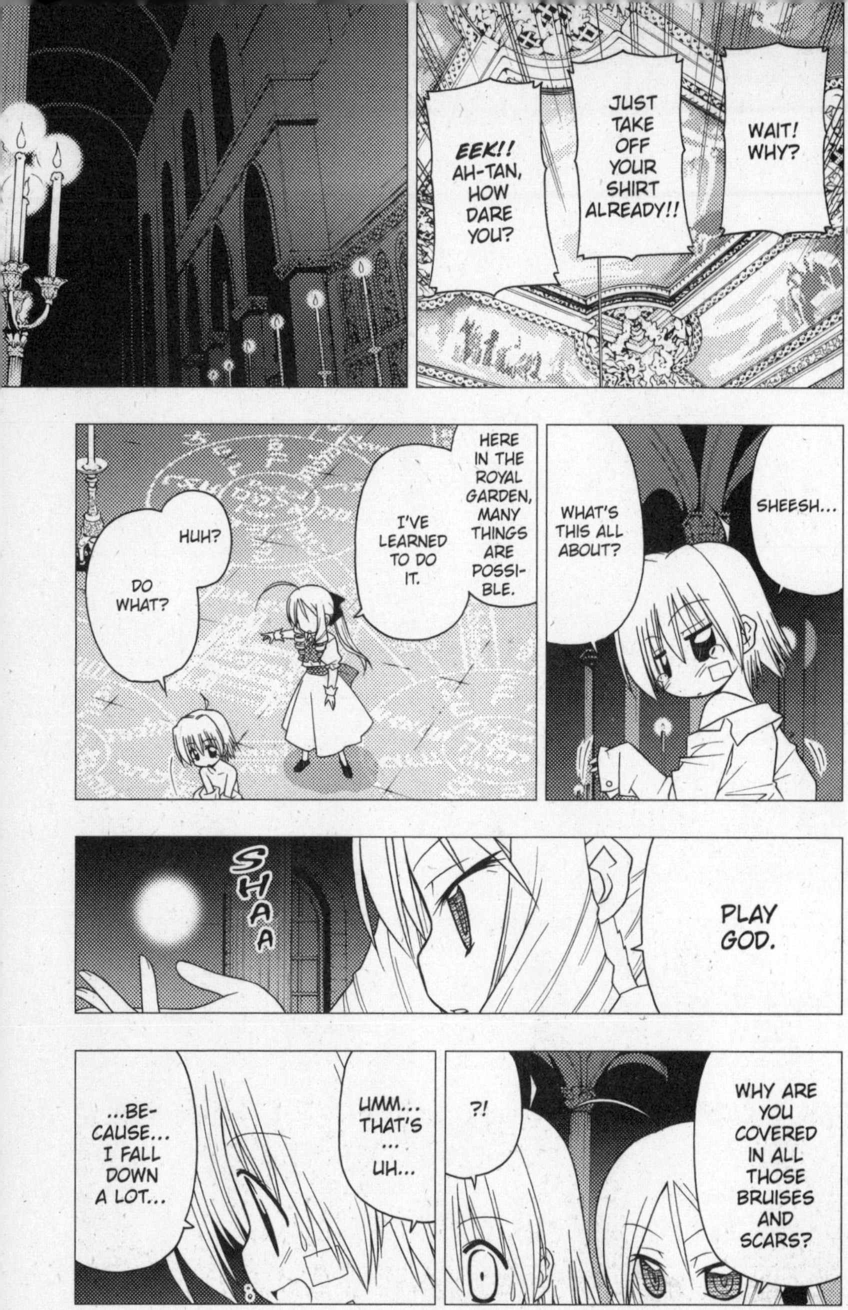
WAIT! WHY?
JUST TAKE OFF YOUR SHIRT ALREADY!!
EEK!! AH-TAN, HOW DARE YOU?
SHEESH...
WHAT'S THIS ALL ABOUT?
HERE IN THE ROYAL GARDEN, MANY THINGS ARE POSSI-BLE.
I'VE LEARNED TO DO IT.
HUH? DO WHAT?
PLAY GOD.
SHAA
WHY ARE YOU COVERED IN ALL THOSE BRUISES AND SCARS?
?!
UMM... THAT'S ... UH...
...BE-CAUSE... I FALL DOWN A LOT...

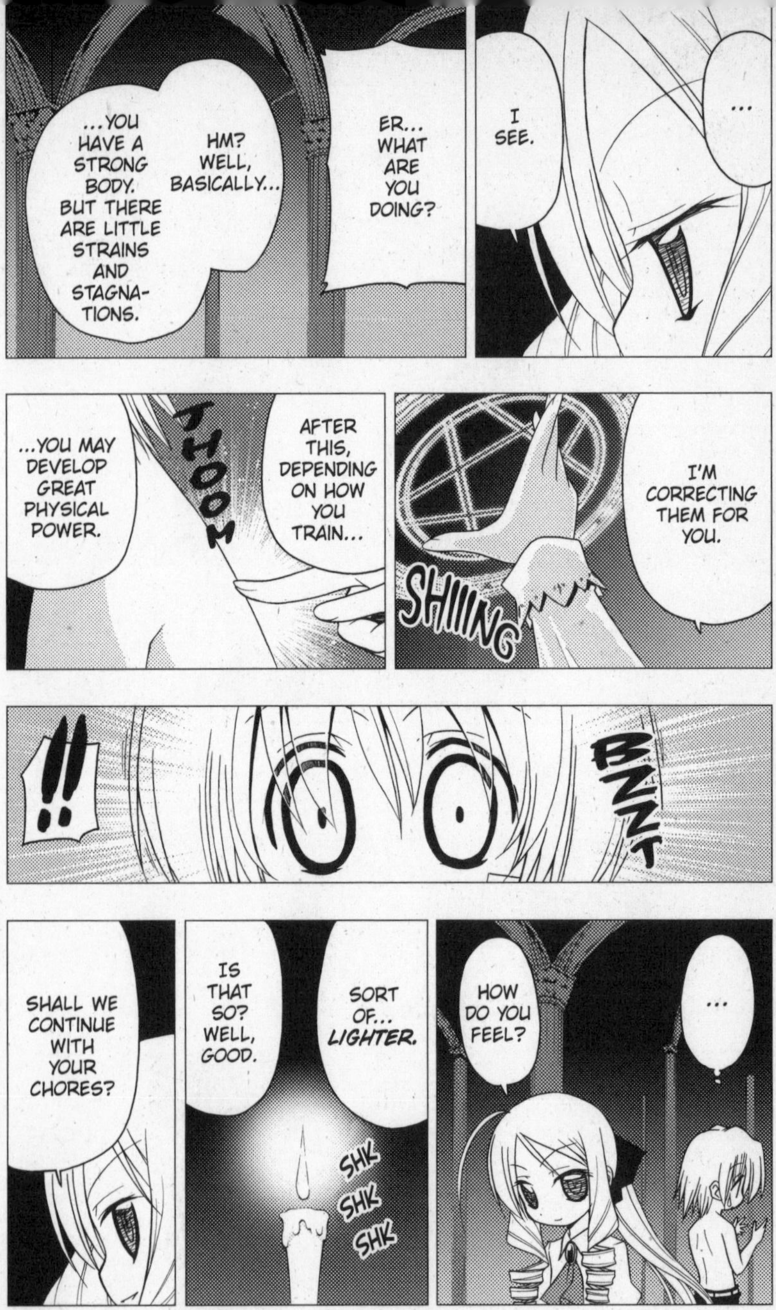
...
I SEE.
ER... WHAT ARE YOU DOING?
HM? WELL, BASICALLY...
...YOU HAVE A STRONG BODY. BUT THERE ARE LITTLE STRAINS AND STAGNATIONS.
I'M CORRECTING THEM FOR YOU.
SHIIING
AFTER THIS, DEPENDING ON HOW YOU TRAIN...
THOOOM
...YOU MAY DEVELOP GREAT PHYSICAL POWER.
BZZT
!!
...
HOW DO YOU FEEL?
SORT OF... *LIGHTER.*
IS THAT SO? WELL, GOOD.
SHK SHK SHK
SHALL WE CONTINUE WITH YOUR CHORES?

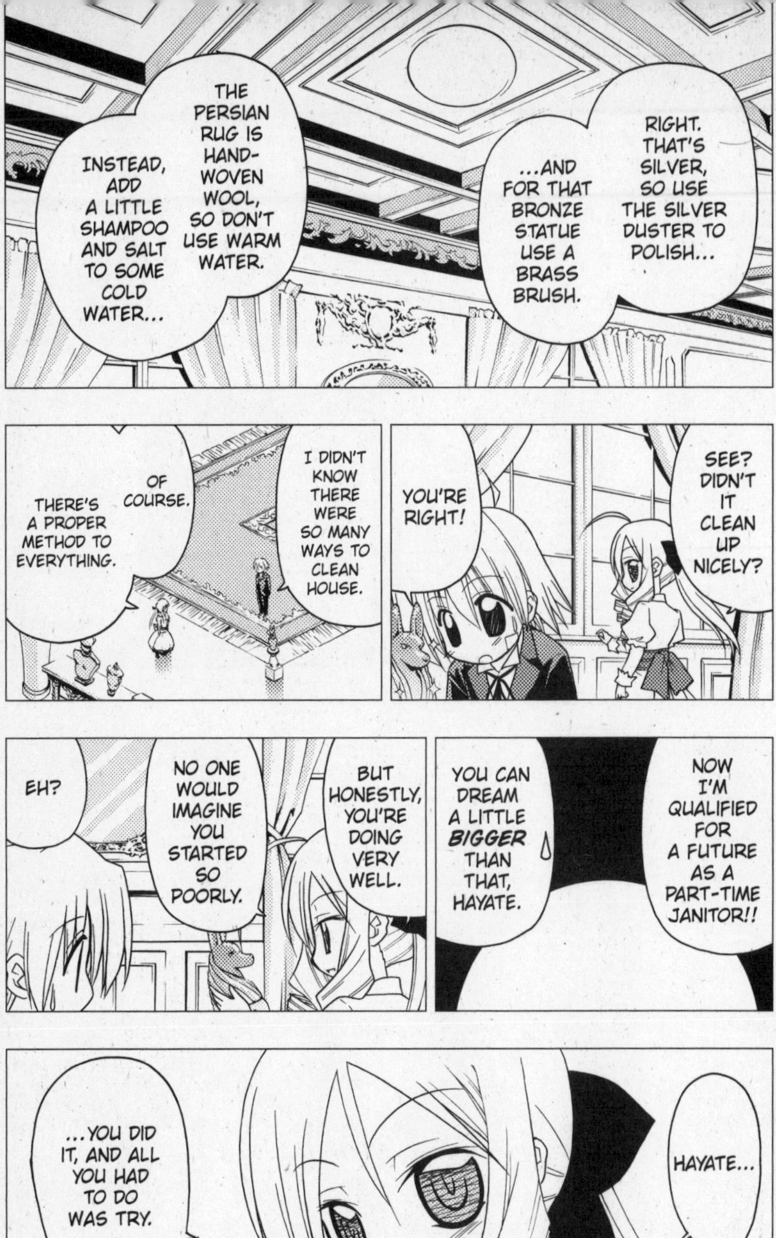
RIGHT. THAT'S SILVER, SO USE THE SILVER DUSTER TO POLISH...
...AND FOR THAT BRONZE STATUE USE A BRASS BRUSH.
THE PERSIAN RUG IS HAND-WOVEN WOOL, SO DON'T USE WARM WATER.
INSTEAD, ADD A LITTLE SHAMPOO AND SALT TO SOME COLD WATER...
SEE? DIDN'T IT CLEAN UP NICELY?
YOU'RE RIGHT!
I DIDN'T KNOW THERE WERE SO MANY WAYS TO CLEAN HOUSE.
OF COURSE.
THERE'S A PROPER METHOD TO EVERYTHING.
NOW I'M QUALIFIED FOR A FUTURE AS A PART-TIME JANITOR!!
YOU CAN DREAM A LITTLE *BIGGER* THAN THAT, HAYATE.
BUT HONESTLY, YOU'RE DOING VERY WELL.
NO ONE WOULD IMAGINE YOU STARTED SO POORLY.
EH?
HAYATE...
...YOU DID IT, AND ALL YOU HAD TO DO WAS TRY.

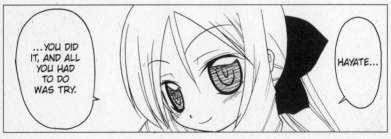

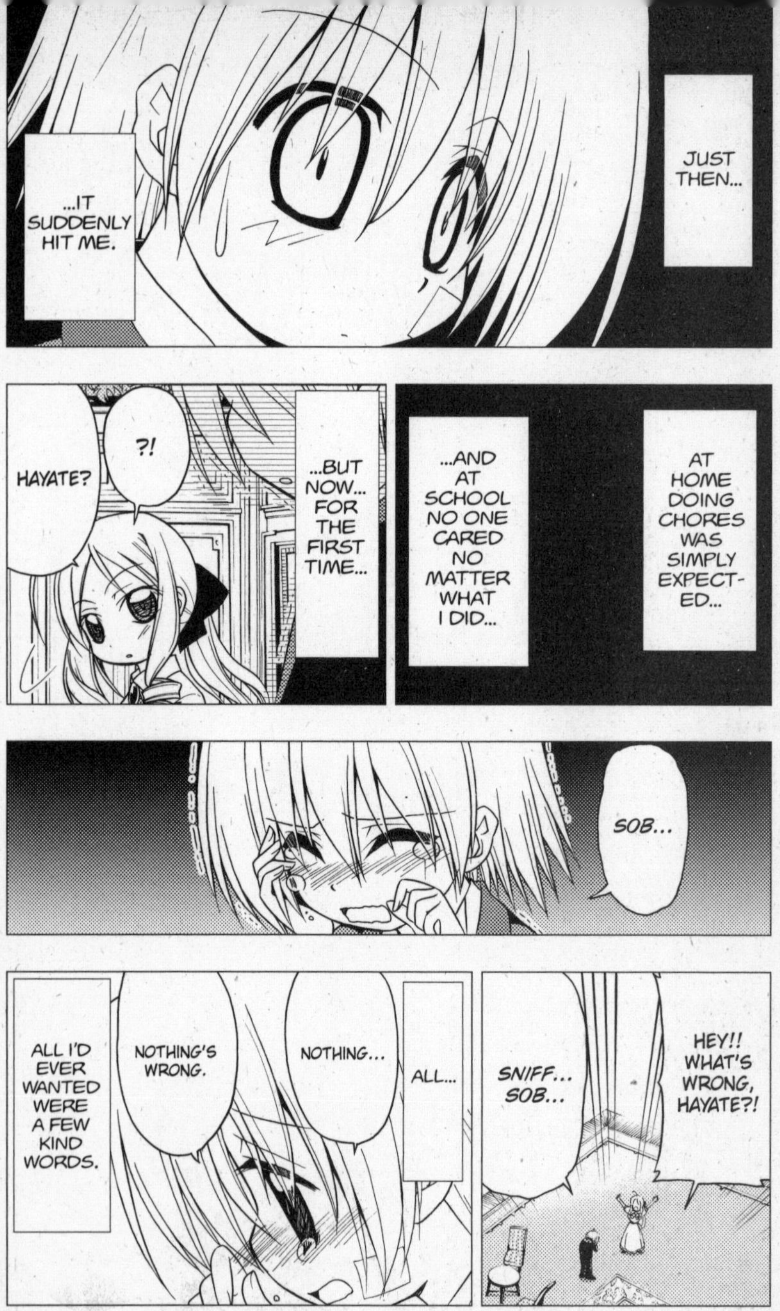
JUST THEN...
...IT SUDDENLY HIT ME.
AT HOME DOING CHORES WAS SIMPLY EXPECTED...
...AND AT SCHOOL NO ONE CARED NO MATTER WHAT I DID...
...BUT NOW... FOR THE FIRST TIME...
?!
HAYATE?
SOB...
HEY!! WHAT'S WRONG, HAYATE?!
SNIFF... SOB...
ALL...
NOTHING...
NOTHING'S WRONG.
ALL I'D EVER WANTED WERE A FEW KIND WORDS.

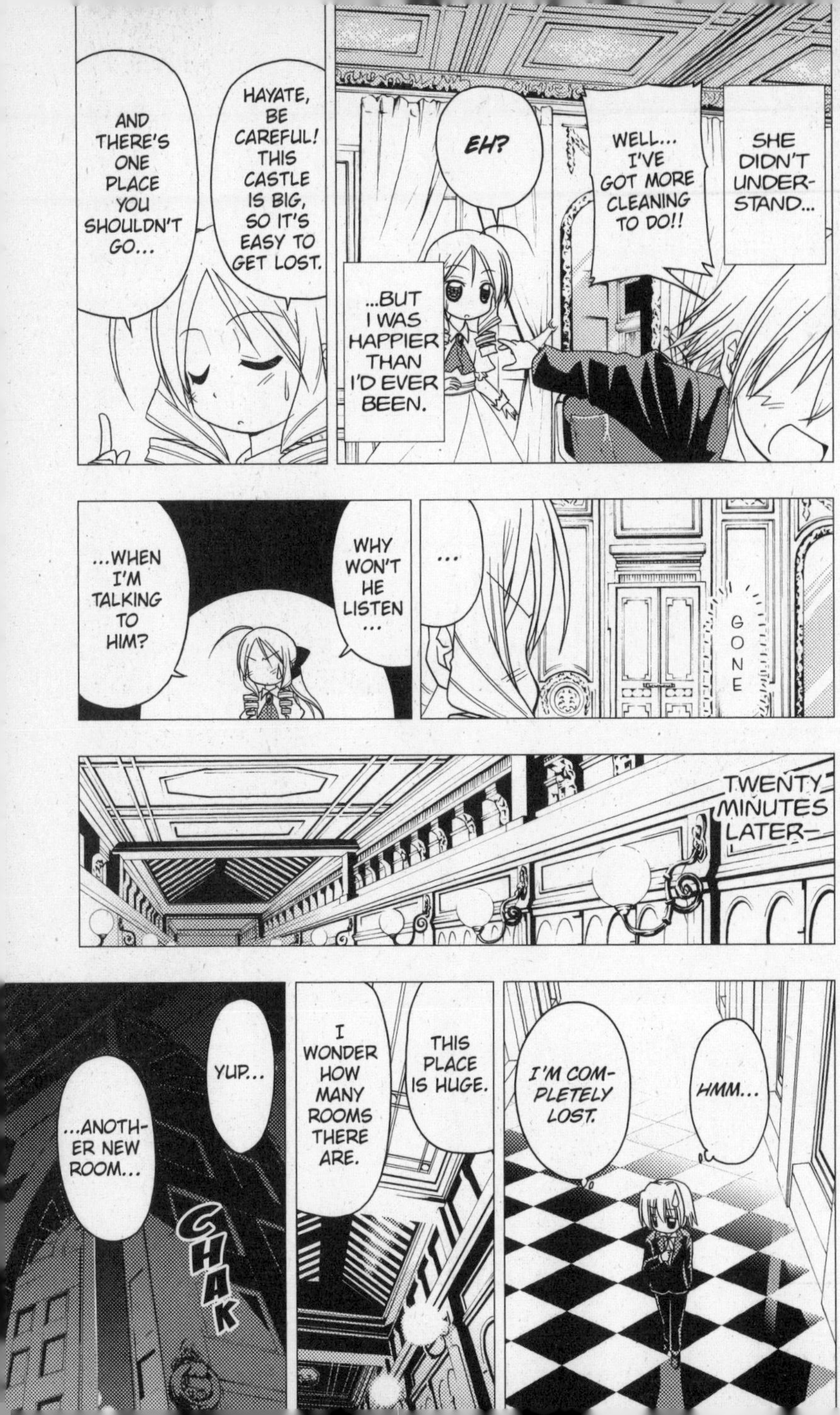
SHE DIDN'T UNDERSTAND...
WELL... I'VE GOT MORE CLEANING TO DO!!
EH?
...BUT I WAS HAPPIER THAN I'D EVER BEEN.
HAYATE, BE CAREFUL! THIS CASTLE IS BIG, SO IT'S EASY TO GET LOST.
AND THERE'S ONE PLACE YOU SHOULDN'T GO...
GONE
...
WHY WON'T HE LISTEN...
...WHEN I'M TALKING TO HIM?
TWENTY MINUTES LATER—
HMM...
I'M COMPLETELY LOST.
THIS PLACE IS HUGE.
I WONDER HOW MANY ROOMS THERE ARE.
YUP...
CHAK
...ANOTHER NEW ROOM...

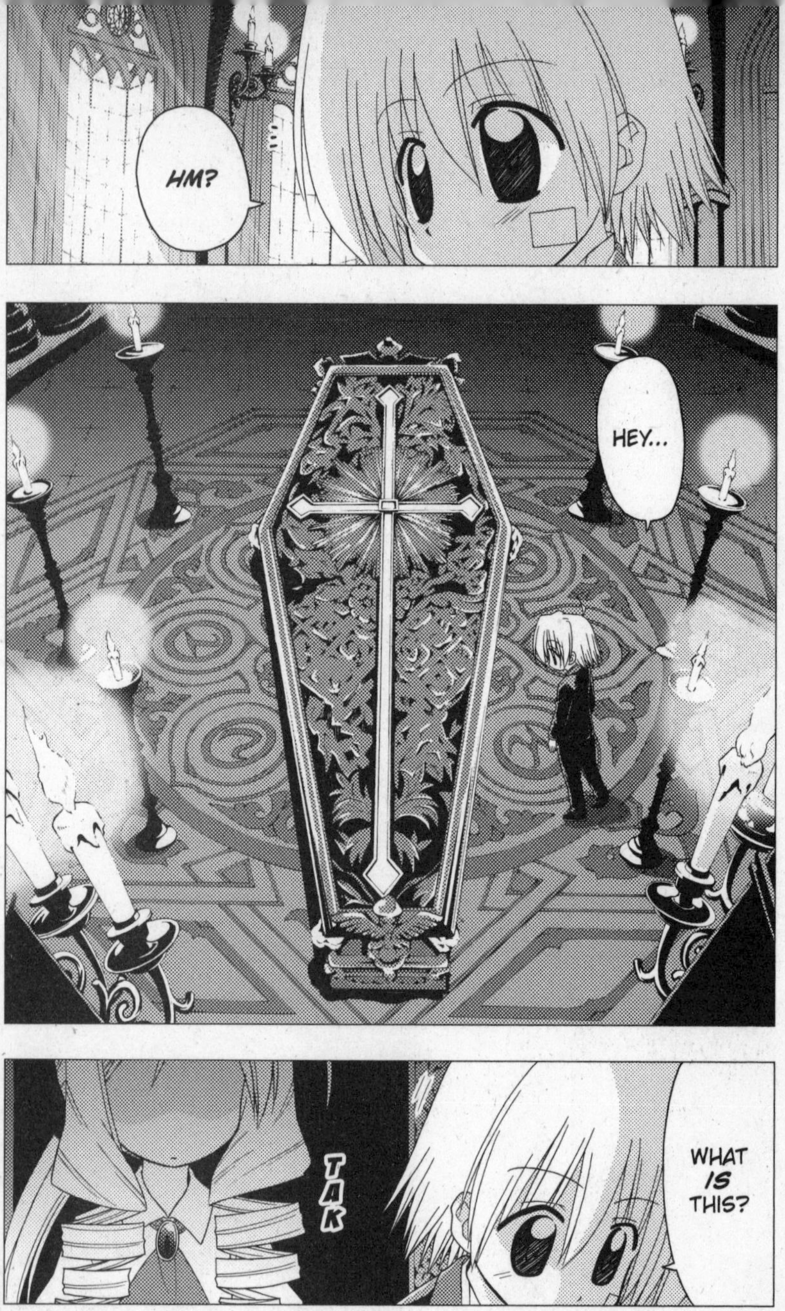
HM?
HEY...
WHAT *IS* THIS?
TAK

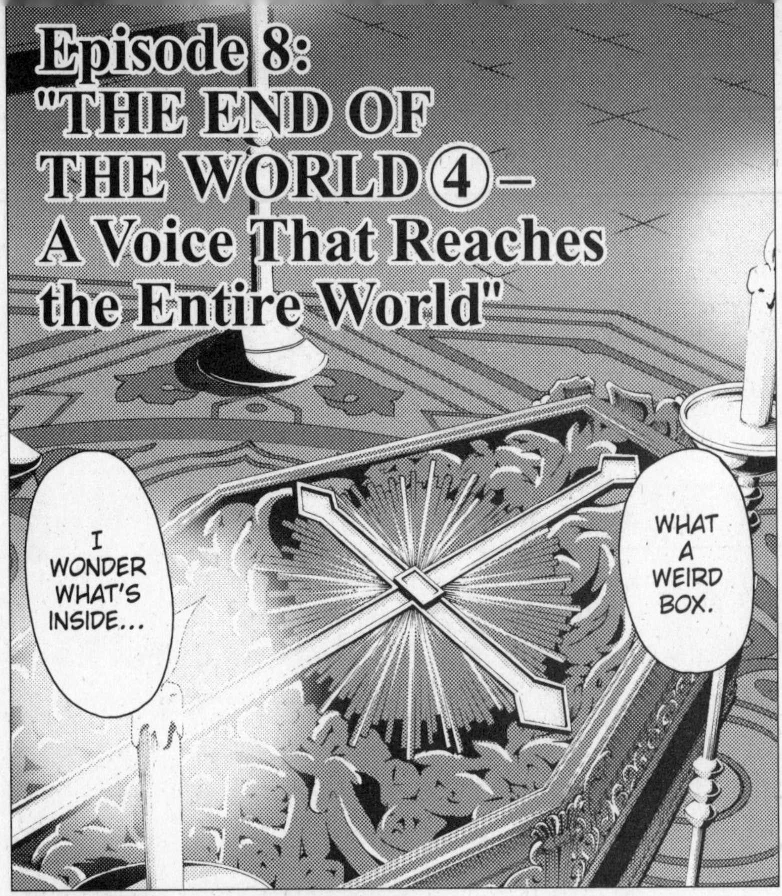
Episode 8: "THE END OF THE WORLD ④ – A Voice That Reaches the Entire World"
WHAT A WEIRD BOX.
I WONDER WHAT'S INSIDE...

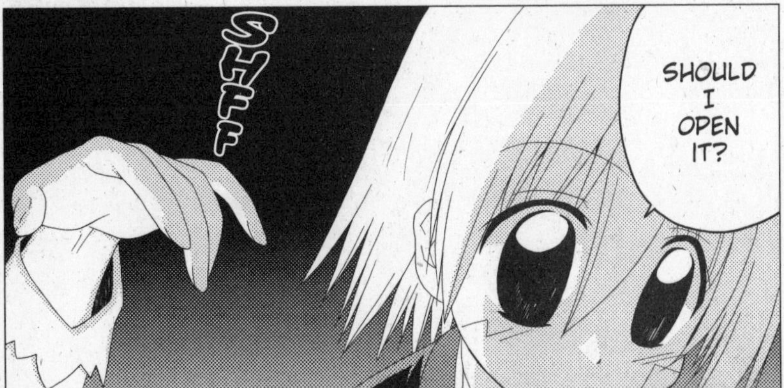
SHOULD I OPEN IT?
SHFF

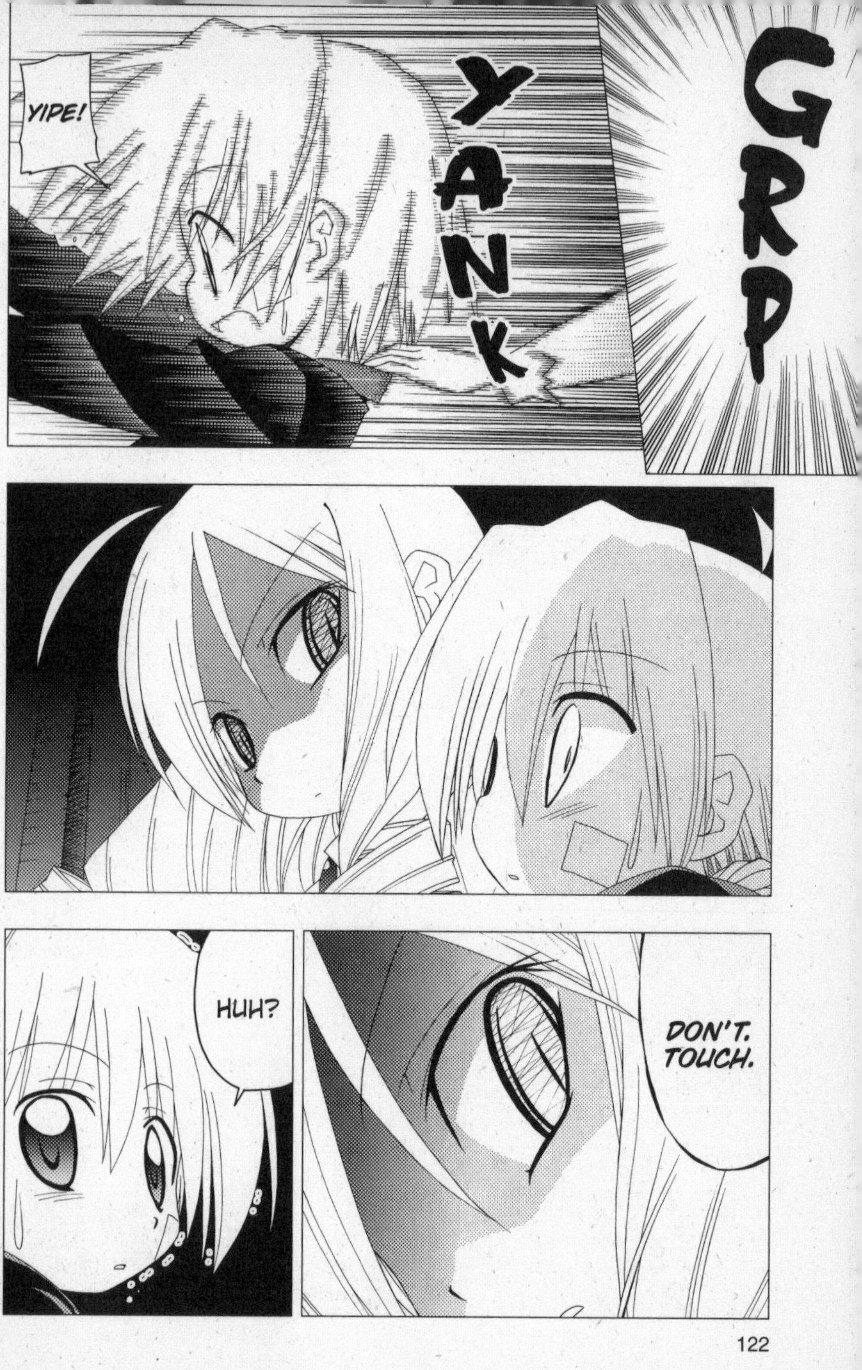
GRP
YANK
YIPE!
DON'T. TOUCH.
HUH?

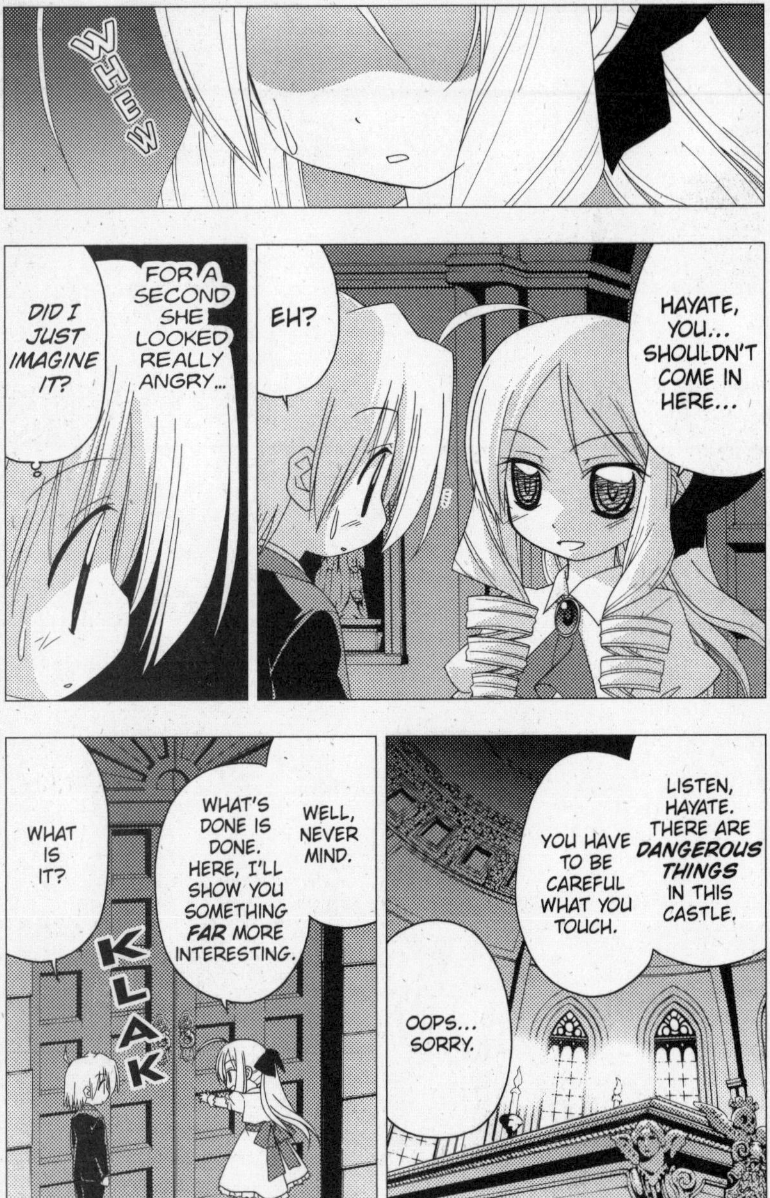
WHEW
HAYATE, YOU... SHOULDN'T COME IN HERE...
EH?
FOR A SECOND SHE LOOKED REALLY ANGRY...
DID I JUST IMAGINE IT?
LISTEN, HAYATE. THERE ARE DANGEROUS THINGS IN THIS CASTLE.
YOU HAVE TO BE CAREFUL WHAT YOU TOUCH.
OOPS... SORRY.
WELL, NEVER MIND.
WHAT'S DONE IS DONE. HERE, I'LL SHOW YOU SOMETHING FAR MORE INTERESTING.
KLAK
WHAT IS IT?

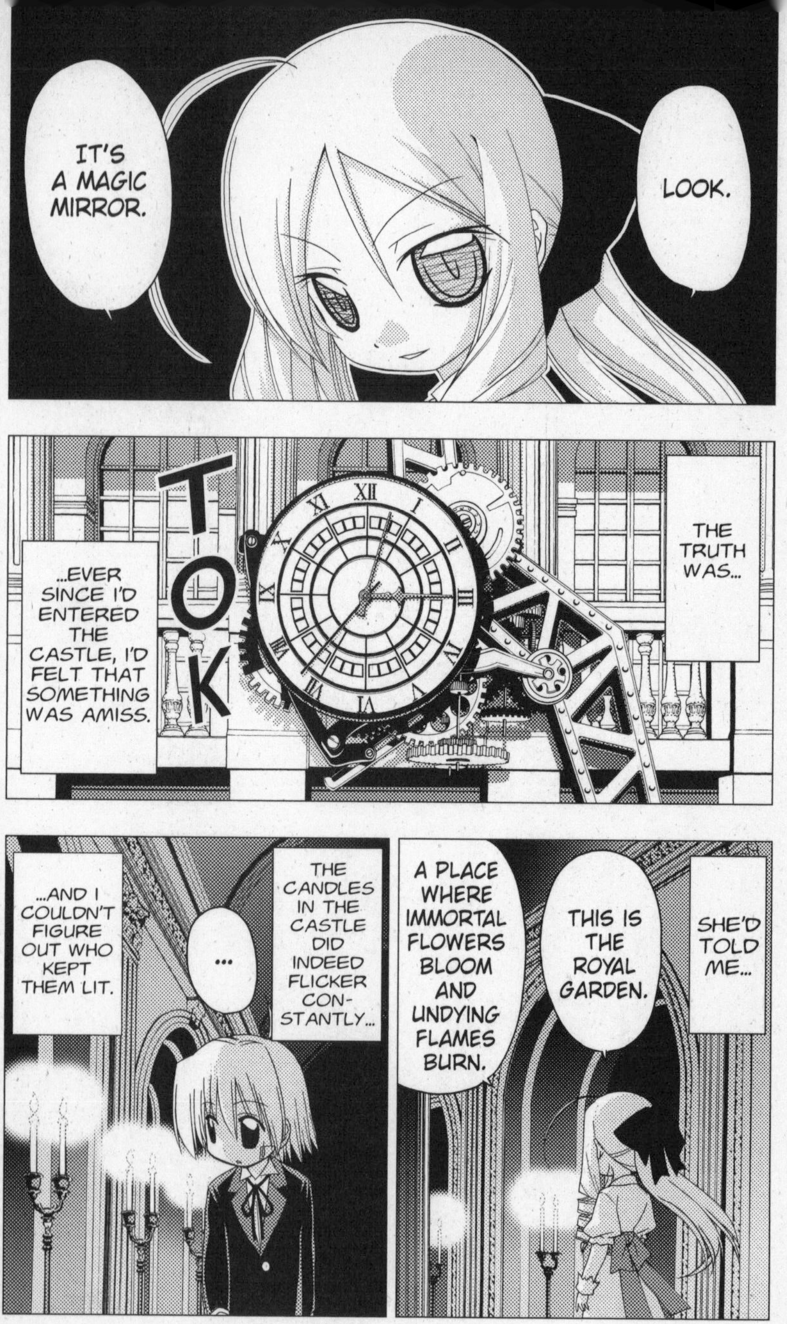
LOOK.
IT'S A MAGIC MIRROR.
THE TRUTH WAS...
TOK
...EVER SINCE I'D ENTERED THE CASTLE, I'D FELT THAT SOMETHING WAS AMISS.
SHE'D TOLD ME...
THIS IS THE ROYAL GARDEN.
A PLACE WHERE IMMORTAL FLOWERS BLOOM AND UNDYING FLAMES BURN.
THE CANDLES IN THE CASTLE DID INDEED FLICKER CON-STANTLY...
...
...AND I COULDN'T FIGURE OUT WHO KEPT THEM LIT.

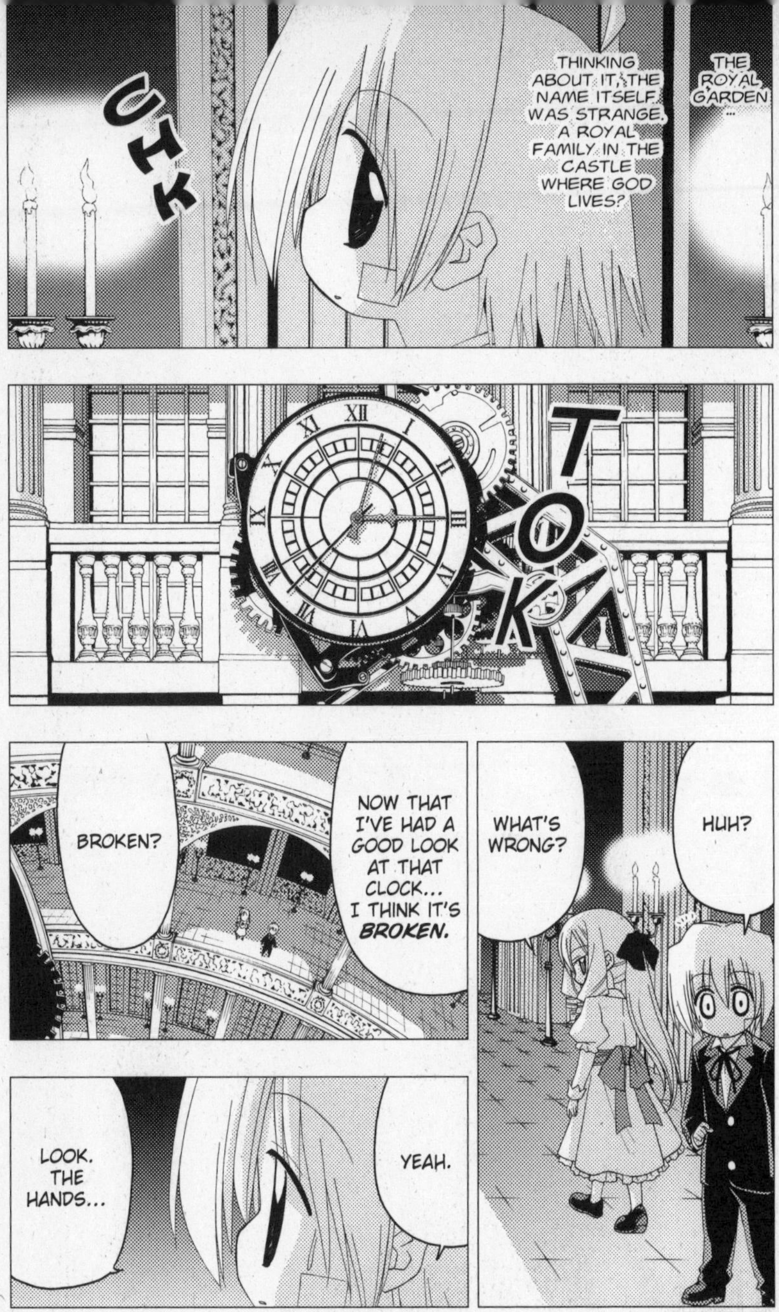
THE ROYAL GARDEN...
THINKING ABOUT IT, THE NAME ITSELF WAS STRANGE. A ROYAL FAMILY IN THE CASTLE WHERE GOD LIVES?
CHK
TOK
HUH?
WHAT'S WRONG?
NOW THAT I'VE HAD A GOOD LOOK AT THAT CLOCK... I THINK IT'S **BROKEN.**
BROKEN?
YEAH.
LOOK. THE HANDS...

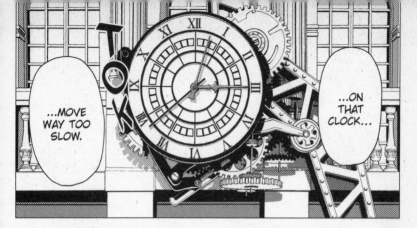

...ON THAT CLOCK...
TOK
...MOVE WAY TOO SLOW.
OH...
YOU DON'T NEED TO WORRY ABOUT THAT.
IT'S WORKING *JUST FINE.*
HUH? BUT...
DON'T WORRY.
BELIEVE ME...
...THAT CLOCK IS ACCURATE.
SOME-THING ABOUT THE CASTLE MADE ME A LITTLE UNEASY.
WHAT ARE YOU DOING?
COME ALONG, HAYATE.
OH! OKAY!
IF I HAD TO PUT IT IN WORDS...

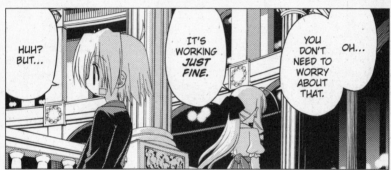

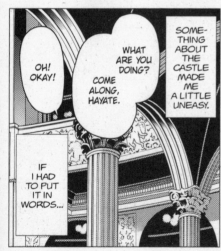

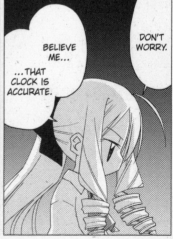

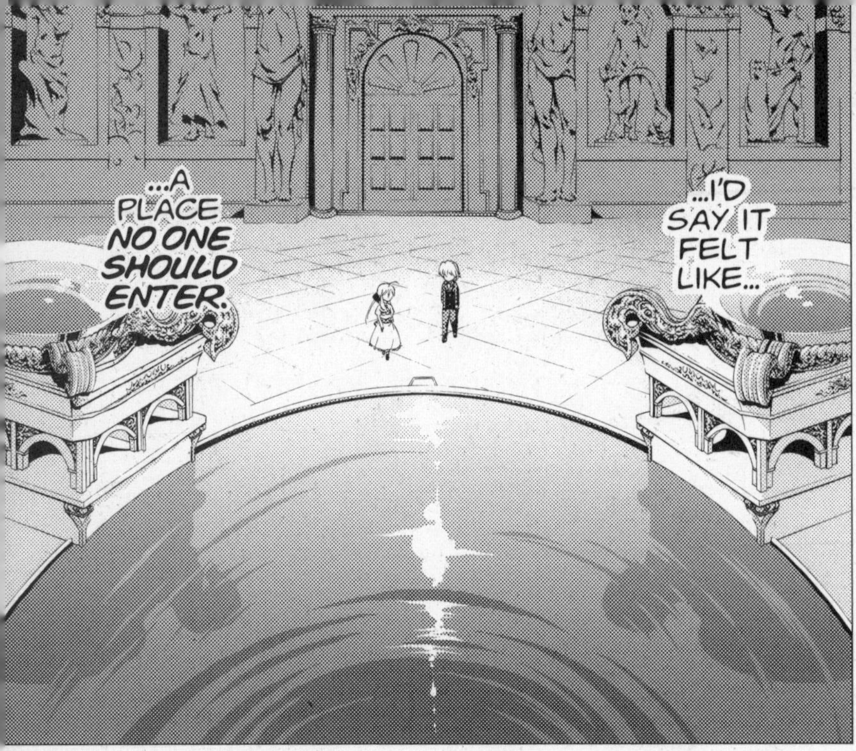
...I'D SAY IT FELT LIKE...
...A PLACE NO ONE SHOULD ENTER.

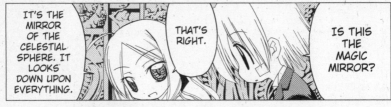

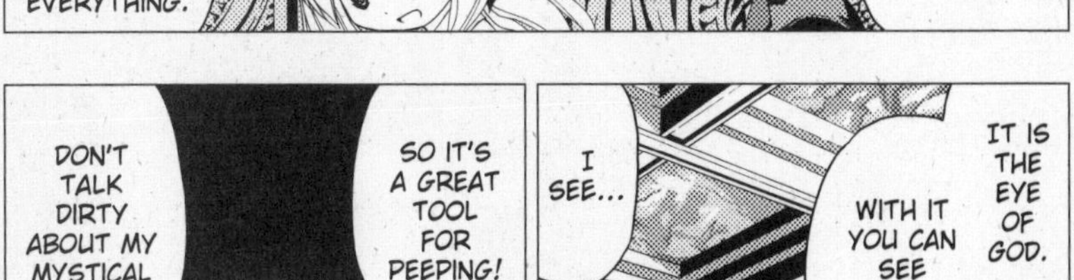
IS THIS THE MAGIC MIRROR?
THAT'S RIGHT.
IT'S THE MIRROR OF THE CELESTIAL SPHERE. IT LOOKS DOWN UPON EVERYTHING.

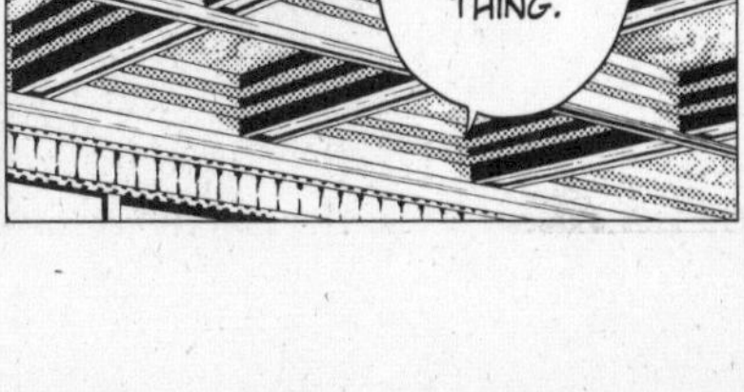
IT IS THE EYE OF GOD.
WITH IT YOU CAN SEE ANY-THING.
I SEE...

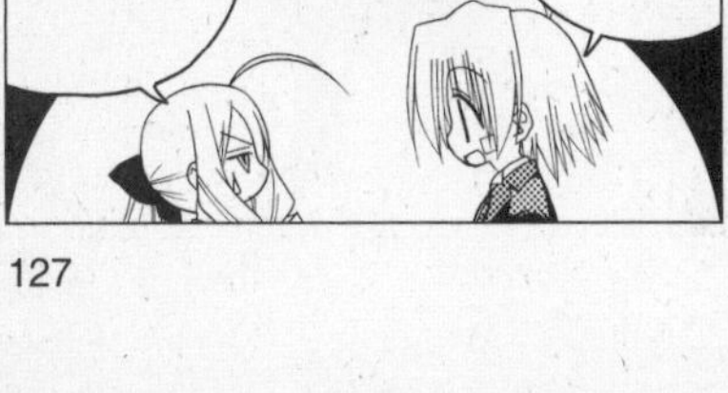
SO IT'S A GREAT TOOL FOR PEEPING! ♡
DON'T TALK DIRTY ABOUT MY MYSTICAL DEVICE!

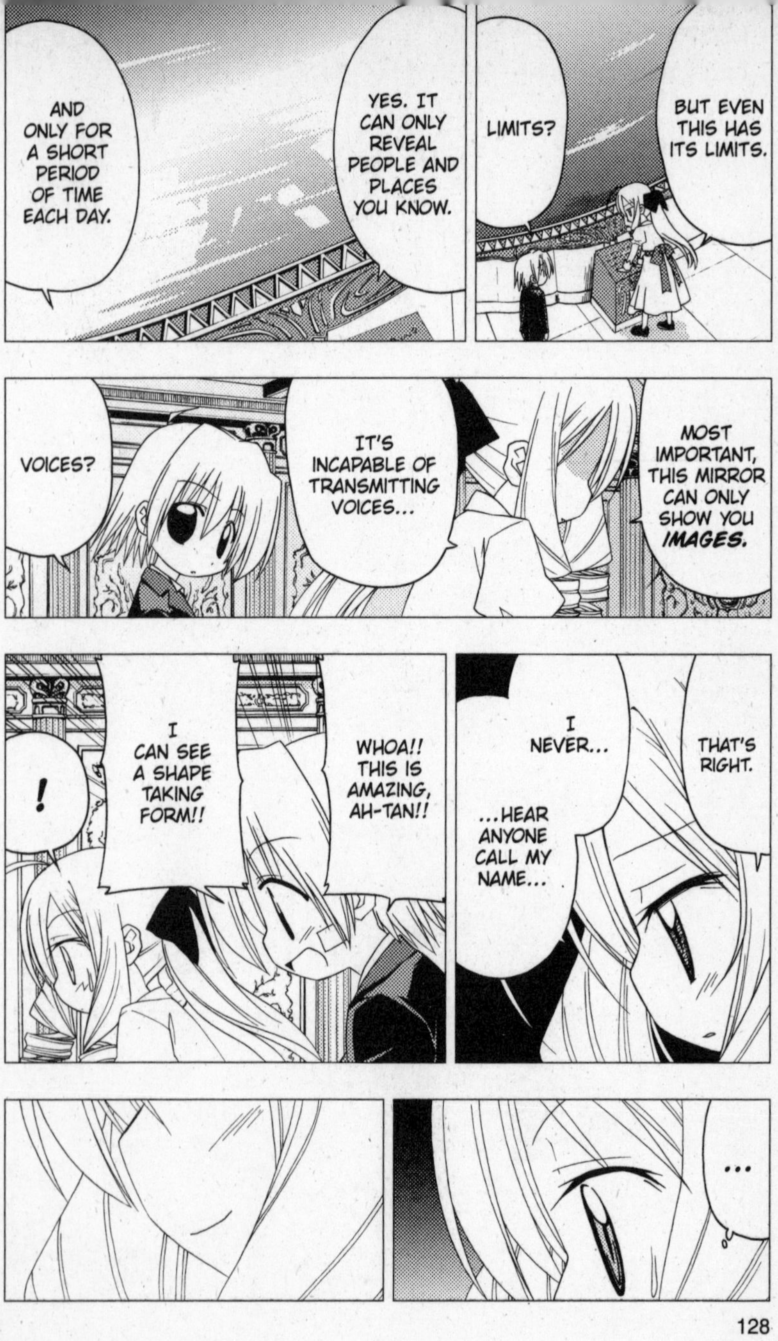
BUT EVEN THIS HAS ITS LIMITS.
LIMITS?
YES. IT CAN ONLY REVEAL PEOPLE AND PLACES YOU KNOW.
AND ONLY FOR A SHORT PERIOD OF TIME EACH DAY.
MOST IMPORTANT, THIS MIRROR CAN ONLY SHOW YOU *IMAGES.*
IT'S INCAPABLE OF TRANSMITTING VOICES...
VOICES?
THAT'S RIGHT.
I NEVER...
...HEAR ANYONE CALL MY NAME...
WHOA!! THIS IS AMAZING, AH-TAN!!
I CAN SEE A SHAPE TAKING FORM!!
!
...

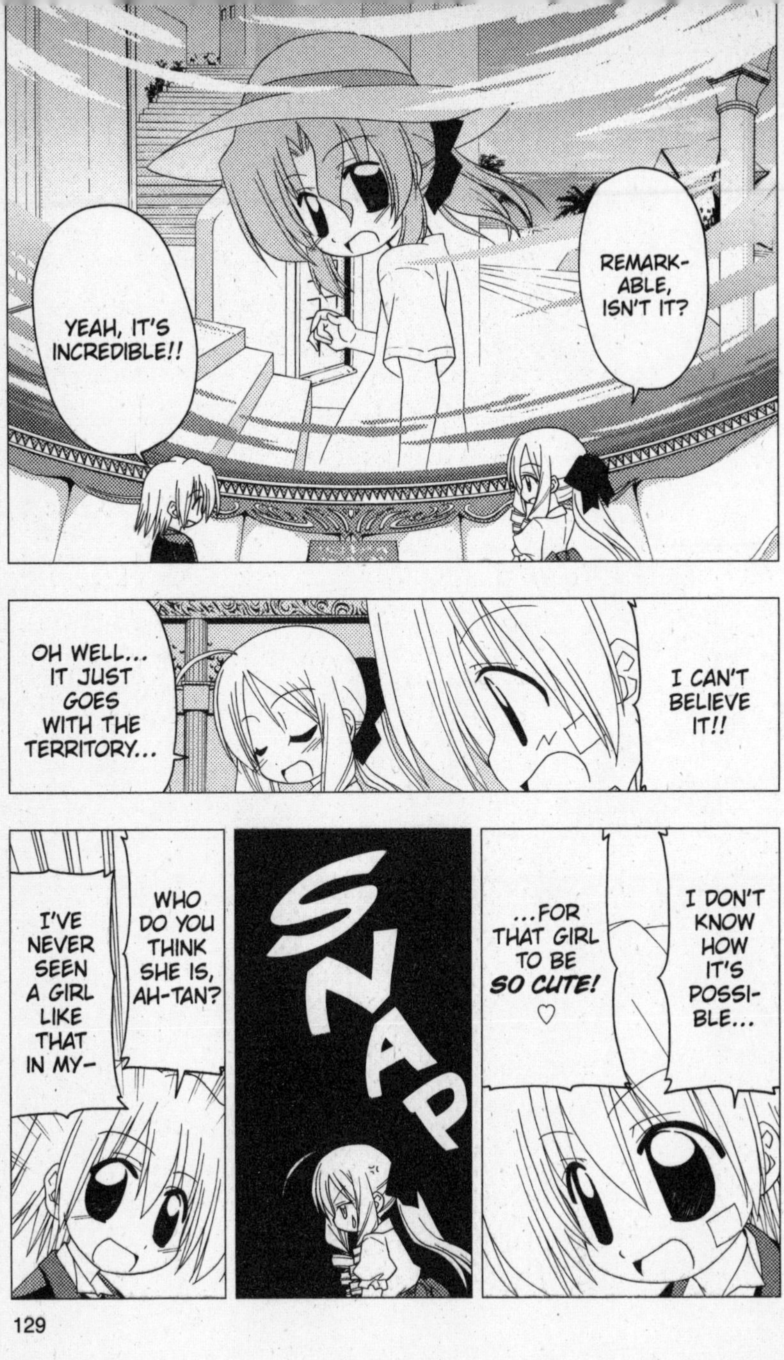
REMARKABLE, ISN'T IT?
YEAH, IT'S INCREDIBLE!!
I CAN'T BELIEVE IT!!
OH WELL... IT JUST GOES WITH THE TERRITORY...
I DON'T KNOW HOW IT'S POSSIBLE...
...FOR THAT GIRL TO BE SO CUTE! ♡
SNAP
WHO DO YOU THINK SHE IS, AH-TAN?
I'VE NEVER SEEN A GIRL LIKE THAT IN MY-

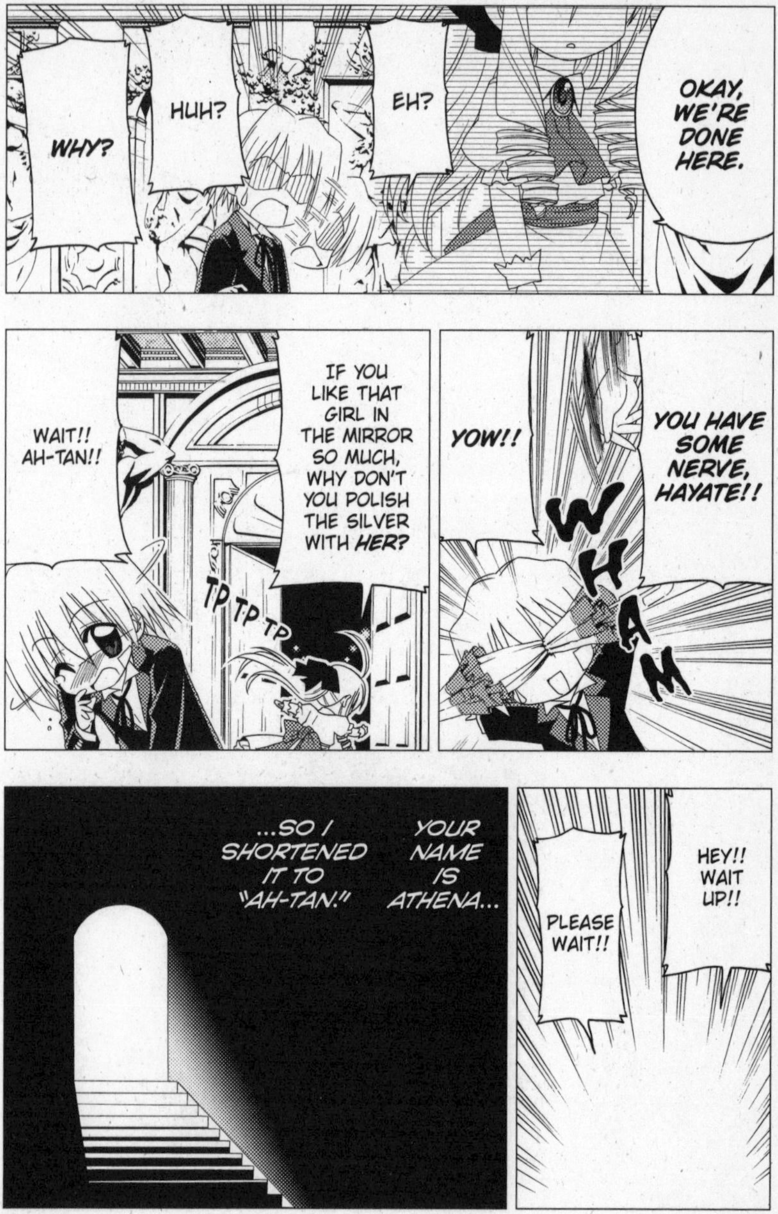
OKAY, WE'RE DONE HERE.
EH?
HUH?
WHY?
YOU HAVE SOME NERVE, HAYATE!!
WHAM
YOW!!
IF YOU LIKE THAT GIRL IN THE MIRROR SO MUCH, WHY DON'T YOU POLISH THE SILVER WITH HER?
TP TP TP TP
WAIT!! AH-TAN!!
HEY!! WAIT UP!!
PLEASE WAIT!!
YOUR NAME IS ATHENA...
...SO I SHORTENED IT TO "AH-TAN."

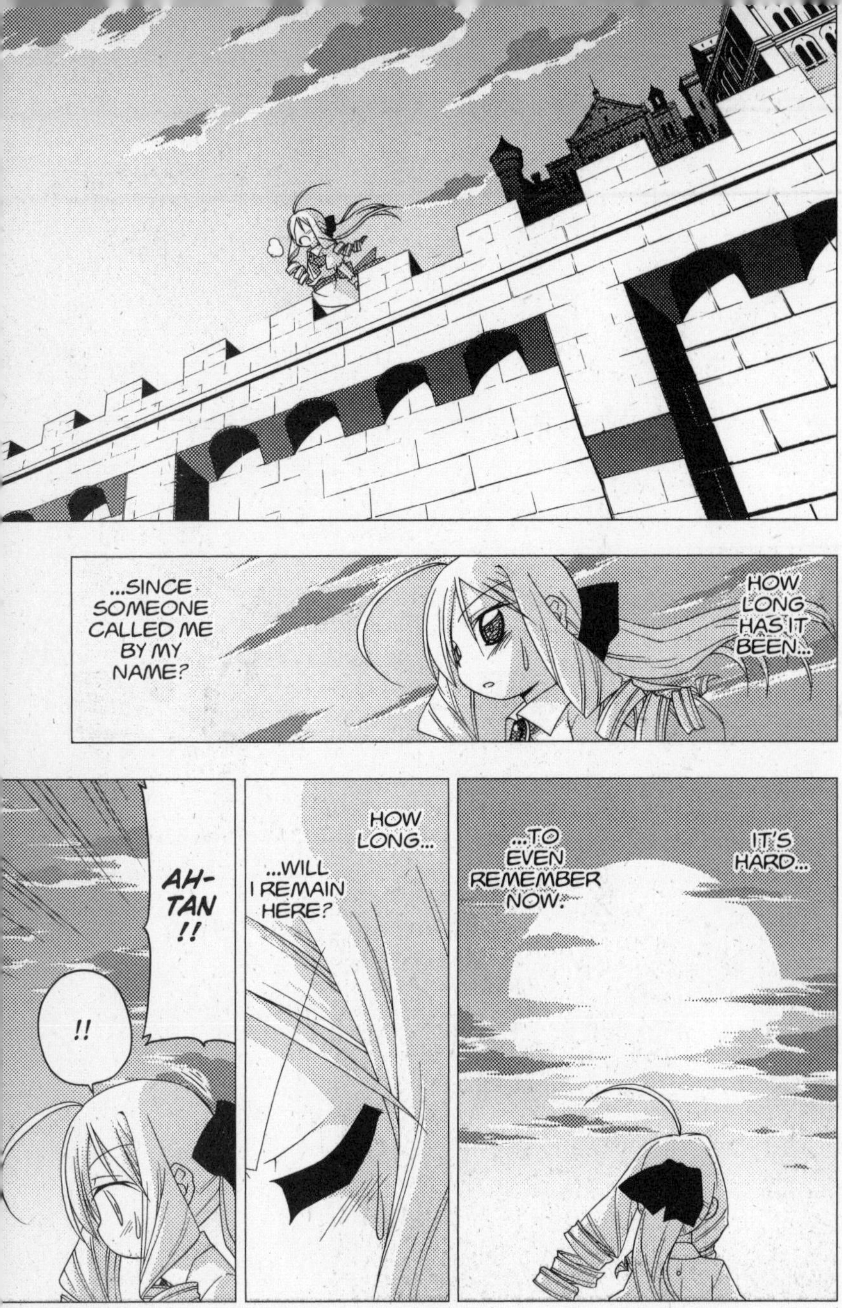
HOW LONG HAS IT BEEN...
...SINCE SOMEONE CALLED ME BY MY NAME?
IT'S HARD...
...TO EVEN REMEMBER NOW.
HOW LONG...
...WILL I REMAIN HERE?
AH-TAN!!
!!

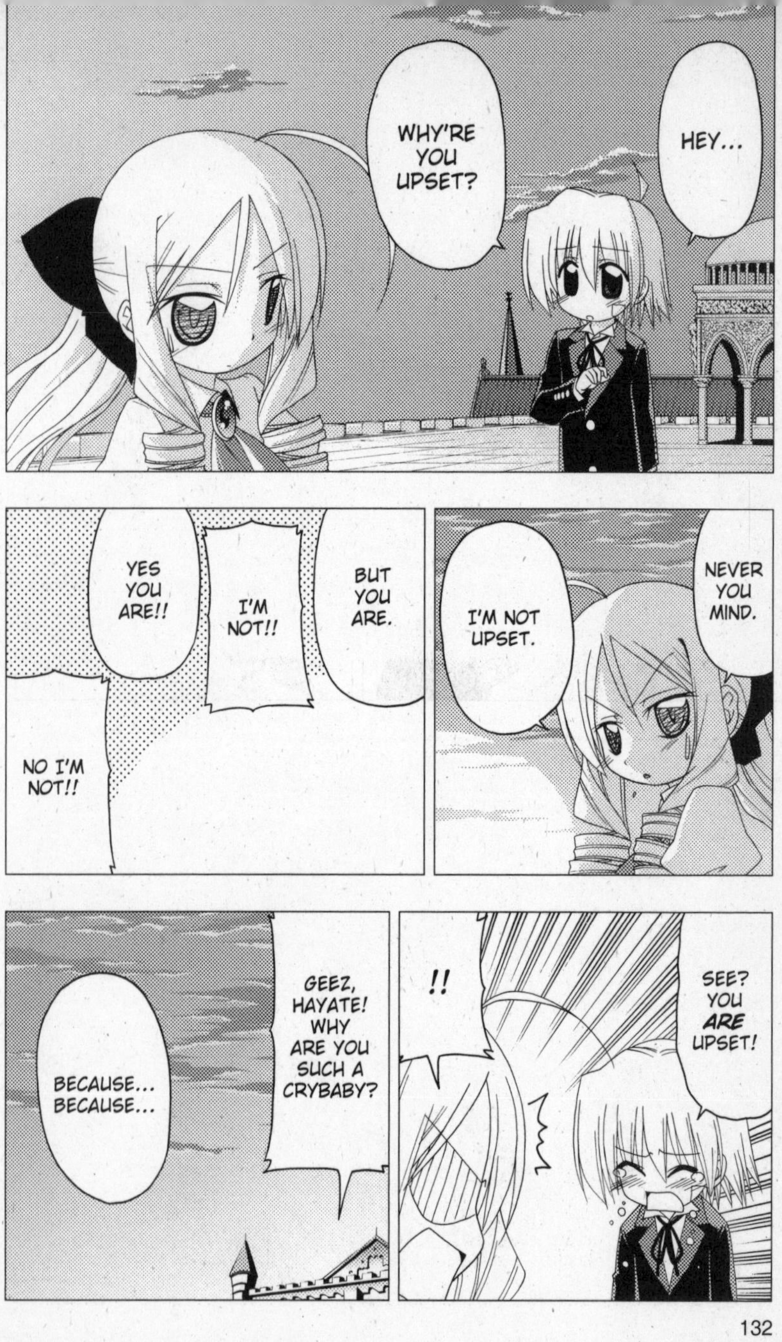
HEY...
WHY'RE YOU UPSET?
NEVER YOU MIND.
I'M NOT UPSET.
BUT YOU ARE.
I'M NOT!!
YES YOU ARE!!
NO I'M NOT!!
SEE? YOU ARE UPSET!
!!
GEEZ, HAYATE! WHY ARE YOU SUCH A CRYBABY?
BECAUSE... BECAUSE...

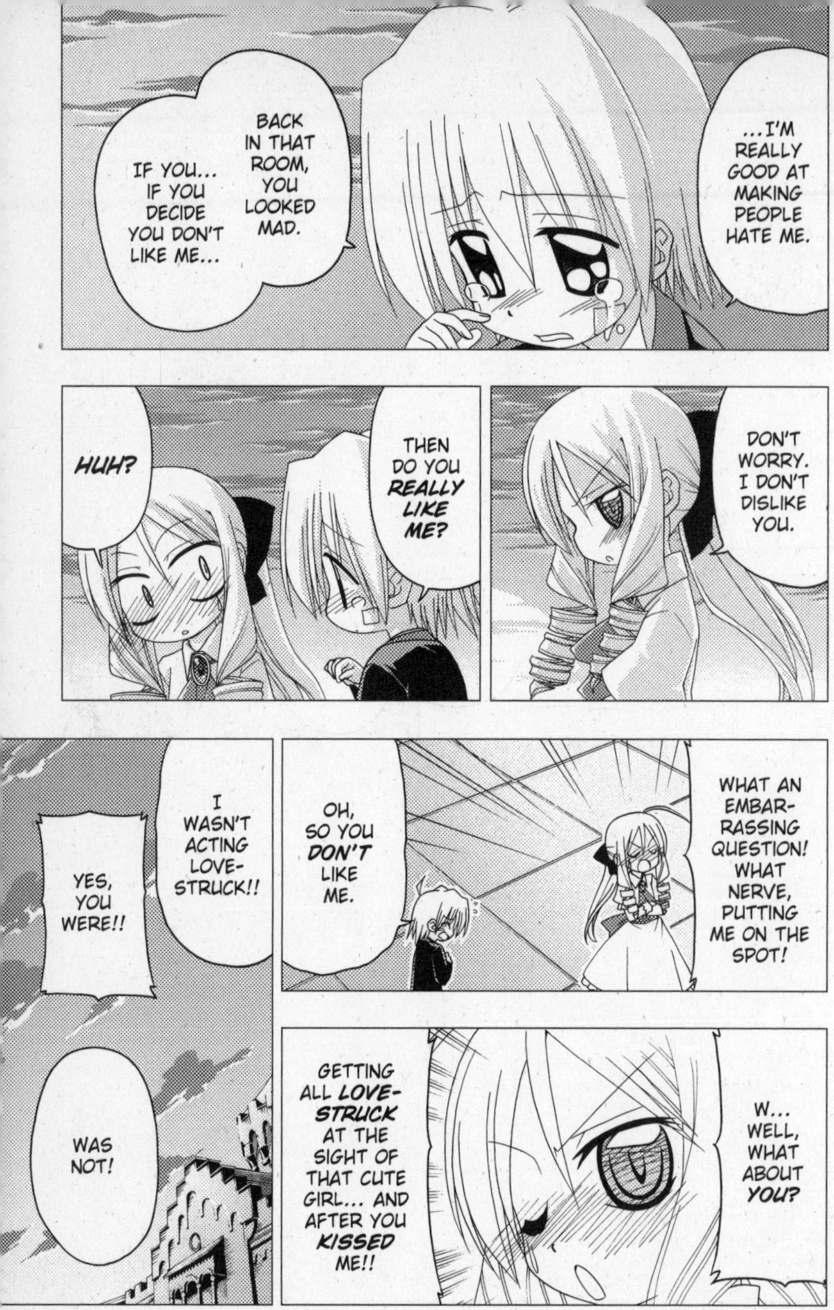
...I'M REALLY GOOD AT MAKING PEOPLE HATE ME.
BACK IN THAT ROOM, YOU LOOKED MAD.
IF YOU... IF YOU DECIDE YOU DON'T LIKE ME...
DON'T WORRY. I DON'T DISLIKE YOU.
THEN DO YOU REALLY LIKE ME?
HUH?
WHAT AN EMBARRASSING QUESTION! WHAT NERVE, PUTTING ME ON THE SPOT!
OH, SO YOU DON'T LIKE ME.
W... WELL, WHAT ABOUT YOU?
GETTING ALL LOVE-STRUCK AT THE SIGHT OF THAT CUTE GIRL... AND AFTER YOU KISSED ME!!
I WASN'T ACTING LOVE-STRUCK!!
YES, YOU WERE!!
WAS NOT!

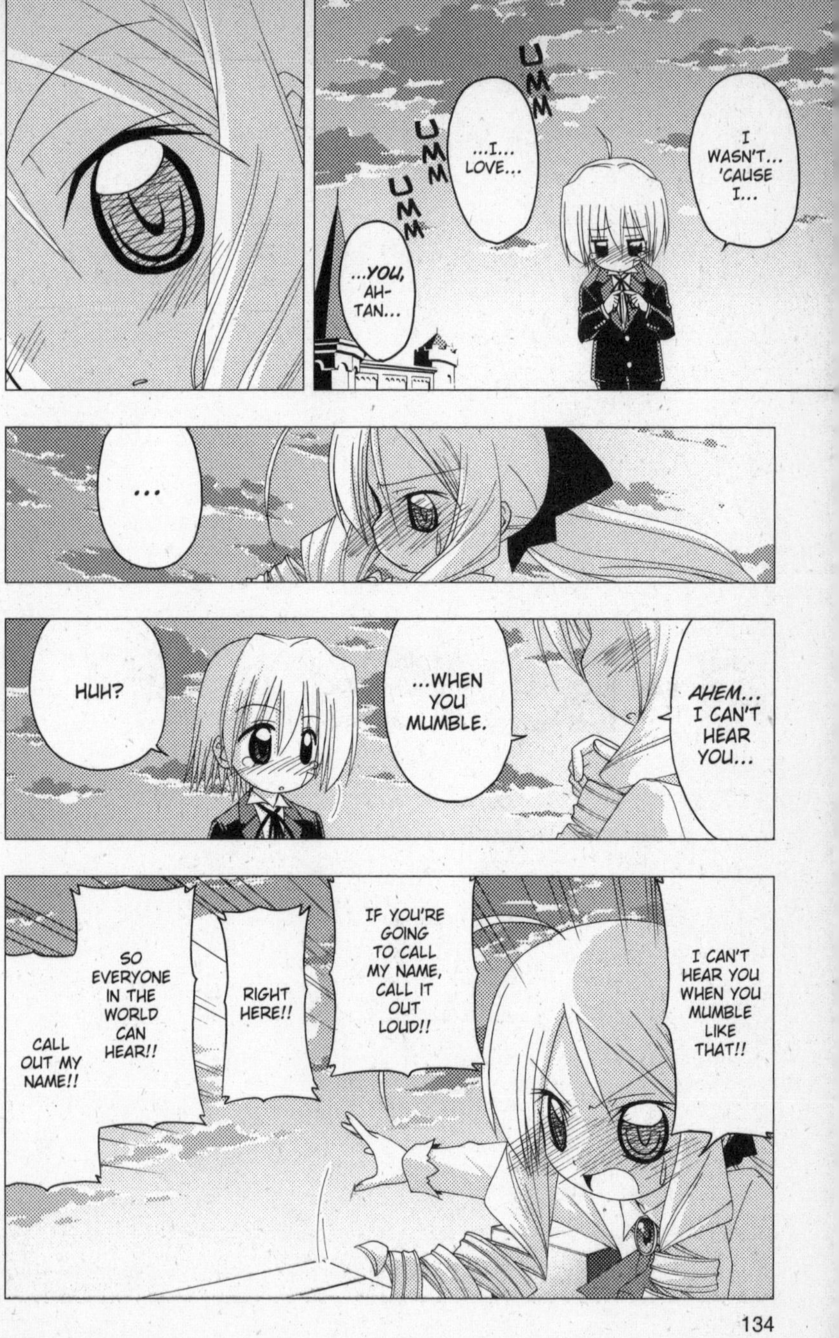
I WASN'T... 'CAUSE I...
UMM
...I... LOVE...
UMM
UMM
...YOU, AH-TAN...
...
AHEM... I CAN'T HEAR YOU...
...WHEN YOU MUMBLE.
HUH?
I CAN'T HEAR YOU WHEN YOU MUMBLE LIKE THAT!!
IF YOU'RE GOING TO CALL MY NAME, CALL IT OUT LOUD!!
RIGHT HERE!!
SO EVERYONE IN THE WORLD CAN HEAR!!
CALL OUT MY NAME!!

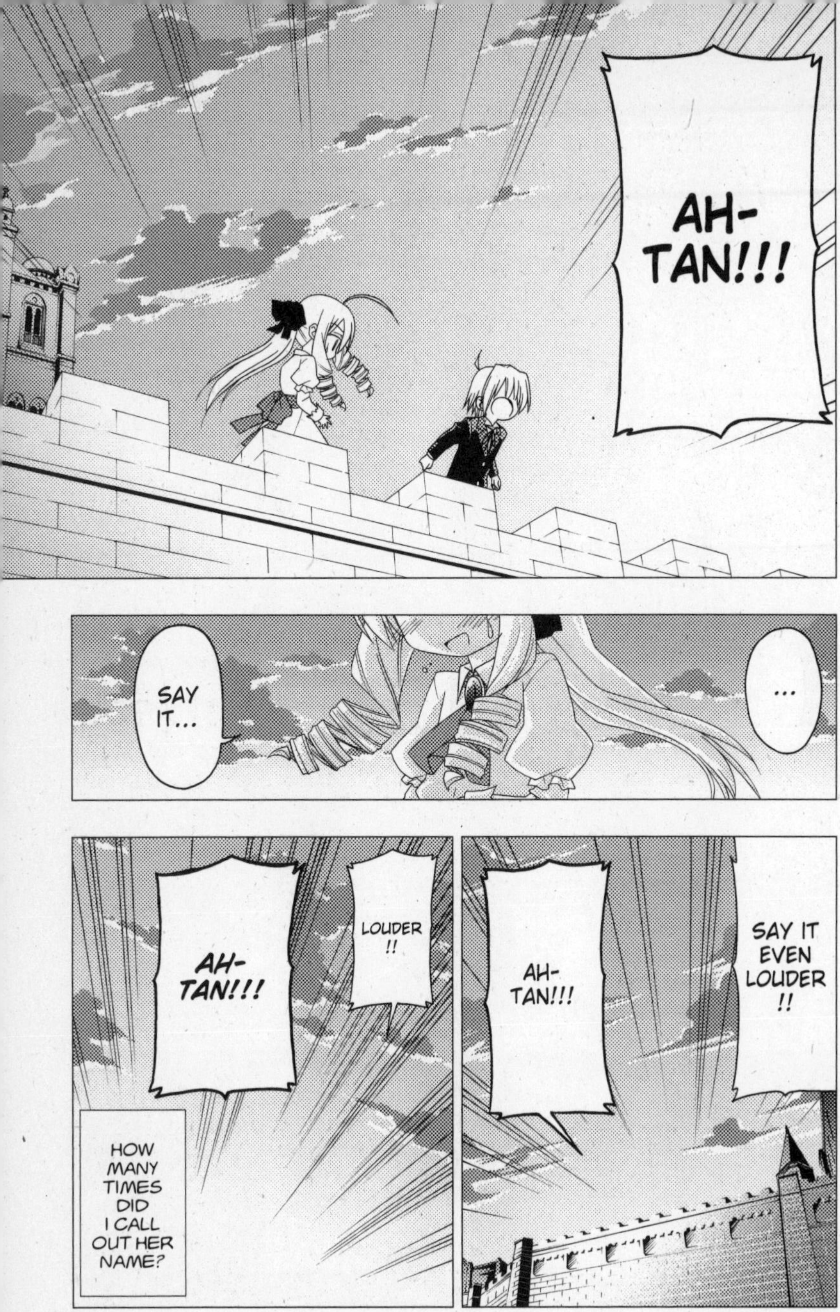
AH-TAN!!!
...
SAY IT...
SAY IT EVEN LOUDER !!
AH-TAN!!!
LOUDER !!
AH-TAN!!!
HOW MANY TIMES DID I CALL OUT HER NAME?

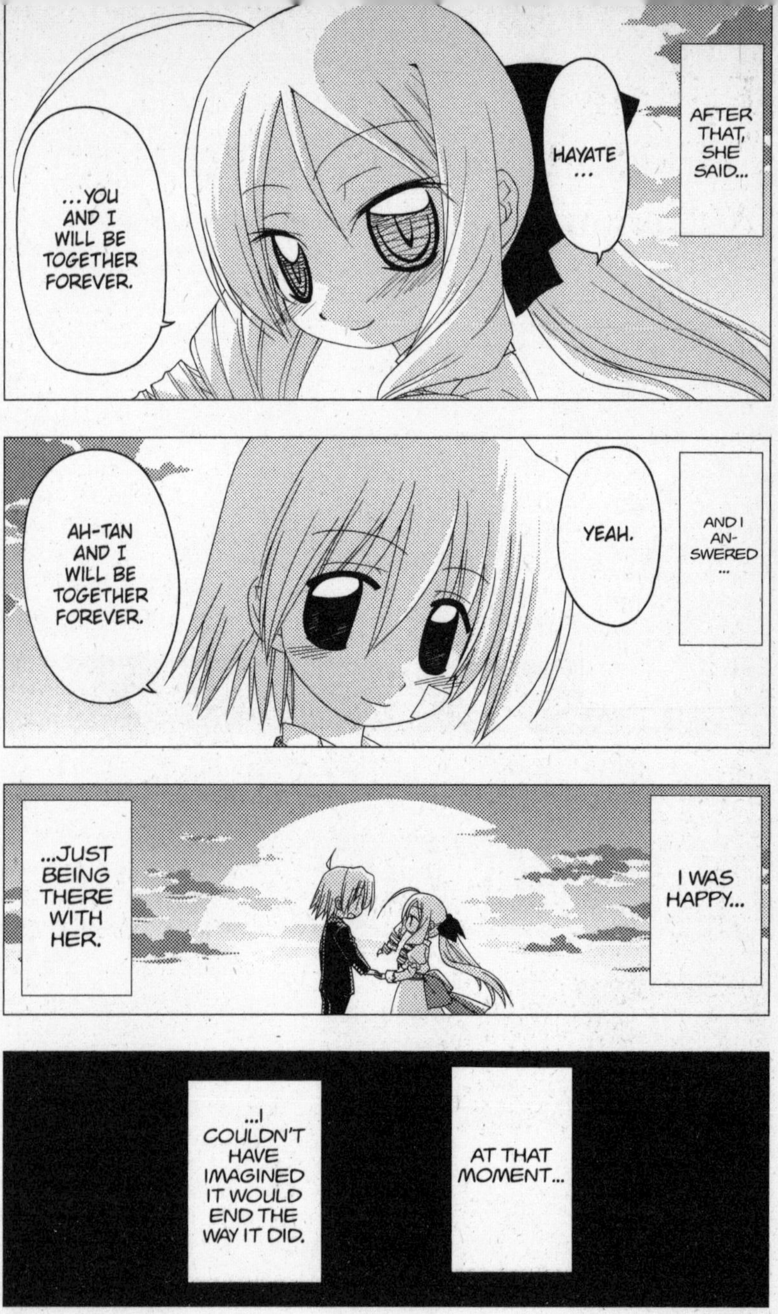
AFTER THAT, SHE SAID...
HAYATE...
...YOU AND I WILL BE TOGETHER FOREVER.
AND I AN-SWERED...
YEAH.
AH-TAN AND I WILL BE TOGETHER FOREVER.
I WAS HAPPY...
...JUST BEING THERE WITH HER.
AT THAT MOMENT...
...I COULDN'T HAVE IMAGINED IT WOULD END THE WAY IT DID.

Episode 9: "THE END OF THE WORLD⑤– A Premonition of the End"

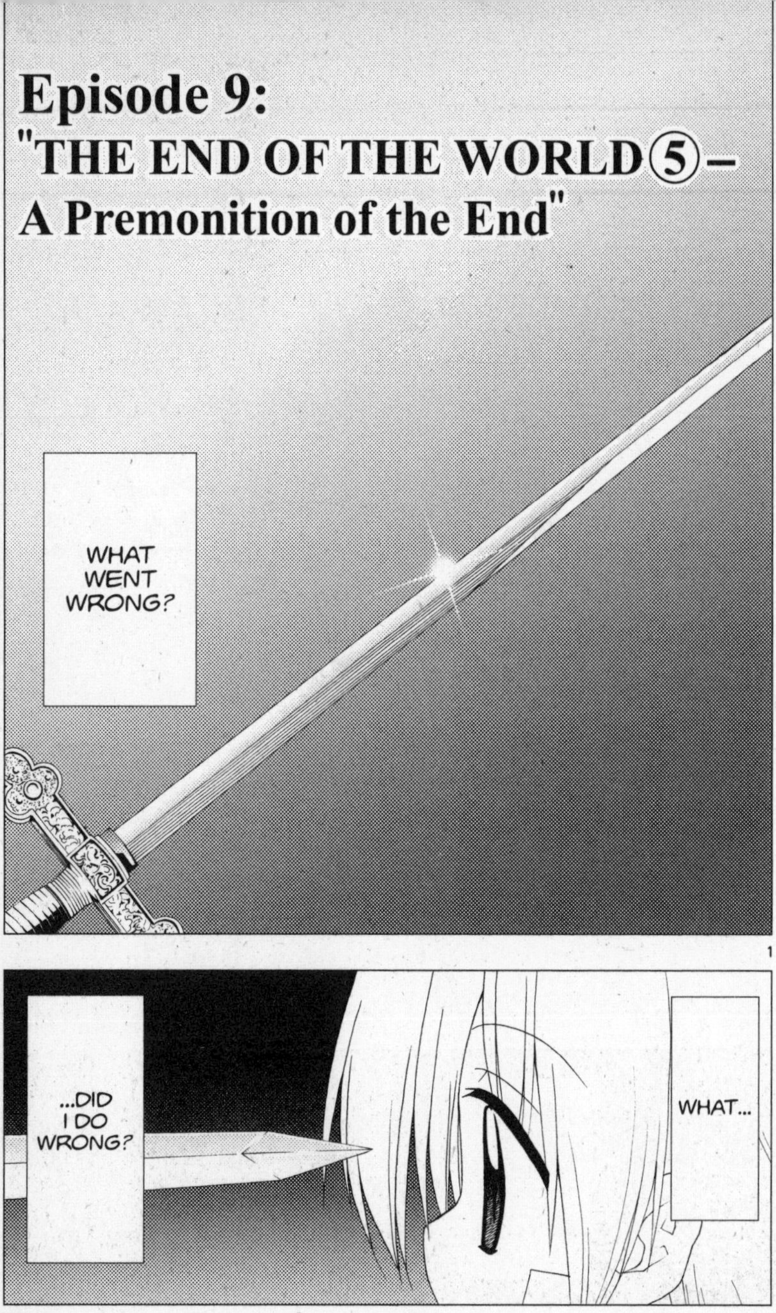
WHAT WENT WRONG?
WHAT...
...DID I DO WRONG?

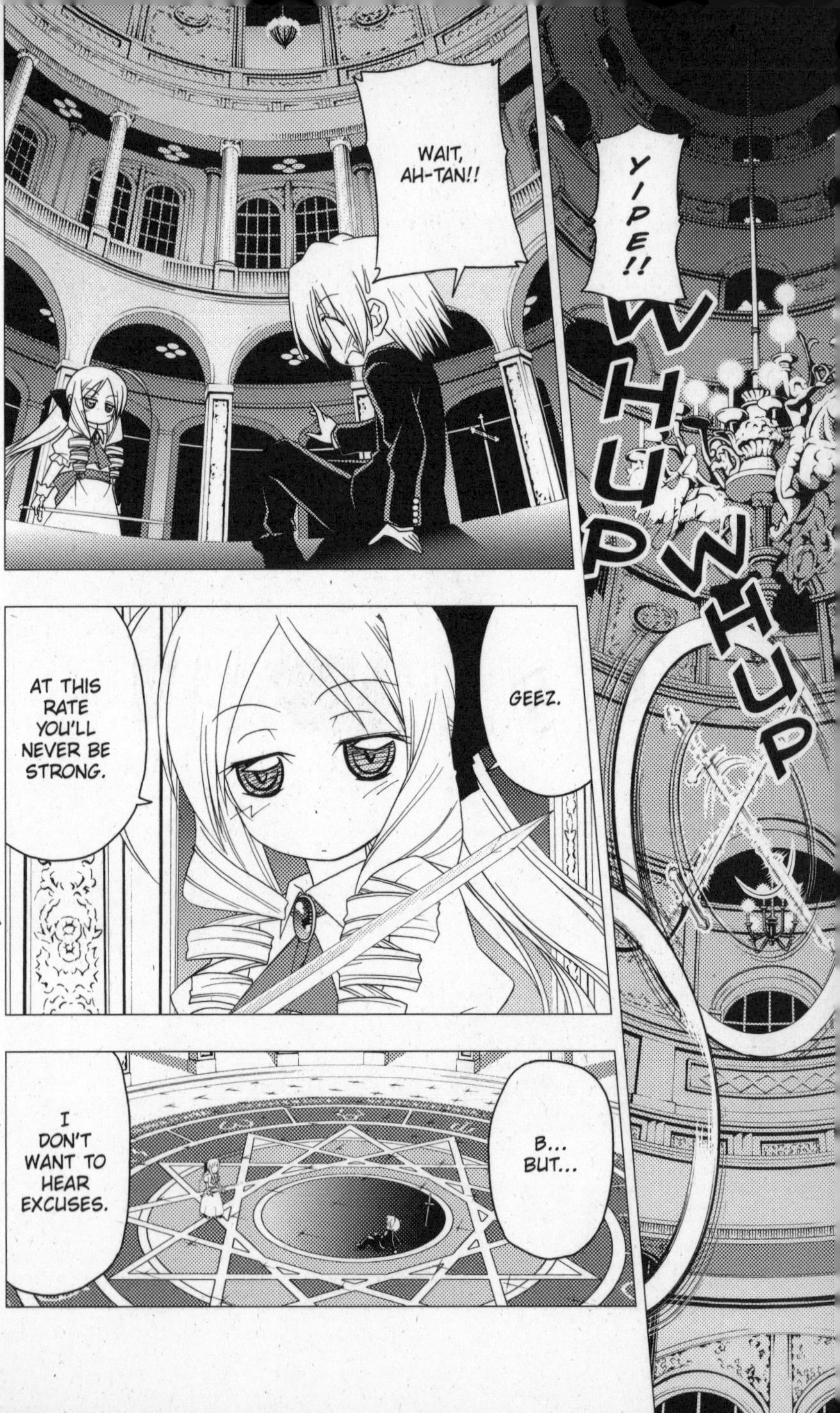
YIPE!!
WHUP WHUP WHUP
WAIT, AH-TAN!!
GEEZ.
AT THIS RATE YOU'LL NEVER BE STRONG.
B... BUT...
I DON'T WANT TO HEAR EXCUSES.

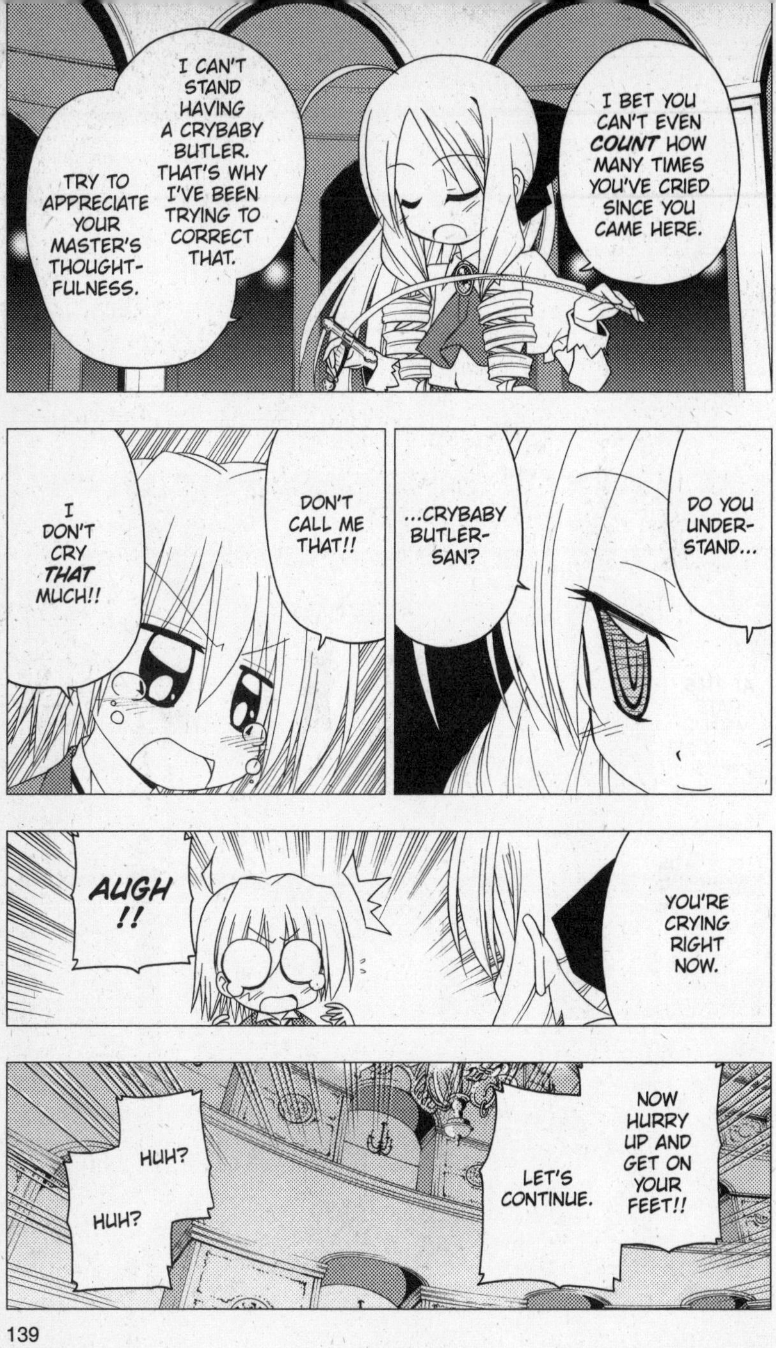
I BET YOU CAN'T EVEN COUNT HOW MANY TIMES YOU'VE CRIED SINCE YOU CAME HERE.
I CAN'T STAND HAVING A CRYBABY BUTLER. THAT'S WHY I'VE BEEN TRYING TO CORRECT THAT.
TRY TO APPRECIATE YOUR MASTER'S THOUGHTFULNESS.
DO YOU UNDERSTAND...
...CRYBABY BUTLER-SAN?
DON'T CALL ME THAT!!
I DON'T CRY THAT MUCH!!
YOU'RE CRYING RIGHT NOW.
AUGH!!
NOW HURRY UP AND GET ON YOUR FEET!!
LET'S CONTINUE.
HUH?
HUH?

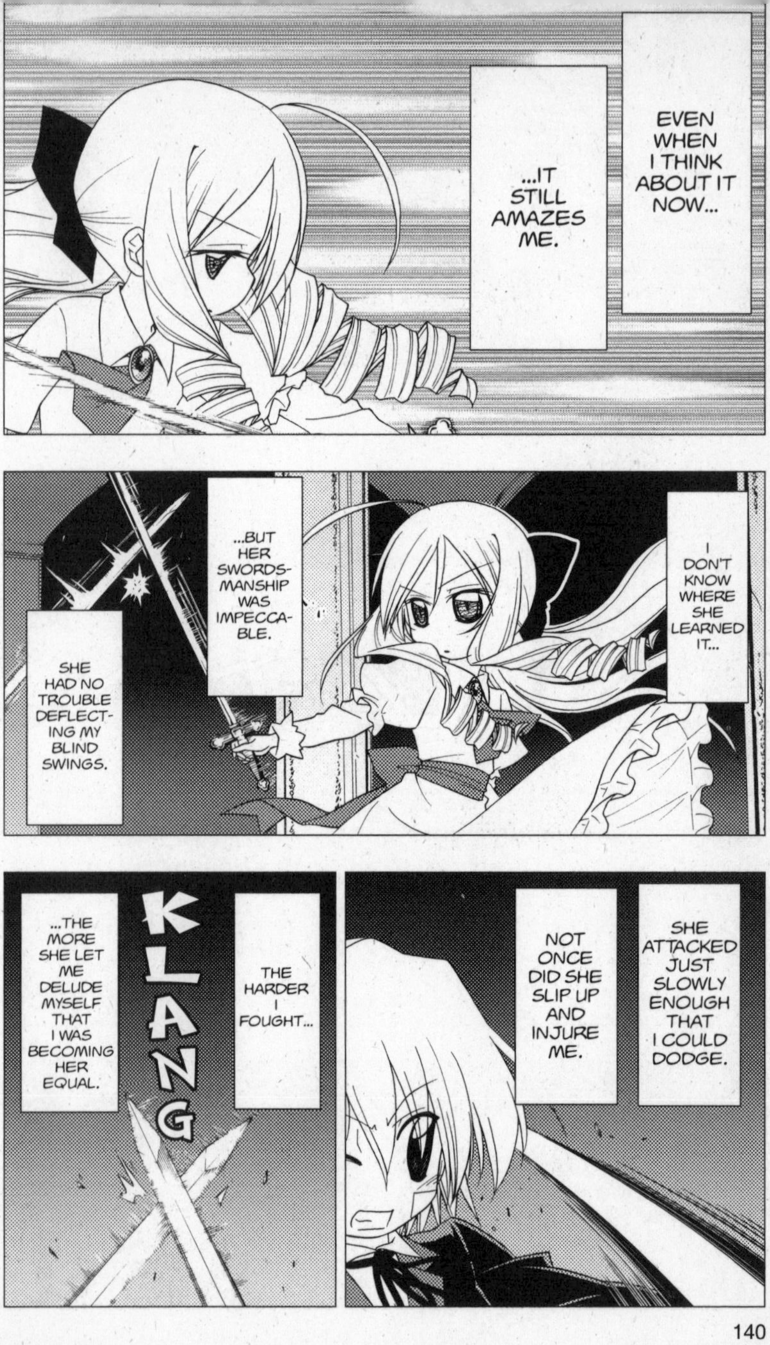
EVEN WHEN I THINK ABOUT IT NOW...
...IT STILL AMAZES ME.
I DON'T KNOW WHERE SHE LEARNED IT...
...BUT HER SWORDS-MANSHIP WAS IMPECCA-BLE.
SHE HAD NO TROUBLE DEFLECT-ING MY BLIND SWINGS.
SHE ATTACKED JUST SLOWLY ENOUGH THAT I COULD DODGE.
NOT ONCE DID SHE SLIP UP AND INJURE ME.
THE HARDER I FOUGHT...
KLANG
...THE MORE SHE LET ME DELUDE MYSELF THAT I WAS BECOMING HER EQUAL.

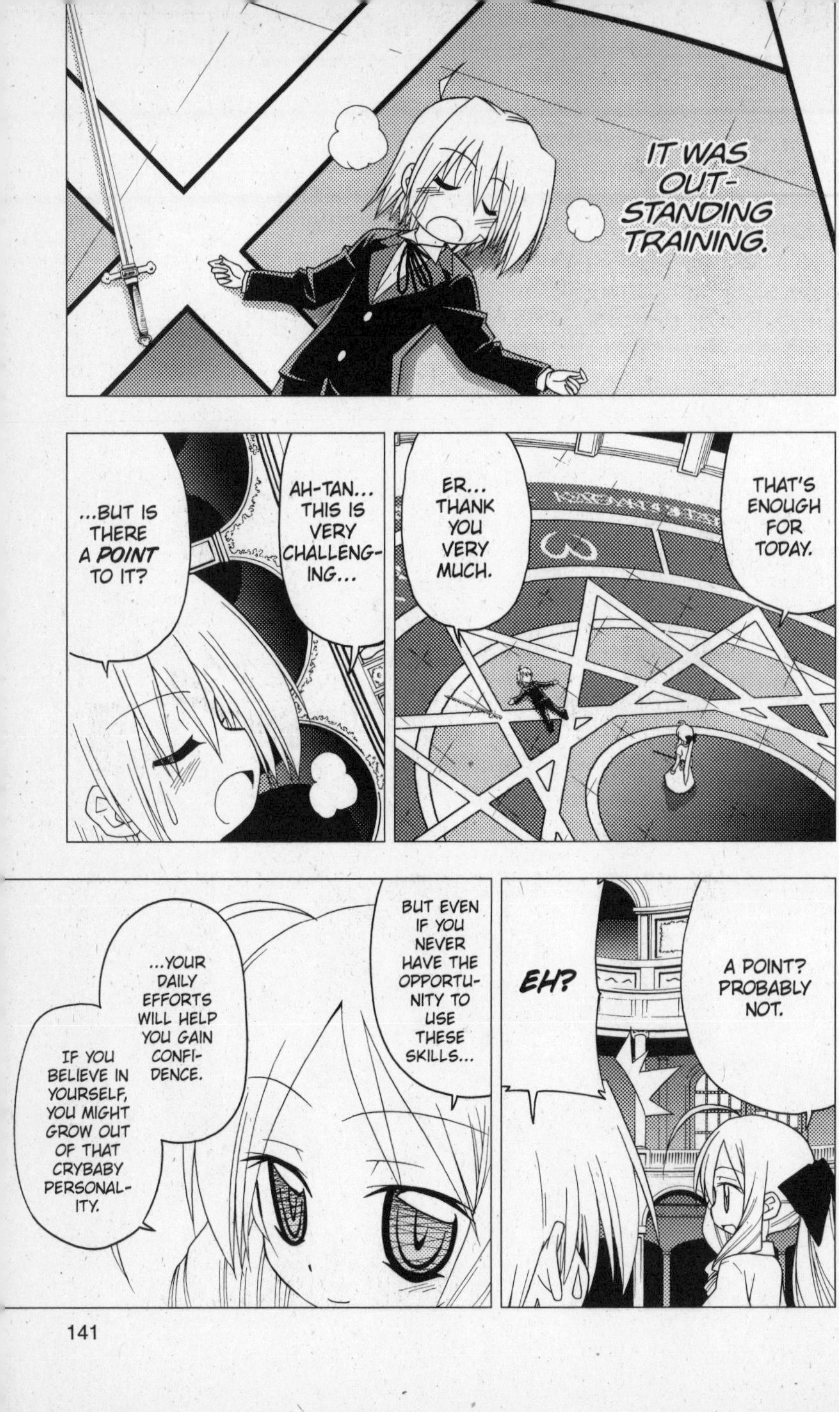
IT WAS OUT-STANDING TRAINING.
THAT'S ENOUGH FOR TODAY.
ER... THANK YOU VERY MUCH.
AH-TAN... THIS IS VERY CHALLENG-ING...
...BUT IS THERE A POINT TO IT?
A POINT? PROBABLY NOT.
EH?
BUT EVEN IF YOU NEVER HAVE THE OPPORTU-NITY TO USE THESE SKILLS...
...YOUR DAILY EFFORTS WILL HELP YOU GAIN CONFI-DENCE.
IF YOU BELIEVE IN YOURSELF, YOU MIGHT GROW OUT OF THAT CRYBABY PERSONAL-ITY.

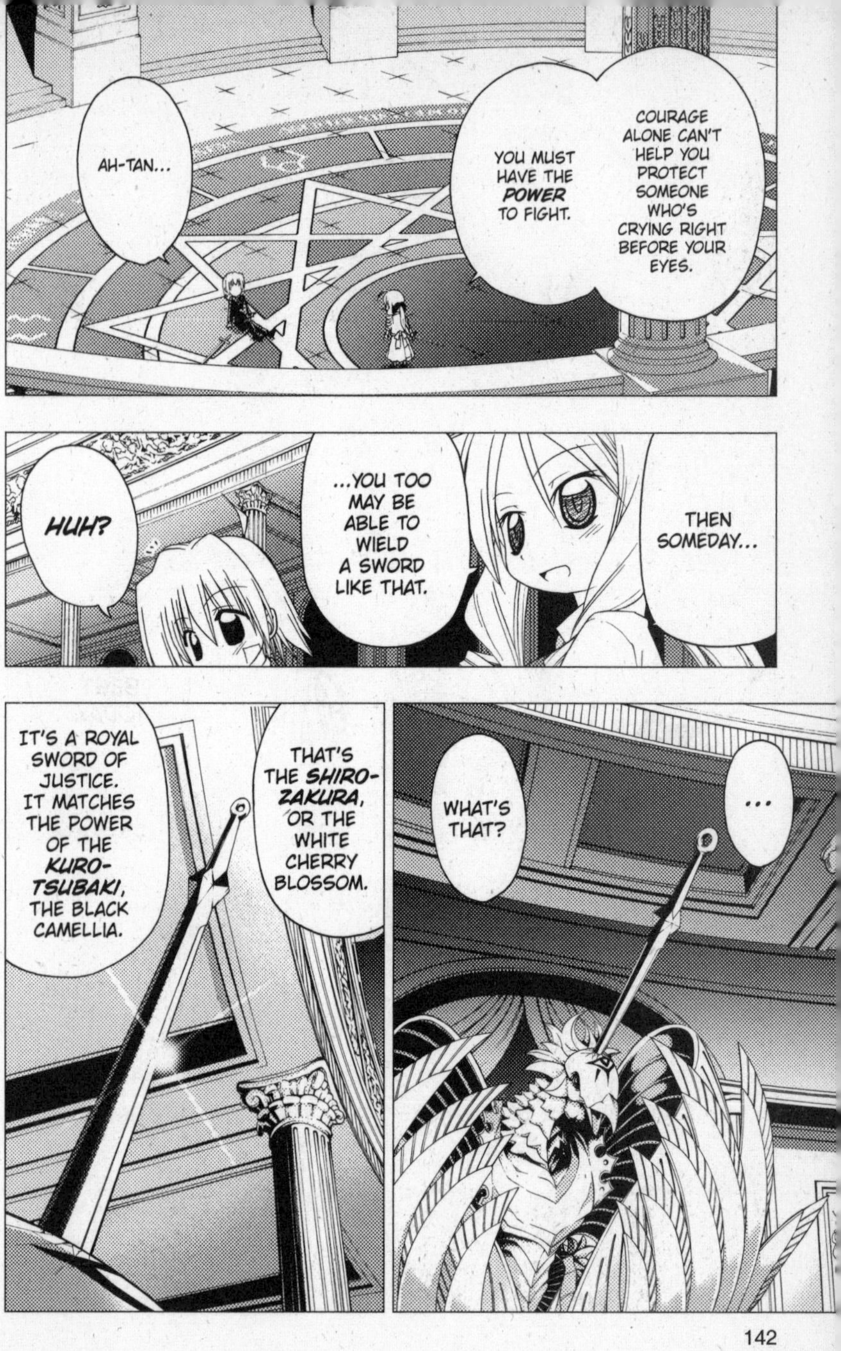
COURAGE ALONE CAN'T HELP YOU PROTECT SOMEONE WHO'S CRYING RIGHT BEFORE YOUR EYES.
YOU MUST HAVE THE POWER TO FIGHT.
AH-TAN...
THEN SOMEDAY...
...YOU TOO MAY BE ABLE TO WIELD A SWORD LIKE THAT.
HUH?
...
WHAT'S THAT?
THAT'S THE SHIRO-ZAKURA, OR THE WHITE CHERRY BLOSSOM.
IT'S A ROYAL SWORD OF JUSTICE. IT MATCHES THE POWER OF THE KURO-TSUBAKI, THE BLACK CAMELLIA.

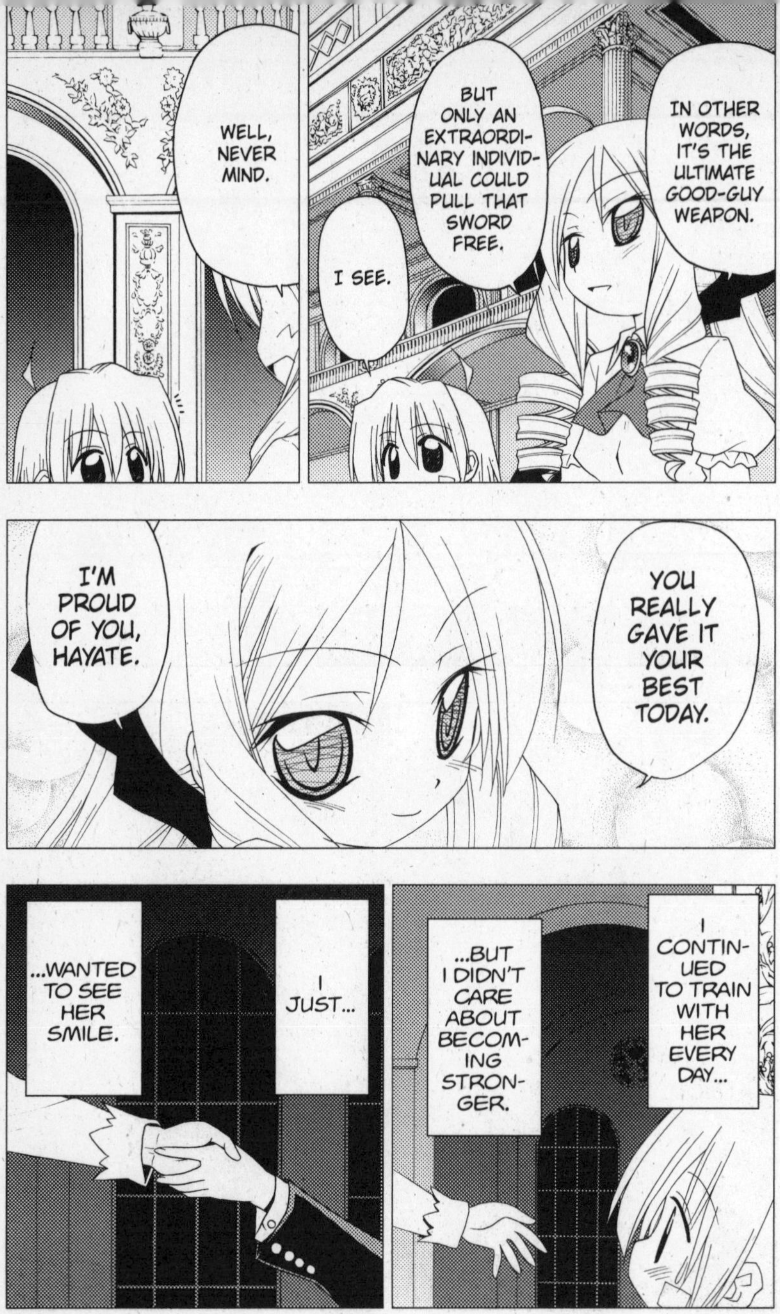
IN OTHER WORDS, IT'S THE ULTIMATE GOOD-GUY WEAPON.
BUT ONLY AN EXTRAORDINARY INDIVIDUAL COULD PULL THAT SWORD FREE.
I SEE.
WELL, NEVER MIND.
YOU REALLY GAVE IT YOUR BEST TODAY.
I'M PROUD OF YOU, HAYATE.
I CONTINUED TO TRAIN WITH HER EVERY DAY...
...BUT I DIDN'T CARE ABOUT BECOMING STRONGER.
I JUST...
...WANTED TO SEE HER SMILE.

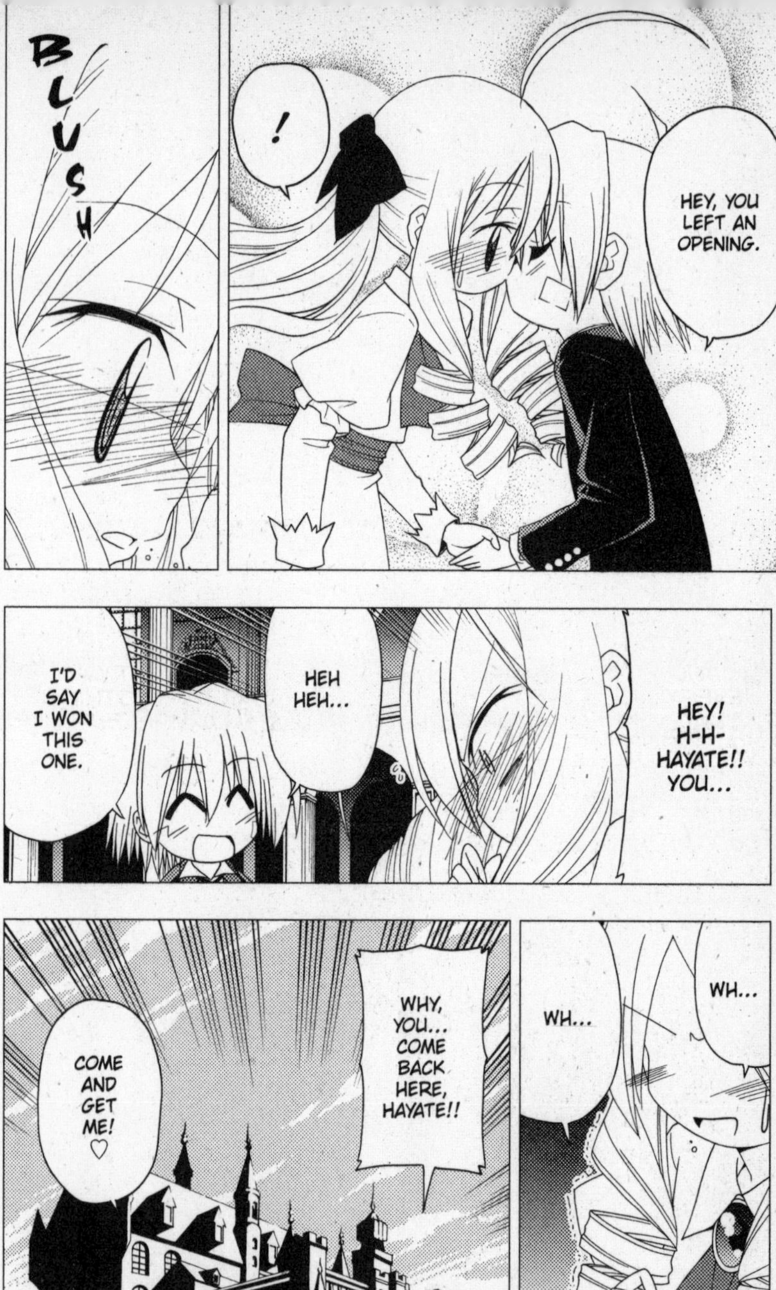
HEY, YOU LEFT AN OPENING.
!
BLUSH
HEY! H-H-HAYATE!! YOU...
HEH HEH...
I'D SAY I WON THIS ONE.
WH...
WH...
WHY, YOU... COME BACK HERE, HAYATE!!
COME AND GET ME! ♡

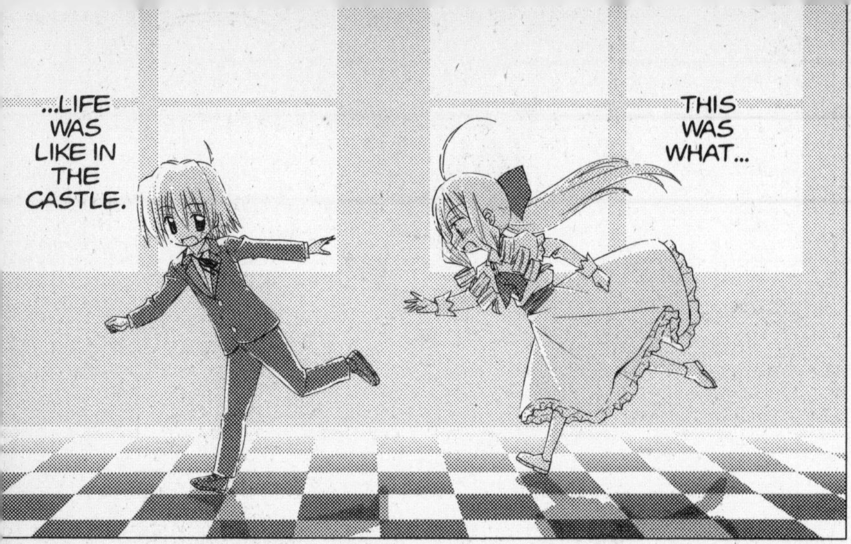
THIS WAS WHAT...
...LIFE WAS LIKE IN THE CASTLE.
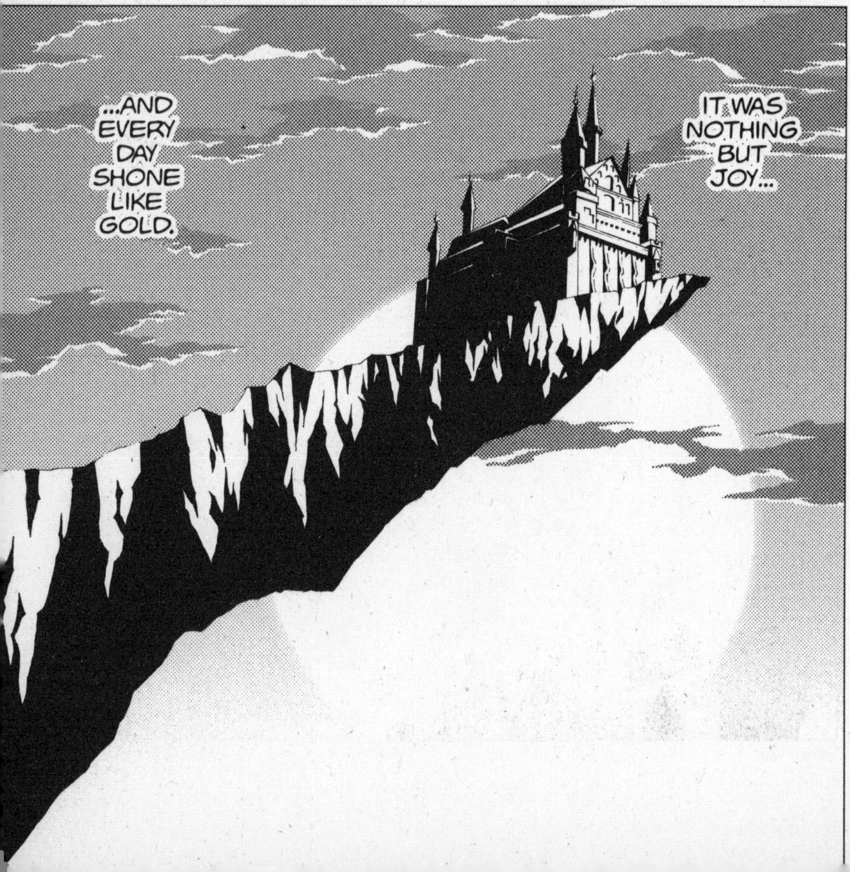
IT WAS NOTHING BUT JOY...
...AND EVERY DAY SHONE LIKE GOLD.

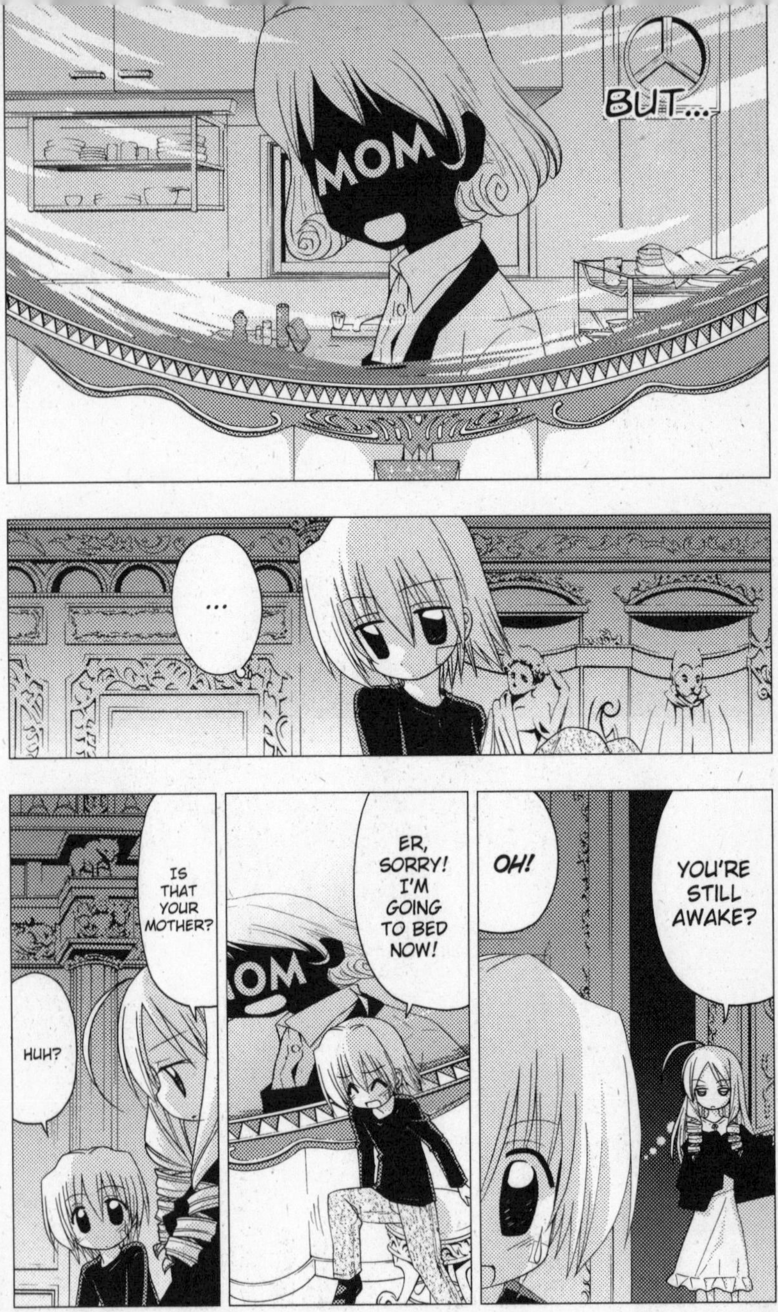
BUT...
MOM
...
YOU'RE STILL AWAKE?
OH!
ER, SORRY! I'M GOING TO BED NOW!
MOM
IS THAT YOUR MOTHER?
HUH?

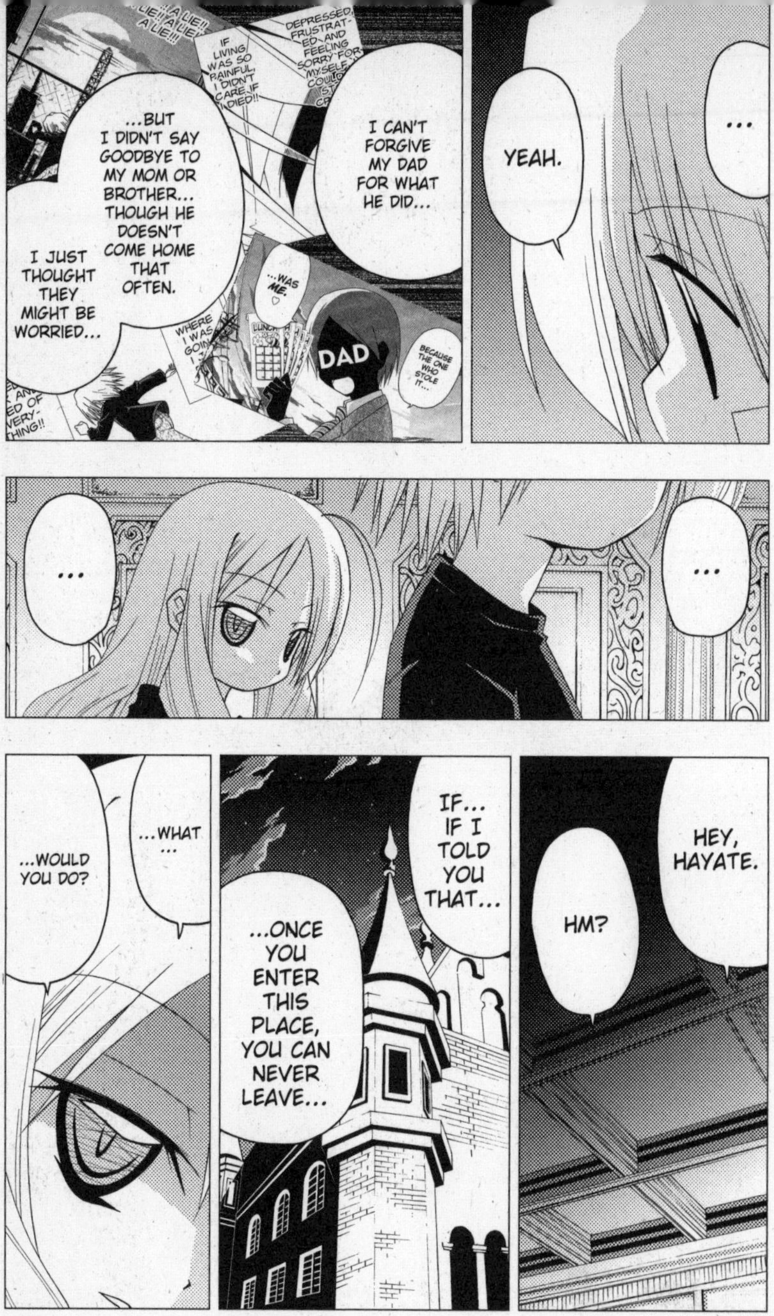
...
YEAH.
DEPRESSED, FRUSTRATED AND FEELING SORRY FOR MYSELF
A LIE!! A LIE!! A LIE!!!
IF LIVING WAS SO PAINFUL, I DIDN'T CARE IF I DIED!!
I CAN'T FORGIVE MY DAD FOR WHAT HE DID...
...WAS ME.
BECAUSE THE ONE WHO STOLE IT...
DAD
LUNCH
...BUT I DIDN'T SAY GOODBYE TO MY MOM OR BROTHER... THOUGH HE DOESN'T COME HOME THAT OFTEN.
I JUST THOUGHT THEY MIGHT BE WORRIED...
...
...
HEY, HAYATE.
HM?
IF... IF I TOLD YOU THAT...
...ONCE YOU ENTER THIS PLACE, YOU CAN NEVER LEAVE...
...WHAT...
...WOULD YOU DO?

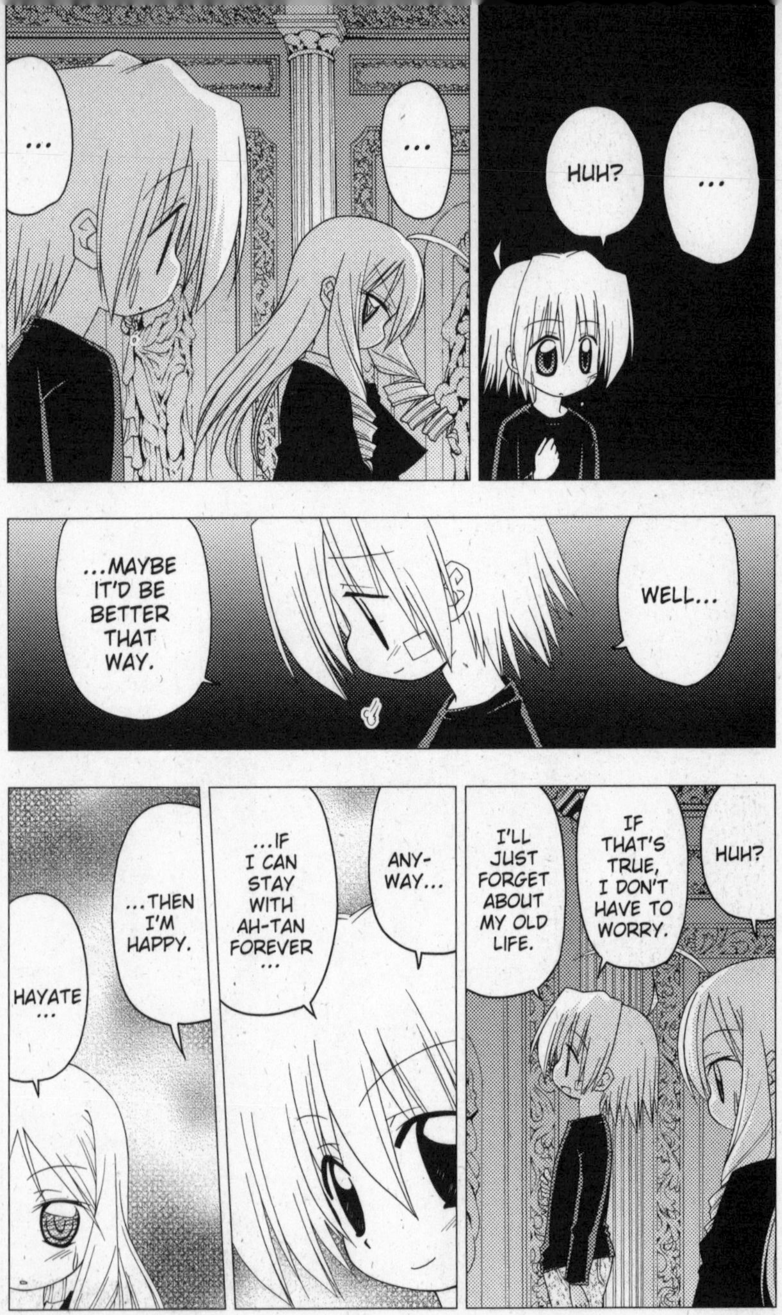
...
HUH?
...
...
WELL...
...MAYBE IT'D BE BETTER THAT WAY.
HUH?
IF THAT'S TRUE, I DON'T HAVE TO WORRY.
I'LL JUST FORGET ABOUT MY OLD LIFE.
ANY-WAY...
...IF I CAN STAY WITH AH-TAN FOREVER...
...THEN I'M HAPPY.
HAYATE...

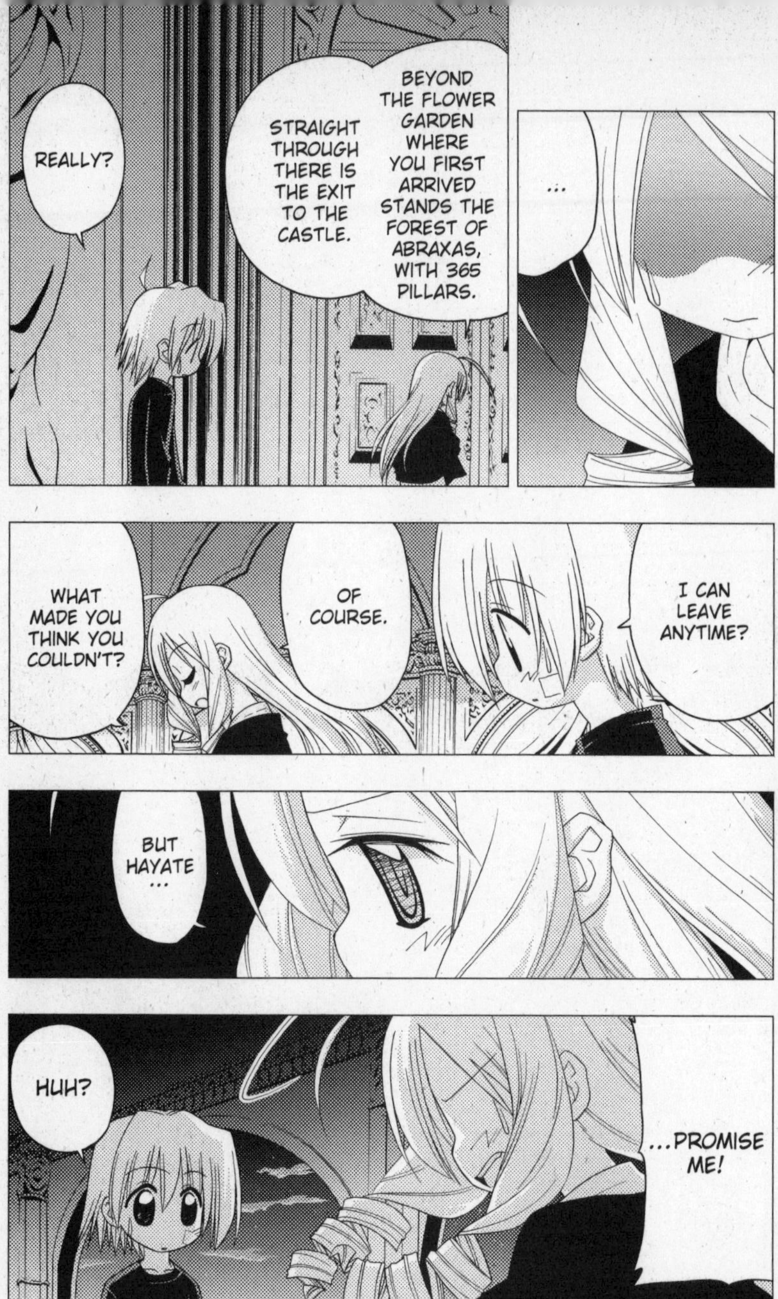
...
BEYOND THE FLOWER GARDEN WHERE YOU FIRST ARRIVED STANDS THE FOREST OF ABRAXAS, WITH 365 PILLARS.
STRAIGHT THROUGH THERE IS THE EXIT TO THE CASTLE.
REALLY?
I CAN LEAVE ANYTIME?
OF COURSE.
WHAT MADE YOU THINK YOU COULDN'T?
BUT HAYATE ...
...PROMISE ME!
HUH?

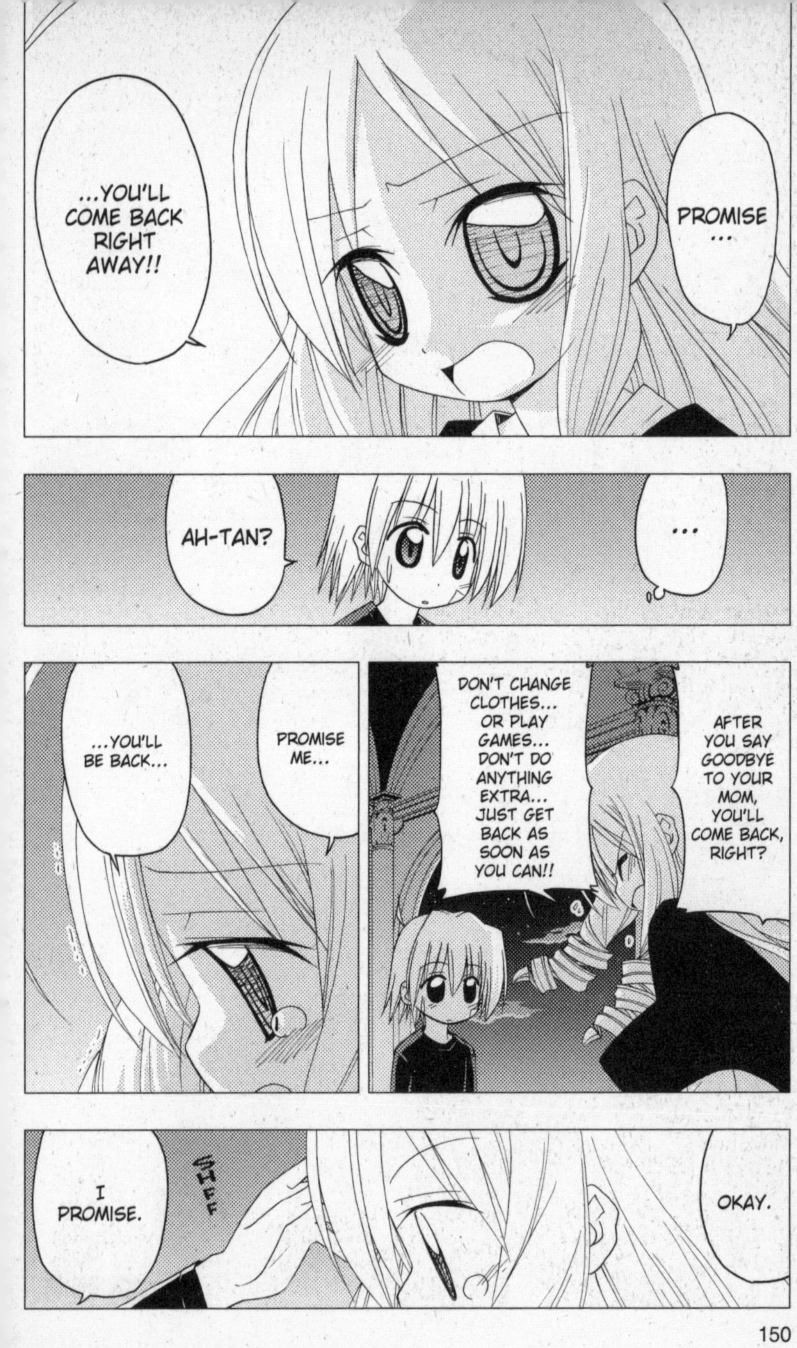
PROMISE...
...YOU'LL COME BACK RIGHT AWAY!!
...
AH-TAN?
AFTER YOU SAY GOODBYE TO YOUR MOM, YOU'LL COME BACK, RIGHT?
DON'T CHANGE CLOTHES... OR PLAY GAMES... DON'T DO ANYTHING EXTRA... JUST GET BACK AS SOON AS YOU CAN!!
PROMISE ME...
...YOU'LL BE BACK...
OKAY.
SHFF
I PROMISE.

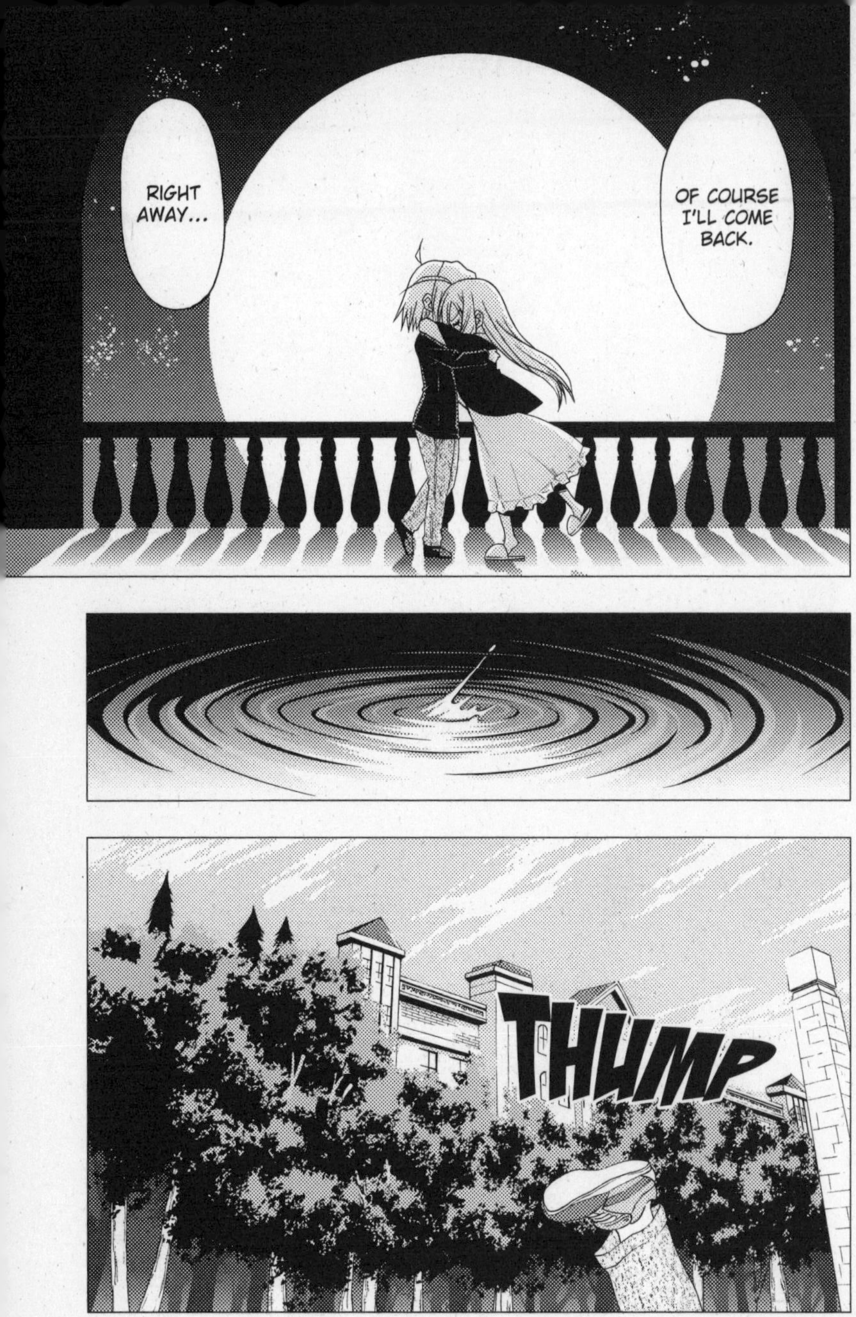
OF COURSE I'LL COME BACK.
RIGHT AWAY...
THUMP

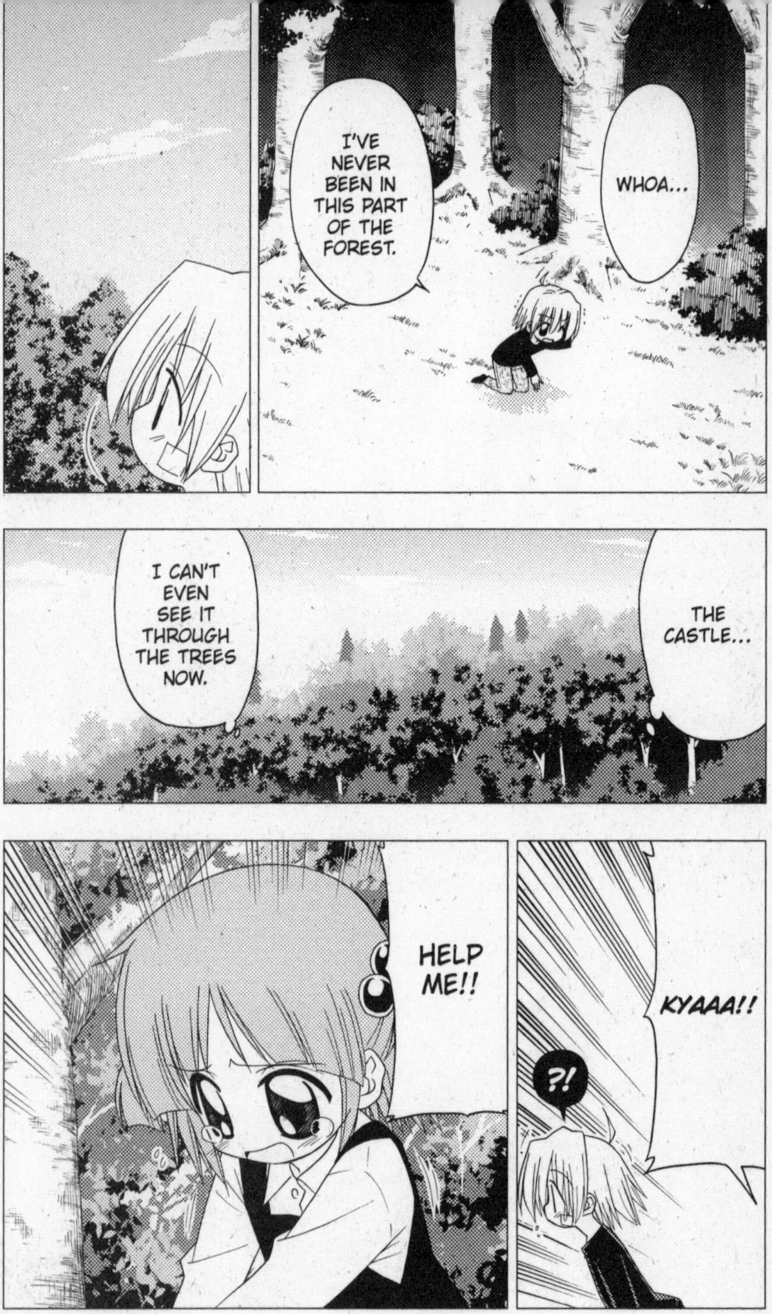
WHOA...
I'VE NEVER BEEN IN THIS PART OF THE FOREST.
THE CASTLE...
I CAN'T EVEN SEE IT THROUGH THE TREES NOW.
KYAAA!!
?!
HELP ME!!

Episode 10: "THE END OF THE WORLD ⑥ – A Will for Power"

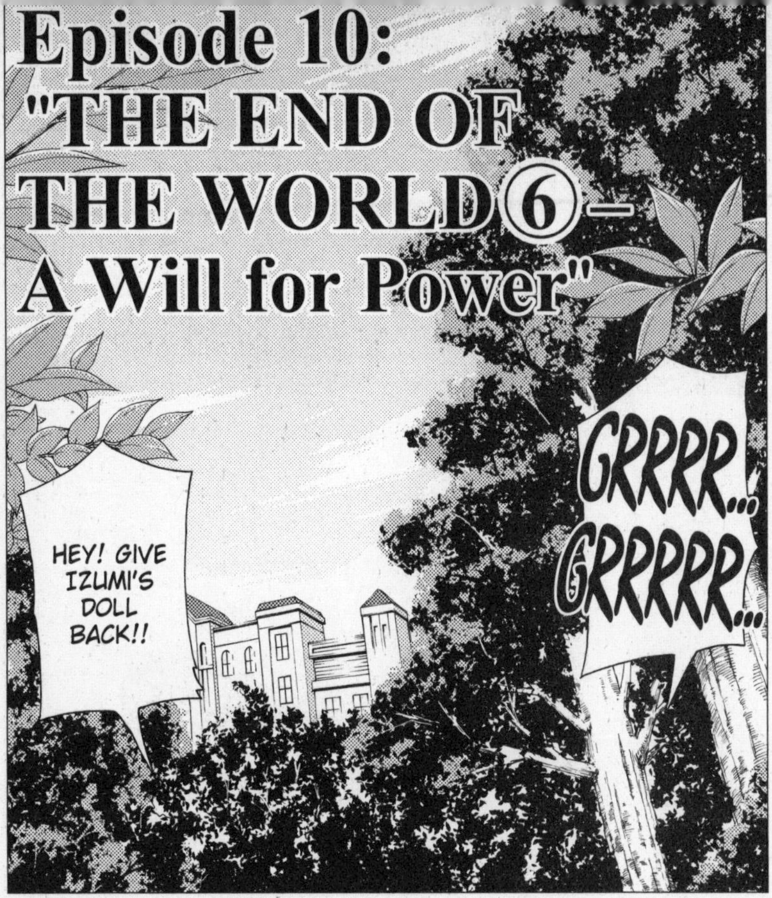
GRRRR... GRRRRR...
HEY! GIVE IZUMI'S DOLL BACK!!

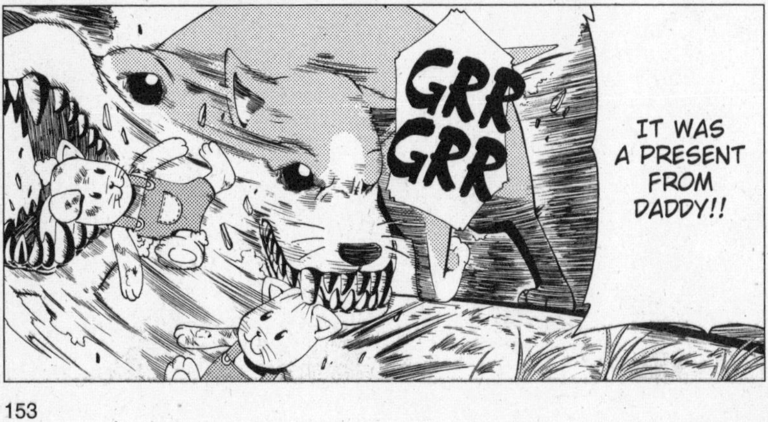
IT WAS A PRESENT FROM DADDY!!
GRR GRR

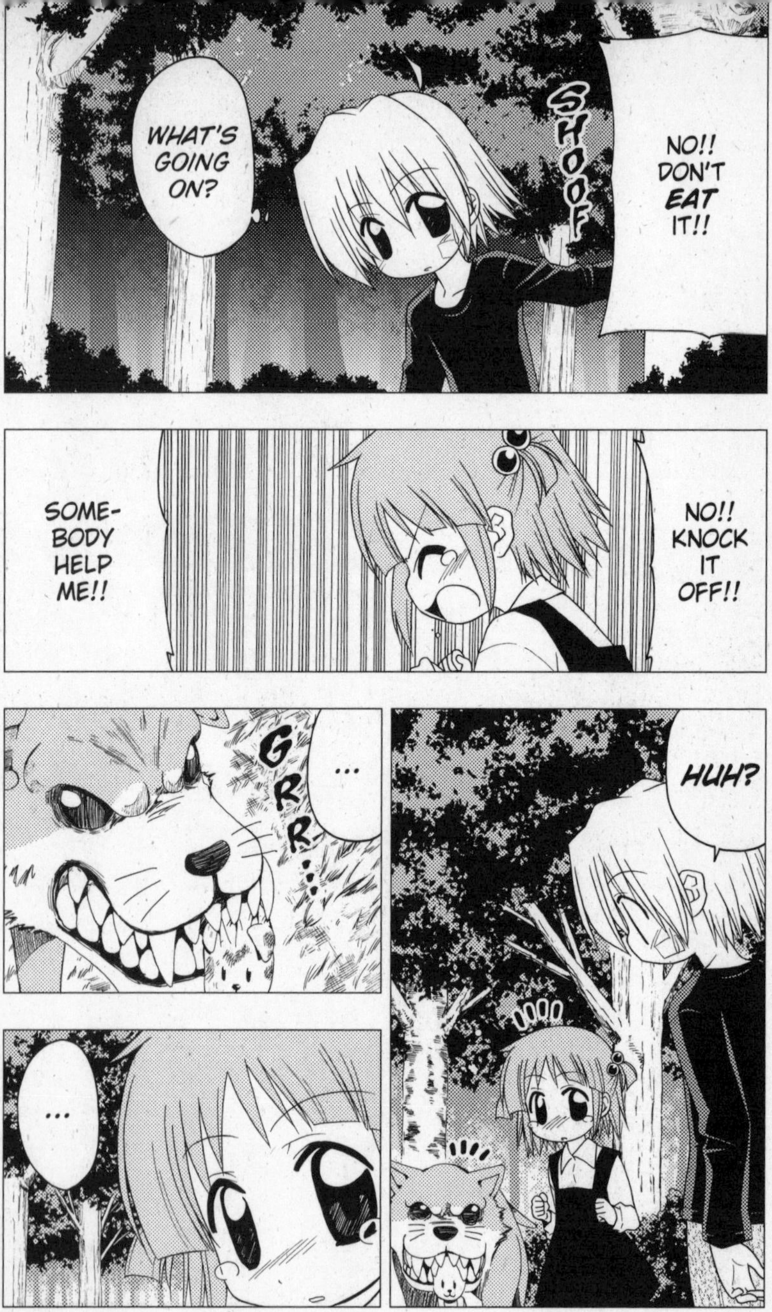

NO!! DON'T EAT IT!!
SHOOF
WHAT'S GOING ON?
NO!! KNOCK IT OFF!!
SOME-BODY HELP ME!!
HUH?
GRR...
...
...

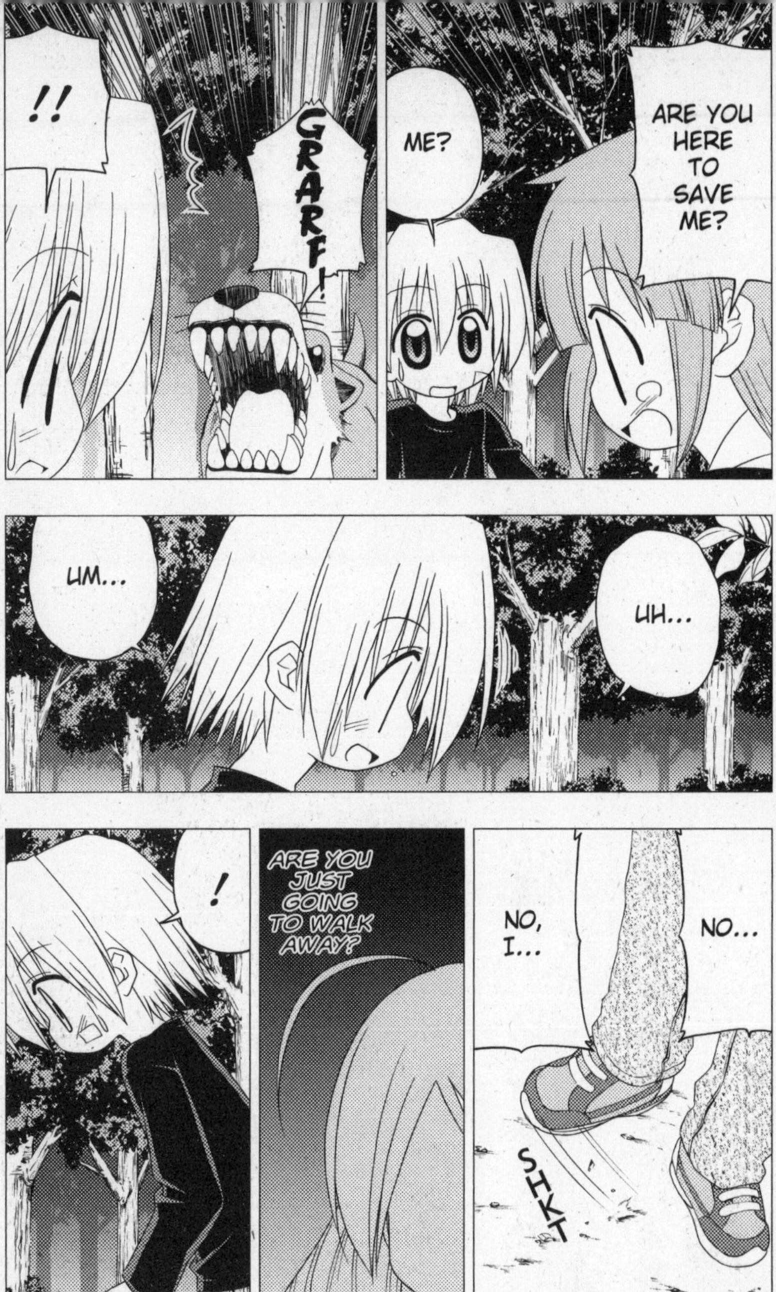
ARE YOU HERE TO SAVE ME?
ME?
GRARF!
!!
UH...
UM...
NO...
NO, I...
SHKT
ARE YOU JUST GOING TO WALK AWAY?
!

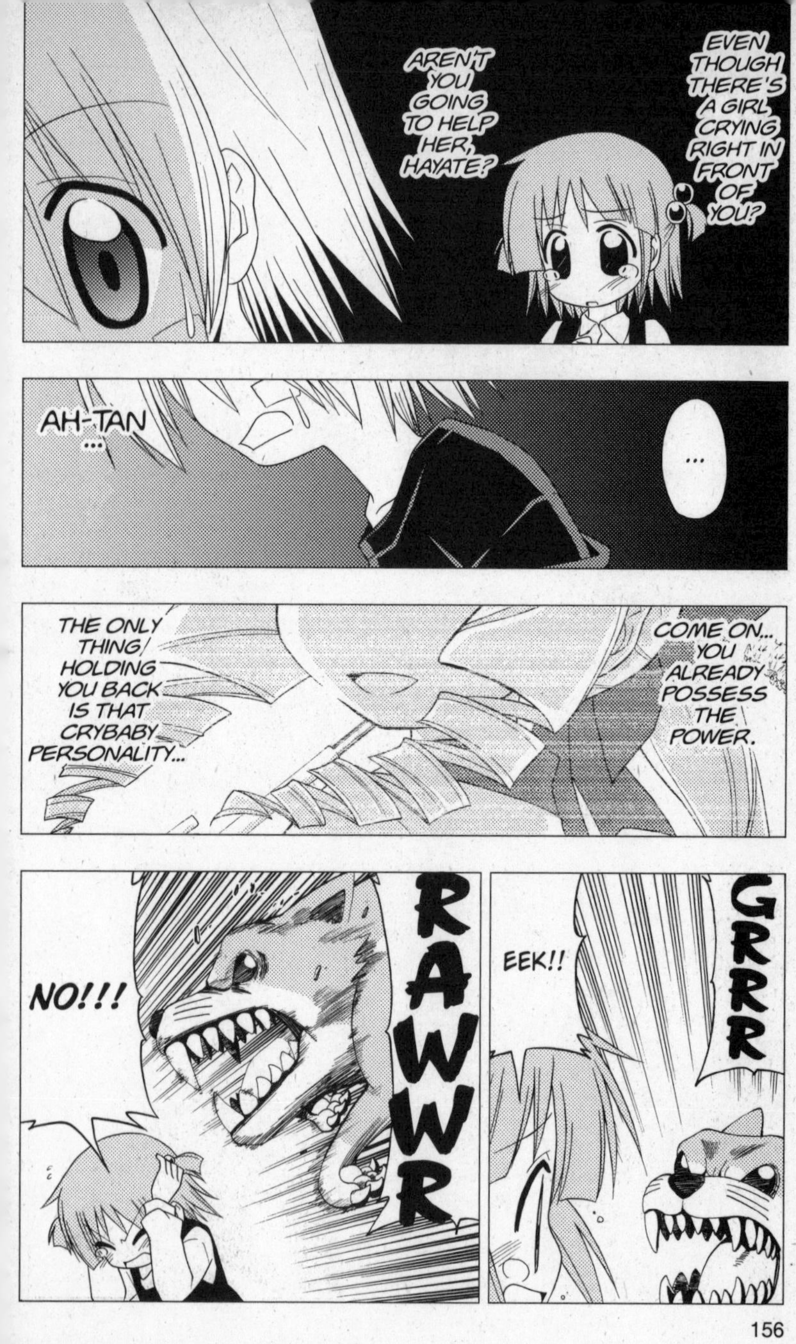
EVEN THOUGH THERE'S A GIRL CRYING RIGHT IN FRONT OF YOU?
AREN'T YOU GOING TO HELP HER, HAYATE?
...
AH-TAN ...
COME ON... YOU ALREADY POSSESS THE POWER.
THE ONLY THING HOLDING YOU BACK IS THAT CRYBABY PERSONALITY...
GRRR
EEK!!
RAWWR
NO!!!

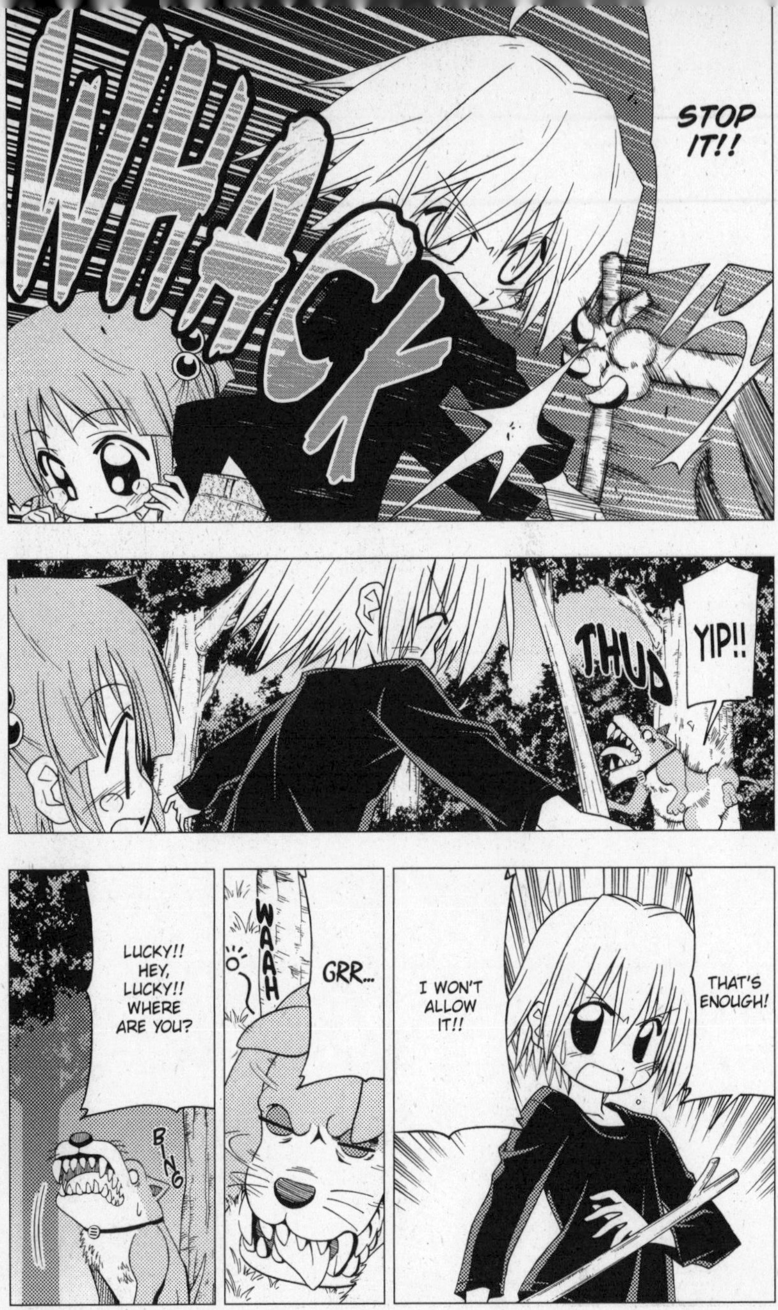
STOP IT!!
WHACK
YIP!!
THUD
THAT'S ENOUGH!
I WON'T ALLOW IT!!
GRR...
WAAH
LUCKY!! HEY, LUCKY!! WHERE ARE YOU?
BING

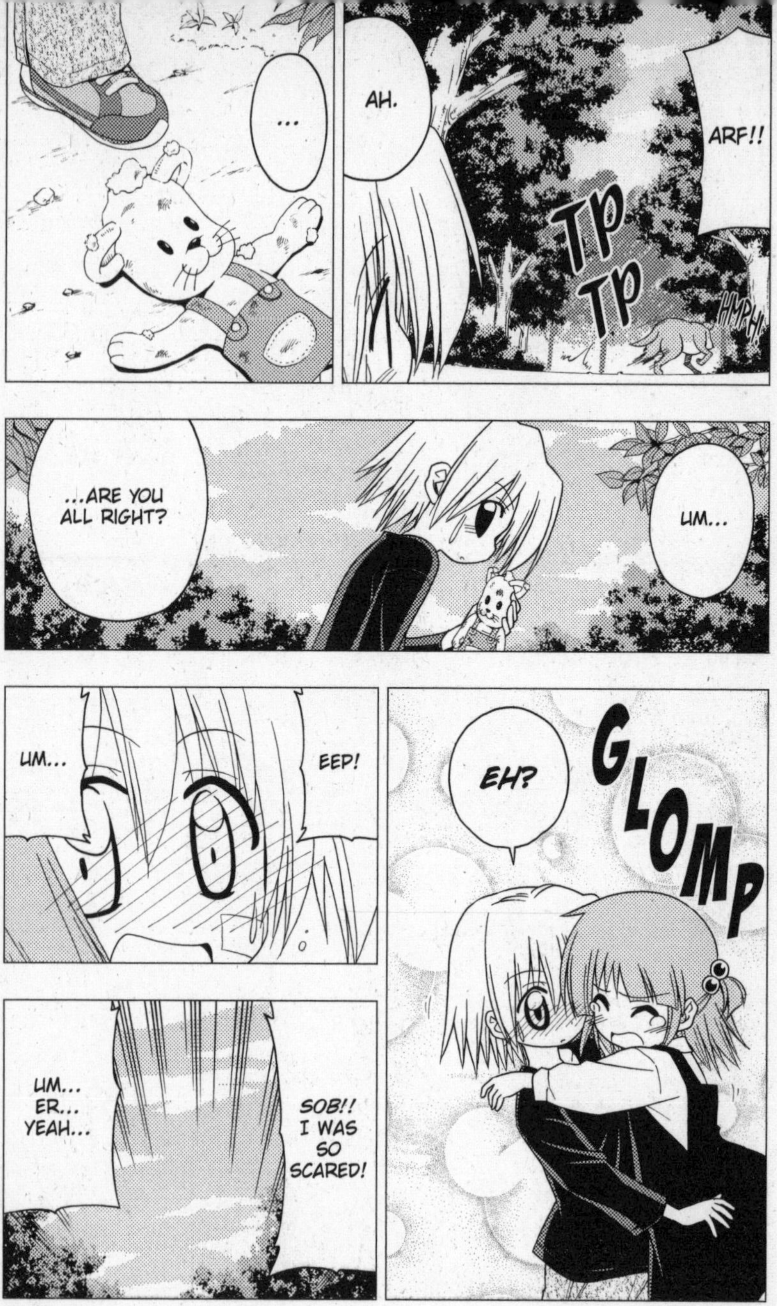
ARF!!
AH.
Tp Tp
HMPH!
...
UM...
...ARE YOU ALL RIGHT?
GLOMP
EH?
EEP!
UM...
SOB!! I WAS SO SCARED!
UM... ER... YEAH...

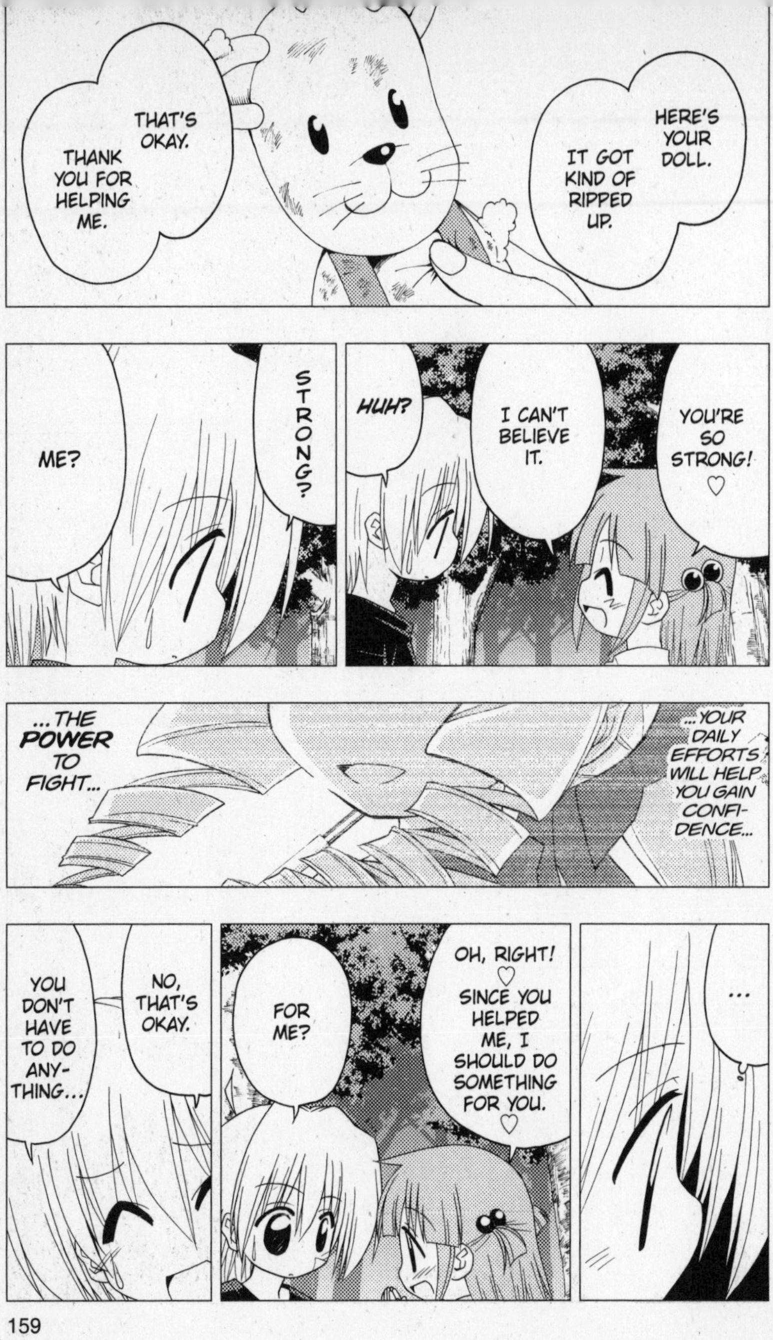
HERE'S YOUR DOLL.
IT GOT KIND OF RIPPED UP.
THAT'S OKAY.
THANK YOU FOR HELPING ME.
YOU'RE SO STRONG! ♡
I CAN'T BELIEVE IT.
HUH?
STRONG?
ME?
...YOUR DAILY EFFORTS WILL HELP YOU GAIN CONFIDENCE...
...THE POWER TO FIGHT...
...
OH, RIGHT! ♡ SINCE YOU HELPED ME, I SHOULD DO SOMETHING FOR YOU. ♡
FOR ME?
NO, THAT'S OKAY.
YOU DON'T HAVE TO DO ANYTHING...

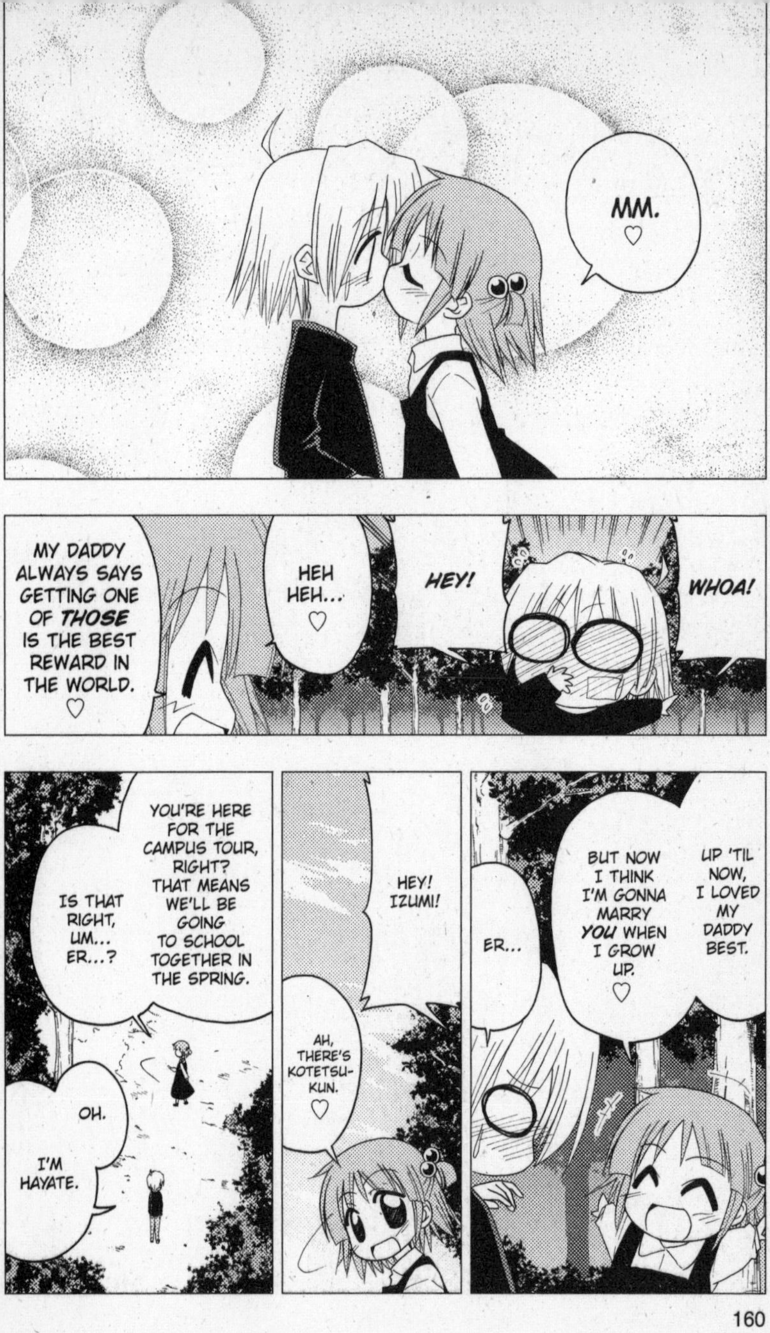
MM. ♡
WHOA!
HEY!
HEH HEH... ♡
MY DADDY ALWAYS SAYS GETTING ONE OF *THOSE* IS THE BEST REWARD IN THE WORLD. ♡
UP 'TIL NOW, I LOVED MY DADDY BEST.
BUT NOW I THINK I'M GONNA MARRY *YOU* WHEN I GROW UP. ♡
ER...
HEY! IZUMI!
AH, THERE'S KOTETSU-KUN. ♡
YOU'RE HERE FOR THE CAMPUS TOUR, RIGHT? THAT MEANS WE'LL BE GOING TO SCHOOL TOGETHER IN THE SPRING.
IS THAT RIGHT, UM... ER...?
OH.
I'M HAYATE.

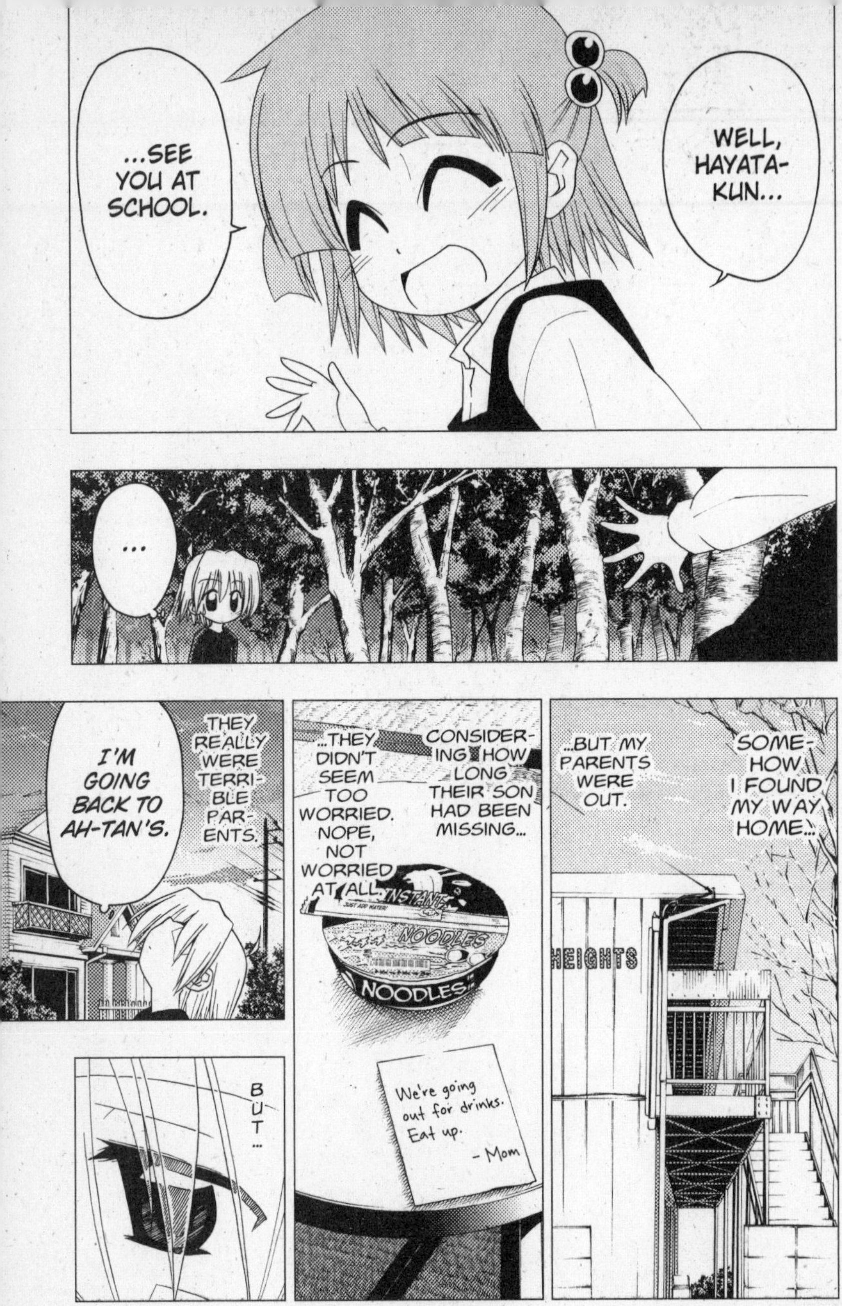
WELL, HAYATA-KUN...
...SEE YOU AT SCHOOL.
...
SOMEHOW I FOUND MY WAY HOME...
...BUT MY PARENTS WERE OUT.
HEIGHTS
CONSIDERING HOW LONG THEIR SON HAD BEEN MISSING...
...THEY DIDN'T SEEM TOO WORRIED. NOPE, NOT WORRIED AT ALL.
INSTANT
JUST ADD WATER!
NOODLES
NOODLES
We're going out for drinks. Eat up. - Mom
THEY REALLY WERE TERRIBLE PARENTS.
I'M GOING BACK TO AH-TAN'S.
BUT...

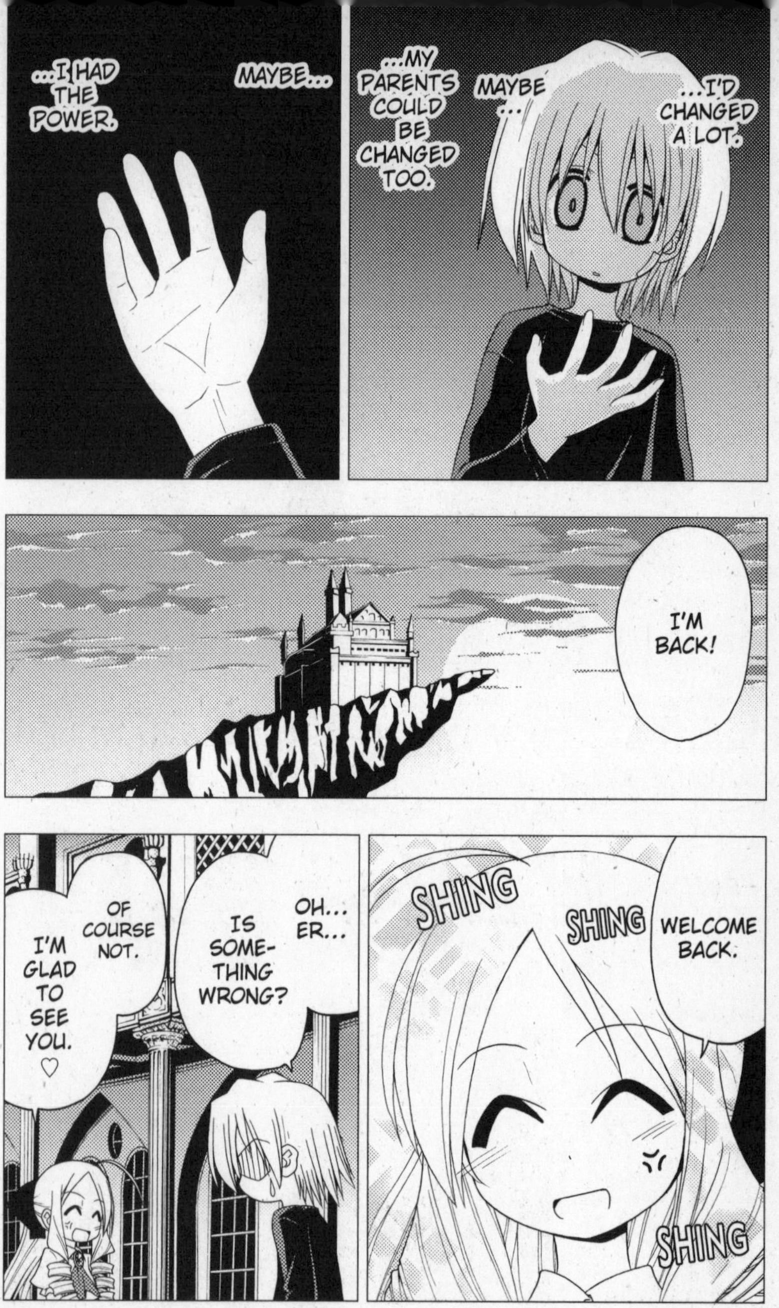
...I'D CHANGED A LOT.
MAYBE...
...MY PARENTS COULD BE CHANGED TOO.
MAYBE...
...I HAD THE POWER.
I'M BACK!
WELCOME BACK.
SHING
SHING
SHING
OH... ER...
IS SOME-THING WRONG?
OF COURSE NOT.
I'M GLAD TO SEE YOU. ♡

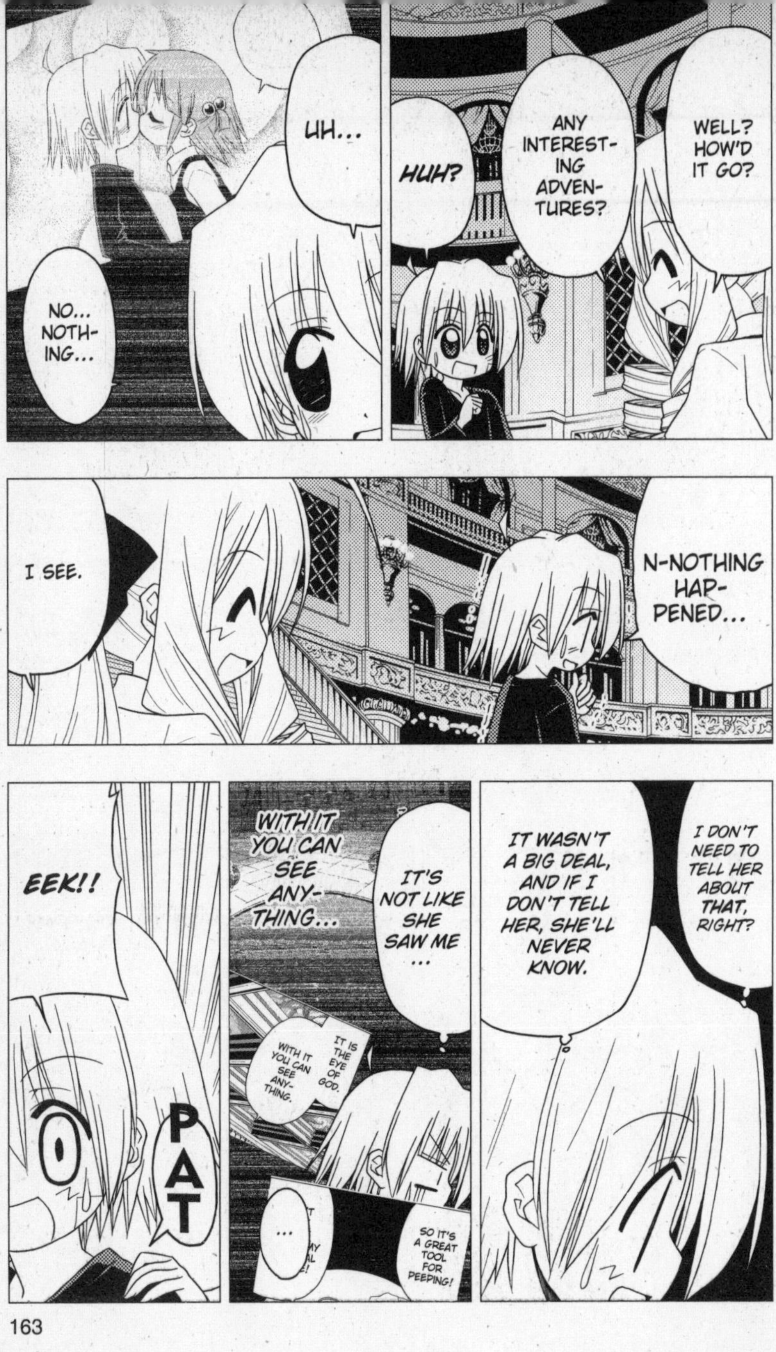
WELL? HOW'D IT GO?
ANY INTEREST-ING ADVEN-TURES?
HUH?
UH...
NO... NOTH-ING...
N-NOTHING HAP-PENED...
I SEE.
I DON'T NEED TO TELL HER ABOUT THAT, RIGHT?
IT WASN'T A BIG DEAL, AND IF I DON'T TELL HER, SHE'LL NEVER KNOW.
IT'S NOT LIKE SHE SAW ME...
WITH IT YOU CAN SEE ANY-THING...
IT IS THE EYE OF GOD.
WITH IT YOU CAN SEE ANY-THING.
...
SO IT'S A GREAT TOOL FOR PEEPING!
EEK!!
PAT

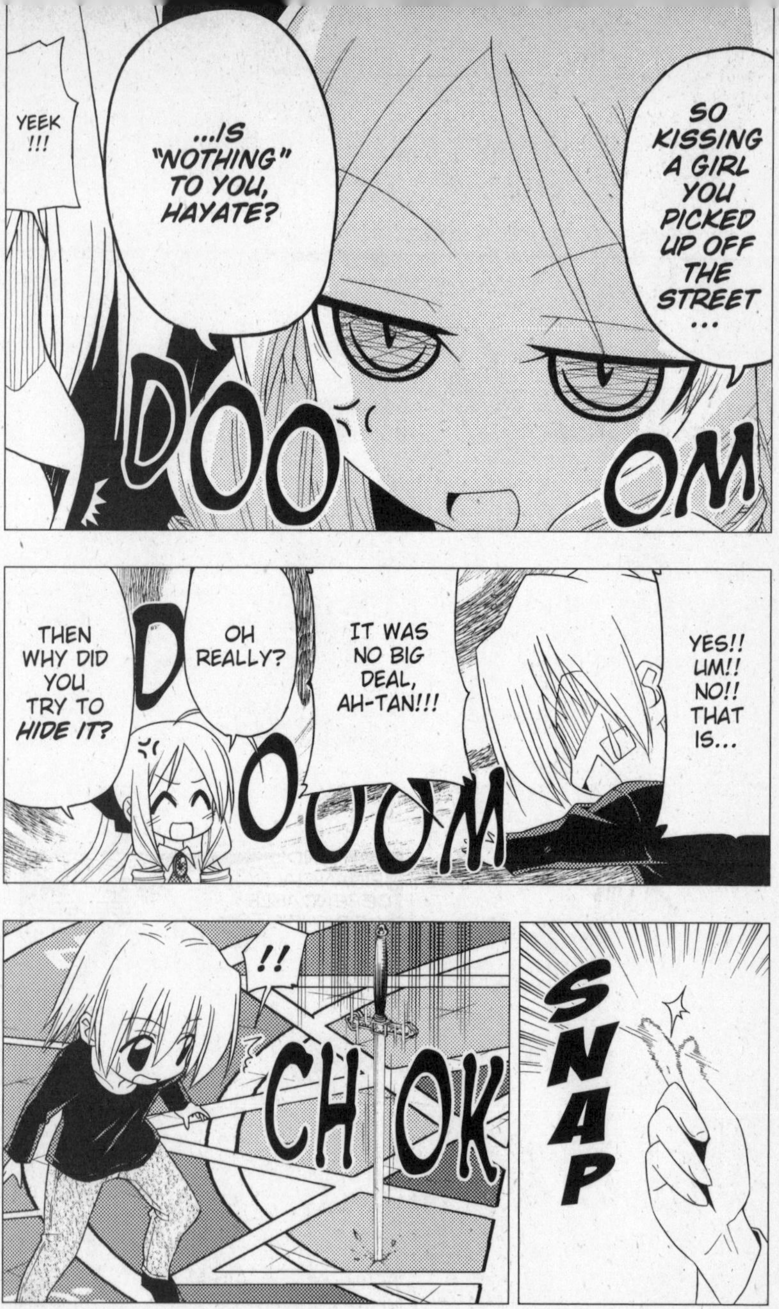

SO KISSING A GIRL YOU PICKED UP OFF THE STREET...
...IS "NOTHING" TO YOU, HAYATE?
YEEK!!!
DOO OM
YES!! UM!! NO!! THAT IS...
IT WAS NO BIG DEAL, AH-TAN!!!
OH REALLY?
THEN WHY DID YOU TRY TO *HIDE IT?*
DOOOM
SNAP
!!
CHOK

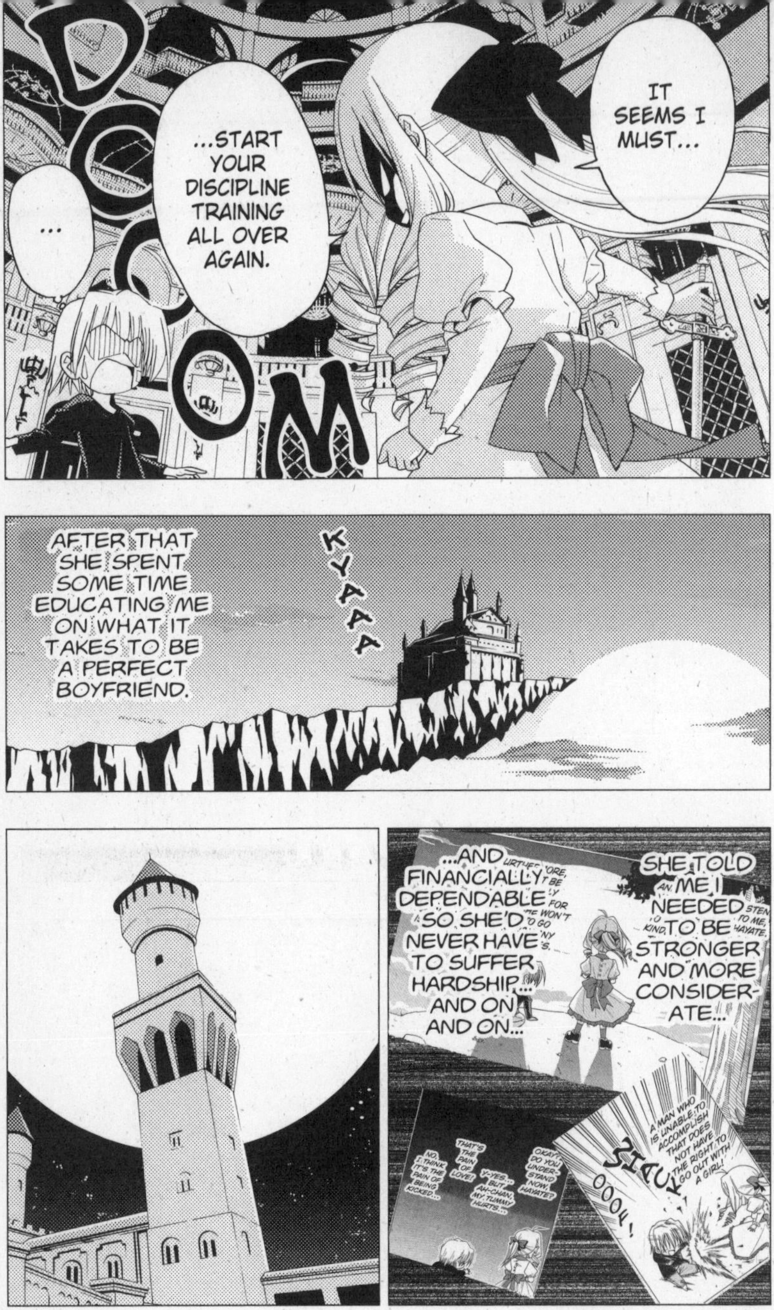
IT SEEMS I MUST...
...START YOUR DISCIPLINE TRAINING ALL OVER AGAIN.
...
DOOOM
AFTER THAT SHE SPENT SOME TIME EDUCATING ME ON WHAT IT TAKES TO BE A PERFECT BOYFRIEND.
KYAAA
SHE TOLD ME I NEEDED TO BE STRONGER AND MORE CONSIDER-ATE...
...AND FINANCIALLY DEPENDABLE SO SHE'D NEVER HAVE TO SUFFER HARDSHIP... AND ON AND ON...
A MAN WHO IS UNABLE TO ACCOMPLISH THAT DOES NOT HAVE THE RIGHT TO GO OUT WITH A GIRL!
OOOF!
OKAY? DO YOU UNDERSTAND NOW, HAYATE?
Y-YES... BUT AH-CHAN, MY TUMMY HURTS...
THAT'S THE PAIN OF LOVE!
NO, I THINK IT'S THE PAIN OF BEING KICKED...

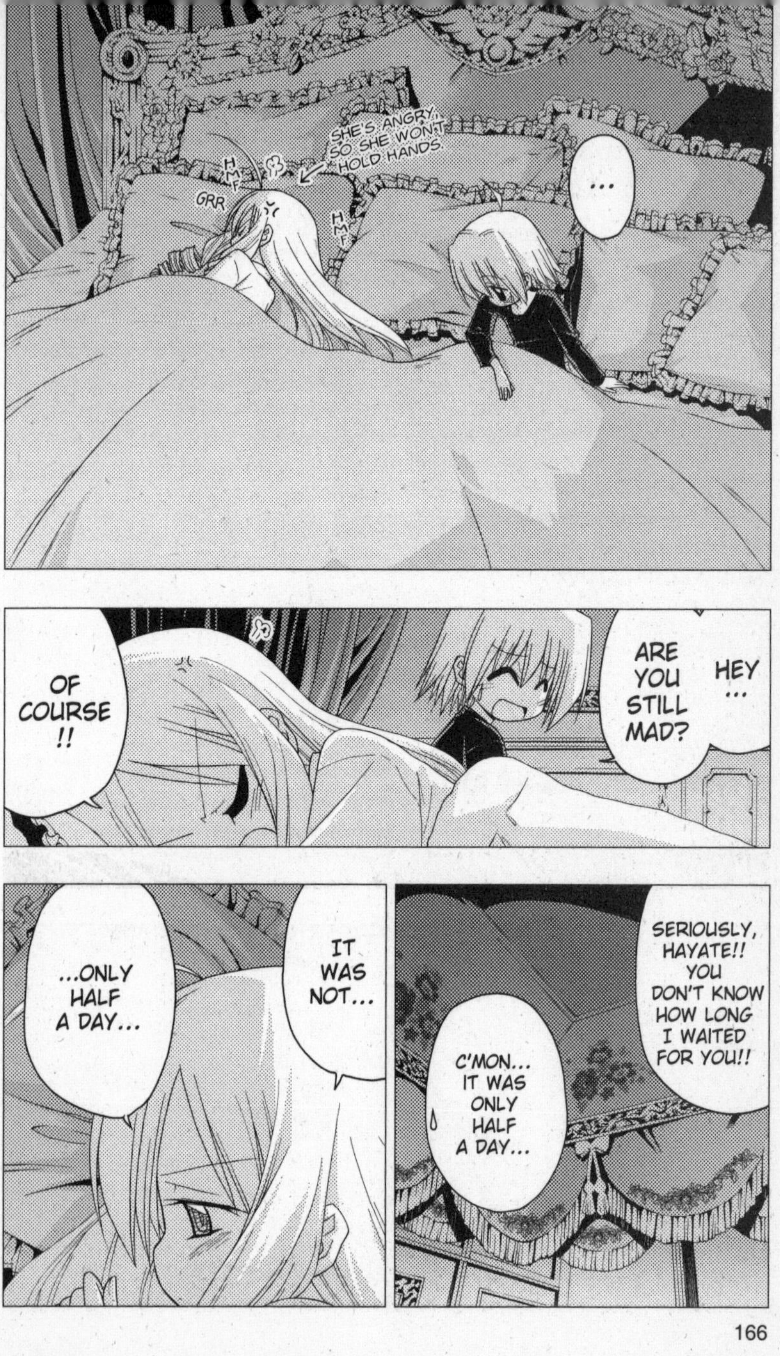
...
SHE'S ANGRY, SO SHE WON'T HOLD HANDS.
HMF
GRR
HMF
HEY...
ARE YOU STILL MAD?
OF COURSE!!
SERIOUSLY, HAYATE!! YOU DON'T KNOW HOW LONG I WAITED FOR YOU!!
C'MON... IT WAS ONLY HALF A DAY...
IT WAS NOT...
...ONLY HALF A DAY...

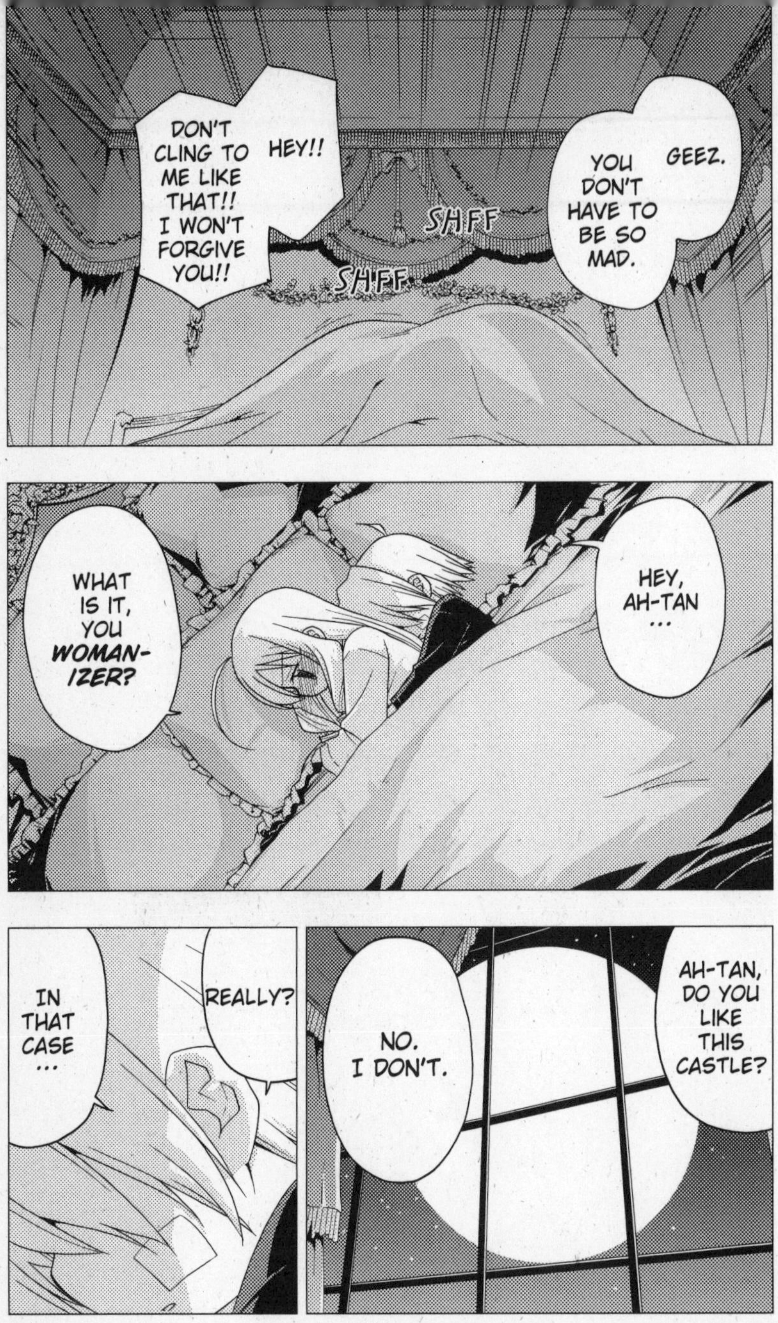
GEEZ.
YOU DON'T HAVE TO BE SO MAD.
SHFF
SHFF
HEY!!
DON'T CLING TO ME LIKE THAT!! I WON'T FORGIVE YOU!!
HEY, AH-TAN...
WHAT IS IT, YOU *WOMANIZER?*
AH-TAN, DO YOU LIKE THIS CASTLE?
NO. I DON'T.
REALLY?
IN THAT CASE...

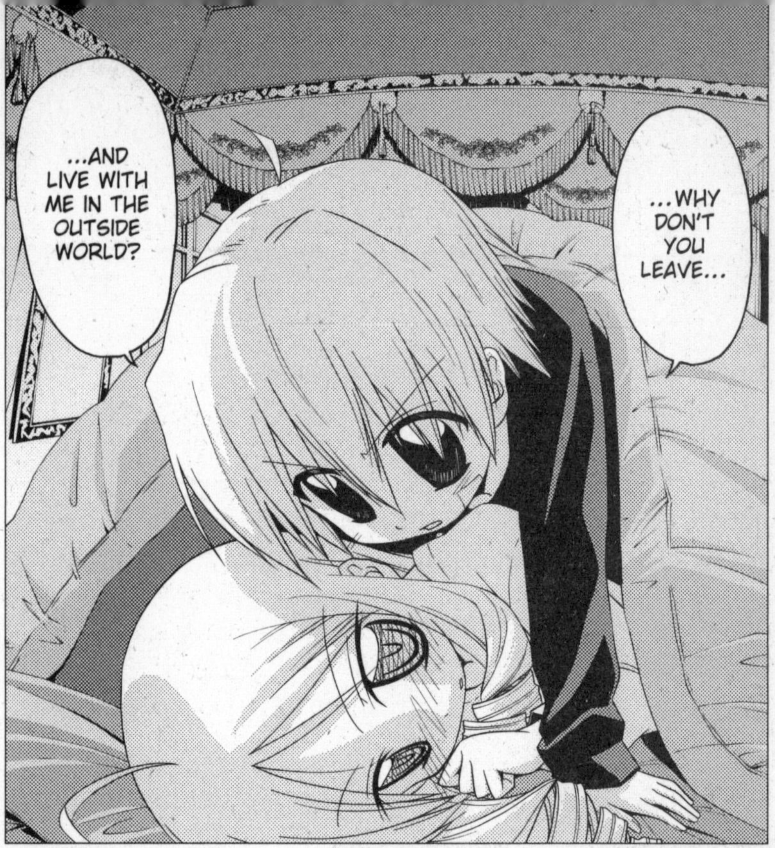
...WHY DON'T YOU LEAVE...
...AND LIVE WITH ME IN THE OUTSIDE WORLD?

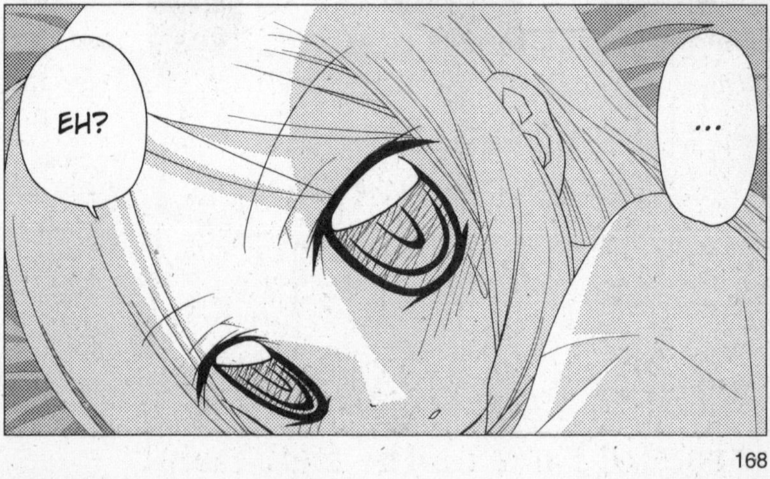
...
EH?

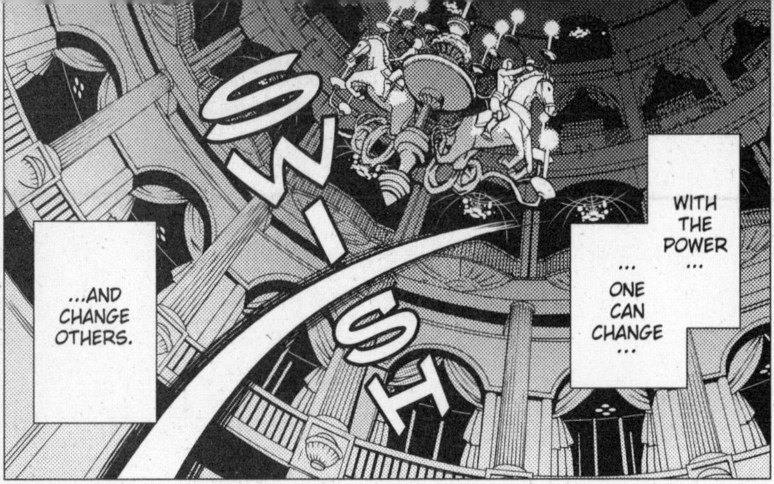
WITH THE POWER ...
... ONE CAN CHANGE ...
SWISH
...AND CHANGE OTHERS.

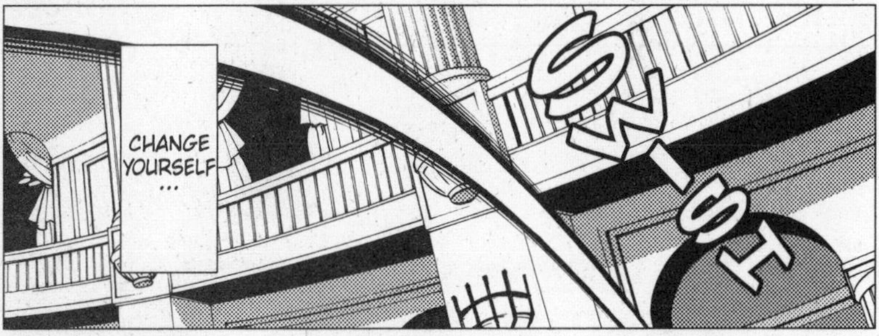
SWISH
CHANGE YOURSELF ...

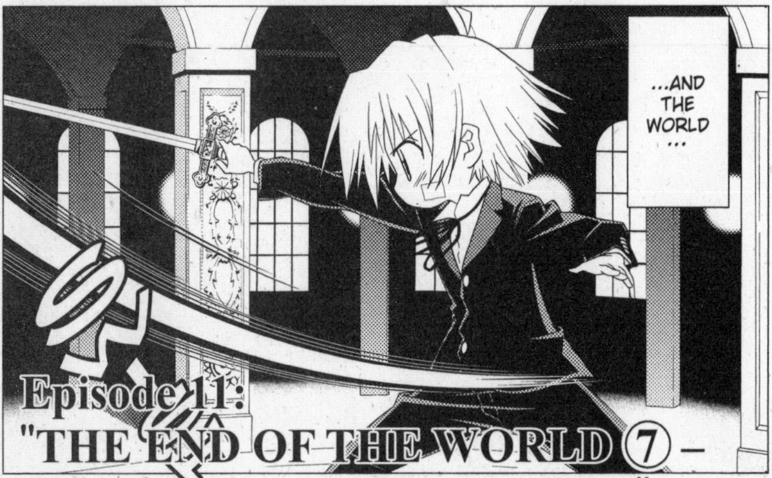
...AND THE WORLD ...
SW

Episode 11:
"THE END OF THE WORLD ⑦ – Proof of Love on the Left Hand"

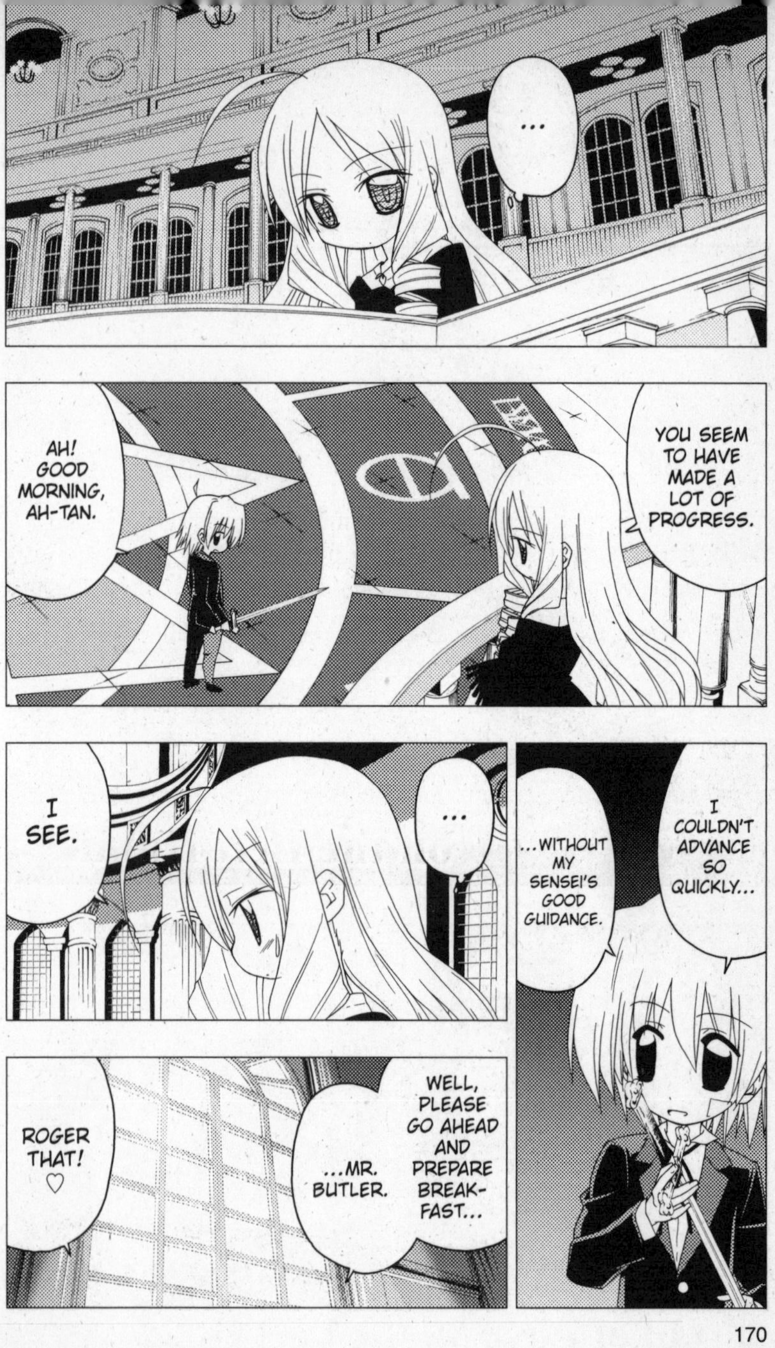
...
YOU SEEM TO HAVE MADE A LOT OF PROGRESS.
AH! GOOD MORNING, AH-TAN.
I COULDN'T ADVANCE SO QUICKLY...
...WITHOUT MY SENSEI'S GOOD GUIDANCE.
...
I SEE.
WELL, PLEASE GO AHEAD AND PREPARE BREAK-FAST...
...MR. BUTLER.
ROGER THAT! ♡

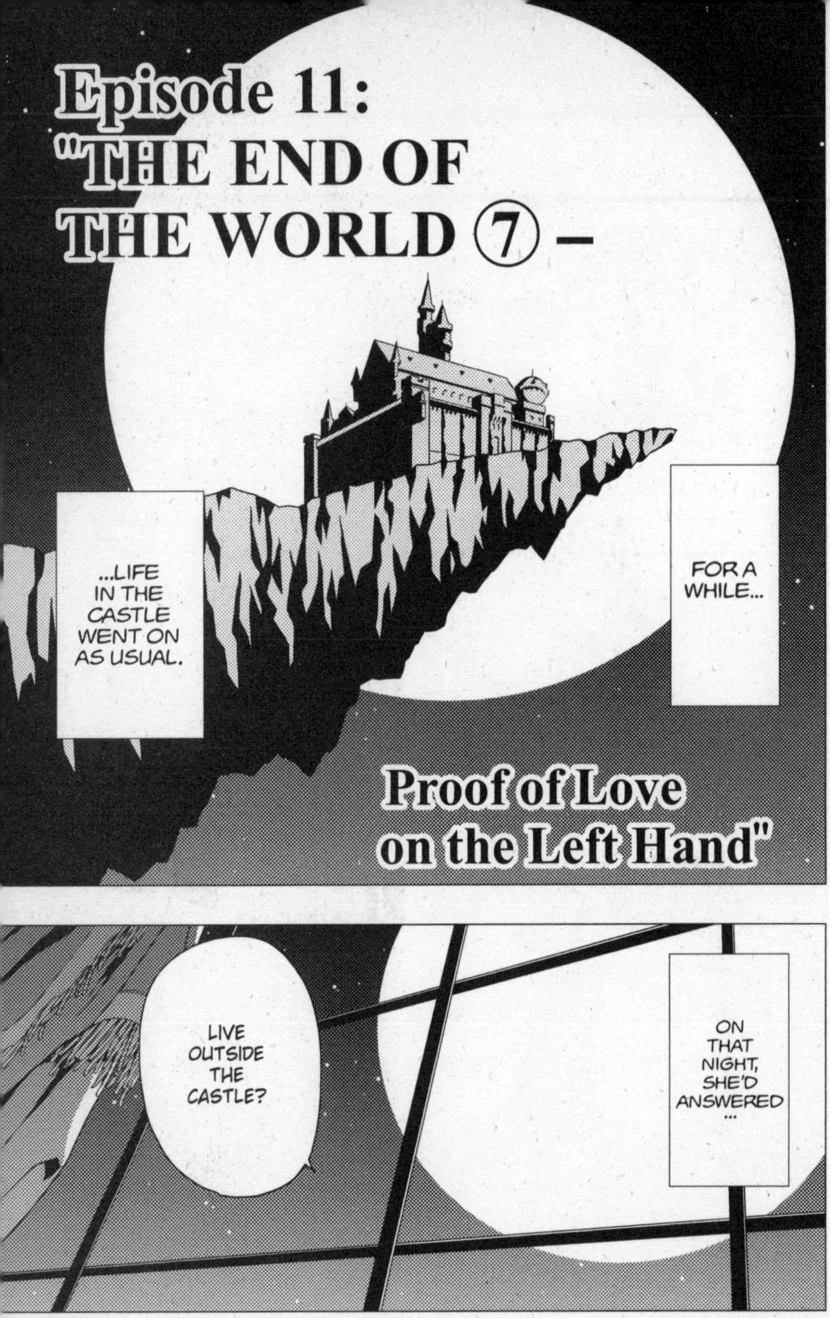
Episode 11: "THE END OF THE WORLD ⑦ –
FOR A WHILE...
...LIFE IN THE CASTLE WENT ON AS USUAL.
Proof of Love on the Left Hand"
ON THAT NIGHT, SHE'D ANSWERED...
LIVE OUTSIDE THE CASTLE?

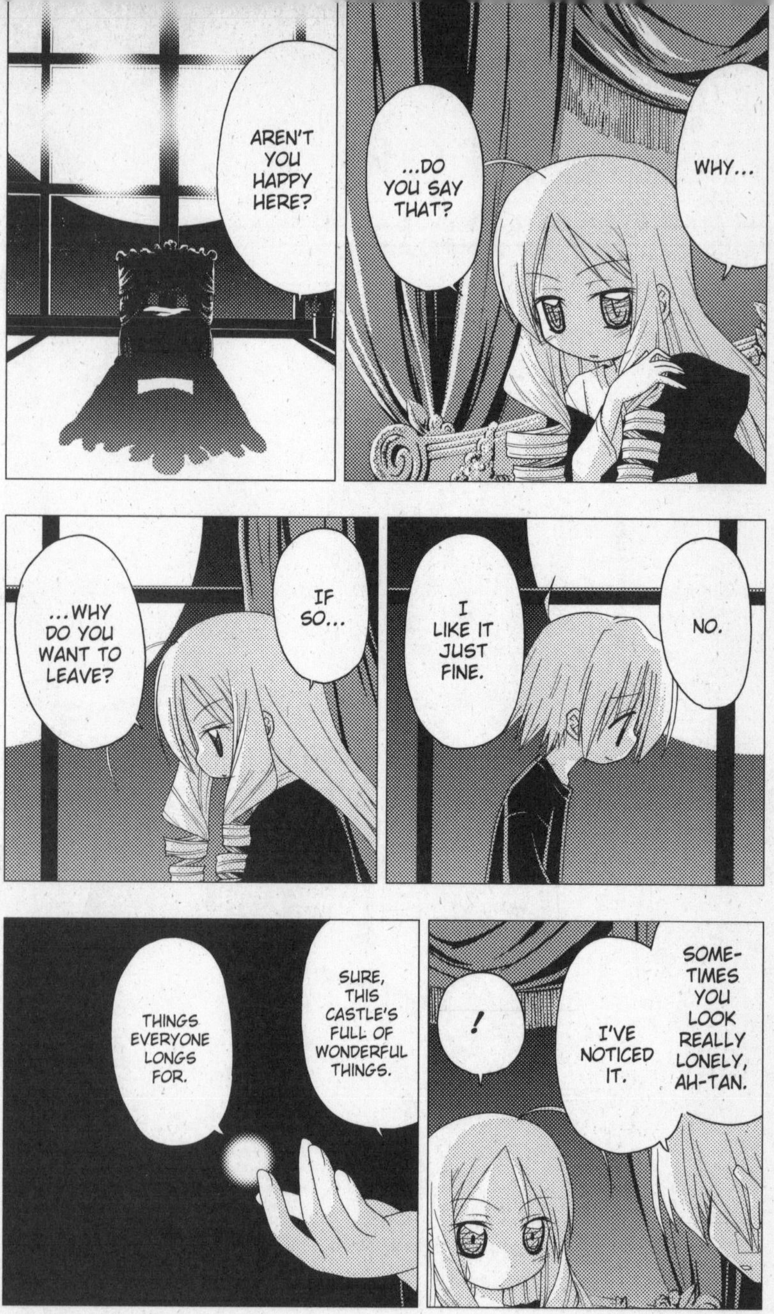
WHY...
...DO YOU SAY THAT?
AREN'T YOU HAPPY HERE?
NO.
I LIKE IT JUST FINE.
IF SO...
...WHY DO YOU WANT TO LEAVE?
SOMETIMES YOU LOOK REALLY LONELY, AH-TAN.
I'VE NOTICED IT.
!
SURE, THIS CASTLE'S FULL OF WONDERFUL THINGS.
THINGS EVERYONE LONGS FOR.

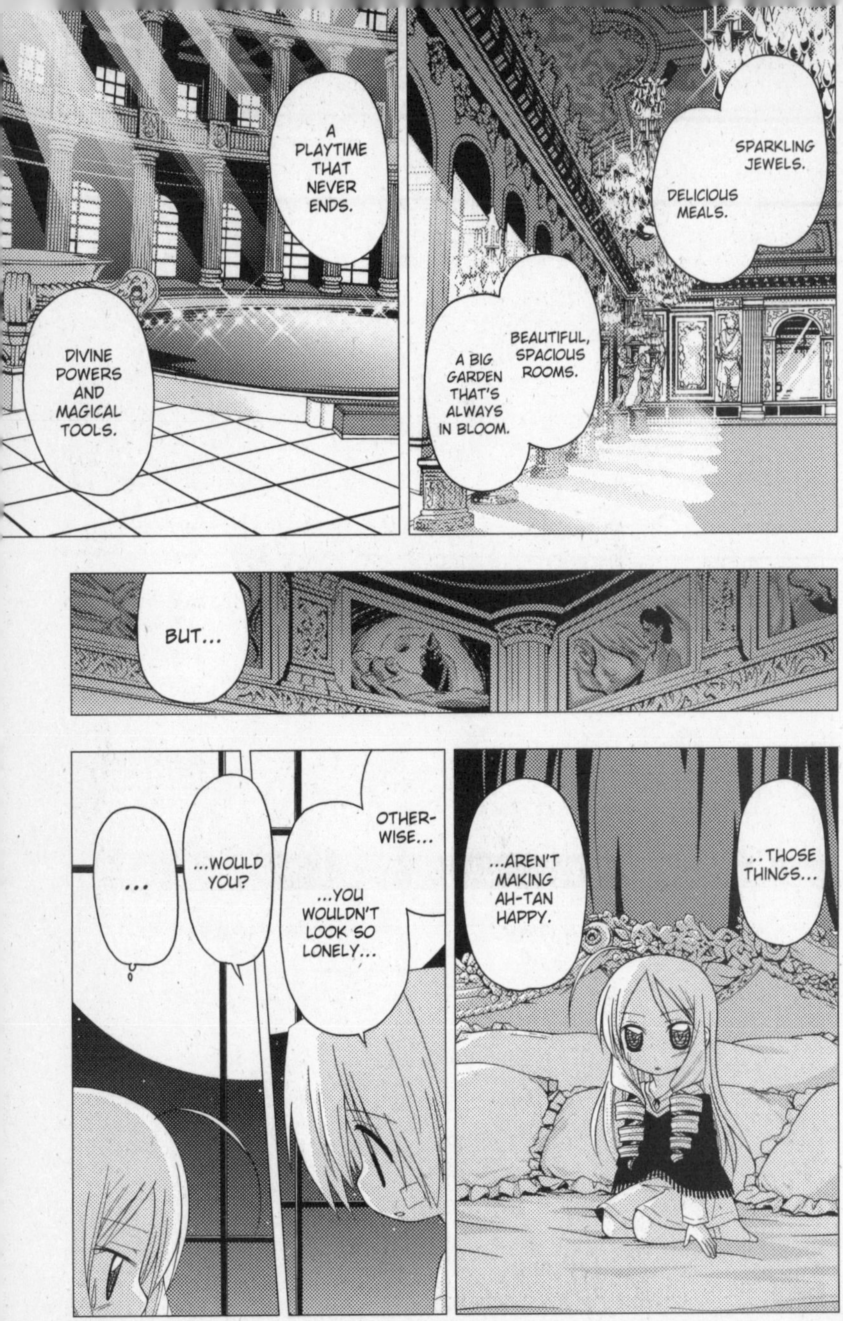
SPARKLING JEWELS.
DELICIOUS MEALS.
BEAUTIFUL, SPACIOUS ROOMS.
A BIG GARDEN THAT'S ALWAYS IN BLOOM.
A PLAYTIME THAT NEVER ENDS.
DIVINE POWERS AND MAGICAL TOOLS.
BUT...
...THOSE THINGS...
...AREN'T MAKING AH-TAN HAPPY.
OTHER-WISE...
...YOU WOULDN'T LOOK SO LONELY...
...WOULD YOU?
...

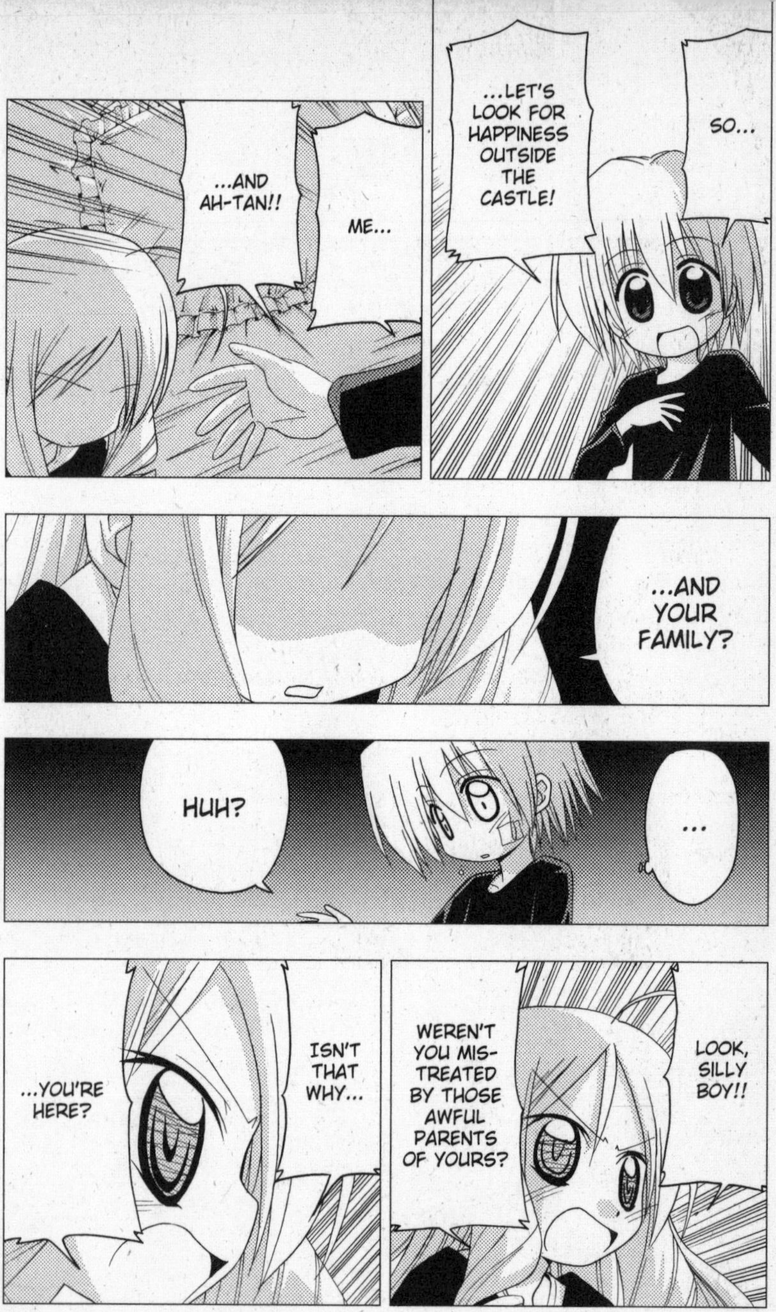
SO...
...LET'S LOOK FOR HAPPINESS OUTSIDE THE CASTLE!
ME...
...AND AH-TAN!!
...AND YOUR FAMILY?
...
HUH?
LOOK, SILLY BOY!!
WEREN'T YOU MIS-TREATED BY THOSE AWFUL PARENTS OF YOURS?
ISN'T THAT WHY...
...YOU'RE HERE?

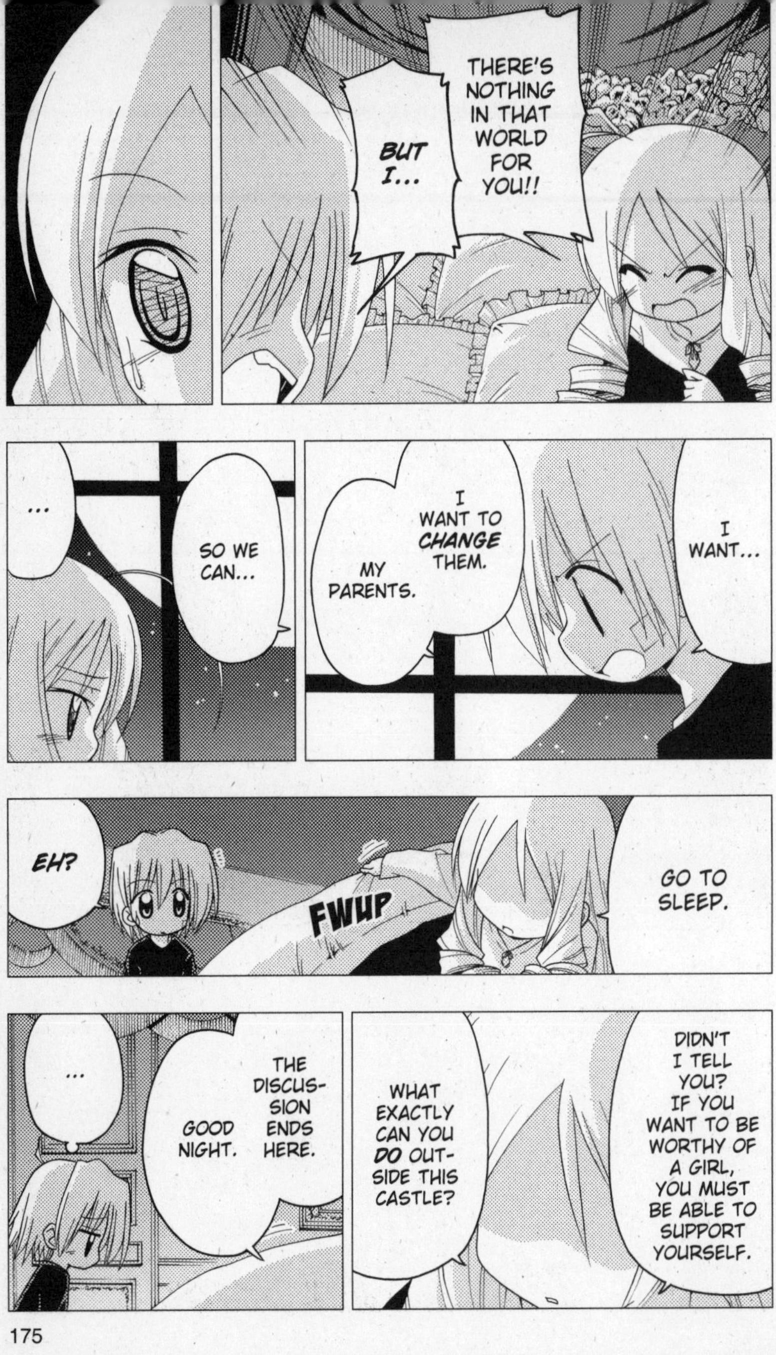
THERE'S NOTHING IN THAT WORLD FOR YOU!!
BUT I...
I WANT...
I WANT TO CHANGE THEM.
MY PARENTS.
SO WE CAN...
...
GO TO SLEEP.
FWUP
EH?
DIDN'T I TELL YOU? IF YOU WANT TO BE WORTHY OF A GIRL, YOU MUST BE ABLE TO SUPPORT YOURSELF.
WHAT EXACTLY CAN YOU DO OUTSIDE THIS CASTLE?
THE DISCUSSION ENDS HERE.
GOOD NIGHT.
...

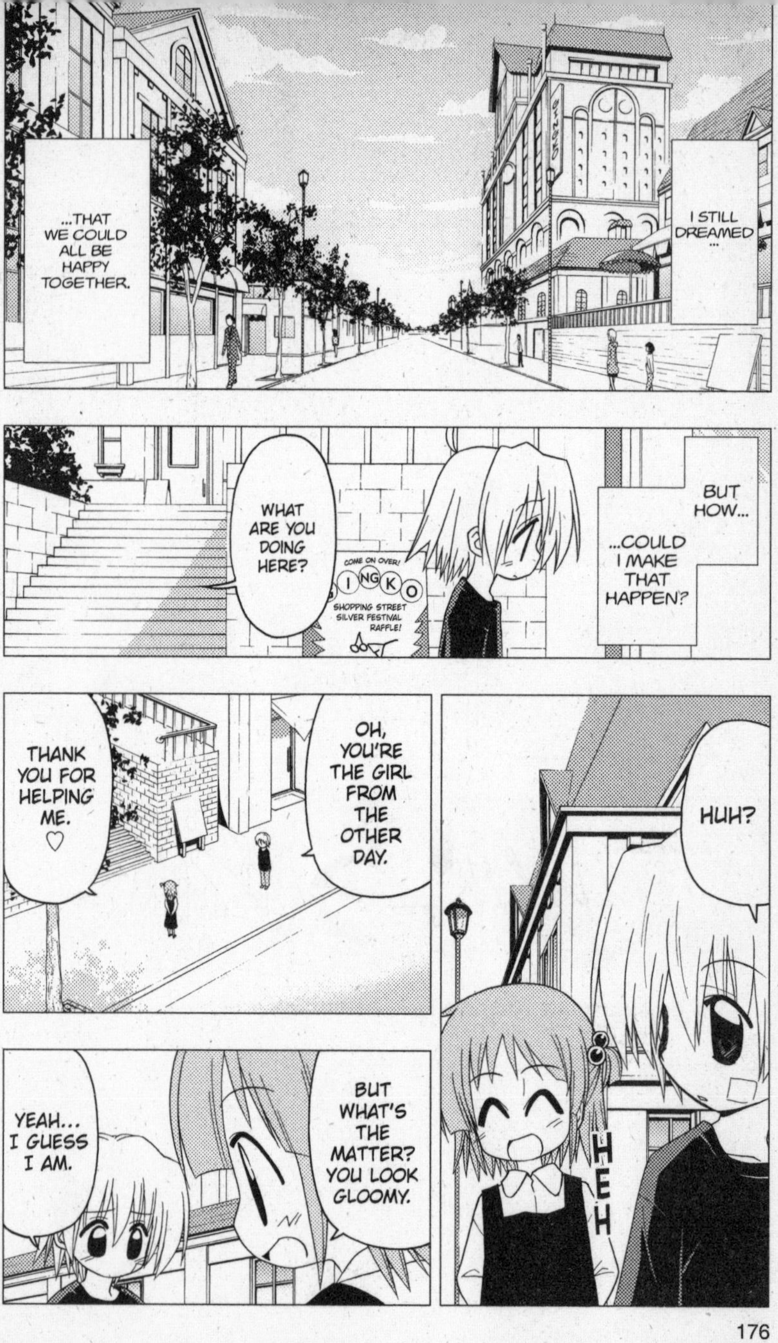
I STILL DREAMED...
...THAT WE COULD ALL BE HAPPY TOGETHER.
BUT HOW...
...COULD I MAKE THAT HAPPEN?
WHAT ARE YOU DOING HERE?
COME ON OVER!
SHOPPING STREET SILVER FESTIVAL RAFFLE!
HUH?
HEH
OH, YOU'RE THE GIRL FROM THE OTHER DAY.
THANK YOU FOR HELPING ME. ♡
BUT WHAT'S THE MATTER? YOU LOOK GLOOMY.
YEAH... I GUESS I AM.

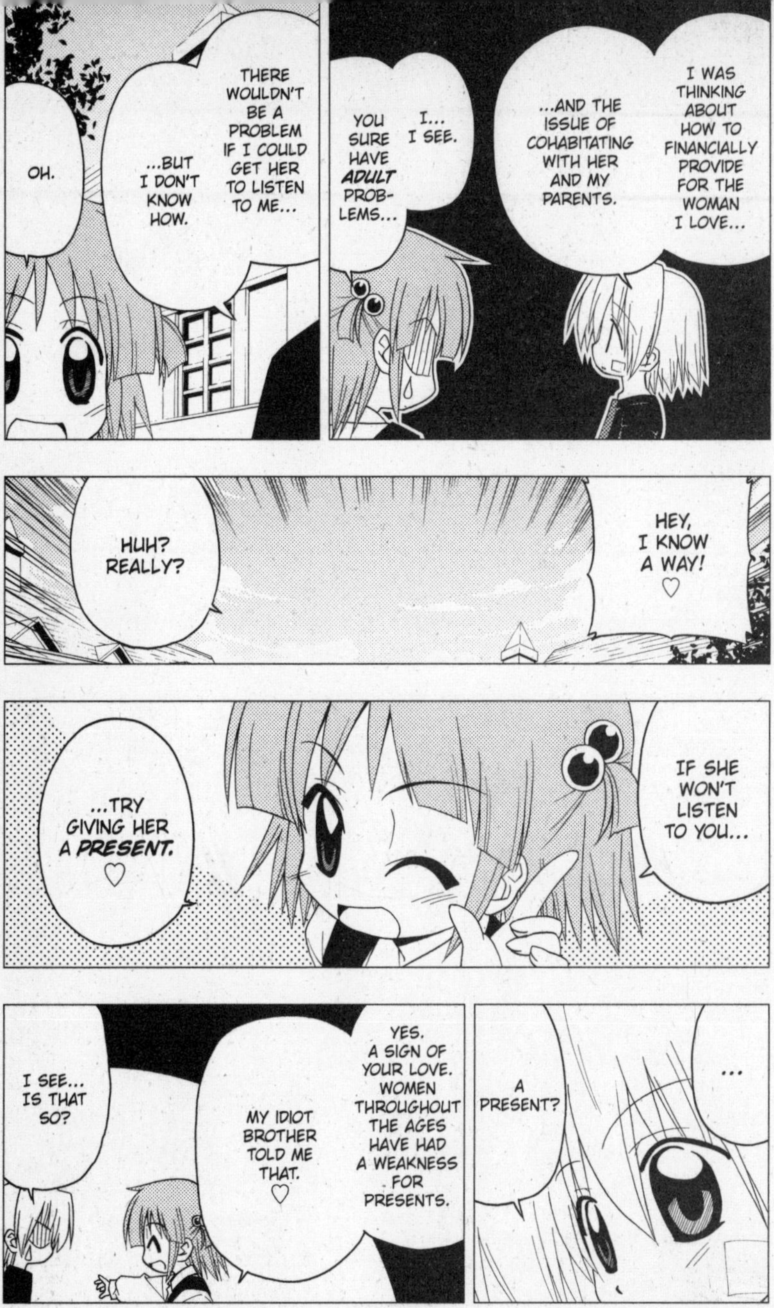
I WAS THINKING ABOUT HOW TO FINANCIALLY PROVIDE FOR THE WOMAN I LOVE...
...AND THE ISSUE OF COHABITATING WITH HER AND MY PARENTS.
I... I SEE.
YOU SURE HAVE *ADULT* PROBLEMS...
THERE WOULDN'T BE A PROBLEM IF I COULD GET HER TO LISTEN TO ME...
...BUT I DON'T KNOW HOW.
OH.
HEY, I KNOW A WAY! ♡
HUH? REALLY?
IF SHE WON'T LISTEN TO YOU...
...TRY GIVING HER A *PRESENT.* ♡
...
A PRESENT?
YES. A SIGN OF YOUR LOVE. WOMEN THROUGHOUT THE AGES HAVE HAD A WEAKNESS FOR PRESENTS.
MY IDIOT BROTHER TOLD ME THAT. ♡
I SEE... IS THAT SO?

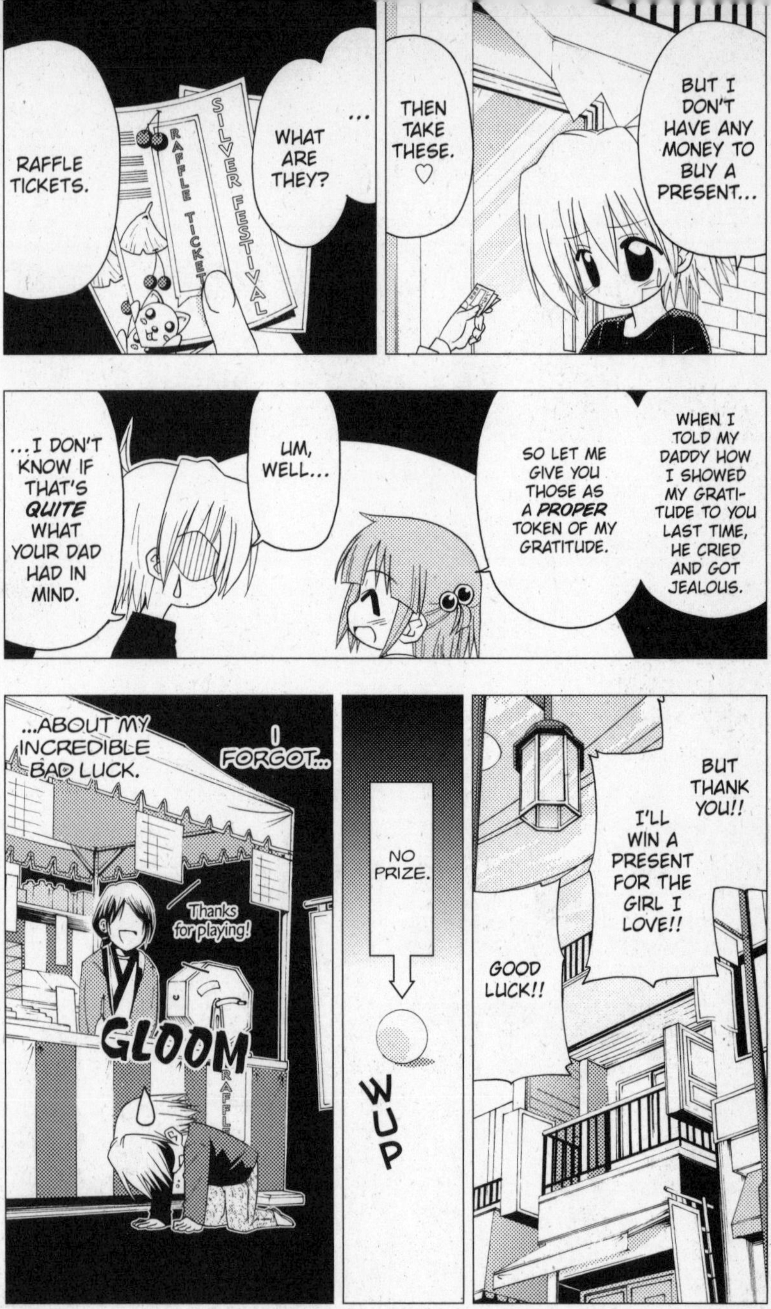
BUT I DON'T HAVE ANY MONEY TO BUY A PRESENT...
THEN TAKE THESE. ♡
...
WHAT ARE THEY?
SILVER FESTIVAL
RAFFLE TICKET
RAFFLE TICKETS.
WHEN I TOLD MY DADDY HOW I SHOWED MY GRATI-TUDE TO YOU LAST TIME, HE CRIED AND GOT JEALOUS.
SO LET ME GIVE YOU THOSE AS A *PROPER* TOKEN OF MY GRATITUDE.
UM, WELL...
...I DON'T KNOW IF THAT'S *QUITE* WHAT YOUR DAD HAD IN MIND.
BUT THANK YOU!!
I'LL WIN A PRESENT FOR THE GIRL I LOVE!!
GOOD LUCK!!
NO PRIZE.
WUP
I FORGOT...
...ABOUT MY INCREDIBLE BAD LUCK.
Thanks for playing!
GLOOM
RAFFLE

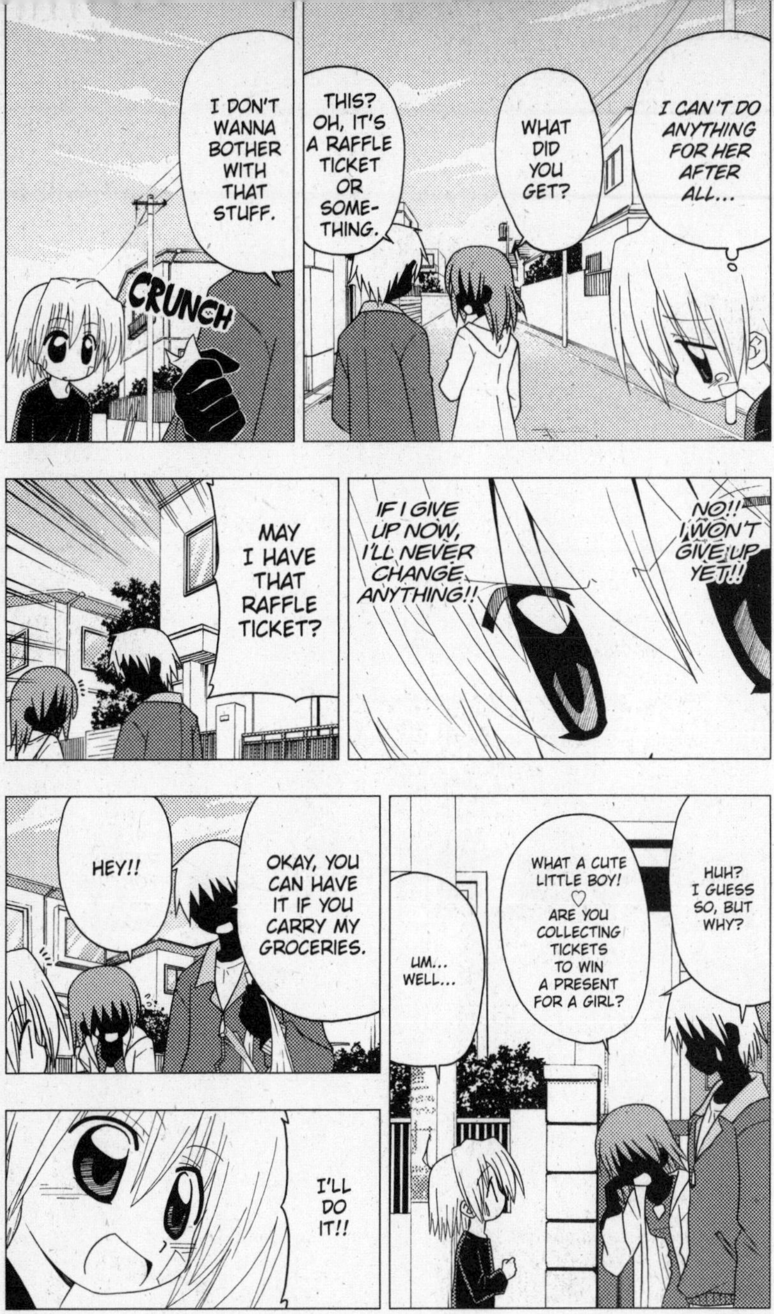
I CAN'T DO ANYTHING FOR HER AFTER ALL...
WHAT DID YOU GET?
THIS? OH, IT'S A RAFFLE TICKET OR SOME-THING.
I DON'T WANNA BOTHER WITH THAT STUFF.
CRUNCH
NO!! I WON'T GIVE UP YET!!
IF I GIVE UP NOW, I'LL NEVER CHANGE ANYTHING!!
MAY I HAVE THAT RAFFLE TICKET?
HUH? I GUESS SO, BUT WHY?
WHAT A CUTE LITTLE BOY! ♡ ARE YOU COLLECTING TICKETS TO WIN A PRESENT FOR A GIRL?
UM... WELL...
OKAY, YOU CAN HAVE IT IF YOU CARRY MY GROCERIES.
HEY!!
I'LL DO IT!!

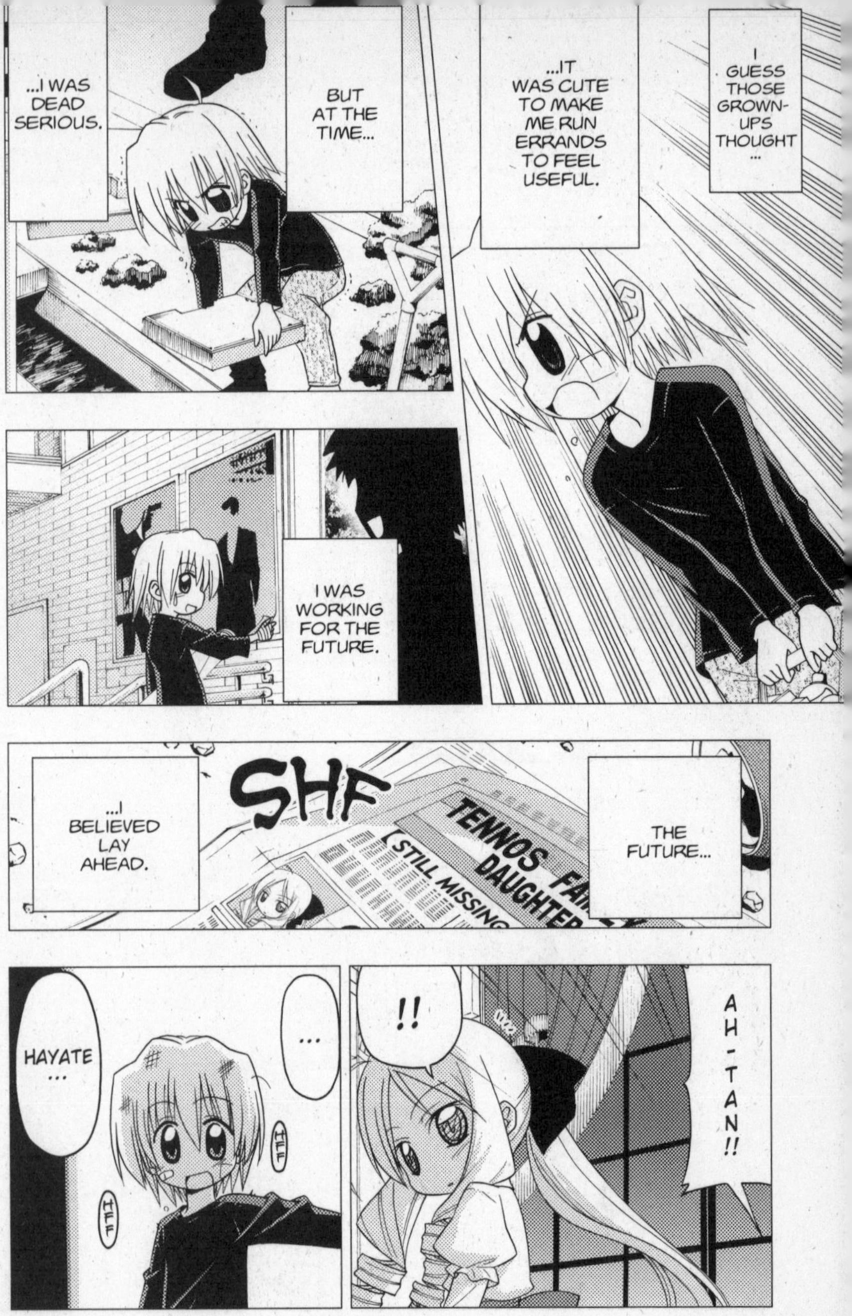
I GUESS THOSE GROWN-UPS THOUGHT...
...IT WAS CUTE TO MAKE ME RUN ERRANDS TO FEEL USEFUL.
BUT AT THE TIME...
...I WAS DEAD SERIOUS.
I WAS WORKING FOR THE FUTURE.
THE FUTURE...
SHF
TENNOS FAM
DAUGHTER
STILL MISSING
...I BELIEVED LAY AHEAD.
AH-TAN!!
!!
...
HAYATE...
HFF
HFF

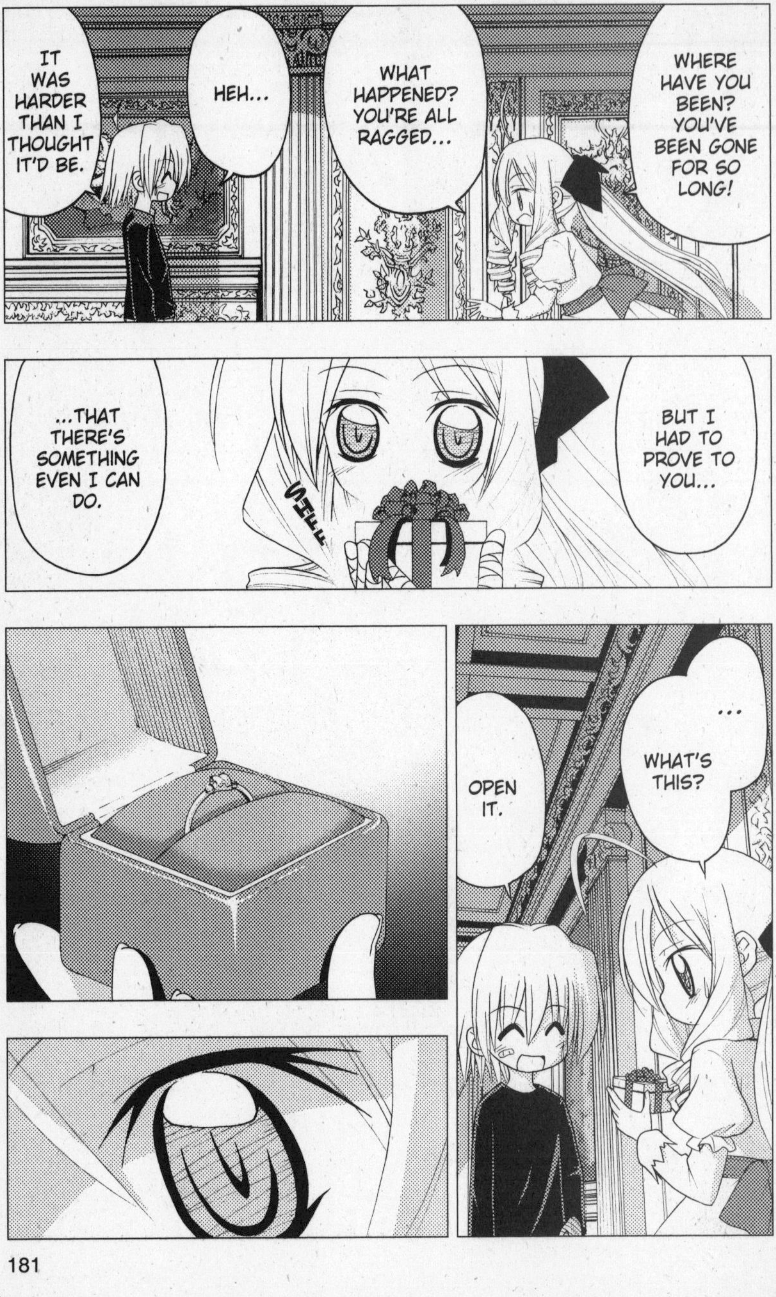
WHERE HAVE YOU BEEN? YOU'VE BEEN GONE FOR SO LONG!
WHAT HAPPENED? YOU'RE ALL RAGGED...
HEH...
IT WAS HARDER THAN I THOUGHT IT'D BE.
BUT I HAD TO PROVE TO YOU...
...THAT THERE'S SOMETHING EVEN I CAN DO.
...
WHAT'S THIS?
OPEN IT.

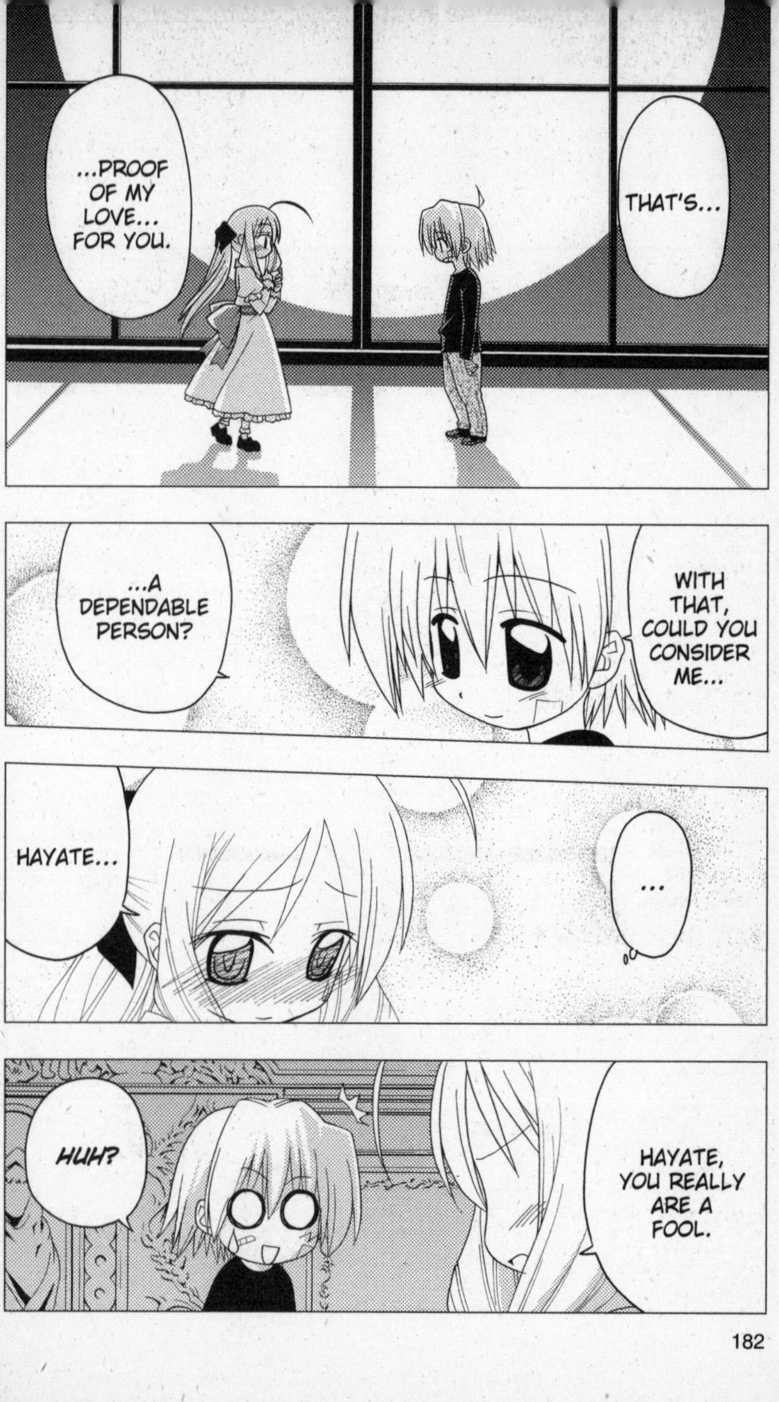
THAT'S...
...PROOF OF MY LOVE... FOR YOU.
WITH THAT, COULD YOU CONSIDER ME...
...A DEPENDABLE PERSON?
...
HAYATE...
HAYATE, YOU REALLY ARE A FOOL.
HUH?

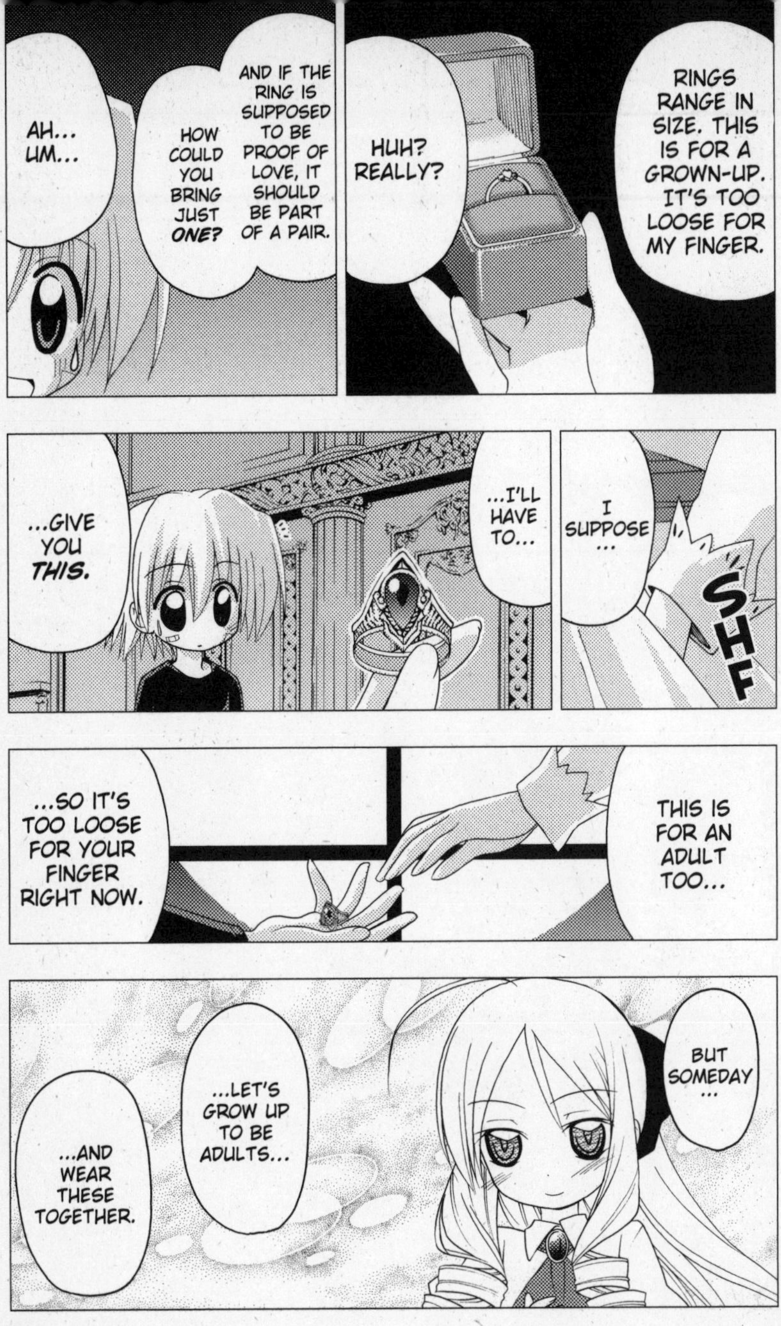
RINGS RANGE IN SIZE. THIS IS FOR A GROWN-UP. IT'S TOO LOOSE FOR MY FINGER.
HUH? REALLY?
AND IF THE RING IS SUPPOSED TO BE PROOF OF LOVE, IT SHOULD BE PART OF A PAIR.
HOW COULD YOU BRING JUST *ONE?*
AH... UM...
I SUPPOSE...
SHF
...I'LL HAVE TO...
...GIVE YOU *THIS.*
THIS IS FOR AN ADULT TOO...
...SO IT'S TOO LOOSE FOR YOUR FINGER RIGHT NOW.
BUT SOMEDAY...
...LET'S GROW UP TO BE ADULTS...
...AND WEAR THESE TOGETHER.

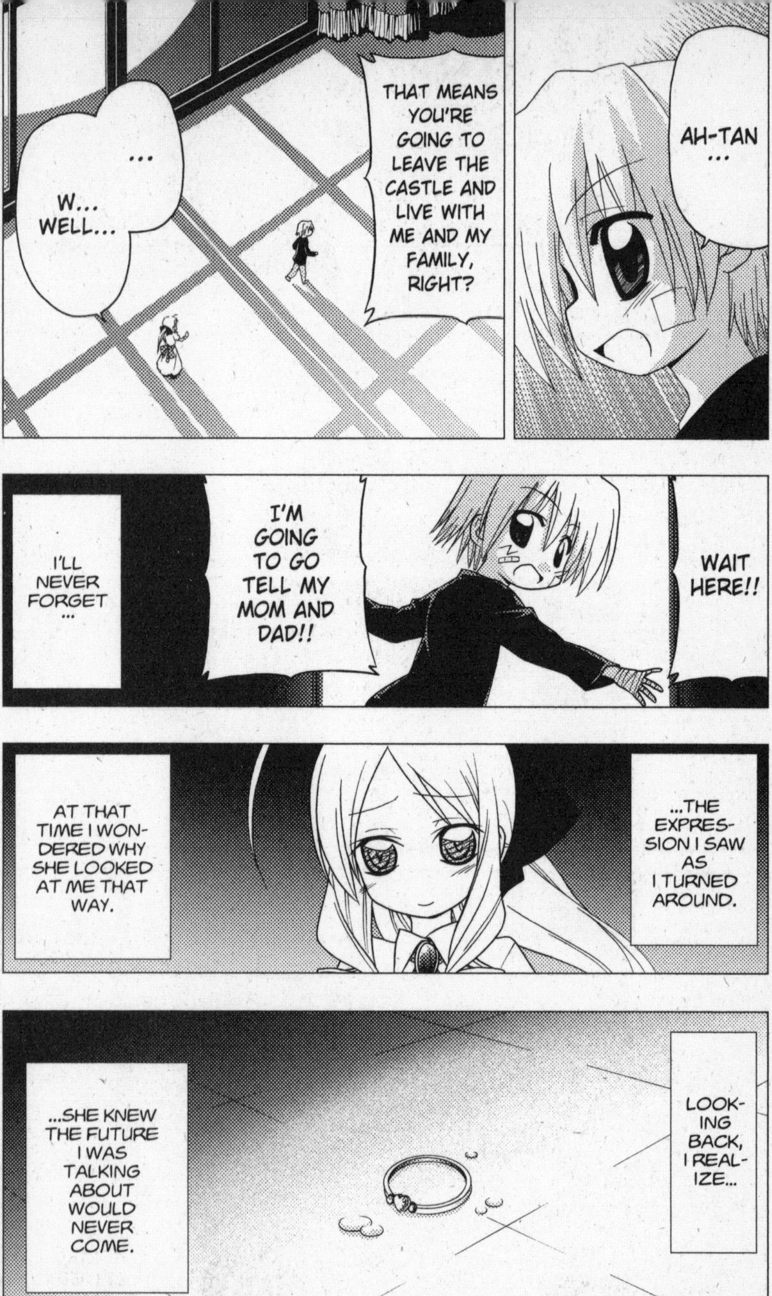
AH-TAN ...
THAT MEANS YOU'RE GOING TO LEAVE THE CASTLE AND LIVE WITH ME AND MY FAMILY, RIGHT?
... W... WELL...
WAIT HERE!!
I'M GOING TO GO TELL MY MOM AND DAD!!
I'LL NEVER FORGET ...
...THE EXPRES-SION I SAW AS I TURNED AROUND.
AT THAT TIME I WON-DERED WHY SHE LOOKED AT ME THAT WAY.
LOOK-ING BACK, I REAL-IZE...
...SHE KNEW THE FUTURE I WAS TALKING ABOUT WOULD NEVER COME.

TO BE CONTINUED

HAYATE THE COMBAT BUTLER

BONUS PAGE

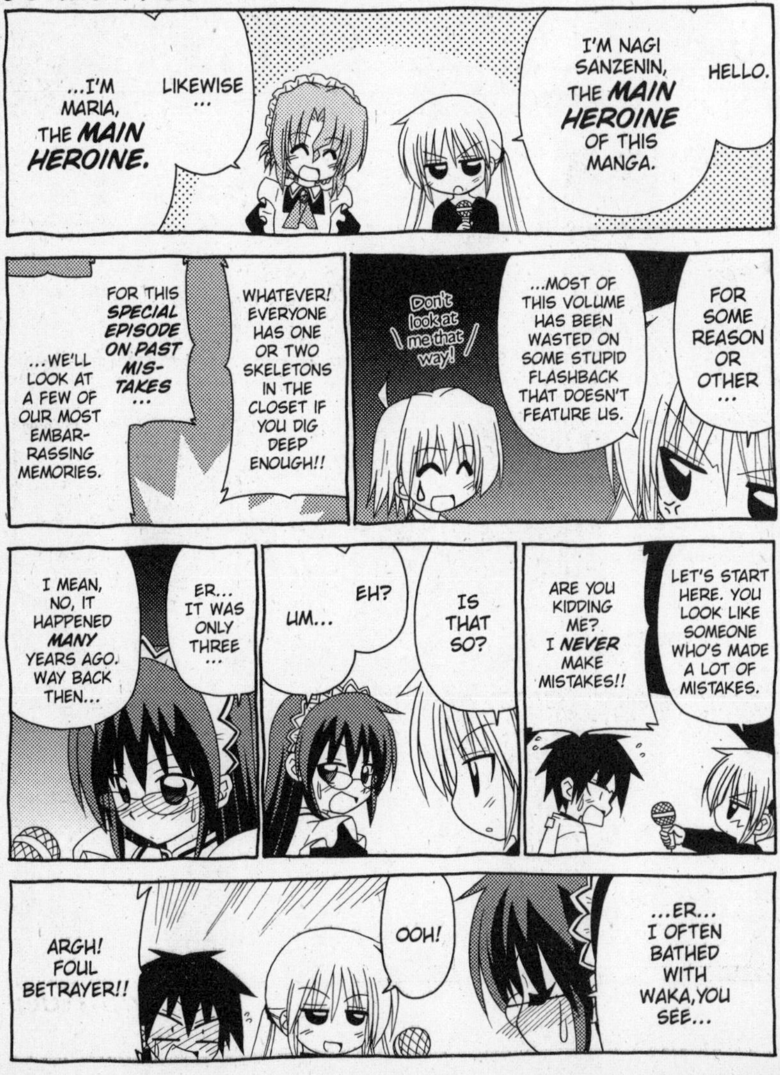
HELLO.
I'M NAGI SANZENIN, THE MAIN HEROINE OF THIS MANGA.
LIKEWISE ...
...I'M MARIA, THE MAIN HEROINE.
FOR SOME REASON OR OTHER ...
...MOST OF THIS VOLUME HAS BEEN WASTED ON SOME STUPID FLASHBACK THAT DOESN'T FEATURE US.
Don't look at me that way!
WHATEVER! EVERYONE HAS ONE OR TWO SKELETONS IN THE CLOSET IF YOU DIG DEEP ENOUGH!!
FOR THIS SPECIAL EPISODE ON PAST MIS-TAKES ...
...WE'LL LOOK AT A FEW OF OUR MOST EMBAR-RASSING MEMORIES.
LET'S START HERE. YOU LOOK LIKE SOMEONE WHO'S MADE A LOT OF MISTAKES.
ARE YOU KIDDING ME? I NEVER MAKE MISTAKES!!
IS THAT SO?
EH?
UM...
ER... IT WAS ONLY THREE ...
I MEAN, NO, IT HAPPENED MANY YEARS AGO. WAY BACK THEN...
...ER... I OFTEN BATHED WITH WAKA, YOU SEE...
OOH!
ARGH! FOUL BETRAYER!!

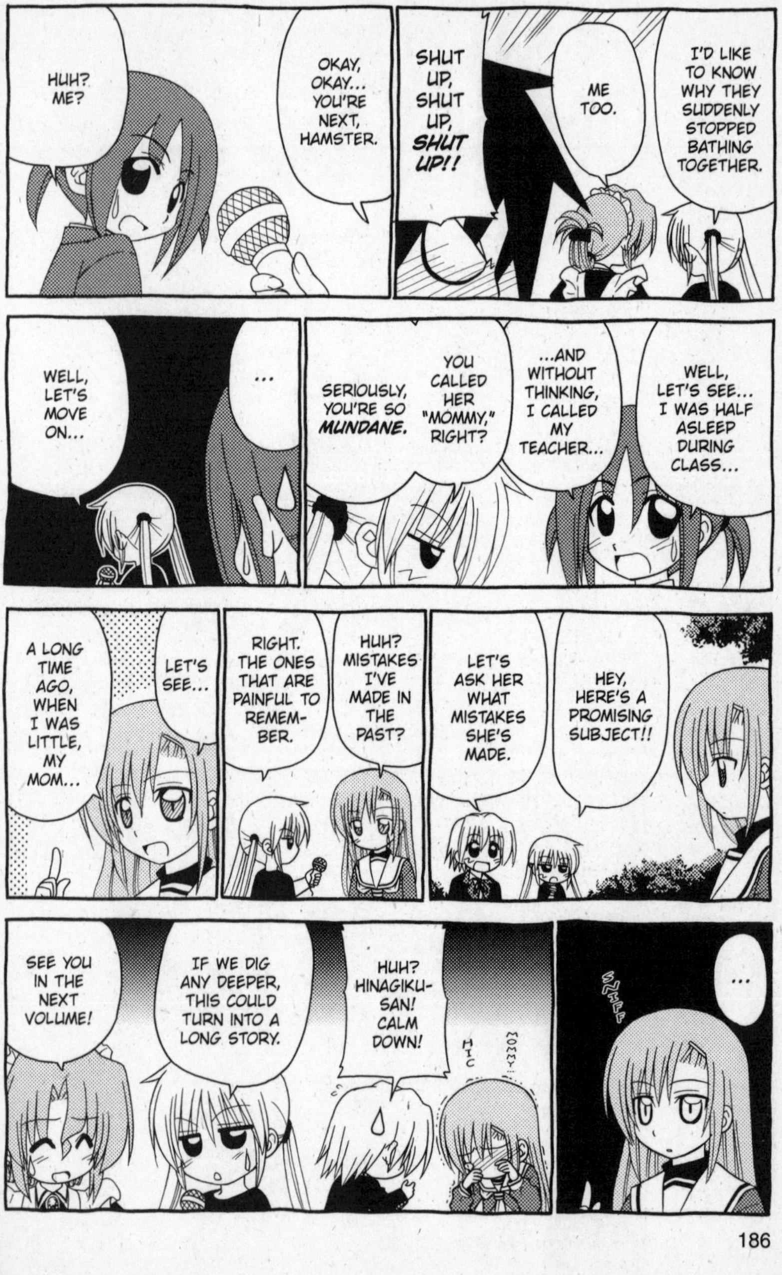
I'D LIKE TO KNOW WHY THEY SUDDENLY STOPPED BATHING TOGETHER.
ME TOO.
SHUT UP, SHUT UP, SHUT UP!!
OKAY, OKAY... YOU'RE NEXT, HAMSTER.
HUH? ME?
WELL, LET'S SEE... I WAS HALF ASLEEP DURING CLASS...
...AND WITHOUT THINKING, I CALLED MY TEACHER...
YOU CALLED HER "MOMMY," RIGHT?
SERIOUSLY, YOU'RE SO MUNDANE.
...
WELL, LET'S MOVE ON...
HEY, HERE'S A PROMISING SUBJECT!!
LET'S ASK HER WHAT MISTAKES SHE'S MADE.
HUH? MISTAKES I'VE MADE IN THE PAST?
RIGHT. THE ONES THAT ARE PAINFUL TO REMEMBER.
LET'S SEE...
A LONG TIME AGO, WHEN I WAS LITTLE, MY MOM...
...
SNIFF
MOMMY...
HIC
HUH? HINAGIKU-SAN! CALM DOWN!
IF WE DIG ANY DEEPER, THIS COULD TURN INTO A LONG STORY.
SEE YOU IN THE NEXT VOLUME!

WELL, WELL... *HAYATE*'S REACHED VOLUME 17.
HOW HAVE YOU BEEN? IT'S ME, HATA.

SOON THE SERIES WILL MARK ITS FOURTH YEAR. I'VE NEVER
MISSED AN INSTALLMENT IN THE WEEKLY MAGAZINE. (TAKE NOTE!)
NOT A SINGLE INSTALLMENT! (C'MON, SOMEBODY GIVE ME A PAT
ON THE BACK!) NOW I'M ABOUT TO HIT THE 200TH EPISODE.
THANK YOU ALL SO MUCH FOR YOUR SUPPORT.

NOW, ON TO *HAYATE*... THIS VOLUME INCLUDES A STORY LINE
ABOUT HAYATE'S PAST THAT'S A BIT DIFFERENT FROM THE USUAL
COMEDY PLOTS. IN VIDEO GAME TERMS, THESE FLASHBACKS ARE
LIKE CUT SCENES THAT CAN'T BE SKIPPED. THEY CONTAIN
ELEMENTS OF THE ORIGINAL PLOT I DEVELOPED FOR THE STORY
BEFORE IT STARTED SERIALIZATION.

I'VE BEEN THINKING FOR SOME TIME THAT I OUGHT TO REVEAL
HAYATE'S BACKSTORY, BUT WHEN THE TIME CAME I REALLY HAD
TO GIVE IT SERIOUS THOUGHT. BECAUSE THE FINAL VERSION OF
HAYATE WAS SO DIFFERENT FROM MY ORIGINAL CONCEPT,
I WAS AFRAID THAT THE FLASHBACK WAS TOO MUCH
OF A DOWNER TO WORK.

I PUT IT OFF FOR A LONG TIME. AFTER GIVING IT A LOT OF
CONSIDERATION, I DECIDED THE MANGA COULDN'T MOVE FORWARD
UNTIL I TOLD THIS STORY. I HAVE MIXED FEELINGS ABOUT
SPREADING THE FLASHBACK OUT OVER TWO VOLUMES,
BUT I HOPE YOU'LL ENJOY THE CONCLUSION IN VOLUME 18.

FOR THOSE OF YOU WHO THOUGHT THAT THIS VOLUME WAS
TOO SHORT ON FUNNY STORIES, THE EPISODES RUNNING NOW
IN THE MAGAZINE ARE ALL UPBEAT AND FUN!! (TAKE NOTE!)
EVERY WEEK!! (C'MON, SOMEBODY... OKAY, NEVER MIND.) ALSO,
I'VE BEEN DRAWING A FOUR-PANEL *HAYATE* WEBCOMIC EVERY
WEEK ON WEBSUNDAY.NET. I'D LOVE FOR YOU TO CHECK IT OUT.

WELL, SEE YOU IN VOLUME 18!
BYE, NOW! ☆

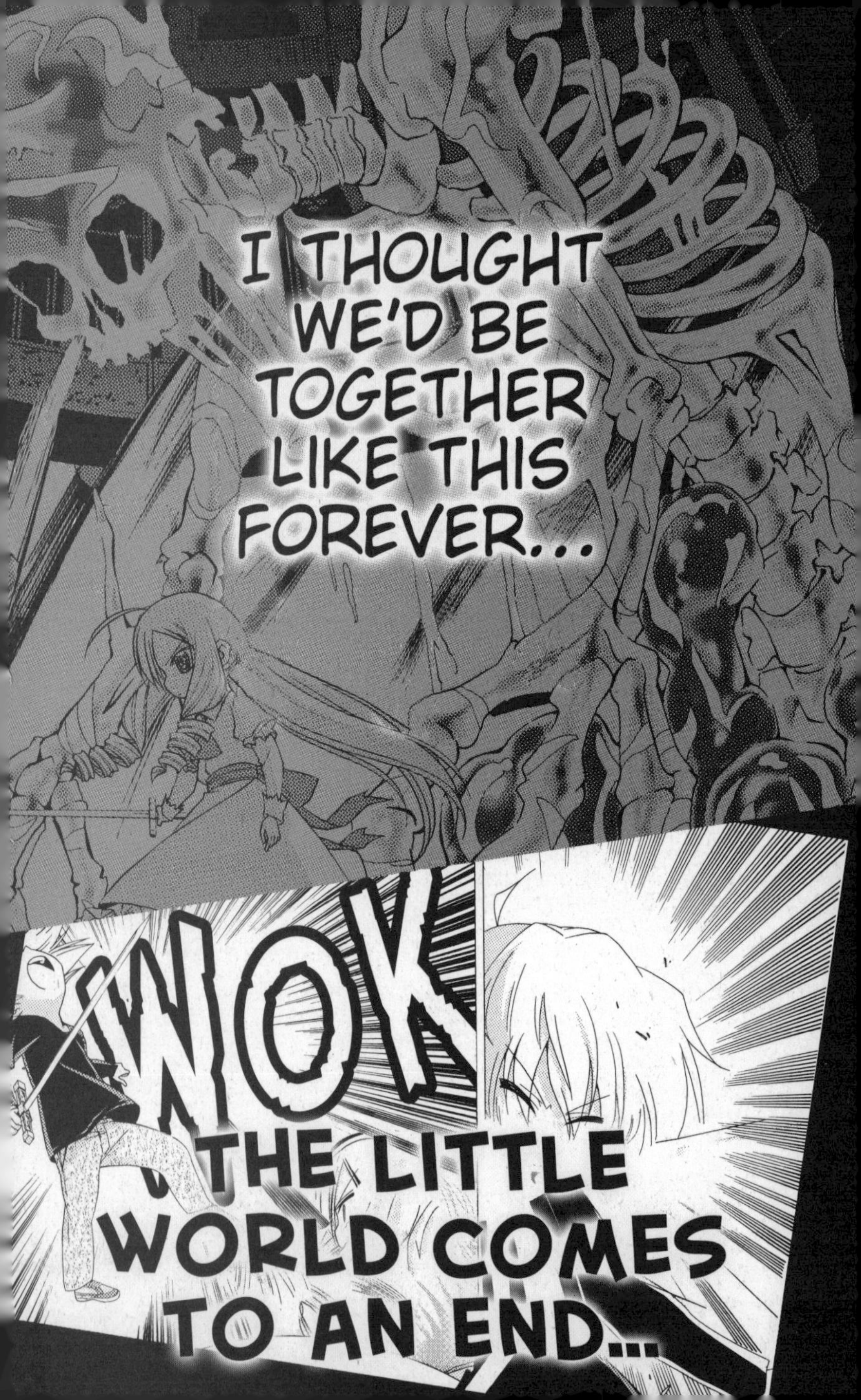
I THOUGHT WE'D BE TOGETHER LIKE THIS FOREVER...
WOK
THE LITTLE WORLD COMES TO AN END...

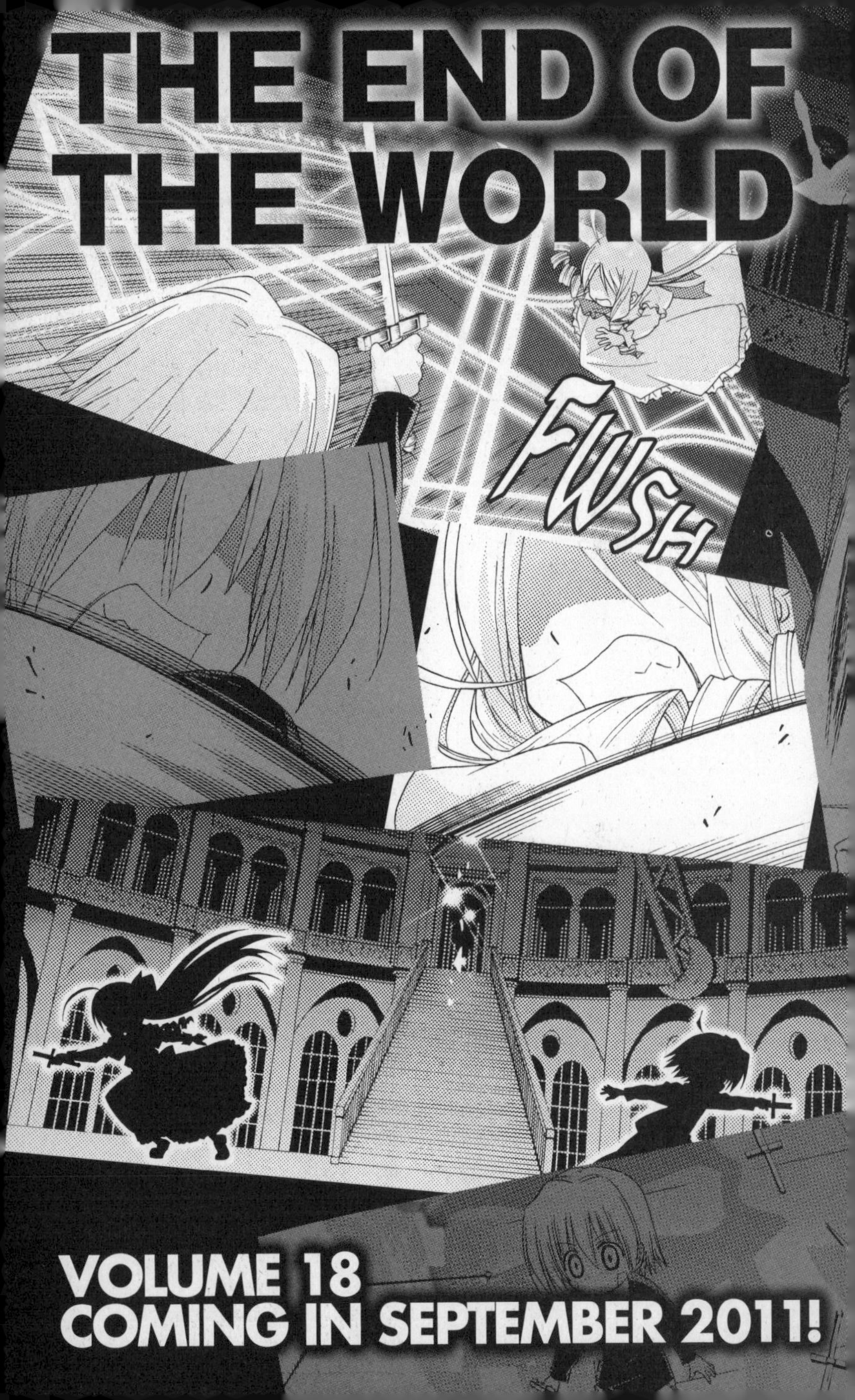
THE END OF THE WORLD
FWSH
VOLUME 18 COMING IN SEPTEMBER 2011!

Butler vs. Maid

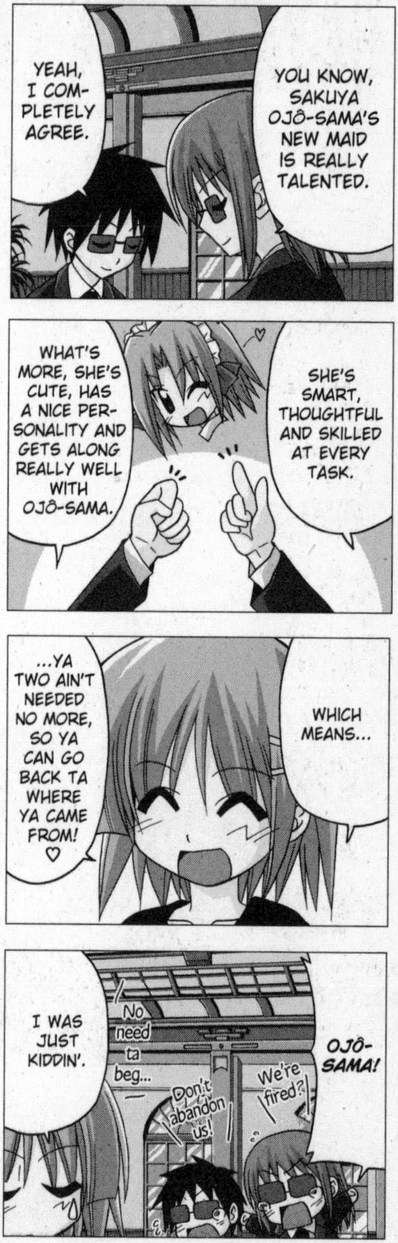
YOU KNOW, SAKUYA OJÔ-SAMA'S NEW MAID IS REALLY TALENTED.
YEAH, I COMPLETELY AGREE.
SHE'S SMART, THOUGHTFUL AND SKILLED AT EVERY TASK.
WHAT'S MORE, SHE'S CUTE, HAS A NICE PERSONALITY AND GETS ALONG REALLY WELL WITH OJÔ-SAMA.
WHICH MEANS...
...YA TWO AIN'T NEEDED NO MORE, SO YA CAN GO BACK TA WHERE YA CAME FROM! ♡
OJÔ-SAMA!
We're fired?!
Don't abandon us!
No need ta beg...
I WAS JUST KIDDIN'.

Maid vs. Zombie

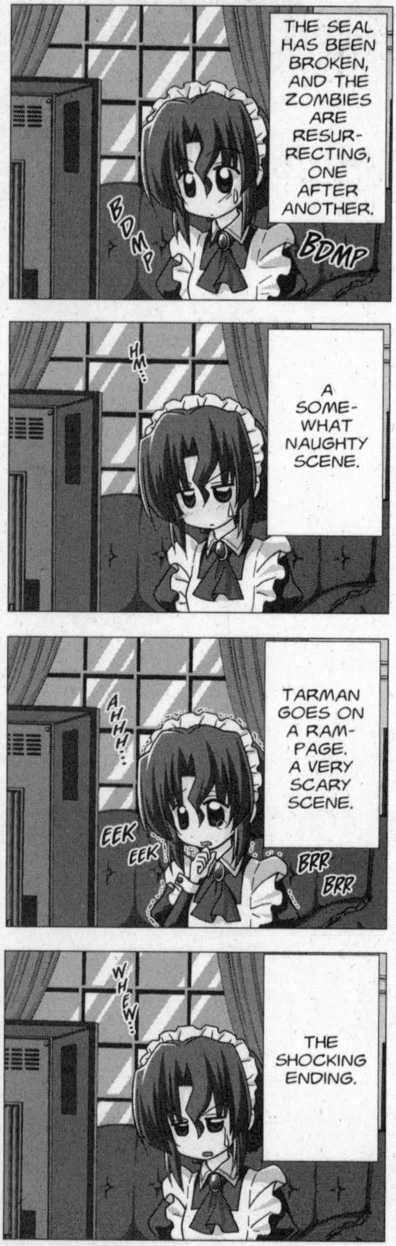
THE SEAL HAS BEEN BROKEN, AND THE ZOMBIES ARE RESURRECTING, ONE AFTER ANOTHER.
BDMP
BDMP
A SOMEWHAT NAUGHTY SCENE.
HM...
TARMAN GOES ON A RAMPAGE. A VERY SCARY SCENE.
AHHH...
BRR BRR
EEK EEK
THE SHOCKING ENDING.
WHEW...

HAYATE THE COMBAT BUTLER!

BAD END (9)

IF THE FLASH-BACK CUT SCENE DOESN'T PLAY...

Ah... The staff credits...
X-1 TURBO Z

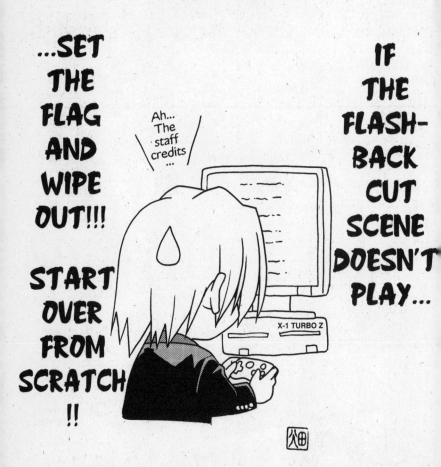

...SET THE FLAG AND WIPE OUT!!!

START OVER FROM SCRATCH!!

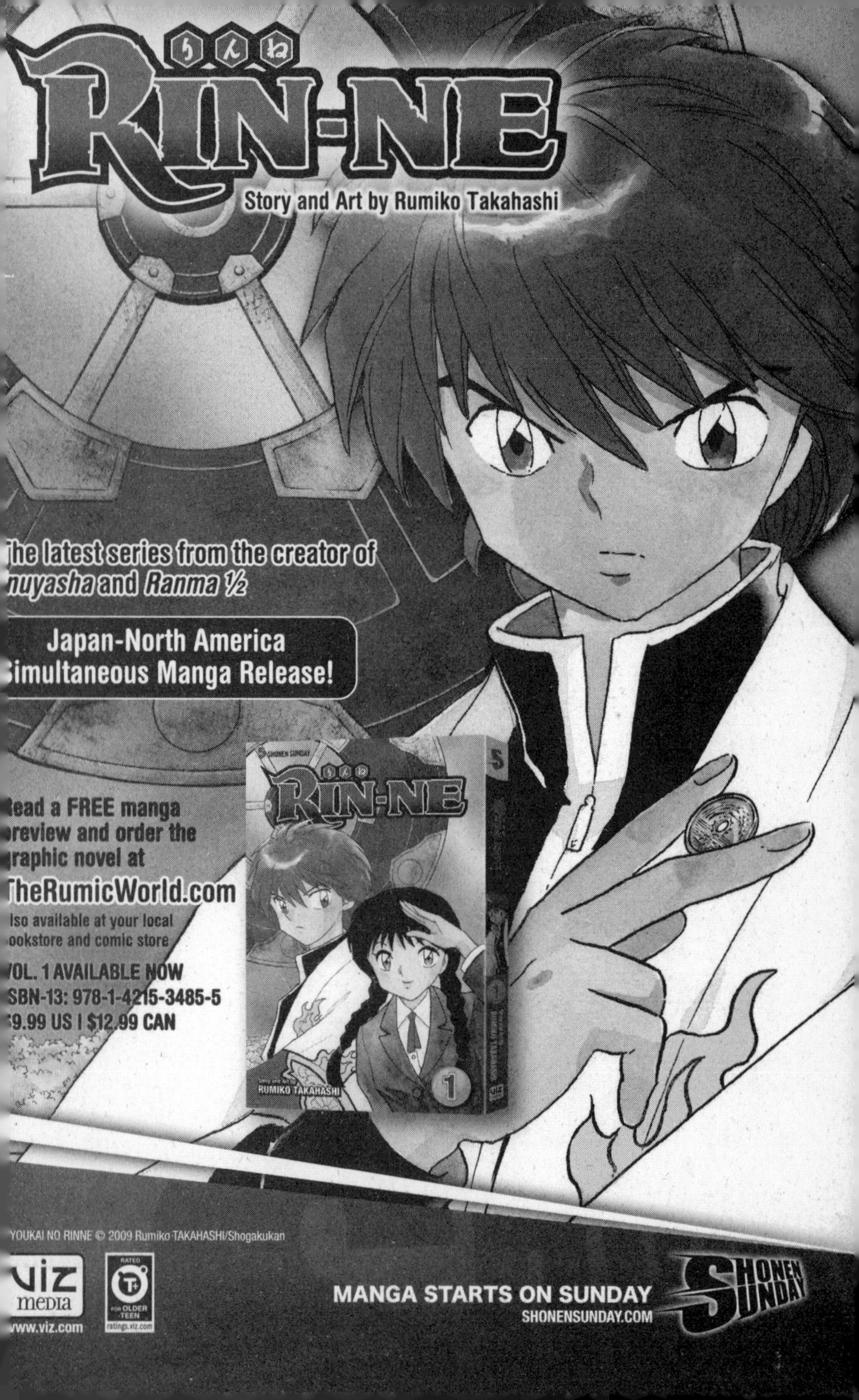
りんね
RIN-NE
Story and Art by Rumiko Takahashi
The latest series from the creator of
nuyasha and Ranma ½
Japan-North America
Simultaneous Manga Release!
SHONEN SUNDAY
RIN-NE
Story and Art by
RUMIKO TAKAHASHI
1
Read a FREE manga
preview and order the
graphic novel at
TheRumicWorld.com
lso available at your local
ookstore and comic store
VOL. 1 AVAILABLE NOW
SBN-13: 978-1-4215-3485-5
$9.99 US | $12.99 CAN
YOUKAI NO RINNE © 2009 Rumiko TAKAHASHI/Shogakukan
viz media
www.viz.com
RATED T+ FOR OLDER TEEN
ratings.viz.com
MANGA STARTS ON SUNDAY
SHONENSUNDAY.COM
SHONEN SUNDAY